WITHDRAWN

THE INDIAN MIDDLE CLASSES
THEIR GROWTH IN MODERN TIMES

THE INDIAN
MIDDLE CLASSES

THEIR GROWTH IN
MODERN TIMES

B. B. MISRA
Ph.D., F.R.Hist.S.

Issued under the auspices of the
Royal Institute of International Affairs

OXFORD UNIVERSITY PRESS

LONDON   NEW YORK   BOMBAY

1961

301.44
M69i

Oxford University Press, Amen House, London E.C.4

GLASGOW NEW YORK TORONTO MELBOURNE WELLINGTON
BOMBAY CALCUTTA MADRAS KARACHI KUALA LUMPUR
CAPE TOWN IBADAN NAIROBI ACCRA

57791
May 1967

PRINTED AND BOUND IN GREAT BRITAIN BY
HAZELL WATSON AND VINEY LTD
AYLESBURY AND SLOUGH

Preface

THIS study is intended to be merely an introductory survey of the Indian middle classes, a subject that remains virtually unexplored. From its very nature it is limited in scope and sketchy in treatment. Even so, it is significant in that it brings out some of the peculiar features which distinguished the Indian middle classes from their Western counterparts. In the West, especially in England, for example, the middle classes emerged basically as a result of economic and technological change; they were for the most part engaged in trade and industry. In India, on the contrary, they emerged more in consequence of changes in the system of law and public administration than in economic development, and they mainly belonged to the learned professions. India's traditional emphasis on literary education combined with Britain's rule and her imperialist economy to make the intelligentsia the dominant strand in the composition of the Indian middle classes.

It was in the course of the research I undertook to write my book on *The Central Administration of the East India Company* that I came across evidence indicating the peculiar nature of social change in India which led me to attempt this separate study.

I wish to express my gratitude to the Royal Institute of International Affairs, London, which offered me the opportunity to undertake this work, and to the School of Oriental and African Studies, University of London, especially to its Director, Professor C. H. Philips, who early in 1958 invited me to accept a senior research fellowship. This enabled me to proceed to London, where I completed the study towards the close of 1959. I am also grateful to the Governing Body of the D.A.V. College, Bihar University, and particularly to its Secretary, Sri Baidyanath Prasad, who gave me ungrudging support and permitted me for a third time to go abroad to undertake research.

During my study leave I was invited to visit the University of

Wisconsin and the University of Pennsylvania as Visiting Professor of Modern Indian History and Civilization. There I benefited from direct contact and discussion with a number of American scholars working in the fields of sociology and economic history. I am particularly indebted to the suggestions made from time to time by Professors Holden Furber and W. Norman Brown of the University of Pennsylvania, and by Professor Wilfred Malenbaum, sometime Director of the International Research Center, Massachusetts Institute of Technology. However, the bulk of the work was done in London, where I had fruitful discussions of many of my problems with Professors C. H. Philips, R. H. Tawney, and the late G. D. H. Cole.

I have pleasure also in acknowledging my debt to the late Acharya Narendra Deo, Socialist leader, whom I last met in London; to Mr. Philip Mason and Mr. L. P. Singh, both of the Indian Civil Service, and to Mr. V. K. N. Menon, Director of the Institute of Public Administration, New Delhi. My thanks are due no less to Mr. A. S. B. Olver, Research Secretary of the Royal Institute of International Affairs, who took a keen interest in my work, and to Miss H. Oliver, of the same Institute, for her care and precision in editing this work for publication. Finally, I wish to express my thanks to Mr. S. C. Sutton of the India Office Library and to his entire staff, whose friendly co-operation was a major factor in the completion of this book. To Mr. D. Matthews I am particularly indebted for reading the proofs and making the index.

B. B. M.

September 1960

Contents

Contents

PART IV
CHARACTER AND ROLE OF THE INDIAN MIDDLE CLASSES

Abbreviations

Beng. Pub. Cons. (or Sec. Cons.): Bengal Public (or Secret) Consultations.

Cal.: Calcutta.

Coll.: Collections.

Com. of Sec.: Committee of Secrecy.

Desp.: Despatches.

G.O.I.: Govt. of India.

HC, or HL: House of Commons, House of Lords.

Home Misc.: Home Miscellaneous series.

I.O.: India Office Library.

Let.: Letter(s).

Moral & Material Progress Rep.: *Statement Exhibiting the Moral and Material Progress and Conditions of India, 1859–*

P.B. Coll.: (India Office), Parliamentary Branch Collection.

P.P.: Parliamentary Paper (see Parliamentary Sessional Papers in Bibliography).

Proc.: Proceedings.

r.: range (I.O. Records location).

Rev. Cons. (or Desp.): Revenue Consultations (or Despatch).

Sels.: Selections.

Statistical Abstract: Statistical Abstract for British India, 1840– (Continued for all India by Union of India Govt.)

Introduction

THIS work, as its title suggests, is historical, not sociological. It is an attempt to trace the growth of the Indian middle classes from about the middle of the eighteenth century to modern times. It is in the main a story of the social policy and changes that occurred in the course of about 200 years of British rule, largely as a consequence of Western education and modern capitalist enterprise, of improved communications and commercial progress, of land reforms and legal administration.

As the character of a social class can by no means be exclusive of its relations with the strata above or below it, an attempt is made to study changes from a sociological angle. But this is done as part of a historical process, not as a study of their present form. My object is to produce a social history, a historical survey of the composition, character, and role of the Indian middle classes. This is a difficult task, since it demands an appreciation of three of the main disciplines immediately involved: history, economics, and sociology. I have some knowledge of the first, but not of the remaining two. Yet in the absence of a work on this subject I have ventured to undertake this as a pioneering project.

CONCEPT OF THE MIDDLE CLASS

The term middle class is much used and since most of us, without the aid of a specialist, understand what we mean when we use it in our everyday conversation, I am not attempting a meticulous definition. While it may be of interest to note the features of the Indian middle classes, and while it may be necessary broadly to know their composition in order to be able to assess their historical role, to attempt to draw the precise limits of the middle class, a heterogeneous social layer, is, in the words of Lewis and Maude, to get 'lured into an almost interminable discussion of the social sciences; and the result, while probably failing to satisfy the expert, would certainly weary the layman'.[1]

The concept of a single social class implies social division which proceeds from the inequalities and differences of man in society, which may be natural or economic. It is chiefly the economic inequality of man that influences, if it does not wholly determine, social differentiation. It arises basically from the difference of relationship which a person or a group bears to property or the means of production and distribution. If an individual is an owner of land, for example, he tends to exercise a relatively superior social significance. But if, on the contrary, he is a mere tiller of the soil that does not belong to him, he finds himself socially scaled down. This is a general principle which applies to all fields of economic production. This principle of relationship to property is qualitative in character in that it determines the quality of social honour, or lack of it, which we call 'status'. Income, earned or unearned, forms part of the total economic factor, but the concept is quantitative rather than qualitative in character. It relates to the physical size of the means capable of acquiring interests in property. A difference of income produces a hierarchy of prestige and power according to variations in its size. It produces qualitative change in the status of an individual or group only when it is converted into a form affecting relationship to property.

Income is, in fact, a means to the creation of wealth. For instance salary receipts if allowed to accumulate unproductively would remain a pure quantitative entity, but the moment they are invested in the purchase of land or an industry, the position changes. The transaction brings about a qualitative change that varies according to the nature and size of the interest so purchased.

The natural or physical inequality of man consists in differences of age, bodily strength, and the quality of mind and character. It causes a difference of income arising from variations in natural abilities. But that difference may in itself be attributable to the inequitable distribution of property through inheritance, a situation which affects the acquisition of natural ability through education.

The civil and political inequality of man is distinct from natural inequality. It consists in the different privileges which some men enjoy to the exclusion of others. Some, for example, are rich,

[1] *The English Middle Classes* (1949), p. 13.

honoured, and powerful, while others are not in spite of there being no difference in natural qualities. That is because of the operation of the economic and social factors. Society is thus divided into classes or groups of people joined together from motives of common economic interest, common ways of behaviour, and common traits of character. Each such class forms a hierarchy of status according to the varying quality of social prestige and power expressed through the standard of living, nature of occupation, and wealth. A social class is in fact a complex phenomenon whose complexity grows with the existence or emergence of a wide range of interests connected with the ownership and management of economic and social institutions.

For most of human history the social inequality of man was regarded as something immutable, an invariable order of things founded on the religious consent of man himself. The Renaissance and the Protestant movements of Europe questioned the validity of a social order based on religious sanction. The American and the French Revolutions went farther. They put this principle into practice. These were middle-class bourgeois revolutions, anti-feudal and secular in their approach to civil and political institutions. They appealed to certain natural rights due to man as man. They introduced *laissez-faire* as the principle of trade and broke the monopoly of political privileges which the owners of feudal estates enjoyed before. The new groups of people, for example the *élite* and the business classes who came to share these rights, did so from no religious sanction. They rose into higher social and political grades merely by virtue of their wealth, education, and power. In other words, they recognized social mobility as a basis of class concept. It meant equality of opportunity to improve one's lot in society. It was a dynamic concept which left the individual to move freely in social space. It became a principle of economic law and social philosophy which guided the conduct of the Western middle-class societies.

Another important element that emerged from the eighteenth-century revolutions was that of self-consciousness. It was a result of the intellectual thinking and progress of secular education that preceded these revolutions. It emphasized the importance of the 'natural rights' of man regardless of the 'estate' to which he might belong. It was the principle of human dignity which formed the basis of struggle against feudalism. It signified adherence to certain liberal values which received the general acceptance of the nation in time. To become a member of a middle-class group it was usual not only for the individual on the basis of these values to feel himself to be so, but likewise to be felt so by others. Thus while the element of social mobility was conducive to progress, the factor of socially accepted consciousness involved fulfilment of conditions precedent to that progress. While one was dynamic, the other was static. Together they constituted an important principle of social mechanics. It was under the influence of this principle that the social history of the democracies proceeded.

THE GROWTH OF THE MIDDLE CLASSES IN ENGLAND

The dynamic concept of a social class is basically an economic concept, for new classes and groups emerge initially from changes in the size and mode of production. The early society with its small-scale handicraft production was, for example, a simple society. The producer owned his implements as well as the articles of commerce he produced. He was a producer-trader because his industrial and commercial functions were indistinguishably mixed up. The master-craftsman was of course there, but he worked with his men under the same roof without any social or functional differentiation. Their relationship was personal, and together they formed a single category of brother labourers.

In England in the fourteenth century the emergence of the trader as a separate social and functional category formed the first step in the rise of a middle class. In the course of the Hundred Years War which stimulated production, especially of cloth, the trading element gradually separated itself from the ranks of the well-to-do master-craftsmen, monopolized certain specific spheres of trade, and organized trade associations which dominated the government of towns. This new element became a distinct group of merchant capitalists who financed the craftsmen, supplied raw materials, introduced new designs, improved quality, and marketed the goods so produced. Every augmentation in the size of their business was a step forward in the degree of urbanization. Before the emergence of joint-stock companies, they united both proprietary and managerial functions in business.

From his earliest urban association the trader was in fact the first burgher or bourgeois, who obtained royal charters and influenced urban governments to protect his trading rights against the inroads of the aristocracy on one hand and the wage demands of the crafts-men on the other. He represented the antithesis of the old régime based on feudal dues and personal service. 'The trading, travelling, money-making middle class', Lewis and Maude justly say (p. 27), 'is presented to us as the antithesis of feudalism, that stable pyramid of society in which each man owed allegiance to his overlord, paying him with services in kind in return for his rule and protec-tion.'

The English merchant capitalists of the fifteenth and sixteenth centuries established schools with an emphasis on the education of the laity to suit their growing requirements of geographical and scientific knowledge. These in time broke down the ecclesiastical monopoly of the educated professions. The trading entrepreneurs navigated the uncharted seas and carried on commerce with the distant parts of the globe. To share the risk of large-scale trading in foreign lands, they introduced a system of joint-stock companies which necessitated an increased division of labour, a separation of proprietary, directional, and managerial groups. The establishment of the English East India Company under the royal charter of 31 December 1600 was perhaps the biggest of the early examples of joint-stock trading.

But since, on account of technological backwardness, production remained essentially domestic in character, social stratification was limited. It progressed only to the extent to which trade and educa-tion necessitated the formation of new functional groups. The result was that, in the absence of factory industry, the wealthy merchants of England bought rural estates where they often retired from the towns, while the younger sons of the aristocracy were apprenticed into trade to build up an urban commercial interest. It is true that this cross-fertilization between town and country created a class of landed gentry who employed capital in the commercialization of agriculture which paved the way for the Industrial Revolution of the eighteenth century. But before this the dominance of the land-owning class had to all intents and purposes remained unaffected.

Indeed it was the exigencies of large-scale mechanical produc-tion that really heralded a new social order, distinct from feudalism and founded not on bondage but free relations. It took time for that revolution to stabilize itself, but generally speaking its first phase of development ushered in an era of *laissez-faire* which broke down the barriers of mercantilism and stimulated trade and industry to an extent never known before. It produced a great concentration of population in the industrial towns which grew considerably in both number and size. It created a class of industrial workers who became conspicuous on account of their capacity for joint action and collective bargaining, arising, as it did, from the concentration of their number. Each step in the advancement of technology was accompanied by a birth and extension of new skills, by an acceleration in the increase of professional groups in both urban and rural areas. Already the establishment of joint-stock companies had resulted in a separation of proprietary and managerial functions in business. The increasing pace of industrial development produced a more complex division of labour, and added to the old directional group a hierarchy of managerial and financial as well as technical and supervisory elements, not only in key industries but also in ever-increasing ancillary branches. Technological advance led to the establishment of a diversified system of education, and with increasing demand for varying degrees of applied and professional skills remunerated at different levels, there arose a much wider range of differentiation between the classes of employed persons.

The increasing number of new groups and categories emerging, as they did, from the expansion of trade and industry, education and professions, added to the complexity of social structure and relationship. History did not march in the direction Marx had indicated during the first phase of capitalist development. Instead of a growing concentration of wealth, the progress of technology and capitalist enterprise brought about a gradual diffusion of its ownership and control. It was in fact large-scale business enterprise that created an ever-increasing class of technicians, administrators, and supervisors, remunerated at various levels for the most part well above those of manual and clerical workers. It was again the growth of capitalist enterprise that from its complexity produced in other fields a large body of the professionals specialized in various branches of knowledge, such as law and medicine, education and journalism. They added to the number of the middle classes.

Capitalism made the middle classes an integral part of a unitary social order. The old trading middle class was called 'middle' because it was situated in between the baronage and the peasant or artisan class. But something more than this was implied by the new middle-class social order; it was not simply that they stood between the capitalist and the worker. There were two other important factors. First, they formed a composite intermediate layer consisting of a wide range of occupational interests but bound together by a common style of living and behaviour pattern. Secondly, they stood for certain liberal, democratic values which they expressed in their social and political conduct. They showed respect for the individual and gave less weight to a religious sanction of authority. Ideologically the new order stood for intellectual freedom and social mobility, liberal individualism and political democracy. A middle-class society thus became identified with a stratified social order representing a new standard of values which its members or groups impressed upon the entire societies in which they lived.

THE INDIAN SITUATION

Institutions conducive to capitalist growth were not lacking in India before British rule. Indian artisan industry and occupational specialization were very highly developed. As will be seen in Chapter I, there existed in addition a separate class of merchants whom the accounts of foreign travellers admired for the great extent of their foreign trade, the quality of their goods, and the magnitude of their wealth. They were organized in guilds designed to regulate prices and to protect trading rights against the interference of royal officials and landed magnates. These were comparable to medieval European trades associations which exercised a great measure of autonomy in the regulation of commerce. India had no joint-stock companies, but Indian traders employed what might be called a sort of managing agency which operated throughout the country. It consisted of a class of middlemen who managed the business of mercantile and banking houses, made advances to producers, and supplied finished goods to merchants.

A money economy had developed in India at an early period of her history. The coining of money was a royal privilege held by certain private families of traders specializing in currency. J. B. Tavernier, who visited India in the time of Aurangzeb, the Mughal king (1658–1707), bears testimony to the purity of both silver and gold coins which circulated in capital cities. The shroffs, a class of money-changers, were an ancient community who specialized in coinage and issued drafts (*hundis*) or letters of credit against the money deposited with them—a system which greatly facilitated the movement of trade. 'Yet modern capitalism', Max Weber rightly observes, 'did not develop indigenously before or during the English rule. It was taken over as a finished artifact without autonomous beginnings.'[2]

The political and social systems of the country were to a large extent responsible for this. The royal officials and priesthood often combined against the bourgeois plutocrats. It is true that such combinations were not peculiar to India; they occurred also in the West. But in the West the mercantile control of municipal governments, especially of the police, rendered them ineffectual. The guild power in India remained purely money power, unsupported by any authority of a political or military nature. It collapsed as soon as the king found it convenient to call in the aid of priestly and knightly elements.

The limitations arising from the existence of caste, the foundation of the Hindu social system, were no less menacing to a merchant guild. Consisting, as it did, of members belonging to different castes, the observance of its rules depended upon the sanction of the caste council (panchayat) concerned. That is where the Brahman and the king stepped in as final arbiters. They played off the superior caste organization against the guild by the threat of punishing recalcitrant members by excommunication. The priesthood thus assisted the king and his officials in the preservation of their dominance over the class of merchants.

The despotism of the Mughal king made the situation of traders still worse. He and his governors, as will be seen, themselves engaged in trade. They used their political power to control prices and to monopolize such specific spheres of trade as they considered profitable to themselves. Mughal despotism differed only in degree, not in kind, from its predecessors. The Indian political

[2] *The Religion of India*, tr. and ed. by H. H. Gerth and Don Martindale (1958), p. 4.

and social systems as a whole were authoritarian and despotic in nature, highly prejudicial to the growth of an independent bourgeois class. Indian merchants were known for their fabulous wealth, but generally they were royal monopolists appointed after the collapse of merchant guilds and dependent for their prosperity upon palace officials or provincial governors.

Ideologically too their situation was equally unfavourable. The priestly and knightly classes regarded trade and industry as inferior callings. The literary classes who followed intellectual professions were ignorant of crafts. The artisans who had the monopoly of craftsmanship received no education. The shrewdness of business classes was proverbial, but their education was limited to commercial accounts. Their knowledge was empirical, descending from the father to the son. Occupational specialization arose from hereditary callings, not from higher education or research, which remained literary in emphasis and divorced from the pursuits of applied skills and sciences.

In spite of the potential of a middle-class bourgeois development, therefore, the immobility of the caste organization and the despotism of bureaucracy precluded such a development. The middle-class elements in society could not become a stratified order, each individual or group having freedom to move in social space and being conscious of a superior status based on the superiority of the values acquired. They remained divided into water-tight status groups according to the caste to which they belonged. They could not form themselves into a unitary middle-class social order comparable to that of Western countries. Cases of caste schisms did arise from time to time to oppose the exercise of hereditary privileges, but they were exceptions. The religious movements of Buddhism and Jainism which supported such schisms, for instance, were pacifist in their approach like the devotional (*bhakti*) movements of the middle ages. They degenerated into sects which later came to be absorbed into the caste system.

Moreover, the caste system was related to the law of property. It formed an integral part of the prevailing land economy. Under the law of inheritance, for example, succession depended upon the performance of caste obligations. And since land constituted a more or less exclusive means of livelihood, except for the artisans who in part earned their living from handicrafts, starvation became the only alternative to the observance of caste rules.

The emergence of a stratified social order depended on occupational and educational diversification. Land economy and limited education were both obstructive to social stratification, but more important still was the backwardness of technology, the existence of a domestic system of production, from which no stratified order could emerge. This small-scale handicraft production afforded little or no scope for a multiplicity of economic functions, such as arose from an increased division of labour under joint-stock business, in large-scale mechanical production or diversified national education. None of these conditions existed prior to British rule. Society was divided into fixed status groups. There were intermediate categories as well but no middle classes of the type described above.

THE RISE OF AN INDIAN MIDDLE CLASS
UNDER BRITISH RULE

Radical changes accompanied the advent of the British in India. In the absence of an adequate political and economic system, they transplanted into India their own form and principles of government and economic organization which they modified only to suit local conditions.

As between European business and British government in India, the relationship differed little from its home pattern. The former exercised considerable influence over the latter. As for Indians, they could join British firms as junior partners, for the membership of a European trade organization was not exclusive, and although the size of the stock held by an individual was significant, the rule of law made no distinction between a European or Indian business man.

The number of Indians able to carry on business on modern European lines was negligible in the beginning. The British attempted as part of their educational policy to create a class comparable to their own, so that it might assist them in the administration of the country and help in the development of its internal resources, necessary for the payment of the increasing imports of British manufactures. In Macaulay's words, this was to be a 'class, Indian in blood and colour, but English in tastes, in opinions, in morals and intellect'.[3]

These ideas and institutions of a middle-class social order were imported into India. They did not grow from within. They were implanted in the country without a comparable development in its economy and social institutions. The Indian middle class which the British aimed at creating was to be a class of imitators, not the originators of new values and methods. The West proceeded to develop education so as to satisfy the needs of an already developed economy. India under the British proceeded to develop education so as to form a class to develop its economy. That was the British theory of 'infiltration' which was to apply to both educational and economic fields.

It was to put the cart before the horse. The traditional Hindu bias against industrial occupation and the administrative requirements of Government led to the whole educational machinery being geared to satisfy the needs of the public service and had the effect of perpetuating the old emphasis on literary education as a virtual monopoly of the upper castes of Hindu society. The development of the country's economy thus long remained the main concern of Europeans. The educated class of Indians who emerged as a result of British educational policy cared more for position and influence in the civil service and councils than for mass education or economic development. New business classes did grow, but not so rapidly as the literary classes. By virtue of their traditional superiority of caste, intellectual pursuits, and political influence, the latter continued to dominate the former except in recent decades during which Indian business had begun to assume a professional character. The respect attaching to higher education and professional skill was gradually imparting to money power a social status which it did not enjoy before.

COMPOSITION OF THE INDIAN MIDDLE CLASSES

The progress of education and the advancement of technology, even though delayed, were tending towards the goal of a middle-class society. India's industrially developed cities produced a social order which in its complexity compared favourably with its

[3] H. Sharp, *Selections from the Educational Records*, pt. 1, 1781–1839, p. 116.

European counterpart. Its component parts, though heterogeneous and even mutually conflicting at times, exhibited in great measure an element of uniformity not only in their behaviour pattern and style of life, but also in their mode of thinking and social values. From the circumstances of their growth the members of the educated professions, such as government servants and lawyers, college teachers and doctors, constitute the bulk of the Indian middle classes. The mercantile and industrial elements which dominate the composition of the Western middle classes are still a minority, limited for the most part to cities like Calcutta and Bombay, Madras and Cawnpore (Kanpur), Ahmedabad and Jamshedpur. But since they form the rising classes, the advanced section of a middle-class bourgeois society, I have given them priority in the following analysis of the Indian middle classes, which consist in the main of the following groups:

1. The body of merchants, agents, and proprietors of modern trading firms, including active partners and directors, exclusive of those at the top, connected with wholesale trading, manufacturing, or financial concerns.

2. The bulk of salaried executives, such as managers, inspectors, supervisors, and technical staff employed in banking, trading, and manufacturing businesses owned privately or otherwise.

3. The higher salaried officers of a wide group of institutions and societies ranging from the chambers of commerce and other trade associations to political organizations, trade unions, philanthropic, cultural, and educational bodies.

4. The main body of civil servants and other public servants, excepting those at the top beyond the ranks of secretaries to government and judges of high courts, but including those of the other public services, such as agriculture and education, public works, transport and communications.

5. The members of the principal recognized professions, salaried or otherwise, such as lawyers and doctors, lecturers and professors, the upper and middle ranges of writers and journalists, musicians and artists, religious preachers and priests.

6. The holders of the middle grades of proprietary tenures of land, such as joint and peasant proprietors, *rentiers*, and farmers of revenue, living on unearned income or partially personal manage-

ment, exclusive of the largest and some of the smallest holders of estates.

7. The body of well-to-do shopkeepers and hotel keepers including the managers, accountants, and other officers employed in the joint-stock concerns operating in such fields.

8. The group of rural entrepreneurs engaged in plantation industry, with a number of salaried managerial hands employed on landed estates.

9. The main body of the full-time students engaged in higher education at a university or comparable level.

10. The main body of clerks, assistants, and other non-manual workers below the managerial and the recognized professional levels.

11. The upper range of secondary school-teachers and the officers of the local bodies, social, and political workers.

As the story of a middle-class society begins with the rise of bourgeois capitalism, this work starts with the study of the rise of commercial and industrial groups in Indian society. It surveys the economic and social policy and the principal changes introduced by British rule, tracing the gradual introduction of organized industry and joint-stock business, a development which was slow in the beginning because of the English East India Company's interest in preserving India's traditional artisan production, which from its cheapness and excellence brought considerable profit to the Company's home and European markets. However, one of the abiding effects of the Company's rule was that India was at least spared the inconveniences of large-scale colonization, and this also saved the Indian merchants and bankers from undue European competition. The class which in fact stood to gain was the commercial middle class of Indian agents employed by the Company, its servants, or free merchants, and the European houses of agency served as models for the Indian entrepreneurs.

The ending of the Company's rule in 1858 resulted in a steep and steady rise in India's external trade, which created capital resources for industrialization, paying for loans incurred on government account for the construction of railways, irrigation, and other public works, as well as maintaining the entire establishment of the India Office and Indian Civil Service. The flow of

British capital and skill contributed to the agricultural and manufacturing industries and also led to the introduction of the managing
agency system, which provided a pattern of industrial organization which shaped the character of India's economic development.
This system differed from the old agency houses in two respects:
first, the capital of the agency houses was mainly in Indian rupees
(in the form of savings of the Company's public servants), and
secondly, the managing agents, especially at first, were mostly
representatives of British companies with sterling capital (whereas
the agency houses had been more distributors than owners of
capital). When these parent companies floated new companies
from the profits they earned, the new companies enjoyed a legal
and functional independence, and this system thus contributed to
the horizontal expansion of more and more new industrial units
while at the same time preserving their vertical integration, under
the direction and management of the pioneering firm. A limited
number of managing agents thus came to control the bulk of the
country's economic power. This financial integration restricted the
growth of the Indian industrial middle classes, while the administrative integration reduced the number of superior executives,
especially directors. The Indian managing houses such as the
Birlas, the Tatas, the Dalmias, and the Thapars, not only adopted
this model but added to it regional and caste prejudices affecting
the appointment of directors and managers, secretaries and engineers. Thus was perpetuated a tendency towards limiting the
selection of business administrators to persons belonging to the
caste or community controlling the businesses concerned. With
the spread of higher education among the traditional business
communities of India, unless their concerns come under public
control industrial administration may become their exclusive
sphere of influence, and the dominance of the old literary classes
may continue by virtue of the lead they gained in the early phases
of British rule. Another consequence of the managing agency
system was the concentration of capital in Calcutta and Bombay
which, together with the growth of education in the Presidency
towns, concentrated the growth of the middle classes in these
towns, tending to cause social instability.

Founded on the rule of law and the principle of *laissez-faire*,
sociologically speaking British rule produced a gradual elevation

of the Indian bourgeoisie as controllers of money power, whose influence became more widespread with the growth of modern towns and cities. Moreover the gradual substitution of custom by law and the growth of a highly centralized administrative apparatus, which took over such duties as had traditionally been performed by village communities or large landholders, encouraged the growth of the middle classes. What shook the foundations of the old society even more were the British land reforms, the cumulative effect of which was to reduce the power of the landholders, to give tenants legal recognition and a prestige they had never enjoyed before, and to transform society from a basis of status to one of contract. Moreover the creation of property in land and the freedom with which that property could be alienated resulted in the growth of a class of money-lenders or rural financiers, and the revenue laws and tenancy reforms led to an unprecedented increase in the volume of litigation to validate disputed claims. This produced a corresponding increase in public business, which necessitated on the one hand hierarchies of officials and on the other professional hierarchies of lawyers. Both swelled the middle classes, who were tending to supplant the influence previously exercised by chief proprietors or village headmen. The extent to which the old social order was facing dissolution towards the end of the nineteenth century is reflected in a telling passage in a report on the condition of the lower classes in 1881–91:

In rural, as in urban, life changes are taking place of which the result is to bring new men to the surface, and to relegate to comparative obscurity the classes on whom the public attention has been up to recent times concentrated ... There can be no doubt that, one by one, the forces which have hitherto held native society together are being loosened, and that the whole masses of the community are being melted as in a crucible, and are gradually losing the form and colour which have hitherto distinguished them, to take what new shape or to reappear in what combinations, it is premature to conjecture.[4]

While it was the bureaucracy that in fact became the most powerful of the new social forces, the growth of the independent

[4] Quoted in J. O. Miller, *On the Condition of the Agricultural and Labouring Classes*, in *Condition of Lower Classes in India, 1881–91* (P. B. Coll. 220).

professions, especially of law, was at the same time tending to the creation of a counterweight to the bureaucracy. These new men came forward as the representatives of the citizenry, and claimed to step into the social vacuum caused by the disintegration of the old order. With the help of the rising Indian bourgeoisie, the educated classes were enabled to become successful rivals of an officialdom controlled by alien rule and not rooted in the land.

Another main effect of British rule which this book attempts to trace is the cultural conflict between East and West. A by-product of the British educational policy of promoting vernacular education in order to spread European knowledge and culture was the revival of Oriental studies on the one hand and the translation into Indian regional languages of English books on the other. The subjection of Oriental studies to Western methods of analysis and scrutiny led to their critical revaluation. The depth of Indian scholarship, the flexibility of Hindu philosophy and the superiority of its ethics enabled Indians to interpret their traditions so as to make them ideologically conformable to the demands of Western liberalism, but the Hindu social system could not be made to conform to a liberalism that was the product of mechanized technology and industrial revolution, of social mobility and a belief in the natural rights of man. In India this conflict emphasized two main trends already present in Indian cultural development—liberal reformism, and reactionary revivalism. The spirit of the new age was represented by the Brahma Samaj in Bengal and the Prarthana Samaj in Bombay, but these middle-class reformist movements had no mass backing, for the bulk of the population was rural, illiterate, steeped in superstition, and profoundly suspicious of the pro-Western educated classes, whom they regarded as Christian. These movements in fact stimulated the spirit of reaction, epitomized in Swami Dayanand Saraswati's Arya Samaj, whose appeal was much wider and whose leader was the first to decry foreign rule and its influence. Men such as Bal Gangadhar Tilak and Lala Lajpat Rai, carrying their revivalist convictions into the political field, ushered in an era of violence which Gandhi had to fight against. But there could be no going back to the Vedas, for the Hindus had become well advanced in Western education and capitalist enterprise, two of the main props of liberalism. They could no longer afford to live in the past, and the most enlightened worked for a cultural synthesis. But the traditional orthodoxy of Islam and the time-lag in the Western education of Muhammadans made revivalism a relatively stronger force in that community, and this was reinforced by the economic decline of the Muslim community. In consequence the Muslim traditionalists dominated the politics of even the educated class of Muslims. The British refusal to extend recognition to Indian aspirations inevitably discredited the moderates, or the liberals, the first champions of constitutional advance in India. Religious bias and political violence followed, and the radical or extremist elements of the Congress tried to produce a mass movement through religious and socially reactionary propaganda. But the religious approach to politics accentuated communal differences, and by the time the goal of responsible government came to be recognized in principle, the situation had got out of control. Thus India became independent but divided in 1947.

Part I

INDIAN SOCIETY
IN PRE-BRITISH TIMES

I

The Merchant, the Artisan, and the
Landed Aristocracy

IN order to establish clearly the character and scope of the growth of the middle classes in India under British rule, it is necessary to give some indication of the structure of Indian society in pre-British times, especially under Mughal rule in the seventeenth century.

Indian society in pre-British times consisted in the main of four elements: the king and his courtiers forming the bureaucratic apparatus of the state, the priestly intellectual comprising scholarly and professional categories, the merchant, called vaishya, and the agriculturist, including both artisans and peasants. Of these four I shall deal first with the mercantile and industrial elements, not because the bulk of the Indian middle classes emerged from this group. On the contrary, the merchant was in fact assigned a third position in order of social precedence; and as for the artisan, he was graded among Shudras, the lowest of the four categories. My object in so doing is to emphasize the fact that in spite of India's commercial progress and industrial efficiency, princely dominance and caste prejudice made impossible the development of large-scale enterprises, with an increasing division of labour which, as in the West, might otherwise have contributed to social mobility as well as stratification.

THE MERCHANT

The observations made by foreign travellers 'would disillusion anyone who may have been tempted to regard the India of the seventeenth century as a country of Arcadian simplicity'.[1] Edward

[1] W. H. Moreland, *From Akbar to Aurangzeb* (1923), p. 145.

Terry, who visited India in the time of the Mughal king Jahangir
(1605–27), refers to a variety of Indian manufactures which
brought a huge mass of wealth into the country. He says that 'as all
Rivers run into the Sea, so many Silver *Streams* run into this
Monarchy, and there stay'.[2] François Bernier, who came nearly
three decades later, is struck with the great quantity of gold and
silver which 'after circulating in every other quarter of the globe,
came at length to be swallowed up, lost in some measure, in
Hindoustan'.[3] He goes on to remark that India's fame consisted
'not only in the production of rice, corn and other necessaries of
life, but of innumerable articles of commerce . . . such as silks,
cotton, and indigo'. The artisan, though 'naturally indolent', had
a reputation for excellence in the manufacture of 'carpets, brocades, embroideries, gold and silver cloths, and the various sorts
of silk and cotton goods which are used in the country or exported
abroad'.

Indeed, the foreign trade of India extended westwards into the
Red Sea as well as eastwards into the Indian Ocean along the
coasts of Ceylon and Burma, Sumatra and Siam. Bernier writes
that all the Indian vessels, whether they belonged to the Indians
themselves or to others, carried 'cargoes of merchandise from
Hindoustan to *Pegu*, *Tanasseri*, *Siam*, *Ceylon*, *Achem*, *Maccasar*,
the *Maldives*, to *Mozambic*, and other places', bringing back to
India 'a large quantity of the precious metals' in the same manner
as they did from the Middle East. Portions of gold and silver
which the Dutch drew from Japan also found their way into India
which made all return payments in merchandise.[4] Jean Baptiste
Tavernier too confirms the excellence and 'enormous quantity' of
Indian muslins, which found markets in 'Persia, Turkey, Mus-
covie, Poland, Arabia, Grand Cairo, and other places'.[5] Sebastien
Manrique, who had visited the country earlier, felt not less surprised at 'the enormous quantity of riches' which the Mughal
emperor possessed in addition to the wealth of his grandees and the
'fortune of the merchants' called *saudagar*.

There were in fact some Indian merchants who dominated the
markets. They acted as great financiers and public creditors. From

[2] *A Voyage to East-India* (1665), pp. 118–19; also pp. 138–9.
[3] *Travels in the Mogul Empire* (1891), p. 202.
[4] Ibid. p. 203.   [5] *Travels in India* (1891), i. 51.

time to time they even financed the 'investment'—the homeward cargoes—of the English East India Company. Virji Vora, the merchant prince of Surat, was one of these. He controlled the wholesale market, buying and selling practically every commodity which changed hands at that port. Apart from foreign trade, he directed the coasting trade, annually sending his men to Calicut where they exchanged opium and cotton goods for pepper over which Virji Vora exercised a virtual monopoly. He maintained branch offices at other great trading centres like Ahmedabad and Agra, Burhanpur and Golconda. His influence was so widespread that even the English East India Company had to reckon with him. With regard to the pepper trade, for instance, its authorities at Surat realized that 'it would obviously be cheaper to deal direct', and not through him. But yet there was no escape. 'Virji Vora', they wrote to London, 'by reason of our continuall mighty ingagements, must not bee displeased in any case', because he was 'a man that hath often supplyed our wants in Suratt with moneys', although for his own ends.[6]

Malaya, a Chetti of South India, was a counterpart of Virji Vora on the east coast, with his headquarters at Pulicat. After his death in 1634 his business was taken over by his younger brother, Chinana Chetti, who was interested in shipping and the farming of public offices. The Serkails dominated the wholesale market at Masulipatam where they would not suffer any merchant to buy or sell except through them. They lent money to the East India Company in the same way as Virji Vora did at Surat. Pyrard de Laval refers to wealthy merchants in the island and town of Goa and says that 'many of the richest of them' farmed the revenue and held 'all the great monopolies, as well as from the king as from private persons'. These monopolies were 'both in merchandise and in other things', so that nothing could be sold 'without the consent of these farmers'.[7]

It was the Khatris of Northern India who attracted the attention of Manrique, who describes them as 'the most distinguished' of the traders engaged in the mercantile profession on that side. 'In some of these houses', he writes, 'I saw such vast sums of money piled up, that if they had been covered over, they would have

---

[6] William Foster, *The English Factories in India, 1642-45*, p. 108.
[7] *The Voyage of François Pyrard of Laval*, tr. A. Gray (1887-8), ii. 74.

struck the ordinary gazer as being merely heaps of grain rather than piles of anything so unusual.'[8] Some of the rich and enterprising families of merchants moved into Bengal which they converted into an extensive field for mercantile operations. Many of these later migrated from Gaur, the ancient capital of Bengal, and settled at Satgaon in the district of Hugli. It is this class of adventurous banyans who first traded with the Portuguese in the sixteenth century and finally collaborated with the English in the eighteenth. The famous house of Jagat Seth was a leading example of this class. Originally living in Nagaur in Rajputana, one of the ancestors of this family, Hiranand Sah, migrated in the middle of the seventeenth century to Patna and then to Murshidabad, where the family finally settled. Fatehchand, one of the descendants and a friend of the English, received the title of Jagat Seth (world banker) from Muhammad Shah, the emperor of Delhi, for controlling the prices of food grains. He was regarded as probably the richest individual merchant of his time.

On the financial side too India was considerably advanced and its machinery of credit fairly widespread. It is true that the business houses themselves held the key positions and united in their firms both mercantile and banking functions. They had developed a remarkable system of credit, exchange, and insurance, bearing heavy risks in the transportation of goods to distant places. As bankers they received deposits and made advances for the produce of the interior. They had branch offices established in the different parts of the country, especially in those that promised favourable trade returns. Bills of exchange, or *hundis*, as they were called by Muhammadan rulers on account of their Hindu origin and association, were drawn up in a regular written character and conveyed by the special couriers of the bankers themselves. But as the system of credit and bills of exchange was known to Indians from remote ages, and as its operation extended in the seventeenth century even to lower levels of administration on account of local variations of coinage, the Indian money-lenders or shroffs, as they were called, resided not only in urban trading centres but also in large villages, where interest on loans and discount on exchange constituted their main source of income. 'In India', writes Tavernier,

---

[8] *Travels of Fray Sebastien Manrique*, tr. C. E. Luard and H. Hosten (1927), ii. 156.

'a village must be very small if it has not a money-changer whom they call *Shroff*, who acts as a banker to make remittances of money and issue letters of exchange.' The acumen which this class brought to bear upon financial transactions impressed Tavernier so much that he came to regard the Jews as much inferior to Indian bankers in point of skill and efficiency. 'All the Jews who occupy themselves with money and exchange in the empire of the Grand Seignier [Ottoman empire]', he comments, 'pass for being very sharp; but in India they would scarcely be apprentices to these Changers.'[9]

In the commercial field too the number of average banyans or merchants seemed not inconsiderable. The contemporary records and the accounts of foreign travellers refer to these frequently. The well-to-do shopkeepers, who commanded greater respect than artisans, formed part of this middle group. But it seems that they were not as prosperous as their counterpart on the financial side, where the high rates of interest on advance and discount on exchange probably assured them a stable income. The shroffs constituted for the most part a wealthy and prosperous community among the Hindus. The average mercantile community, on the contrary, had, besides facing the risk of trade, necessarily to toe the line set for them by big monopolists.

But although immensely rich and to some extent even richer than their European counterparts in their stocks of precious metals, the Indian merchants were no entrepreneurs. For reasons indicated in the Introduction they contributed to the stability of the caste order which blocked technological change and occupational mobility. Considerable quantities of bullion flowed into India, but there it stayed. In the words of Bernier, it was 'swallowed up' and to a great extent even 'lost' to productive enterprise and organizational expansion. Manrique refers to 'piles' of precious metals that he saw stored in the business houses of the Khatris. But he makes no mention of what part of their accumulated capital they released for circulation.

Bernier attributes the lack of productive investment to the despotic political system of the country. He says that from a sense of insecurity most of the wealthy people buried their gold and silver 'at a great depth', and instead of assuming an air of indepen-

[9] Tavernier, ii. 28–29.

dence and living in comfort, studied the means by which they could appear 'indigent'. He goes on to add that the general practice among all merchants, whether Hindus or Muslims, but specially among the former, who controlled almost exclusively the trade and wealth of the country, was to keep money concealed lest it should excite the cupidity of a local governor or officer possessing 'both power and inclination to deprive any man of the fruits of his industry'.[10] Despotism in fact discouraged the circulation of precious metals and withdrew wealth from productive undertakings. The melting of considerable quantities of these metals to make ornaments or for the manufacture of gold and silver cloths produced a similar effect. Another significant point that one has to bear in mind about the Indian trading community, especially under the effective rule of the Mughals, is that unlike its Western counterpart it acted in subservience to the princely order, not in opposition to it. Drawn originally from the ranks of well-to-do master-craftsmen, the English traders and organizers of industry became a class of merchant manufacturers who wrested charters of liberty from the king, dominated municipal governments, and used their political power to further their trade privileges. This rising class of burghers or bourgeoisie acted as the spearhead of social leadership. It modified, disrupted, and finally supplanted feudalism. It became the leader of the *laissez-faire* economy and the Industrial Revolution. It limited the powers of government and fought for democracy.

The Indian traders had no charters of liberty, no municipal rights, no police or political backing. They had their merchant guilds. But, as Max Weber rightly points out, the king and his bureaucracy remained dominant, and used the priestly apparatus of superior caste organization to reduce recalcitrant elements to obedience.[11] On the defeat of guild power a merchant prince often became a royal monopolist subservient to the bureaucratic apparatus of the state. His interest was then to effect the concentration of economic power, not its diffusion.[12]

---

[10] Bernier, pp. 224–5.   [11] Weber, p. 90.

[12] The case of Virji Vora may be cited as an illustration. Within his sphere of influence he would not permit any merchant to deal directly with any firm other than his own. He awed 'all Banyan merchants to his observance' (see Foster, *Eng. Fac. in Ind., 1642–5*, p. 18). In one case a merchant at Surat thought of

Indeed, the traditional segregation of occupational groups, the supremacy of the literary and bureaucratic classes, and the hegemony of commercial monopolists were some of the factors which prejudiced the growth of the middle classes. Their general tendency was to keep society rigid and divided principally into two categories: the rich and the poor. It is perhaps in this sense that Bernier, in spite of his mention of varied occupational groups existing under the Mughals, recognizes these two categories only, even in Delhi, the Mughal capital, where according to him there was 'no middle state. A man must either be of the highest rank or live miserably'.[13] He gives reasons and quotes himself as an example to show that he had to lead a 'miserable' life in spite of his pay being considerable and he being not 'sparing of money'; because it often so happened that he did not have the 'wherewithal to satisfy the cravings of hunger' on account of 'the *bazars* (markets) being so ill supplied, and frequently containing nothing but the refuse of the grandees'.[14] Thus the supply of consumer goods, including food grains, was insufficient and the aristocracy had the first claim to the purchase and use of whatever choice goods were available in the market.

Tavernier's account supports this view, though from a different angle. He gives a picture, among others, of two of the largest cities of India, Agra and Golconda; and while describing the houses in each, he classifies them into two groups: those of 'the nobles' (at Agra) being fair and well built, but those of 'private persons' having nothing fine about them 'no more than in all the other towns of India'.[15] As for Golconda, he says that merchants, brokers, and artisans lived side by side with 'all the common people' outside the city, which was 'inhabited only by persons of quality, the officers of the King's house, the ministers of justice, and military men'.[16] He gives a similar picture of the economic and social development of Burhanpur, which constituted a con-

---

defying his orders and bought from the English East India Company a consignment of coral, but his fear was so great that for two years he did not dare to avow the transaction. The goods remained in the English warehouse 'unrequested' and 'unregarded'. Likewise at Masulipatam the local monopolist would suffer 'Noe merchant to buy or sell there, but such as deale for him'.

[13] Bernier, p. 252.   [14] Ibid. p. 205.   [15] Tavernier, i. 105.
[16] Ibid. p. 152.

siderable command, conferred only on a member of the royal family.[17]

It is clear that under the Mughals the intermediate group of merchants had no independent significance. For one thing, they were not treated as men of quality. Far from enjoying a social prestige in any way comparable with that of their European counterparts, they always ran the risk of being reduced to mere artisans or workmen. Niccolao Manucci, an Italian traveller, declares that even the most successful merchants were found wanting in courage and independence, especially in capital towns where the rule of the Mughals was most effective. Their wealth brought them estimation in their tribes and might also make them worthy objects of royal consideration, but it by no means elevated them to a position of dignity held by the official or landed aristocracy. He even goes so far as to say that although wary and crafty, they were as a class timid and chary of giving any direct answer for fear of punishment.[18] The medieval towns themselves were in fact more or less enclaves in the midst of a peasant economy, where even professional and intellectual classes were mere place-holders in a patrimonial and bureaucratic state.

India's western seaboard, however, presented a pattern of economic development which was relatively free from Mughal influence. While its geographical situation provided an element of mobility in the movement of trade, the superior strength of foreign trading vessels held out a promise of protection against the rapacity of a local governor. The Indian trading community there could thus operate with freedom and security of private property. Duarte Barbosa, for instance, affirms that even the Muhammadan merchants of the Malabar coast lived with the Hindus in a single community, followed their law of property, spoke their language, and traded with them without fear of Government. Before the advent of the Portuguese these Muhammadans controlled all the trade and navigation, and Barbosa cites instances to show that their

[17] Tavernier, p. 51. While deposing before a parliamentary committee in 1781, the Brahman emissary of Peshwa Raghunath Rao, by name Honwontrow, who had been to England with letters to the king and the East India Company, referred to only two classes of persons in point of income in the Maratha country: those who were 'rich' and others 'of low condition' (Rep. Sel. Com. HC, 1781–2, p. 39a, in P.B. Coll. 16A).

[18] See *Storia do Mogor*, tr. and ed. W. Irvine (1907–8), i. 143–5.

spirit of independence led them even to take up arms in the preservation of their rights. The Nairs, who constituted the landed and military aristocracy, could not suppress them. Even the Nair king often had to pacify them either by threats or cajolery.[19] The Portuguese seemed to subdue them for a time, but although weakened, they held their ground and recovered again on the decline of that power.

Gujarat was yet another province where the business community exercised a certain amount of independence. This community consisted in the main of a numerous class of Hindus, including Jains; the English called these merchants 'banyans'. Before the ravages of the Marathas every town of Gujarat was inhabited by wealthy merchants attached to commerce as a hereditary pursuit.[20] They travelled to distant countries where they settled for years before returning home. In India itself they had spread along the western coast as far as Calicut where they traded with a variety of foreign elements called *pardesis*. Their business also extended inland, particularly to Benares (Banaras), Bihar, and Bengal, with which they maintained a regular trade in silk and cotton piece-goods. Barbosa was surprised to find that they dwelt 'in great houses and streets of their own as the Jews are wont to dwell in our land'.[21] Pietro della Valle also made a similar observation: not only public men, he said, but any private individual might live in these parts 'with as much grandeur and equipage as he pleases. . . . Hence generally, all live much after a genteel way', especially because living was cheap and servants available in abundance for not more than three rupees a month.[22]

In addition to the port towns, which imparted mobility to the movement of its trade, Gujarat possessed certain other advantages of its own. Excepting Brahmans and banyans, all other castes would occasionally take to looms, which contributed to the cheapness and excellence of its manufactures. Then there were Bohras who, although Muhammadans, compared favourably with Jews in dress

[19] *The Book of Barbosa*, ed. M. L. Dames (1918–21), ii. 82.

[20] Charles Malet to Governor-General, 8 Aug. 1788 (app. 6 to 3rd Rep. Sel. Com. of Court of Directors, 1792–3, P.B. Coll. 28).

[21] Barbosa, ii. 73. The Gujaratis and Muhammadans together held the coasting trade right from Coromandel, Ceylon, the Maldives to Ormuz in Persia (ibid. p. 81).

[22] *The Travels in India of Pietro della Valle*, ed. E. Gray (1892), i. 41.

and manners as well as in genius and capacity for business. Virji Vora (Bohra), who has already been mentioned, was the leader of this community at Surat in the first half of the seventeenth century. To these may be added another, perhaps the most important, advantage that Gujarat had over other provinces. It contained nearly the entire Parsi population in India. The Parsis constituted a remarkable race of business men who came over in the eighth century from Ormuz to escape Muhammadan persecution in Persia, their original homeland. 'Since then', writes Hamilton,

the Parsis have resided in larger or smaller communities, dispersed in cities and villages along the coast of India, from Diu to Bombay, and although very enterprising traders, embarking frequently on distant and perilous voyages, few settle out of their own country, by which term they mean the space above defined, and within which limits they have accumulated to the number of about 150,000 families.[23]

The Indian textile and shipbuilding industries as well as banking and insurance constituted their main fields of enterprise.

A relatively free growth of trade in these parts was due to some extent to the moderation of Government, for these areas were never completely subdued by any invader, Rajput or Jat, Turk or Mughal. But in no small measure it was also due to the care which the Hindu banyans generally took not to have their credit injured in case their business failed. In Gujarat there was a peculiar custom under which a merchant, before his crash, set up a blazing lamp in his house or office and then kept away until his creditors had completed the examination of his effects and obtained a full knowledge of his property. So great was his care to keep his credit that he would not wear 'the tail of his waistcloth hanging down' until his creditors declared him as fairly acquitted.[24] Such banyans were held in great esteem for their perfect honesty and uprightness of conduct. Religiously too they were quite free from persecution. They had secured from the Mughal Government an order which prohibited cow slaughter and left them in the full exercise of their religious rights. They used their freedom to expand commerce as well as in support of charitable institutions, including hospitals for men and animals. It is not surprising therefore that Virji Vora,

[23] Walter Hamilton, *Description of Hindostan and its Adjacent Countries* (1820), i. 614.
[24] Ibid. p. 616.

the monopolist merchant of Surat who awed 'all Banyan merchants to his observance', found one of their number acting against his will and by-passing him by a direct negotiation of trade with the English East India Company.[25]

These facts lend support to the view that the shape of commercial development on the western coast of India differed from the inland pattern. It resembled to some extent that of the precursor of the English middle class, the merchant-manufacturer or commercial capitalist who monopolized specific branches of trade and organized industry by the advance of capital, improvement of quality and sale of finished goods. These were the functions which the Gujaratis and other coastal merchants also exercised, with a measure of independence and mobility peculiar to them. They constituted a potential opposition to feudalism to the extent to which their situation enabled them to carry on their urban trade without much let or hindrance. But socially the position of Hindu merchants here was much the same as elsewhere. Their occupation was hereditary and their status inferior to that of priestly as well as landed and military aristocracy. They never sprang from among the ranks of craftsmen as their English counterparts frequently did. Their ability and character combined with their wealth to raise them in public esteem, but they could not climb the rungs of the social ladder so as to move into positions held by the nobility; nor could they ever intermarry with them. Caste stood in the way: it did not allow wealth to supersede status by birth. Indian society was in fact not a money-dominated society with freedom for individuals to move up or down the social scale according to economic circumstances. However, a fair sprinkling of Parsis, Bohras, and Jains, who formed a separate community regardless of caste barriers, made all the difference. It introduced into that region a nucleus of social mobility which would later contribute to progress on Western lines.

Among the inland towns of the Mughal empire Benares held a peculiar position of its own. As a centre of Hindu culture and learning, it remained to a large extent free from the imposition of Mughal authority. The mildness of its government contributed to the development of trade and industry to a degree never attained by those parts of the province more immediately under Mughal

[25] See above, p. 26 n. 12.

rule. Many reputable shroffs flocked to it from a sense of security and converted the city into a nucleus of banking operations. Their money dealings extended to all parts of India, particularly to Surat where their bills of exchange were most current.[26] Thus places comparatively free from the despotic rule of the Mughals were more favourable to business than those effectually under it. Despotism introduced an element of insecurity which restricted the flow of capital. The ordinary merchants remained subordinate to magnates, and the magnates in turn to local governors, who had the option of entering the market and preventing competition whenever they wished to.

The Marwaris, one of the major business communities of India, represented precisely the type which grew under bureaucratic influence. Originally residents of Marwar, which in Akbar's time included the districts of Ajmer, Jodhpur, Sirohi, Nagaur, and Bikaner, they spread far and wide over the whole country. Probably the desert and mountainous tract of their homeland, with scanty rains and limited manufactures, held out little promise for a full expression of their business ability and skill. The militarism of Rajputs and the predatory hordes of Mairs[27] perhaps pushed them in the same direction and persuaded this enterprising class to move out in quest of fresh woods and pastures new.

The Marwaris were divided into a number of sections called Oswal, Mahesri, Agarwal, Porwal, Srimal, Srisrimal, Vijayawargi, Saraogi, and Khatri.[28] They traded in goods of local consumption, chiefly grain, cotton, and opium. Those who specialized in banking and money-lending were called Seths and Mahajans. According to the *Gazetteer of Ajmer-Merwar*, the heads of a number of firms trading in other parts of India lived at Ajmer where their sole business was banking and money-lending.[29] The Mughal government recognized their title of Seth and, as we have seen, conferred it on Fatehchand (Jagat Seth) whose ancestors had come from Nagaur in the seventeenth century. Many of the Marwaris were Jains, of whom there were a great many in parts of Marwar and

[26] See Rep. Com. HC on Petitions, 1781, p. 41 a–b.
[27] See C. G. Dixon, *Sketch of Mairwara* (1850).
[28] C. K. M. Walter, *Gazetteers of Marwar, Mallarni &c.* (Cal., 1877), p. 24.
[29] This business declined since the enactment of a law prohibiting sales of land in execution of decrees (J. D. Latruchet, *Gazetteer of Ajmer-Merwar*, pp. 50–51, 95–96).

who had their shrine at Mount Abu. Together they constituted a numerous class of banyans scattered all over India in larger or smaller groups. Situated at great distances from their native land and locally segregated as a community known for its crafty and usurious habits, the Marwaris established a pattern of behaviour at once timid and parsimonious. They usually submitted, since they were illiterate and inferior in caste, to the arbitrary proceedings of local officials. Manucci's description of banyans was particularly applicable to this class.

The pomp that surrounded the Mughal palace by no means signified the people's prosperity. The system of government was such that nobody felt secure. It encouraged hoarding both on the part of private individuals and government officers. It is often argued that the pay of the vast army as well as the upkeep of magnificent courts and their ostentatious officials sent precious metals into circulation in the purchase of every article of luxury. It is true that this encouraged industry and kept the country's economy going. But, as will be seen, the men engaged in production were treated more or less as forced labour. They could not bargain. Moreover, they satisfied the requirements of only a small and limited part of the country's population, the king and his officers, who alone consumed luxury goods. As for the great bulk of the countrymen, their dress was cheap and simple, little subject to change for ages. The rules of caste also obliged them to adhere to a particular mode of apparel.[30] The products of industry thus went into the coffers of the king's bureaucracy, and did little to improve the lot of the producers themselves.

The king's monopoly and the risk of official interference constituted yet another obstacle to private enterprise. These tended to narrow down the area of free trade and to kill the competition necessary for economic prosperity and thus prevent the emergence of new functional groups as elements of a stratified society. As has been said, before investing any capital private merchants had to reckon with the possibility of local governors or their nominees appearing in the market to buy or sell any commodity at a rate not determined by the principle of free competition but by the will of men in authority. The king himself was in this respect the sole banker and carried on business on his own account. He advanced

[30] See 3rd Rep. Sel. Com. of Court of Directors, 1792–3, p. 9.

loans and granted monopolies to whomsoever he wished. There could be no objection to the state interfering with the movement of trade in the interest of the community, but no attempt on the part of the sovereign or his officers to monopolize staple commodities, including even food grains, with the sole object of enriching himself or his agents could ever be justified. In 1632 the governor of Surat monopolized the entire available supply of food grains, and he did so at a time when Gujarat was in the grip of a terrible famine. Mir Jumla was another governor who was notorious for imposing his authority to advance his trade concerns.[31] The *English Factory Records* of the period are indeed replete with instances where local officers intervened, even in defiance of the standing orders of Government.

An interesting case arose in 1633 when the Mughal king granted one Mannodas (Manohar Das) the exclusive right to buy all indigo grown in the kingdom.[32] In return, he was to pay at the end of three years a sum of six lakhs of rupees out of his profits and another five lakhs towards the repayment of a loan made to him out of the royal treasury. But since the English and the Dutch were the main export dealers in indigo, it was feared that they might combine to abstain from buying. It was therefore stipulated that in case the foreign merchants declined to buy from Manohar Das, and the whole quantity of indigo remained in his hands, he was to be excused from all payment to the king except in respect of the loan. It may be noted that the English themselves had first been asked to farm the indigo areas on the terms offered by Manohar Das, but they refused. They could not afford to be so oppressive as a fellow countryman. 'Whatever authority the King may give', they argued, 'it would be impossible for them to deal as rigorously with the people as their fellow-countrymen can.' Instead of buying indigo from Manohar Das at fifty rupees a maund against a market price of less than half, the English persuaded the Dutch to form a covenant that both nations 'shall for the year ensuing forbear to buy indigo anywhere in this kingdom' and that for the duration of this contract neither company would

---

[31] Foster, *Eng. Fac. Ind.*, *1646–50*, pp. 98, 137, 139, 166, 198, 213, 273

[32] Ibid. *1630–33*, pp. 324–5. The indigo produced in the whole of the country amounted to nearly 1,500 maunds, of which Biana (near Agra) indigo came to one-third.

export any indigo in their ships either for Muhammadans or other persons. This broke down the monopoly arrangement and the market returned to normal.

But such instances of combination were only few and far between. In the ordinary course of business it was open to a governor or his agent to monopolize any article of trade likely to bring considerable profit to him. This practice, as we have said, was ruinous to social progress in that it penalized the social class which should have received the benefit of trade and the produce of industry. It tended to prevent the growth of an intermediate class in point of income. A study of the contemporary records suggests that, consistently with its own interest, the English East India Company wished to negotiate directly and to by-pass the rich monopolists and rapacious governors. But since in the early days it could not afford to antagonize either, the intermediate commercial group had to remain contented with the leavings of the grandees.

THE ARTISAN

So far as the quality of industrial production was concerned, India enjoyed in the seventeenth, and even in the eighteenth, century a reputation in no way inferior to that of any other country. It stood unequalled especially in the manufacture of cotton fabrics, shawls, and luxury goods, including gold and silver cloths, brocades, and embroideries as well as those which specialized in the cutting, polishing, and setting of precious stones. Della Valle tells us that cotton linen was 'for the most part very fine in comparison of those of our Countries'.[33] Pyrard admires the shops of jewellers and goldsmiths, of carpet weavers and silk mercers.[34] On his way from Patna to Agra, Manrique visited Benares and found the city 'very rich on account of the abundance of its merchandise, especially its very fine cotton cloth'. He says that the town and its suburbs maintained as many as 7,000 looms and produced rich head-dresses 'variegated with gold, silver, and various coloured silks' which were exported to 'Turkey, Persia, and Corazane' and many other countries where European shady hats were not in use.[35] Writing in a period of decline, in 1840,

[33] Della Valle, i. 43.   [34] Pyrard, ii. 64.   [35] Manrique, ii. 146–7.

Hugh Murray, a member of the Royal Society of Edinburgh, admired the quality of the Indian loom which according to him

had reached a perfection to which those of no other country except Britain, and that very recently, could make even an approach. The delicate and flexible form of the Hindoo, the pliancy of his fingers, and the exquisite sense with which they were endowed, even his quiet indefatigable perseverance, all render him peculiarly fitted for this description of employment. The muslins of Dacca in fineness, the calicoes and other piece-goods of Coromandel in brilliant durable colours, had never been surpassed.[36]

Earlier, in the course of his visit to Bengal, Pyrard seemed equally impressed by the superiority of its cotton and silk manu-factures.

The inhabitants, both men and women [he writes] are wondrously adroit in all manufactures, such as of cotton cloth and silks, and in needlework, such as embroideries, which are worked so skilfully, down to the smallest stitches, that nothing prettier is to be seen anywhere. Some of these cottons and silks are so fine that it is difficult to say whether a person so attired be clothed or nude.[37]

What struck Peter Mundy was the quality of saltpetre and indigo manufactured at Agra, of calico made at Broach, and of *tassar* silk produced in Patna.

W. H. Moreland's masterly study of India's economy under Akbar and three of his successors reached a similar conclusion. It confirmed the excellence of Indian manufactures, especially of cotton and silk textiles, where India exercised a virtual monopoly of the home market and also those of neighbouring and remote countries. Making allowance for certain errors, he says, 'it is still to my mind indisputable that in the matter of industry India was more advanced relatively to Western Europe than she is to-day.'[38]

But the excellence of manufactures in India did not generally signify any social advancement of the manufacturers. To the fixedly low estimation attaching to all handicrafts under the rules of caste, was added the military nature of government and its

---

[36] *Historical and Descriptive Account of British India* (1843), ii. 442.
[37] Pyrard, i. 329; also Barbosa, ii. 145–6.
[38] *India at the Death of Akbar* (1920), pp. 155–6.

peculiar pattern of distribution which deprived the great bulk of the people of any reserve of wealth.

No artist [says Bernier] is expected to give his mind to his calling in the midst of a people who are either wretchedly poor, or who, if rich, assume an appearance of poverty, and who regard not the beauty and excellence, but the cheapness of an article: a people whose grandees pay for a work of art considerably under its value, and according to their own caprice, and who do not hesitate to punish an importunate artist, or tradesman with the *korrah*, that long and terrible whip hanging at every *Omrah's* (noble) gate.[39]

He goes on to suggest that the situation under which the artisans worked was such that they could 'never hope to attain to any distinction' or to effect any savings with which to 'purchase either office or land'. Nor would they ever venture to 'indulge in good fare or to dress in fine apparel', even if they could afford to.

The Indian artisans and handicraftsmen possessed the skill and ingenuity necessary to rise into the higher income and social groups. Bernier noticed that though 'destitute of tools' they produced in several cases 'handsome pieces of workmanship' without any supervision or assistance. But they had no education to support their skill or to sustain the quality of their workmanship. An occupation descended from father to son. And since occupation and status went by birth, the possibility of functional or social upgrading was generally ruled out. 'The embroiderer', observes Bernier, 'brings up his son as an embroiderer, the son of a goldsmith becomes a goldsmith. . . . No one marries but in his own trade or profession; and this custom is observed almost as rigidly by *Mahometans* as by the *Gentiles*.'[40] Della Valle tells us that none of the descendants of a caste could ever depart from the calling of their race. He adds that they 'never rise nor fall'.[41] Society was thus in a state of stagnation, not of progress.

Max Weber, the great German sociologist, also maintains that the professional castes, particularly those of industry, were, and still are, 'the very pillars of rigid caste segregation and tradition— alongside pure peasant castes, for which a rigid traditionalism goes without saying'.[42] Their attachment to customary pursuits is so

---

[39] Bernier, p. 228. [40] Ibid. p. 259. [41] Della Valle, i. 78.
[42] Weber, p. 104.

great and tenacious that, for example, in spite of the modern capitalist environment of a metropolitan city, such as Calcutta in the first decade of this century, 80 per cent. of the laundrymen followed their traditional pursuits; so did more than 50 per cent. of the Hindu caste of fishermen, street-cleaners, basket weavers, pastry cooks, domestic servants, and even goldsmiths.

Though famous for their industry and accumulation of property, the ancient professional castes impeded the advancement of technology because of their tenacious adherence to traditionalism and 'a mutual segregation of the various branches of production'.[43] The artisans were no doubt possessed of skill, but they received no education to enable them to command respect or to know the theory of professional skills. Education was the virtual monopoly of the upper castes, the twice-born, especially of the Brahmans. There was no occupational mobility which might otherwise have resulted in a combination of skill and education. A Karma-ordained social system like that of the Hindus hindered such mobility. It tended to obstruct the indigenous growth of modern capitalism. Weber remarks that 'a ritual law in which every change of occupation, every change in work technique, may result in ritual degradation is certainly not capable of giving birth to economic and technical revolutions from within itself, or even of facilitating the first germination of capitalism in its midst'.[44] Intellectual and industrial pursuits remained poles apart.

Manufactures were carried on essentially on small-scale domestic levels. The artisan depended upon production for the market. There was the merchant and the urban artisan, but the latter was more often dependent economically upon merchant guilds. The weavers, for example, possessed their hereditary looms and they provided for local consumption, except in cases where they received advances from a merchant or his agent who collected from them his stock for the general market. It often took considerable time for a buyer to assemble small lots from individual producers before these could be made up into a full consignment for dispatch to a central market or for export. This small-scale production in fact dictated the decision on the part of Europeans to establish 'factories' and to appoint 'factors' or agents to buy the articles of trade and store them for periodical transportation. The early

[43] Weber, p. 105.   [44] Ibid. p. 112.

European factories were thus no more than mere warehouses which later grew into manufactories or centres of production. Peter Mundy found it very difficult to procure goods even in a large city like Patna during his visit there in 1632, when he was told by one Gongerum (Ganga Ram), a reputable broker who dealt in coarse linen, that 'there might bee invested 2 or 3,000 rupees a Moneth; but before that would bee effected, it would require 40 or 50 days, I meane before wee should receive the Cloth ready Merchantable [for sale]'.[45] It was to obviate this difficulty that Hughes, an English factor of Agra who had visited Patna in 1620 in search of *tassar* silk and calico, recommended the establishment of a factory there for 'continual residence'.

Thus in addition to the existing political and social systems, the domestic size of production as well as the practice of selling goods directly to tradesmen left little scope for the division of labour and the consequent rise of an industrial middle class. Buying through a broker or middleman was not unknown. It was practised wherever direct dealing was considered impracticable. But the broker operated more as an agency of supply than as the means to industrial organization. He worked either under a private merchant or a European company. If an independent person, practising on his own, he charged commission on the amount of the transaction made. Whether independent or otherwise, he also made his profits from the difference in the price paid by his principal and that paid to the producers. Though associated with manufactures in a manner supposed to be supervisory and to an extent even managerial in so far as he was to ensure a proper return to the advances made, he used his position to build up fortunes more by a deterioration of quality than by its improvement. The interest of the manufacturer and of the trader stood to suffer under the middleman. His agency was therefore discouraged, although he formed an indispensable appendage to European factors, ignorant of local languages and customs, rates and practices. Moreland is right when he says that 'the management of business had not been separated from the work of manufacture and that production was carried on by artisans without superior capitalist direction'.[46]

---

[45] *The Travels of Peter Mundy in Europe and Asia*, ed. R. C. Temple (1914), p. 146 and App. D, pp. 362–3.

[46] *India*, p. 184.

The Mughal king was however the biggest capitalist. According to Bernier, he possessed manufactories called 'karkhans' where the most skilled workmen were employed in the manufacture of embroideries, silks, brocades, and fine muslins; of precious stones and ornaments, as well as in a number of other arts, including painting and varnishing, joining and turning, tailoring and shoemaking. The royal workshops represented a higher stage of production, for the artisans worked under the superintendence and direction of an officer of Government who presumably supplied the materials and ensured the quality of designs and workmanship. But while the element of superior direction was official and dependent on Government, the income of the artisans even here bore no relation to their productivity. In spite of the king's patronage, 'the great majority of the workers had nothing to hope for beyond the continuance of the conditions which afforded them a bare subsistence'.[47] In so undeveloped a country, the state's monopoly of production seriously arrested the evolution of an industrial middle class—the product of free competition and a money economy.

What the king did at the centre the governors followed in the provinces. The artisans were not free to contract or to sell their produce at a profit so as to effect savings and form a reserve. The Dutchman Pelsaert, who was in Agra from 1621 to 1627, deplored that besides low wages the workmen had to submit to the oppression of the local governor and other officers of Government. 'If any of these', he wrote, 'wants a workman, the man is not asked if he is willing to come, but is seized in the house or in the street, well beaten if he should dare to raise any objection, and in the evening paid half his wages, or nothing at all.'[48] Bernier, as has been seen, confirms this view and adds that nothing but sheer necessity or blows from a cudgel kept an artisan employed.

He never can become rich [Bernier comments], and he feels it no trifling matter if he has the means of satisfying the cravings of hunger, and of covering his body with the coarsest raiment. If money be gained, it does not in any measure go into his pocket, but only serves to increase the wealth of the merchant. . . .[49]

[47] Moreland, *India*, p. 188.
[48] F. Pelsaert, *Jahangir's India*, tr. W. H. Moreland and P. Geyl (1925), p. 60.
[49] Bernier, p. 229.

And as the artisans had partially to depend on agriculture, any failure of their crops brought disaster to them. The famine of 1630–2, for instance, reduced the weavers to a state of penury, particularly in Gujarat where according to Peter Mundy hardly one out of ten survived that great catastrophe. For the duration of the famine they could with difficulty supply twenty to thirty pieces in comparison with forty or fifty scores which they did before.[50] Mundy explains the sufferings of the manufacturers by saying that the rich and strong engrossed and took everything they could for themselves.

THE LANDED ARISTOCRACY

Wealth was obviously concentrated in the hands of the upper class of nobility, landed or commercial. In view of the country's technological backwardness, however, the landed nobility dominated the commercial group through their control over the military and bureaucratic apparatus of the state.

The Mughal amirs or nobles constituted only a section of the country's superior landed interest. They formed part of the mansabdari establishment[51] to which every officer of Government was primarily recruited and graded according to the number of horsemen he was paid for. An amir was paid either in cash from the royal treasury or by an assignment of land revenue called jagir. Akbar stressed the former mode of payment, but in the seventeenth century the latter was becoming more and more popular. The grant of jagir was also one of the forms in which the meritorious service of an officer was often recognized. This system of assigning the public revenues in lieu of salary encouraged the formation of vested interests in land arising from a continued power to collect revenue from and manage the same, especially in parts remote from the capital, where offices tended to be hereditary under a weak centre. In places where a class of landed gentry or small landholders existed in one form or another before the Mughal empire, the grant of jagirs tended in effect to reduce this class to a state of subservience to the jagirdar who stepped in as part of a higher superstructure.

In the distant provinces of the empire like Bengal or parts of

[50] Mundy, ii. 245–6, 276.   [51] See below, p. 46.

Bihar the government entrusted the collection of revenue either to certain ancient families of rajas or zamindars, such as the Rajput chiefs of Monghyr, Ramgarh, or other frontier districts, who had perhaps migrated from the north-west, or to such other men of local influence as stipulated to pay a fixed sum annually to the royal exchequer. The zamindar functioned more or less as a semi-official agency operating locally in subordination to a district executive officer called faujdar, whom he assisted in the preservation of the peace and, if necessary, placed at his disposal the entire police contingents engaged in the collection of revenue or night patrolling. Some of the rajas maintained an auxiliary armed force which they supplied to Government whenever called upon to do so. They even performed a number of odd duties, such as the supply of victuals and other necessaries required by an army in the course of its march through their zamindari.

At least in the early part of the eighteenth century, in most districts of Bengal there existed, in addition to big zamindars, a class of small landholders called taluqdars. They were comparable to the village zamindars of the Upper Provinces where the word 'taluqdar' signified a superior landed interest like that of a jagirdar or Bengal zamindar. The counterpart of village zamindars or small middle-class landed gentry existed likewise in Madras and parts of western India, but they were all subject to the immediate rule of an overlord wherever Government decided to impose one. Socially, the appointment of a farmer of revenue holding a long lease had a similar effect, although he was inferior in status to a hereditary zamindar, who was not required to furnish any security for the payment of his revenue.

The holders of jagir or free grants of land called *madad-i-ma'sh* (subsistence grant) represented yet another type of major landed interest. Such grants were under the administration of a separate functionary called Chief Sadr. The object was to support such institutions or individuals as engaged in Islamic studies or other cultural pursuits of a religious or charitable nature. These grants were in fact made in return for such services as lay beyond the scope of the regular mansabdari establishment. They differed from the jagirs allowed to officers of Government in lieu of salary. They were part of *waqf* or charity land granted for life or in perpetuity. *Soyurghals* were another kind of charitable endowment made out of *waqf* land, but these were 'not confined to members of religious classes',[52] nor was their grant restricted to *waqf* land. It was also made out of waste or even crown lands carrying of course certain immunities from taxation in each case. Abu Fazl gives a list of learned scholars, including qazis and muftis, who were granted quite considerable jagirs. For instance Maulana Alauddin, a scholar from Laristan who had once been Akbar's tutor, held 4,000 bighars as *soyurghal* in Sambhal.[53]

These various types of assignees constituted elements of what might be called a feudal structure of society where the rajas or zamindars received from the king their arms and fiefs with knightly ceremonies. Their seignorial rights, however, arose from tax-farming and the military and fiscal fiefs of a bureaucratic state rather than from any legal recognition of the same in respect of village lands. In the words of Max Weber, 'these were a product, not of feudalization, but of later prebendalization of political authority'.[54] For, as will be seen later, villages in most parts of India were immediately owned either individually or collectively by a class of proprietors variously known as mirasdars, village zamindars, or lambardars. Custom even recognized the occupancy rights of a resident peasant, although the exercise of such rights depended upon the discretion of the immediate overlord.

The upper class of nobility did possess the means, though not the will, necessary to effect some material progress. They were men of capital which they could have invested profitably in the improvement of agriculture, but the majority of the higher order of the landed aristocracy cared little to acquire a knowledge of the subject. Although born to considerable estates, most of them even lacked incentives to educate themselves. They were receivers of rent rather than entrepreneurs in agricultural production. While their contemporary English counterpart was being fast induced to organize agriculture so as to produce a saleable surplus, the Indian landholders, frequently given to vice like other men of rank, thought of nothing but of extorting the utmost possible from the labouring tenantry. Moreover, since the landed interest was dominated by the upper-caste Hindus, who regarded mercantile pur-

[52] A. K. S. Lambton, *Landlord and Peasant in Persia* (1953), p. 115.
[53] Abu Fazl, *The Ain i-Akbari*, tr. H. Blochmann (1873–94), i. 540.
[54] Weber, p. 66.

suits as inferior, the commercialization of agriculture was an object foreign to them. The trading or banking interests could afford to buy zamindaris and settle down as rural capitalists. Many of the shroffs in fact advanced loans to zamindars to clear off the arrears of revenue. But as a zamindari was more of an office than property, and as its transfer was subject to the previous permission of Government, it was not without risk to have it transferred and to take possession of it against the will of the overlord. Probably from their distant urban situation the shroffs were unwilling to undertake the risk of an agricultural investment. Those who made advances did so from motives of interest, and that too on the personal security of the debtor. These circumstances perhaps prejudiced the rise of rural capitalism in the pre-British period.

It is true that in between the big zamindars and the cultivating tenants there did exist in some form or other a class of small land-holders. They were called taluqdars and mukarraridars in Bengal and Bihar, village zamindars in parts of Bihar and the upper provinces, and mirasdars in the south of India.[55] One of their common features was, and still is, that they traced their origin to a common ancestry and that they held the villages as coparceners. But on these, as we have said, was superimposed a higher order of landed interest called zamindars in Bengal, taluqdars or jagirdars in Oudh (Avadh), inamdars in Bombay, and poligars in Madras.[56] It was this superimposition that obstructed the growth of small land-holders into a landed middle class comparable to the English yeomanry or landed gentry, and it was this superimposition again that the revenue laws of the British tended later to weaken or even to remove.

One regular feature that characterized the Indian landed aristocracy was that it was imposed by conquest and maintained itself in power unchecked by popular institutions. Though not wholly cut off from the community, if was never renewed from below. Even the village zamindars of the Upper Provinces, for example, traced their ancestry to certain Rajput conquerors from the north-west. In the absence of a law of primogeniture, their descendants in time were reduced to small tenure holders, whom the English termed 'village zamindars'. Force came into play again when the jagirdars

[55] S. S. Iyengar, *Land Tenures in the Madras Presidency* (1921), pp. 94–95.
[56] Ibid. p. 112.

or taluqdars were imposed upon them after they had been so reduced. Similarly, the holders of *ghatwali* tenure in Bihar were at one time Rajput conquerors from the north-west. These immigrants kept themselves aloof from the local population and maintained themselves in power with the support of the Mughal king. They maintained their racial purity and would not allow the marriage of their daughters to locally-born Rajputs. The mirasdars of the south were Brahman usurpers of the land originally belonging to local tribesmen.

The Nairs of Malabar, who constituted a landowning military aristocracy, held the poliyas, a low-caste people, in great disdain. Thévenot says that if a Nair felt the breath of a poliya, he considered himself polluted, and was obliged to kill the man and make certain ablutions to restore his purity. No poliya was allowed to enter a town. If he wanted anything, he cried for it with a loud voice outside the town, and left the money at a certain place appointed for the purpose. Some merchant then brought the commodity he wanted and collected the money so left. The Nairs were bound in fealty to their king, from whom they held their jagirs in return for military service. The Rajputs also held their fiefs from their overlord on a similar condition. With them all commands were hereditary. The vassal served his lord, the lord his raja, and the raja the suzerain. Akbar became the suzerain and left the whole system intact.

The Mughals in their turn introduced a degree of despotism which can hardly be paralleled in India. Conquest naturally formed the basis of their nobility, which consisted in the main of foreign Muslim adventurers, particularly from Persia and Afghanistan. Abul Fazl's list of Akbar's amirs (nobles) indicates that very few of the Indian Muslims occupied higher posts in the army and civil service. There was a fair sprinkling of Hindu nobles in the hierarchy of the Mughal administration. Of the 415 amirs and mansabdars on Abu Fazl's list, for example, 51 were Hindus.[57] With the extension of the empire, their number increased and was doubled in Shah Jahan's time, but these were not recruited from among the Indian merchants. They were either foreign adventurers or such of the Rajput princes as the king considered politically dependable and socially superior.

[57] *Ain*, i. 236.

The alien character of the official aristocracy, the incorporation of its members regardless of any consideration of their educational equipment, and the complete absence of any service rules or conditions reduced them to a state of servility to the king. He 'raises them to dignities, or degrades them to obscurity, according to his own pleasure or caprice'.[58] The whole basis of the Mughal official hierarchy, called the mansabdari system, was indeed founded on autocracy. By way of justification, Abu Fazl attributes it to the inherent baseness of human nature whose 'passions' and 'wickedness' he considers worse than those of animals. And since these could not be suppressed by a monarch alone, he appointed mansabdars to do so under his guidance.[59]

The costly presents which the superior officers of Government had to make to the king, their own large establishments of wives and entourage, and their extravagant spending on the pomp and splendour of courts constituted a dead weight on the country's resources. The Mughal bureaucracy and army together obstructed the flow of money and material advantages to levels other than their own, or, in some measure, to those of their hirelings and retinues.

The amirs lavished no small treasures on palaces and tombs to satisfy personal vanity. Works of a productive nature and of public utility did not receive as much of their attention as gladiatorial shows and the new year's pageantry. Public works were probably more an object of private benefaction that of the royal treasury. Contemporary records and accounts of foreign travellers indicate that the roads were in a very bad condition and transportation extremely slow and risky.[60] This tended to reduce the movement of trade and made famine relief altogether impossible. Dr. P. Saran admires the efforts of Government in the construction of dams and bridges, but he has only two examples under this head to mention for the whole empire. He also refers to the provision of a regular medical service, and says that the Government spent 2,000 rupees annually on the purchase of medicines.[61] This petty amount reflects its apathy rather than redounds to its credit. The

---

[58] Bernier, p. 212.   [59] *Ain*, i. 236–7.
[60] Foster, *Eng. Fac. Ind., 1637–41*, p. 2; also Della Valle, i. 95; Manrique, ii. 145.
[61] *The Provincial Government of the Mughals* (1941), p. 419.

only major work of public benefit was the erection of caravan *sarais* or rest-houses, which were relatively widespread. But here too the motive was to facilitate, by a regular supply of rest-house horses, postal communication which was not to be used for private purposes.

The prodigal nature of the Mughal aristocracy possibly arose from the fact that it was hardly rooted in the country or even hereditary. The grandsons of the greatest amirs had often to serve in the ranks as common soldiers. Under the system of what was called 'escheat', the king exercised his right to inherit their estates and other savings. From a letter written by Aurangzeb to his father it appears that as soon as an amir breathed his last, or before he died, it was customary to put royal seals on his coffers and to beat the servants to make them disclose the whole property.[62] Pelsaert gives a clear picture of how on the death of an amir his effects were appropriated by the king and his children obliged to begin life afresh. He writes:

Immediately on the death of a lord who has enjoyed the King's *jagir*, be he great or small, without any exception—sometimes even before the breath is out of his body—the King's officers are ready on the spot, and make an inventory of the entire estate, recording everything down to the value of a single pice, even to the dresses and jewels of the ladies, provided they have not concealed them. The King takes back the whole estate absolutely for himself, except in a case where the deceased has done good service in his lifetime, when the women and children are given enough to live on, but no more. . . . And so you may see a man whom you knew with his turban cocked on one side, and nearly as unapproachable as his master, now running about with a torn coat and a pinched face; for it is rarely that such men can obtain similar employment from other masters, and they go about like pictures of death in life, as I have known many of them to do.[63]

The official aristocracy of the Mughals thus lacked both economic stability and psychological security. Unlike the English aristocracy, it had no roots in an ancient society. It constituted the upper crust of a hierarchical society, but since it formed an exclusive caste, it had no chance of being replenished except by a recruitment of foreigners who made hay while the sun shone. Their

[62] Moreland, *From Akbar to Aurangzeb* (1923), pp. 277-8.
[63] Pelsaert, pp. 54-55.

rapid advancement and promotion in the service were as easy as their sudden decline and ruin. Pelsaert remarks that under the Mughals 'wealth, position, love, friendship, confidence, everything hangs by a thread'.[64] This produced a sense of insecurity which reacted in turn on the general pattern of social behaviour characterized by want of firmness and straightforward dealings.

[64] Pelsaert, p. 56

II

The Authoritarian Basis of Society

AUTOCRACY as a basis of the Indian political system may be traced in some degree to the patriarchal nature of its vast rural communities dominated by Hindus. The growth of urbanization, with its mixed and mobile population, conduced to sociability which tended to militate against autocracy, but since, unlike the English ones, the Indian medieval towns possessed no charters of liberties nor any form of popular municipal government, they could not operate as an effective check on the arbitrary proceedings of officials. Even the upper stratum of the business communities could not afford to ignore them. Moreover the Mughal towns were after all enclaves situated in a vast rural surrounding where money was still a scarce commodity. Rural societies thus continued to be governed by three of their main institutions, the joint family, caste, and village community.

The joint-family system was, and still is, a characteristic feature of the Hindu social system. It signified common property, common rituals and common meals. It represented practically a primitive, communistic form of production where on account of undeveloped technology and ignorance of advanced agricultural science and methods, the collective endeavours of the family, and then of the kin and the community, were necessary to make the local economy and defence possible. But as the Hindu family was a patriarchal institution, the father acted as chief and maintained its unity by an exercise of exclusive discretion in the disposal of the entire property.[1] Added to this was the sanction of religion, on which the whole concept of property was founded among both Hindus and Muhammadans. The sons of a father were naturally

[1] In his *Judicial System of the Marathas*, p. 2, V. T. Gune shows that the disposal of property was subject to the general consent of the village community.

bound to him in loyalty as subjects of a king, especially in the absence of such other avenues of employment as the growth of education, technology, and industry later created under British rule.

Whatever its other effects, the minute fragmentation of inheritance to which the whole system gave rise proved inimical to the formation of capital which might otherwise have contributed to prosperity and progress. While on the one hand it encouraged idle dependence on patrimony, stifling disposition to innovation and a variety of productive occupations, it led on the other to the formation of uneconomic holdings which dissipated both energy and capital. Except in the case of certain ancient families of rajas, who allowed the exclusive right of inheritance by primogeniture in opposition to Hindu or Muhammadan law, the descendants of the greatest landed proprietor were bound in time to sink to ordinary landholders or even poor farmers.[2] Indian merchants and bankers too were not free from the ruinous effects of the law of inheritance. They built temples and tanks and left considerable fortunes to their sons, but by the time their savings came to be subdivided in the third or fourth generation, the successors had become too poor even to be able to repair the works erected by their ancestors.

In England, whereas the aristocratic principle of primogeniture saved landed property from disintegration, the early growth of joint-stock companies ensured an increasing flow of capital which made the agricultural revolution possible. The process of cross-fertilization benefited both landed and commercial interests and later became the harbinger of the Industrial Revolution. The English yeomanry and merchants set up their own schools and colleges which became centres of education for the laity, both literary and scientific. While primogeniture had the effect of freeing younger sons to join commercial and colonial enterprises, the less rigid emphasis on aristocracy by birth made the task easier for common people to climb the social ladder. Cross-fertilization in fact set in motion a process of competition where career was open to talents. In India the joint-family system, with a divinely-

---

[2] See Beng. Govt. Let. to Court, 6 Mar. 1793, para. 8, in Rep. Sel. Com. HC, 1808–12 (P.B. Coll. 55), p. 100. The principle of primogeniture was not recognized by Cornwallis, who abolished the custom introduced by certain principal zamindars.

ordained status by birth, was opposed to any progress of society. Although individual enterprise was not lacking, and instances of rapid rise in fortunes were numerous under a despotic government, the gradual fragmentation of property prejudiced the formation of any stable and permanent economic interest which arises from a long and sustained enjoyment of undivided property rights. 'Although rapid rise and sudden fortunes', commented Mountstuart Elphinstone, 'are more common in India than in Europe, they produce no permanent change in the society; all remains on the same dead level, with no conspicuous objects to guide the course of the community, and no barrier to oppose to the arbitrary will of the ruler.'[3]

CASTE

Caste, as has been said, was another course of social stagnation. Its ritual basis and occupational immobility obstructed the transformation of *status* into *contract* as the principle of social organization. It was a Brahmanical institution based on the law of Karma, whereby a man's status in this life is determined by his actions in past lives. Under this law all living creatures, including human beings, remained subject to a repeated process of transmigration or a cycle of birth, death, and rebirth unless by virtue of their good deeds they secured a merger with the *Brahma*, the supreme being, who was believed to be absolute and unchangeable. Caste was thus supposed to be a divinely-ordained social system under which every individual was born to a fixed state of existence, to which were assigned a fixed occupation and a fixed status. These were subject to improvement or promotion to a higher status according to the quality of the deed performed, but no individual could be entitled to this except after rebirth. The philosophy of the Hindu social system in fact recognized no 'natural rights' of man. It hindered occupational mobility, precluded social criticism, and made for authoritarianism as the principle of the Hindu social system.

The assimilative powers of Hinduism were so great that not only alien ruling classes but even the devotional sects such as Jainism and Buddhism, which arose in revolt against Brahmanism, were

[3] *The History of India*, 6th ed. (1874), p. 224.

incorporated into the caste order. Integration into the Hindu community provided religious legitimation for the ruling stratum. As Max Weber has said (p. 16):

> It not only endowed the ruling stratum of the barbarians with recognized rank in the cultural world of Hinduism, but, through their transformation into castes, secured their superiority over the subject classes with an efficiency unsurpassed by any other religion.

The history of India is no doubt replete with instances of popular movements which arose from time to time to challenge the validity of hereditary privileges. These also questioned the sanctity of Brahmanical ritualism and animal sacrifice as the basis of *moksha* or freedom from rebirth.[4] Brahmanism had, for example, to contend with the Ajivikas, Jains, and Buddhists who recognized no caste ritualism or sacrifice. Of those, the Buddhists were by far the most popular. They kept open house to all, regardless even of nationality, and Buddhism spread far and wide into regions remote from the country of its origin. But though important elsewhere it decayed in India, where these early movements degenerated into sects and were finally assimilated as part of the Hindu caste order.

Vaishnavism was another popular movement based on the principle of loving faith called *bhakti*. It was preached among others by Vasudevakas, later called Bhagavatas. The religious and philosophical principles of the early *bhakti* movement were expounded in the *Bhagavad Gita*. These were comparable to the teachings of the Upanishads, universal in appeal and liberal in concept. Like Buddhism, its followers stressed the piety and purity of human thought and conduct as a value superior to rites and sacrificial ceremonies. To these must be added the worshippers of Shiva called Lingayats, who formed part of the popular movements directed against the Brahmanical hegemony. The *bhakti* movements of the middle ages likewise incorporated the liberal traditions of the early periods and tried to reconcile the cultural conflicts arising from the impact of Islam in India. These degenerated into sects and gave rise to distinct monastic orders, where the upper castes became identified with the prevailing caste order and

---

[4] Nirvana, the Buddhist concept of spiritual liberation, was comparable to *moksha*.

the lower remained insignificant as a social force. Since the devotional movements were essentially renunciationist in outlook, and since they generally represented the lower orders of the agricultural population, Brahmanism remained more or less the dominant force in the country. Unlike the contemporary religious renaissance of Europe, which contributed to the rise of capitalism, the liberal traditions of Indian religious movements remained unsupported prior to British rule which, through education and economic development, created both social and economic bases of liberalism.

The recurrence of famine in India was another factor militating against caste rigidity. Starving people of different castes moved in large groups in search of food and broke the bonds of commensality to save themselves from total extinction. In a report of 15 February 1778 Captain James Browne, Collector of the Jangal Tarai district of Bhagalpur, describes the social effects of famine, and points out how on the failure of crops in the plains a considerable number of inhabitants fled to the hills where hardy grains, requiring no water for growth, could be available in plenty. They remained with the hill tribes for the duration of the famine, but on their return found that they had forfeited their caste. 'They were held in so abominable a light', says Browne, 'that no person would trust or employ them; this necessity, and perhaps some influence from the example of the hill people, soon made them robbers; and being well acquainted with the low country, they were more dangerous than the hill people by far.'[5] The sociability produced by a state of famine was thus a temporary phenomenon. Socially, its permanent effects were more ruinous.

Caste tended to be weakened by yet another factor. Nothing could prevent a despot from raising a low-caste man to a position of dignity, and once a person was so raised he acquired a social significance by virtue of wealth and power. A whole community of Kayasths rose in status through royal patronage.[6] They constituted a class of clerks and writers, and though not highly paid, exerted considerable influence on the Mughal Government because of their

---

[5] B.M. Add. MS. 29210, f. 162b.

[6] Colebrooke holds that they were regarded as low in social prestige (see *Asiatic Researches*, v.58). Weber (p. 76) says that 'the kayasths undoubtedly were shudras'; see also Weber, p. 75.

shrewdness and knowledge of Persian, as well as their partiality to alcohol which commended them to royal favour.[7] They rivalled the Brahmans in everything connected with the pen. But these trends were limited to great urban centres, and that too in the north. Elsewhere the dominance of Brahmans continued, and with it the superiority of their caste carrying certain values, such as simplicity of dress and piety to parents, temperance and abstinence, learning and character, service and sacrifice. Pietro della Valle was impressed with their 'doctrine of morality' which held 'not onely Adultery, but even simple Fornication, a great sin'. As a matter of fact they were opposed to commerce of any kind with slaves, male or female. Such of them as were dedicated to spiritual learning and divine worship were held in great esteem and regarded as 'the most noble of all'.[8] They exercised a virtual monopoly of all Hindu learned professions like those of astrologers and physicians, scholars and priests. In the south, where Muslim influence was weak, they even monopolized all secular occupations connected with writing and public business, extending from the minister of state down to the village accountant. In Bengal their position was no less dominant, although intellectual pursuits were equally shared by Kayasths.[9] In western India too Brahmanism reigned supreme in spite of the spread of Christianity. J. H. van Linschoten, for example, says that the villages around Goa had for the most part become Christian; and yet these Christians differed little 'from the other heathens', because 'they can hardly leave their heathenish superstitions'.[10]

Both Pelsaert and Pyrard agree that the influence of Brahmans was not confined to the Hindus. By virtue of their knowledge of astronomy and 'fortune-telling' it extended to 'all the Moslems', who, like the Hindus, would not 'undertake a journey until they have enquired what day or hour is auspicious for the start'.[11] Peter Mundy quotes a specific instance where on his return journey from Burhanpur in June, 1632, the Mughal king Shah Jahan himself stayed out in a garden near Agra till midnight when he was brought

[7] See Manucci, ii. 449–50.

[8] Della Valle, i. 82 and 88; also Terry, pp. 248–51.

[9] J. N. Das Gupta, *Bengal in the Sixteenth Century* (Cal., 1914), pp. 155–8.

[10] *The Voyage of J. H. van Linschoten to the East Indies*, ed. A. C. Burnell (1885), i. 230.

[11] Pelsaert, p. 77; see also Pyrard, i. 371–5.

to his castle, 'close shut up in a palanquin', because the astrologers had so advised.[12]

The village community was a conglomeration of caste groups, each pursuing its hereditary calling and enjoying its fixed status. It was a pattern of rural organization where because of almost exclusive dependence on land in the absence of money economy a village provided locally for all such services as were needed to make the community compact and self-sufficient. Two developments, however, had materially affected what is supposed to be its corporate character. First, before the coming of the British, the influence which dominated a village community was that of a particular kin, especially of Brahmans and Rajputs, who owned most villages, either as village zamindars in the upper provinces and parts of Bihar or as taluqdars in Bengal; as mirasdars in the south or inamdars in the west. The other occupational groups worked in subservience to the dominant landed interest of a village. A kin had offshoots not limited to a village community in that its members held villages in joint ownership. The binding force in such cases was not the community but the kin. Secondly, the superimposition of a higher order of landed interest tended in effect to weaken both the village and the kin loyalty, and made the members subject to the rule of an overlord differently named in the different parts of the country. Fundamentally the inferior occupational groups functioned more or less in bondage in all situations. But with the imposition of a superstructure even the class of independent landholders, who previously paid directly to Government, was subjected to another class of superior intermediaries.

The institution of the village community has in the past occasioned as much controversy as that of caste. Great scholars like Maine and Baden-Powell, Majumdar and Altekar, Matthai and Mukerjee have studied it from different angles and thrown adequate light on the subject. However, since the object here is only to show how far this institution was connected with the growth or otherwise of rural societies, it is sufficient to quote a relevant and remarkable statement made before the parliamentary Select Committee of 1831–2 by Sir C. T. Metcalfe, one of the most experienced and enlightened officers of the East India Company.

[12] Mundy, ii. 194.

The village communities [said Metcalfe] are little republics, having nearly everything that they want within themselves, and almost independent of any foreign relations. They seem to last where nothing else lasts. Dynasty after dynasty tumbles down; revolution succeeds to revolution; Hindoo, Pathan, Mogul, Mahratta, Sik, English, are all masters in turn; but the village communities remain the same. . . . If plunder and devastation be directed against themselves, and the force employed be irresistible, they flee to friendly villages at a distance; but when the storm has passed over, they return and resume their occupations. If a country remain for a series of years the scene of continued pillage and massacre, so that the villages cannot be inhabited, the scattered villagers nevertheless return whenever the power of peaceable possession revives. . . . This union of the village communities, each one forming a separate little state in itself, has, I conceive, contributed more than any other cause to the preservation of the people of India, through all the revolutions and changes which they have suffered; and is in a high degree conducive to their happiness, and to the enjoyment of a great portion of freedom and independence.[13]

Although recorded in an admiring sense, Metcalfe's note inadvertently establishes beyond doubt the immobility of rural societies, tending to continuity rather than growth. It betrays indigenous satisfaction with a deplorably low standard of living arising from exclusive dependence on agriculture and the village industries subservient to it. It shows a lack of enterprise and pioneering spirit necessary for a growing society to explore new and productive careers to improve its living conditions. The peasantry were inextricably bound to their hearths and homes because no better opportunities existed. This view of the village community is thus one which fits in well with a rigid and static concept of society. It doubtless preserved the community, but its members became parochial in thought and behaviour, particularly in the absence of any national system of education. They thought in grooves, and that hardly beyond the confines of their village or the circle of their kin or clans outside. The up-and-down movement of the peasant population arising from a desire to make pilgrimages doubtless militated against parochialism and conduced to sociability, but as such movement was occasional and limited to the well-to-do and higher grades in the social scale, the great bulk of the rural communities remained stagnant, and if they moved at all

[13] Sel. Com. HC, 16 Aug. 1832, app. to Rep. III (735 III), p. 331.

it was only side by side. No concept of a nationhood could grow in such rural societies so long as family, caste, or kin exercised the first claim on the loyalty of their members.

Thus in pre-British times, although there existed potential elements for a middle-class growth in society, a unitary middle-class social order did not exist. The smaller-scale artisan industry of that period could not conduce to its growth. Autocracy and its peculiar pattern of distribution were also inimical to it. These gave incentive to monopoly, tended to kill competition, and held up the circulation of money necessary for the emergence of new income groups. There were large cities where money transactions took place in considerable quantity, but these were mainly restricted to central or provincial capitals which were only few in number. Middling towns at district and subdivisional levels had not yet come into being. Social stratification could not proceed because technology was simple and suited to handicrafts, education limited to few, and society based on caste.

ELEMENTS OF A MIDDLE-CLASS GROWTH

None the less, there were elements which formed the basis for a later middle-class growth on modern lines. They consisted of a number of functional groups which in point of income as well as respectability came next to the upper class of aristocracy, official, landed, or mercantile.

The official element comprised the mansabdars, so called because every one of them was invested with a mansab (rank or office) as a commander of so many horsemen, which determined his pay and position in the imperial service. In point of precedence a mansabdar came next to an amir, whose lowest command was 200 horsemen under Akbar and 500 under Shah Jahan. But as the ministerial staff of higher grades also formed part of the mansabdari establishment, the intermediate category of mansabdars, it may be assumed, consisted of all those whose commands range between contingents of ten to below 200 in Akbar's time and 500 in Shah Jahan's.

Under Akbar the total number of mansabdars amounted to 1,388; under Jahangir they rose to 2,064.[14] Next to these in point

[14] J. de Laet. *The Empire of the Great Mogol*, tr. J. S. Hoyland (Bombay, 1928).

of precedence came *qhadis* or gentlemen troopers who supplied their own horse and formed a separate organization, with a diwan and paymaster appointed under one of the amirs as their chief.[15] Many of these gentlemen troopers later served on the staff of various offices and worked even as adjutants and special messengers.

While the provincial governors and departmental heads were appointed from among the amirs, officers who administered the affairs of sarkars or districts were those who belonged to the rank of mansabdar and who carried on their executive, revenue, and judicial business. In the district, as in the provincial, headquarters, particularly in the department of revenue, there existed a considerable class of subordinate officers and clerks, variously known as mutsaddis and muharrirs, munshis and poddars, who were generally Hindus.[16] Judicial officers and functionaries, especially those in charge of the canon law, were however all Muslims. The subordinate and ministerial staff at all levels, as well as the religious, revenue, and judicial appointments often tended to be hereditary; at least the British found them so when they took over in the eighteenth century.

The members of learned professions constituted another element. Whether Hindus or Muhammadans, they were conscious of their superior position arising from the social superiority of their calling as well as of their caste and official connexions. Since the pursuit of education was regarded as a religious exercise, the Muhammadan members of these professions were supported by grants of landed property called *waqf*. This perhaps explains why one scarcely notices reference to state-managed seminaries designed to impart regular professional training. The *Ain* mentions the scope of Oriental studies which Abu Fazl perhaps drew up for general guidance. It included logic and mathematics, history and philosophy, grammar and law, theology and metaphysics, astrology and astronomy, medicine and general sciences. But there is no evidence of the extent to which the state associated itself with the management or maintenance of these studies. The results of the inquiries conducted by William Adam in 1835 on the state of

[15] *Ain*, i. 249.
[16] 4th Rep. Com. of Sec. HC, 1773, pp. 216–27, showing the establishment of the Khalsa, or chief revenue office, at Murshidabad for 1767–8.

The Authoritarian Basis of Society

education in Bengal and Bihar, however, lend support to the view
that these were in one form or another maintained by endowments
granted by local rajas or zamindars, that among the Hindus the
higher branch of Oriental studies was pursued exclusively by
Brahmans, and that the children of other twice-born castes acquired
a knowledge of simple arithmetic and accounts, reading and writing, imparted through local vernaculars by schoolmasters who subsisted either on the charity of wealthy persons or of local communities.[17] R. Thornton's *Memoir on the Statistics of Indigenous
Education within the North-Western Provinces of the Bengal Presidency* provides a very similar account of education supported by
private benefactions.

The next chapter will deal with the learned professions in some
detail. Here the main professions of the pre-British period, which
comprised those of physicians and astrologers, of scholars and
priests, will be briefly reviewed.

Speaking of the medical profession, Edward Terry, himself a
physician, comments that 'the Natives of *East India*, in all their
violent hot diseases, make very little use of Physicians', and that
they 'use much fasting as their most hopeful remedy'.[18] Tavernier
confirms Terry and adds that throughout his travels in the country
he found no physicians except those who attended 'Kings and
Princes'. The common people, he continues, used indigenous herbs
which they knew 'to be proper for the diseases which occur in a
family'.[19] Bernier too mentions physicians, but says that they were
all hereditary like most other trades and professions.

The able works of Dr. Thomas A. Wise and Dr. J. F. Royle are
indicative of the fact that the ancient Hindus had made considerable progress in the studies of anatomy and physiology, of medicine
and therapeutics.[20]

The Aryan Brahmins [Wise says] proud of their learning and moral
influence among the Turanian mass of the people of Hindostan, were

---

[17] See *Adam's Reports on Vernacular Education in Bengal and Behar*, ed.
J. Long (1868). These reports contain valuable statistical information covering
population, educated castes, and professions.
[18] Terry, p. 244.   [19] Tavernier, i. 200–1.
[20] T. A. Wise, of the Bengal Medical Service, wrote *Commentary on the Hindu
System of Medicine* (1845) and *Review of the Hist. of Medicine* (1867), covering
Hindu, Buddhist, and Chinese systems. Dr. Royle, of the Medical Staff of the
Bengal Army, wrote *An Essay on the Antiquity of Hindu Medicine* (1837).

satisfied with their riches, their fine climate, and fruitful soil. Insulated in their position, they appear to have been satisfied with the knowledge and power which they had acquired at a very early period; and affectionately attached to their own country, they retained for ages their opinions and practices.[21]

But while the West developed a more careful and practical mentality, with an emphasis on evolving scientific methods, the Hindus exhibited skill and perseverance rather than a searching spirit of innovation and experiment, especially necessary for surgical advancement.

Tavernier does not seem much to exaggerate when he writes that 'regarding surgery, the people of the country understand nothing about it'.[22] He says this because for the simple surgical operation of letting out a little blood from his tongue the King of Golconda had to call in a Dutch surgeon, Peter de Lan, who charged 800 pagodas, equivalent to about £320. In medicine, however, the Hindus were relatively more advanced in the seventeenth century, and Linschoten, who visited Goa in 1630, bears testimony to the fact that they commanded great respect and trust among all.

These Heathen phisitions [he writes] doe not onely cure there owne nations [and countriemen], but the Portingales also, for the Viceroy himselfe, the Archbishop, and all the Monkes and Friers doe put more trust in them, then in their owne countrimen, whereby they get great [store of] money, and are much honoured and esteemed.[23]

In addition to physicians, there was another class of practitioners who knew nothing of medicine as a science but practised the art according to prescribed routines. They were more or less quacks yet better respected than those who claimed to cure diseases by incantations.[24] There were yet others who, although unlettered, administered herbs from experience which was passed from one generation to the next. It was this class of medical practitioner who treated village folk of practically no means. Those who possessed some knowledge of medicine preferred to serve wealthy families on a monthly pension which amounted to any sum between fifteen and twenty rupees.[25]

[21] Wise, *Rev. of Hist. of Med.*, i. xiv–xv.   [22] Tavernier, i. 301.
[23] Linschoten, i. 230.   [24] *Adam's Reports*, p. 139.   [25] Adam, 1st Rep., p. 117.

The profession of astrologer, as has been noticed, had a strong hold on the mind of the people, both Hindus and Muhammadans, who superstitiously regarded them 'as so many infallible oracles' and believed that the stars had an influence 'which the astrologers can control'.[26] Bernier divides them into two groups. The first consisted of a large number of ordinary 'bazar astrologers' who resorted to market places where they remained seated in the dust with a large book representing 'the signs of the zodiac'. The other group comprised those who frequented the court. Bernier calls them 'crafty diviners' whom wealthy persons granted large salaries and 'never engaged in the most trifling transaction without consulting them'.[27] Pyrard and some other travellers testify to the popularity of this profession in western India also.

Among the Hindus the priestly profession was an exclusive right of the Brahmans. Its upper grade included learned Brahmans called *raj-pandits* or *raj-gurus*, who associated themselves with the performance of only such sacramental ceremonies as related to the families of rajas or wealthy persons.[28] The job of a priest for lower-caste people was however considered an inferior calling and practised in most cases by a class of uneducated Brahmans. W. H. Wiser of the American Presbyterian Church conducted an interesting socio-economic survey in one of the villages of the United Provinces, and published its results in what he called *The Hindu Jujmani System*.[29] While throwing light on the principle of interrelatedness in village services, the book establishes beyond doubt the heritable nature of the rural occupations which had fixed standing and status through the ages. The element of reciprocity in the service relationship of occupational castes persists even now. It is adjusted by mutual understanding or even by a transfer of service rights to those who can perform the duties on the spot. The priest formed an integral part of what Wiser describes as the *jujmani* system, but dominated it by virtue of his caste superiority and economic power.

The profession of scholar comprised, among others, philosophers and law-givers, grammarians and astronomers, writers and poets. Local rajas and princes endowed them with lands for instruction as well as for the maintenance of scholars. Even in the early nine-

[26] Bernier, p. 243.   [27] Ibid. p. 245.   [28] See *Adam's Reports*, p. 116.
[29] Published in Lucknow, 1958.

teenth century these endowments were found to be still in existence. Adam took note of them especially in the districts of Burdwan and Nadia, which had built up a reputation in Sanskrit studies, though not equal to that of Benares, which earned his admiration. In Tirhut he felt equally impressed with the patronage which the rajas of Darbhanga had extended to Oriental learning and scholarship.[30]

Abu Fazl's list of scholars suggests that in Akbar's time the total number who received royal patronage amounted to 140, of whom 32 were Hindus and 108 Muhammadans.[31] Most of the Muhammadan scholars were foreigners, and those among them who claimed a knowledge of science were actually men versed in theology, Islamic law and jurisprudence, serving as they did as qazis and muftis in Mughal courts.

At the start of Muslim rule the Hindus were averse from learning Persian, the language of the state. Although despised and suppressed on religious and political grounds, they held their own in trade and industry, revenue and finance. Before Akbar's time even the converts, still less the Hindus, who rose to positions of dignity were few and far between. His liberal policy, however, tended to popularize Persian education, and Todar Mal, his Hindu revenue minister, introduced Persian into revenue accounts previously maintained in local vernaculars. The Hindus successfully competed with the Muhammadan scholars in literary achievements, and by the time Shah Jahan came to the throne, even excelled them in literary refinement. The result was that Sa'dullah, his distinguished Muslim minister, was replaced by Rai Raghunath and Chandra Bhan, known for their skill in letter-writing and power of composition in Persian. 'One-half of the Persian literature of the 18th century', writes Blochmann, 'is due to Hindus. Their *dîwâns* (poetry) are as numerous as their *inshás* (model letters); their Persian grammars and commentaries are most excellent, and they have composed the most exhaustive dictionaries and the best critical works on the Persian language.'[32]

The increasing use of Persian by the Hindus resulted in Shah Jahan's time in the formation of a common language called Urdu

---

[30] Adam, 3rd Rep., p. 196.   [31] *Ain*, i. 437–47.
[32] 'A Chapter from Muhammadan History', *Calcutta R.*, Apr. 1871, p. 322. See also C. A. Storey, *Persian Literature* (1927).

or Hindustani, which on account of its indigenous origin gave a fillip to Indian elements in the Mughal service and counteracted the infiltration of foreigners, Persians or Afghans. Already under Aurangzeb Hindu officers had become so numerous that they could defy any attempt on his part to uproot them from his administration. This trend continued and perhaps asserted itself still more on the decline of the Mughal empire; for even in the Upper Provinces, the heart of Mughal rule, the Hindus constituted by far the greatest part of the army belonging to the Nawab of Oudh. While giving evidence before the parliamentary Committee of 1781, one of the military officers of the East India Company admitted this fact and stated that many of the principal officers of the army were Hindus, and that amongst them were several of those who held high commands. The nawab, he said, was 'more attentive to the Hindoo Officers than to those of his own Religion in order to attach his Gentoo Subjects more to his Person and Government'.[33]

In the absence of a national system of education, however, the scholarly professions were dependent on royal favour or private munificence. Abu Fazl cites a number of instances in which learned men had either to lose their jagirs or their very life for a show of independence. Abdul Qadir, whose duty it was to say daily prayers at the audience hall of Fatehpur Sikri, where scholars assembled for debates and discussions, had his considerable jagir cancelled because he refused to say prayers at the private residence of Akbar.[34] Maulana Alauddin, who had for a time served as Akbar's teacher, happened to occupy a seat at a *darbar* (audience hall) in front of that of a leading officer of Government. When asked to go back, he retorted: 'why should not a learned man stand in front of fools?'[35] The result was that he had to leave the hall, to which he never returned again. Mir Nurullah, an eminent jurist and for a long time qazi of Lahore, offended the emperor by a 'hasty word' for which he was executed.[36] Despotism and dependence in fact afforded little scope for the exercise of intellectual freedom. There was no press to bring public opinion to bear upon Government. All that existed in this regard was a class of experienced clerks called wakianavis (*waqia-navis*) who reported on the

---

[33] Rep. Com. HC, 1781, on Petitions &c. rel. to Administration of Justice in Ind., p. 40b.
[34] *Ain*, i. 544.   [35] Ibid. p. 540.   [36] Ibid. p. 545.

orders and doings of the king and his various departments both at the centre and in the provinces. These reports too were corrected and finally approved by the king or one of his officers before they were made public or copied for preservation.

Thus the study of the professions, as of commerce, industry, or agriculture under the Mughals, presents an almost identical picture of development, the upper crust in each case being identifiable in some degree or other with the aristocratic element of society, while the middle was reduced to the common category of the lower. For instance, the commercial monopolists and wealthy merchants attempted to fleece their dependent traders in the same way as the superior rajas or jagirdars did the small proprietors or landed gentry. The operation of this principle of conduct did not stop here. It extended to all levels of society and culminated with the king. The result was that wealth always had a tendency either to remain buried or to flow into the coffers of the rich and stay there. This tendency applied in no small measure to the scholarly professions as well. Here too a wide gap existed between professional practitioners at the top and those below. The elements to fill up the intellectual and social void between a learned physician and a veritable quack, between a royal and a 'bazar astrologer', between a *raj-pandit* and a village schoolmaster, or between a *raj-guru* and a village priest, were for the most part wanting.

On the commercial side, however, a significant change was taking place in the seventeenth century. A class of brokers was fast growing in association with the trading companies of the West. In the following chapter it will be shown how this class, in spite of limitations, established itself as a stable middle-class bourgeois interest, sharing the benefits of increasing trade and opportunities for educationed employment. Suffice it to say here that their knowledge of broken English commended them as interpreters to foreign factors, who employed them to manage their business, to advance money to manufacturers, and to collect the finished goods for warehousing or transportation. The members of this class were the first to rise in status on money power. C. R. Wilson cites an interesting example from Govindpur which later formed part of Calcutta. In 1679, he says, when the captain of an English vessel sent over to ask the local bankers for 'a *dobhash*, meaning an interpreter or broker':

the simple villagers mistook the word *dobhash* for *dhoba*, a washerman, and accordingly sent one, named Ratan Sarkar. Luckily the man could understand a little English, and was so intelligent, that his new employers were quite satisfied with him, and thus the quondam washerman was promoted to the dignity of being the English interpreter in Bengal.[37]

[37] *The Early Annals of the English in Bengal* (1895–1911), i. 59. 'Dobhash' was a common word used for a broker in Madras. In Bengal the English generally called him a banyan or gomastah.

Part II

A CENTURY OF GROWTH UNDER THE EAST INDIA COMPANY

III

The Commercial Middle Class

THE growth of the Indian middle classes in modern times proceeded from certain new conditions which developed under the rule of the East India Company, especially after the abolition of its trading monopoly in 1833. These new conditions were, for example, the mild and constitutional character of Government and the rule of law, the security of private property and the defined rights of agricultural classes, a national system of education and a period of continued peace, an economy of *laissez-faire* and a liberal policy of employment and social reform.

A cumulative effect of these factors was to encourage the free circulation of capital, productive enterprise, and a system of large-scale production on a joint-stock principle and method. These created new demands which modified the old pattern of consumption. They introduced new relationships which tended to transform society from a basis of status to contract. The exigencies of a large-scale production in fact led to technological progress, the improvement of communications, and the construction of the railways which, besides creating new forms of employment, set in motion a degree of social mobility that India had never attained before. In these and in other matters a sound beginning was made, and while much remained to be done later, the shape of things to come had already emerged by the time the Company handed over to the Crown in 1858. This chapter traces the manner in which these new factors contributed to the emergence of the modern middle classes, and the way in which the classes so formed differed from those of the earlier period.

THE MAIN FEATURES OF BRITISH RULE

Majority Rule

Unlike the despotism of the Mughals, the English East India Company evolved a committee form of government, which precluded the arbitrary proceedings of individuals, howsoever highly situated. It sprang from the Company's corporate character and commercial needs. Naturally suspicious of its servants operating in foreign dominions thousands of miles away from London, the Company considered it inexpedient to concentrate power in the hands of a single functionary who might misuse it to the prejudice of the Company's interest. This necessitated the establishment of a government by majority. When the Company acquired territories in India the executive head of its Government was in time invested with powers to annul a decision of his council. But the old rule of the majority continued in that he could not act except through the council; for every decision taken against the views of the majority, he had to give reasons in writing which could be altered, modified, or accepted by the Company in London.

The Dominance of Civil Authority

The dominance of the civil authority over the army was another feature which distinguished the Company's rule from that of the Mughals. This too arose because the Company was in origin a purely commercial concern, not a body of conquerors. The idea of armed fortification developed later in view of the state of political insecurity in the country. But at no time was its military authority permitted to act independently of its civil Government.

It is true that in the beginning there was no legislative authority apart from the executive Government, but the rules enacted by the latter were designed to operate as a check on its own conduct. These and a number of other features which it is not within the scope of this work to examine here contributed to the mildness of the Company's rule. They were responsible for the general respect and security of private property, for the circulation of capital and productive investment.

A Mobile Naval Power

Unlike the Mughals again, the British were a naval power, mobile from their very circumstances. Places like Surat and Madras, Bombay and Calcutta were vital to them because of their access to the sea. They entered the vast land mass of India by means of river or road transport, and repaired to these ports whenever the situation so demanded. Their original establishments consisted of a number of 'factories' built at sea ports as well as in the interior, especially along rivers and at important centres of trade. They were called 'factories' because the Company's agents or 'factors', as they were designated, lived there and carried on its import and export trade. Starting with the factory at Surat built in 1612, the Company made considerable progress in a few decades, and towards the end of the century it had consolidated its position by erecting fortifications at each of the settlements of Madras, Bombay, and Calcutta. Its factories in the interior were subordinate to one or other of these settlements. When it later came to acquire territories, these were similarly annexed to the settlements on the principle of contiguity, and administered from them for a long time before separate units could be formed to suit administrative convenience. Madras, Bombay, and Calcutta thus held positions of pre-eminence which none of the subsequent inland capitals ever enjoyed. The growth of the Indian middle classes was naturally concomitant with the emergence of these first modern towns in India.

Trading Settlements as the First Centres of Growth

The royal charter of 31 December 1600 invested the East India Company with exclusive trading rights and powers to punish the violation of its monopoly. Like any other foreign merchants, however, its servants in India were subject to the law of the land, and it was not before 1618 that Sir Thomas Roe, a British ambassador at the court of Jahangir, the Mughal emperor, secured for the Company certain rights including the immunity of its servants from the jurisdiction of the Mughal courts. They were declared free to follow their own law and religion within the bounds of each of their factories.[1] An English factory thus became

[1] John Bruce, *Annals of the Hon. East India Co.* (1810), p. 204.

I.M.C.—6

an extra-territorial unit carrying on trade as well as exercising administrative and judicial functions.

The Company's rule of law and the mildness of its Government tempted foreigners as well as Indians to reside within the limits of its settlements or subordinate factories. It is true that the residence of Indians there by no means freed them legally from the jurisdiction of the country courts. But it often happened that the Europeans bribed the judges deputed by local government to administer justice to their countrymen.[2] Moreover they provided shelter to those who asked for it. They extended this protection openly after 1660 when the internecine wars and the instability of India's political affairs under Aurangzeb dictated, in the interests of trade and commerce, the policy of fortified settlements. Sir Charles Fawcett quotes the measures which Gerald Aungier, the Governor of Bombay, took in 1669 to encourage the settlement of foreign merchants:

Among the measures adopted by Aungier to encourage foreign merchants to settle in Bombay was one giving them protection for five years from liability to be arrested or sued in Bombay for previous debts contracted elsewhere. It had been found that without this protection they were much molested by arrests and suits brought in the court of judicature. In November 1677 this privilege was extended so as to exempt all inhabitants of Bombay from liability to be sued by foreigners on bonds or other obligations.[3]

Although the English had erected Fort William in Calcutta in 1696 to protect their interests from internal disorders, Bengal remained subordinate to Madras until 1700, when it became the seat of an independent presidency. Here too protection was extended to those who needed it, and while the English could not openly oppose Murshid Quli Khan, who in effect governed Bengal until 1727 from his capital at Murshidabad, they did influence the Mughal emperor, who in 1717 granted them thirty-eight villages in the vicinity of Fort William. Their growing influence excited the jealousy of the nawabs at Murshidabad; the grant of the villages remained a paper transaction, but the settlement at Calcutta continued to grow. It attracted both foreign and Indian

[2] Cowell, *History and Constitution of Courts and Legislative Authorities in India*, 2nd ed. (Cal., 1884), p. 16.

[3] *The First Century of British Justice in India* (1934), p. 66.

merchants, who found greater security there. Weavers and other industrial workmen also flocked to it in great number to avoid the exactions of men in power.[4]

By the middle of the eighteenth century the settlements of Madras, Calcutta, and Bombay had forged ahead as important centres of trade and commerce. They were the first of the modern towns to become subject to Western influence and cultural interaction. Politically, they were the headquarters of the Company's power in the East. They each had a fortified settlement with a President and Council who exercised the executive function of Government, levied taxes, appointed judges, and preserved the peace with the help of the Presidency police and armed forces. The factories subordinate to them in the interior each had a chief and council who managed local affairs subject to the final orders of the nearest president and Council. That is how the Company grew extra-territorially. But with the country's political instability its task became increasingly difficult. Any attempt to assert or extend its trading rights embroiled it with local governors. It was not until after its victory at Plassey in 1757 that the Company could afford to dictate to the Nawab of Bengal or ignore its foreign competitors.

Bengal Takes the Lead

It was the British victory at Plassey that made the Nawab of Bengal a nominee of the Company and created a situation in which the British had the power and the Nawab the responsibility of administration. Mir Jafar was installed as Nawab, but since he could not satisfy their financial demands, he had to retire in favour of Mir Kasim, who ceded three of his districts to the Company in return for favours shown to him. But he too did not last long. The Company's servants and their agents, called gomastahs, tried to engross the entire trade of the province and insisted that they were exempt from imperial transit dues. Mir Kasim's opposition led to the war of 1763 in which the Nawab of Oudh and the emperor of Delhi came to his support. In 1764 the British were victorious and restored Mir Jafar. It was in these circumstances that the Company deputed Lord Clive to stabilize its affairs in Bengal. In 1765 he

[4] J. Long, ed., *Selections from Unpublished Records of Govt.* (1869), pp. 23, 32, 64–65.

secured from the Mughal emperor the Diwani (right of collecting the revenue) of Bengal, Bihar, and Orissa, which brought under the Company's control the entire revenues and civil administration of these three provinces, thereafter known as the Diwani provinces.

The Presidency of Fort William in Bengal thus became by far the most important of the three Presidencies. Calcutta became the seat of the Company's central Government, established under the Regulating Act of 1773. The Governor and Council at Fort William became the Governor-General and Council, invested with the civil and military government of the three provinces, with powers to superintend the other two Presidencies in making war or peace. A Supreme Court of Judicature was established at Fort William.[5] It supplanted the old Mayor's Court instituted in 1728 under a royal charter to administer justice to British subjects as well as to those residing within the limits of each of the three settlements. Bengal later undertook to supply the bulk of the finances required for the Company's wars and territorial acquisitions.

It was again in Bengal that a regular system of district administration was first evolved and perfected. This was to some extent modified to suit local conditions, but the basic pattern of the district staff continued, and exists even today, on the model and with many of the features belonging to the original office of Collector which Warren Hastings established in 1772. The civil and criminal courts too were first modelled in Bengal and later adopted in other provinces with local variations. Both Madras and Bombay as well as the North-Western Provinces introduced the Bengal model of the Sadr Diwani Adalat (civil) and Faujdari Adalat (criminal) courts, which finally merged with the Supreme Court under the Indian High Courts Act of 1861.

From the peculiarity of its political circumstances Bengal thus stole a march over the other two Presidencies. It went ahead of them in economic and social development much as in administrative and educational progress. And since Calcutta was the headquarters of the central Government until 1912, the Bengalis enjoyed certain opportunities which could never be available in its subordinate or inland capitals. In 1829 Lord William Bentinck tried to have the capital shifted to Allahabad, since it was centrally

---

[5] Supreme Courts were set up in Madras and Bombay in 1801 and 1823 respectively.

situated and more convenient for administrative purposes, but naval considerations led the home authorities to reject the scheme. Thus until 1832, when a separate board of revenue and courts of Sadr Diwani Adalat and Faujdari Adalat were first established at Allahabad, the jurisdiction of the Presidency of Bengal extended as far as Delhi and Nagpur. Calcutta naturally monopolized the benefits of trade and commerce as well. The new middle classes first arose here and then spread gradually, as in other Presidency towns, to provincial capitals and district and subdivisional headquarters. The settlement of Fort William possessed the maximum strength of the European population in India. Of the total number of 2,016 Europeans in 1828, as many as 1,595 lived in Bengal, especially in Calcutta: Madras had only 116 and Bombay 236, the remaining 69 being resident elsewhere.

Calcutta was in fact the first among the Presidency towns to become effectively influenced by European ideas and institutions. These filtered downwards to provincial or district levels through the media of civil servants and commercial residents, who operated through the agency of the Company's courts and factories respectively. To these must be added Christian missionaries, free merchants, and European planters, who likewise carried liberal traditions to the interior of the country. Schools and colleges came later. These constituted the various nuclei for the growth of the modern middle classes on the basis of money economy and Western education. New functional groups arose with an increase in the size and variety of business. They included, for example, engineers and overseers, technicians and supervisors, managers and inspectors, deputies and assistants. Even such groups which existed earlier tended to become more and more specialized and regulated so as to facilitate inspection. These trends will be examined in the following pages, and since the modern middle classes in the West arose through money power, it is appropriate to begin with the commercial middle class in India.

THE COMMERCIAL MIDDLE CLASS

Composition

The predecessors of the commercial middle class which began to emerge in the second half of the eighteenth century were groups of persons engaged in carrying on business as agents to mercantile and banking houses. They were variously known as gomastahs or munibs, vaishyas or banyans. In Madras they were identified as dobhash, or interpreters. But the English generally called them banyans or brokers.

They performed a variety of functions connected with the transaction of business. Jadow, for example, was the Company's broker and interpreter at Agra during 1611–13. He received and advanced money on behalf of his principal, kept his accounts, managed his household affairs, and negotiated with Mughal courtiers such business as his English factor wished to transact with the emperor. Jadow's relatives were also in the Company's service at Broach, Surat, and Burhanpur, where they performed similar duties, assisting their English masters in the supply of the Company's 'investment' and the sale of their goods. Sundar Das was another of his relations who accompanied Peter Mundy in 1632 from Agra to Patna to purchase cotton and silk goods. The Company maintained separate cart and camel brokers whose business it was to buy and sell carts, bullocks, and camels used in the transportation of merchandise by caravans.

Dr. Fryer states that on his arrival at Masulipatam (Madras Presidency) in June 1673, he noticed that a number of Indians appeared on board ship. Unlike the boatmen who carried the English treasure to the shore, they were clad in a more stylish garb, with a head-dress of calico-coiled turban, light vest, and loose trousers. They all spoke English, offered their services for a small wage, and awaited on the passengers to execute their business. James Rennell, the Company's Surveyor-General, estimated the number of such interpreters in Bengal at about 1,000. They understood English, lived in the principal cities, and served as interpreters to Europeans.[6]

In addition to brokers and interpreters, there was another group of men called shroffs whom the Company employed as poddars or cashiers because of their specialized knowledge of currency. Their appointment was essential, for in the seventeenth century India's currency differed widely from place to place. Tulsi Das Khan Parak was one such shroff in the Company's service at Surat in 1651. Like his father and brother who had preceded him, Tulsi

[6] Rep. Com. HC on Petitions, 1781, p. 39a.

served as a cashier on a small salary of £25 a year.[7] It seems that his business was also to negotiate loans for his principal; for on his failure to do so the Company engaged another shroff, Beni Das, who agreed to 'furnish them [the Company] with money up to 200,000 rupees at ⅝ per cent. per month'. Beni Das also acted as a broker negotiating the payment of certain compensation due from a native ruler.[8]

Paikars (spelled Pykars) were yet another group of middlemen who contracted to supply goods on the basis of advances made to them. They were especially engaged in the supply of cotton piece-goods in Bengal, and were so called because they went on foot (*paik*) into the interior and collected the finished goods from individual producers. Ram Ganga was such a paikar. He advanced money to the weavers in Dacca, advised them on the kind of cloth to be supplied, collected and stored the goods in his house, and then handed them over to the Company in return for advances received from time to time.[9]

Dallals were a different type of middleman. They charged commissions as gomastahs or agents did, but in their business transactions they were seldom responsible for the payment of the goods sold or bought by them. Besides, they were not stockists.[10] A gomastah could be both a stockist and agent carrying on business on the responsibility of his principal.[11] He could do his own business and be an agent to a number of firms at the same time. When he maintained his own firm in addition to his agency business, he was personally responsible for any money received on his own behalf and not on behalf of his employer.[12] But it often so happened that the agent forwarded his own business on the good-will of his master, and received deposits in his own name under the shield of his principal.

These various types of brokers were to be found with the foreign

[7] Foster, *Eng. Fac. Ind., 1651–4*, pp. 42, 106.
[8] Ibid. pp. 119, 108.
[9] 9th Rep. Sel. Com. HC, 1782–3, app. 51, p. 218.
[10] See Cause 16, 1806, *Reps. Select Causes, Sudder Dewanny Adawlut*, p. 69.
[11] Ibid. p. 13. Nowell (Indigo Planter) vs. Motee Ram, gomastah of Rachpal Das. Nowell received a loan and dealt with Motee Ram as a banker who advanced money, but this he did on behalf of his principal whose business failed. Nowell lost his case.
[12] Ibid. p. 129.

companies as well as the indigenous mercantile and banking houses. But those who were in the service of Europeans were comparatively better off. The shroffs engaged by the British even hired ships to carry on external trade on their own account.[13]

These brokers, whom the British denominated indiscriminately as gomastahs or banyans, were the people who constituted the spring-board of a rising commercial middle class in the latter part of the eighteenth century. They were the people whom the British employed as intermediaries in one capacity or another. It was they who assisted Clive in the overthrow of Siraj ud-Daula, the Nawab of Bengal. This group included men like Jagat Seth and Omichand, leading merchants and bankers who brought about the Nawab's defeat at Plassey. But the numerous gomastahs whom the Company's servants employed in the transaction of their private as well as the Company's business were the kind of men who stood to gain as a class after that victory.

A Junior Anti-Feudal Ally of the British

As against the Nawab and his officers, zamindars, and retainers, there was an identity of interest between the Company's servants and their agents, European or Indian. The clash between the English and Mir Kasim in 1762 brought out this fact more openly. The negotiations which the Governor of Fort William, Henry Vansittart, conducted with Mir Kasim at Monghyr shows that Mir Kasim was not opposed to the Company's import and export goods passing 'unmolested, and free of Customs, as usual'.[14] His opposition was directed to the gomastahs of the Company's servants, for his fear was that 'if the *English* Gomastahs were permitted to trade in all Parts and in all Commodities Custom free, . . . they must of Course draw all the Trade into their Hands', and deprive his Government of all its customs revenue.[15] His aim was to keep his Government free from the influence of these agents. That is why he emphasized that

none of the Company's Servants, Agents, Gomastahs, or other Person employed by them, shall be permitted to hold Offices under the Country

---

[13] Moreland, *From Akbar to Aurengzeb*, p. 158.
[14] 3rd Rep. Sel. Com. HC, 1772–3, app. 32, p. 340b.
[15] Ibid. p. 341a.

Government, nor to purchase, rent, or hold Lands, Gunges, or Markets, nor to lend Money to the Zemindars or Collectors; as all these are Sources of Dispute between the Company's People and the Government's.[16]

This was clearly an attempt on the part of the Nawab to exclude them from the enjoyment of the various opportunities which the political superiority of their European masters had made available to them. If put into effect, the Nawab's proposals would tend to keep them bound to brokerage and not permit them to rise to the level of the merchants above.

At the start the Company's Government at Fort William did try to some extent to restrain the upward movement of their agents. It proposed that they might carry on their trade freely even as merchants, but that if a dispute arose from any use of force on their part in 'buying and selling', they were not to sit in judgement in their own case. They were advised to have the matter decided by an officer of the Nawab's Government who might summon them to appear before him.

But the Europeans at Dacca opposed this policy of making the gomastahs subject to the control of the Nawab's officers. Since they considered them useful in transacting all kinds of business, especially in the provision of cloth, they took steps to protect them and their other employees from the jurisdiction of the Nawab's men. If authorized to try their cases, the Dacca Europeans feared, the officers of the country's Government might on the slightest excuse summon and confine them whenever they thought proper. Thus they openly declared that in the protection of their gomastahs lay their 'chief badges of honour' and the interest of their nation. Obviously there was a complete identity of interest between them and their Indian gomastahs. Together they constituted a challenge to feudalism, hostile as they were to the old régime dominated by the landed aristocracy and a band of retainers. They fought Mir Kasim in 1763, and their victory over him was a joint victory. It is true that their alliance led to the spoliation of the Nawab's treasures, which found their way to Europe. But the gains of those who were either Indians or Europeans with stable interests in India must in economic and social

[16] Ibid. p. 341b.

terms be regarded as a liberation of the hoarded capital which
came into productive circulation.

The social prestige of the new commercial middle class arose
on the basis of wealth and power, not from nobility of birth or
personal distinction. In the new cities the old values of simplicity
and piety, of integrity and honesty, of abstinence and austerity
were ceasing to carry weight. The gomastahs used their wealth
and influence to destroy the old régime and its administrative
apparatus. The contemporary records of the Company indicate
that they exhibited rudeness in their behaviour, and often acted
in a manner contrary to the established code of conduct even in
relation to the Nawab's officers of rank.

To quote an instance. In September 1777 trouble arose between
one Shakarullah, the faujdar (district executive officer) of Tirhut,
and Imam Buksh, a saltpetre agent of the Company. The faujdar
had sold a log of wood to one of the officers of his department.
On hearing that one of Imam Buksh's men was chopping it up
with the assistance of a peon, he sent for them and informed them
of this transaction. The woodcutter remained with the faujdar,
but the peon left to inform his master, Imam Buksh. Accompanied by a large number of armed men, the Company's agent
proceeded to the faujdar's court, pillaged it, robbed the treasury,
dragged the faujdar out, beat him and took him unconscious to his
house. The prisoners used this opportunity to escape from the
common jail. Some people of the locality then interceded, got the
faujdar back, and brought him to his residence.[17] It was in these
circumstances that the old office of faujdar was abolished and
that of European magistrate instituted under a regulation enacted
on 6 April 1781.

Factors Conducive to Growth

Sharing of Gains with Europeans. The commercial middle class
grew with the extension of the Company's trade and its territorial
acquisition. The first of the immediate circumstances responsible
for its sudden rise was, as has been said, the sharing of gains
between the Company's servants and European agents.

The sudden, and, among many, the unwarrantable Acquisition of
Riches, [said Clive] had introduced Luxury in every Shape, and in its

[17] *Calendar of Persian Correspondence*, v. no. 655.

most pernicious Excess. .... Every Inferior seemed to have grasped at Wealth, that he might be enabled to assume that Spirit of Profusion, which was now the only Distinction between him and his Superior. .... In a Country where Money is plenty, where Fear is the Principle of Government, and where your Arms are ever victorious, ... it is no Wonder that Corruption should find its Way to a Spot so well prepared to receive it. It is no Wonder that the Lust of Riches should readily embrace the proffered Means of its Gratification, or that the Instruments of your Power should avail themselves of their Authority, and proceed even to Extortion, in those Cases where simple Corruption could not keep Pace with their Rapacity.[18]

In the acquisition of wealth by means fair or foul, the Company's servants and their gomastahs justified themselves openly. The new broker-merchant made no further attempt to study how to appear indigent, as his predecessor under the Mughals had done. The large sums of money or presents

were so publicly known and vindicated, that every one thought he had a Right to enrich himself, at all Events, with as much Expedition as possible; the Monopoly of Salt, Beetle, Tobacco, &c. was another Fund of immense Profits to the Company's Servants, and likewise to such others as they permitted to enjoy a Share, while not a Rupee of Advantage accrued to the Government, and very little to the Company, from that Trade.[19]

Security and Respect for Private Property. The mildness of the Company's government, its regard for the rule of law and respect for private property left a person free in the enjoyment of his gains, regardless of the manner in which these were acquired. These were open to misuse, but the sense of security arising from these conditions did encourage the circulation of capital and tended to modify the old pattern of living.

The committee form of the Company's Government at times acted as a shield to protect the interest of an individual found guilty of peculation. An interesting case arose in 1752 when J. Z. Holwell took over the management of the Company's zamindari of Calcutta. He questioned the honesty of his assistant, Govind Ram, who managed the Calcutta lands on a monthly pay

[18] Clive to Court, 13 Sept. 1765 (3rd Rep. Sel. Com. HC, 1772–3, app. 73, p. 391a).
[19] Ibid.

of Rs. 50 or £5. On the basis of the evidence he collected, Holwell charged Govind Ram with embezzlement to the extent of a lakh and a half of rupees. He recommended to the President and Council that he be held in custody and that his property be sequestrated. But instead of arrest or the confiscation of his property, they gave him a week's notice to explain his conduct. He defended himself on the basis of a custom which acquiesced in the indulgence of certain farms which a person in his circumstances might acquire to maintain the equipage of an officer of some status. Holwell then retorted that according to the customs of the country his offence was punishable by lash, fetters, and the confiscation of his property. The Council however disagreed and opposed the punishment as inadmissible under a regular process of law. Govind Ram was allowed to retain all the wealth he had acquired. Shortly after the battle of Plassey he was even raised to the office of deputy zamindar.[20]

Ramchand and Naba Krishna were among others who made fortunes out of the English victory at Plassey. They were in Clive's confidence, but they concealed from his notice the real contents of the defeated Nawab's treasury, which ran into crores of rupees. They shared this booty with Mir Jafar and a few others. While Ramchand left a fortune of more than a crore, Naba Krishna assumed the title of a raja and spent lakhs over the funeral ceremony of his mother.

The Company's respect for private property thus left an opening for ordinary persons to attain higher status. Cases occurred in which ordinary banyans in the service of the Company or of an English firm rose to positions of wealthy merchants and shipowners. Madan Mohan Datt, a grandson of Ram Chandra Datt of Hathkola, who was a simple banyan of the East India Company, became a leading banker and owner of several ships.[21] Ram Dulal Day was a still more striking example of a low-paid gomastah who became wealthy. He began as a gomastah on four to five rupees a month and later became a clerk in the house of Messrs. Fairlie & Company at Calcutta. There he acquired a knowledge of business and became an independent broker. He was then introduced to certain American ship captains whose cargoes he supplied

[20] See *Calcutta R.*, iii (1845).
[21] L. N. Ghose, *The Modern History of the Indian Chiefs, &c.*, ii. 19.

at rates cheaper than those of the established English houses of agency. That is how he came to leave a fortune of about £400,000.[22] His son, Ashutosh Day, bought the assets and became one of the assignees of the famous house of Messrs. Palmer & Company when the house collapsed in 1830.[23] He was one of the directors of the Union Bank of Calcutta in 1835. Indeed the success with which the rule of law operated in the field of free enterprise, contributed considerably to the growth of the commercial middle class. As will be seen, a similar consideration of economic security guided the British in the introduction of land legislation to stabilize the ownership of landed property.

Removal of Inland Duties on Trade. Before the Company took over the direct administration of Bengal in 1772 the zamindars collected a number of miscellaneous taxes and levied inland duties on the transit of all trade goods through their zamindaris. This practice arrested the growth of a trading middle class in two ways: first, by restricting the flow of commerce; and secondly, by subjecting the merchants to the control of zamindars.

Warren Hastings enacted a regulation which divested the zamindars of their power to collect and levy such taxes, but the regulation remained inoperative, for Barlow's report of 1787 on trade in Benares indicated that in spite of Hastings's enactments to the contrary, illegal imposts continued to be collected in Benares, which Hastings had annexed to Bengal in 1781.[24]

The greatest part of the trade carried on between the Company's provinces and the internal parts of India [the report added] must pass through the district of Benares. The town of Mirzapore situated on the banks of the Ganges is the centre of this important trade.[25]

Merchants from the Deccan, the North-Western Provinces, and Nepal came there in search of European goods and the rich manufactures of Bengal. The district was equally important for trade in cotton piece-goods, shawls, and silk. But the imposition of heavy duties on the import of Bengal silk and the collection of illegal

[22] Sel. Com. HC, 1831–2, II: Finance & Accounts—Trade, p. 160.

[23] See *Bengal Directory* (Commercial), 1835.

[24] I.O., Beng. Pub. Cons., 26 Dec. 1787, r. 3, v. 30, f. 656.

[25] Ibid. The principal merchants who traded from Bengal to the Deccan were called 'sunnasees' (Sanyasis), 'a religious sect remarkable for their wealth and integrity in commercial transactions' (ibid. ff. 651–2).

imposts at times from village to village seriously impeded the movement of trade and provided a fillip to zamindars and their agents to oppress the merchants.

Much of the trouble proceeded however from the vagueness of the previous regulations. Lord Cornwallis accordingly specified the goods liable to duty and fixed the rates in each case. These were payable only to Government at a customs office maintained for the purpose. The landholders were not to collect any duty whatsoever. They were not to exercise any authority over the merchants or impede their trade. The latter could prosecute them in the courts for any exaction. That is how the Company's Government secured the independence of the trading community.[26] It was again to secure freedom of trade that Cornwallis subjected the Nawab of Benares to the immediate control of a British Resident who in 1793 took over its entire administration. It was in fact the interests of trade that often embroiled the Company with the country powers.

Early Restrictions on European Colonization. The early restriction of the Company on European colonization formed part of the policy to preserve its monopoly interest, but there were also other considerations which guided it in its opposition to European infiltration.[27] In India most of the land was in the occupation of Indians. To eject them in favour of Europeans was considered a dangerous as well as an unjust measure. If the Company in the beginning of its rule were to encourage their settlement in India, especially in Bengal where lands were settled on a tax-farming basis, they might have engrossed most of the lands; for no Indian would venture to bid against a British subject. A more serious consideration was the danger to which Indians might have been exposed in the interior where the jurisdiction of the indigenous or even of the Company's courts did not extend to British subjects. Moreover, if they or their agents were to hold land on a tax-farming basis, the Company feared that it might not be able to recover the arrears of revenue except by a process of the Supreme Court of Judicature involving considerable expense and delay. Then there was a political danger too. It was felt that any attempt on the part of individuals to explore the several parts of India might

[26] See Beng. Govt. to Court, 16 Mar. 1793, Rev. Dept., para. 6.
[27] See 9th Rep. Sel. Com. HC, 1782–3, app., pp. 844a–845a.

embroil the Company's Government with country powers. Colonization was therefore regarded as 'highly injurious'.[28] Under the orders of the Company free merchants and European agents were not permitted to go up country beyond Calcutta to trade in the interior.

In spite of these restrictions, however, 'a great number of Europeans, stragglers from ships, and others' had dispersed all over the upper provinces in the dominion of the Nawab of Oudh by the second half of the eighteenth century.[29] The Company's Government at Fort William therefore directed them to be secured and brought to Calcutta. All Europeans, Portuguese and Armenian agents were ordered in 1765 to settle their business and return to Calcutta by a specified date. They were not permitted to go up country under any pretence, nor were they to employ any other agent except 'Bengal natives'.[30]

The withdrawal from the interior of Europeans or agents other than 'Bengal natives' thus excluded all competition for Indian agents. This was an opportunity which accelerated the growth of the Bengali commercial middle class. It is true that to secure a wholesale compliance with the orders of the Government in those days was not attainable. But the fact that disobedience was punished establishes beyond doubt the Company's determination not to permit the infiltration of Europeans in the interior. William Bolt, one of its servants, was dismissed and sent to England in 1767. His Armenian agent was put under arrest at Patna and brought down to Calcutta. This anti-colonization policy was continued and later incorporated in the India Act of 1784, which restricted the residence of such Europeans as were not in the Company's service to within ten miles of the Presidency towns.

The Company was, however, not opposed to Europeans being encouraged to improve the cultivation of India's staple articles of commerce, such as indigo or sugar. Its principle in this respect was 'to give free scope to the internal powers of their territories, in Agriculture and Manufactures, and a free vent, by exportation, to the commodities thus raised'.[31] In conformity with this prin-

---

[28] Rep. Sel. Com. Court of Directors, 1792–3 (P.B. Coll. 28), p. 13.
[29] 2nd Rep. Sel. Com. HC, 1772–3, p. 295a.
[30] See Beng. Sel. Com. Proc., 1765, quoted ibid. pp. 293b–295a.
[31] 4th Rep. Sel. Com. HC, 1808–12, p. 17.

ciple, it improved the cultivation of indigo by introducing in Bengal and Bihar a process of manufacture followed in America and the West Indies. Although originally an Indian product, it had lost its market in the West on account of the bad quality of the dye produced from the juice which the Indian peasants extracted in their old and antiquated manner. The Company introduced the new process of manufacture in 1783. But after improving the quality of production it left European planters in 1785 to carry on the trade, and made advances to them to put them on their feet.[32] The application of European skill and capital raised the quality and quantity of its production to such an extent that Bengal and Bihar alone could supply the entire need of Europe.[33] Writing in the first quarter of the nineteenth century William Milburn commented:

This article has attracted much attention, and speculation has urged its production very far. The average crop of nine years, ending 1821–22, was 89,200 maunds; the following year it was 108,904 maunds. . . . A large supply, it was stated, might be obtained in Bengal; perhaps as much as 150 or 200,000 maunds, little short of 15 millions of pounds. . . . the demand of all Europe was estimated at 3 millions of pounds per annum . . . but supposing it to exend to 4 millions, Bengal could supply the whole. The quantity of indigo exported from Calcutta in 1821, was 32,887 factory maunds, and the average annual export in 7 years, 63,139 factory maunds. The home (Bengal) consumption is estimated at 4 per cent of the produce.[34]

The new mode of manufacture was later introduced in the Upper Provinces along the Gangetic plain and in Madras. The speed with which the cultivation of indigo proceeded may be judged from the fact that the amount of advance made on the crops increased from £19,000 in 1791 to £137,000 in 1795, more than seven times in a period of four years.[35] The value of the export trade, on the other hand, rose from £724,934 in 1814 to £1,917,160 in 1827.[36]

The large-scale production of indigo created in rural areas a

---

[32] Mins. of Ev. II, Sel. Com. HC, 1831–2 (735 II), p. 93.
[33] *Sketch of Commercial Resources and Monetary and Mercantile System of British India* (1837), p. 35.
[34] Milburn, p. 291.   [35] Murray, ii. 437.   [36] Ibid. p. 452.

clerical and supervisory group of persons called *amlas*, and another group of contractors whose business it was to distribute advances and supply the plants. In addition to these, there emerged a middle-class landed interest, who held land on lease on behalf of an indigo factory (for before 1830 planters were not permitted to buy lands of their own). Together these groups constituted a class of persons who might be called rural bourgeoisie. Besides their salary and middlemen's profit, their income arose from a money-lending business in which they invested their savings as means to acquire indigo lands. Unlike the old zamindars they were a class of intelligent, enterprising, and independent peasant proprietors who partly cultivated their own lands and partly let them to others. The formation of agricultural capital began with them, and the establishment of an indigo factory served as a nucleus in that formation. Sociologically, the commercialization of other agricultural products, like sugar or opium, tea or coffee, produced similar results.

In the early part of its rule the Company thus exercised a protective influence which encouraged the growth of the Indian commercial middle class and gradually introduced the benefits of European skill and capital which helped in the development of India's commercial resources.

The English Houses of Agency. The houses of agency provide another example of the Company's policy of controlled economy. By means of European skill and capital they developed the internal resources of the country, and they did this without much prejudice to its trade and industry. They pooled the savings of the Company's civil and military servants, employed these in the stimulation of the country's internal powers, and acted as a sluice gate in regulating the influx of British goods, to the advantage of Indians. Many of them, especially Bengalis and Parsis, received training in European methods of business organization, and set up their own firms on joint-stock principles. The agency houses in fact operated as means to introduce what was European without destroying what was Indian.

Their contribution to the growth of the Indian middle classes lay in the expansion of trade and the commercialization of India's staples, in the pooling of capital and the introduction of paper currency, in the specialization of business administration and the consequent growth of ancillary services, in the exercise of restraint on Government and freedom of trade.

The history of these houses of agency, especially of Messrs. Alexander & Company, goes back as far as the year 1769–70 when the rising prices and the Company's requirements arising from its policy of supervising the administration of the Diwani provinces through the agency of its own servants led to the establishment of a number of European firms designed chiefly to supply the needs of Government.

Indeed speculation had started as early as the English victory at Plassey. The subsequent revolutions at Murshidabad, which led to the acquisition of the Diwani in 1765, poured vast fortunes into the coffers of individuals and rapidly increased the number of Europeans resident in the Diwani provinces. These fortunes soon overflowed the usual channels of remittance through the bills of the Company. But the Company had not yet adjusted itself to the new situation that demanded a change in the established mode of a purely commercial remittance. Many of the illicit fortunes acquired by individuals found their way into Europe through foreign channels, for the East India Company would not permit them to use its own channels. When once opened, these foreign channels continued to remit British treasure so long as there was no alternative. In the beginning, foreign companies used to give bills on Europe for the money advanced to them in India, and they employed this money in the purchase of Indian goods, which provided the funds for the payment of those bills in Europe. The result was that in a period of three years (1766–9) the bullion imported into Bengal amounted to Rs. 55,50,000 only as against an export of merchandise and treasure to the amount of Rs. 5,61,00,000, with an adverse balance amounting to Rs. 4,88,50,000. This was exclusive of the trade carried on by private European merchants,[37] who soon afterwards became, clandestinely and unlawfully, parties in the trade carried on by foreign companies, where many of them were supposed to be the real, though concealed, principals.[38]

The establishment of the agency houses in Calcutta was in

[37] See Verelst's letter, 5 Apr. 1769, in 8th Rep. Com. Sec. HC, 1772–3, pp. 413–14.
[38] 4th Rep. Sel. Com. HC, 1808–12, app. 47, suppl., p. 9.

fulfilment of a historic need. They supplied the alternative to the remittance of British capital through foreign companies. Their formation possibly proceeded immediately from the restrictions imposed on the residence of private merchants in the interior, especially after the transfer of the Company's civil administration from Murshidabad to Calcutta in 1772. Prohibitory enactments against civil servants being connected with private trade or holding tax-farms was perhaps also responsible for some of the most ambitious of them opting in favour of a mercantile career. The firms of Alexander & Company, Palmer & Company, Colvin & Company, Fairlie-Fergusson & Company, Cruttenden-Mackillop & Company, and Mackintosh & Company were some of the earliest and most prominent of the English houses that enjoyed the patronage of the Company.

But once established in Calcutta, these houses developed a more or less Indian interest, for they became the depository of the savings of the Company's servants, and in order to be able to pay interest and have their own capital, they invested these deposits in business and productive enterprises. In the course of a statement made before the parliamentary Select Committee on 24 March 1832 Thomas Bracken, a partner in the house of Alexander & Company, thus explained the origin and peculiar features of the agency houses:

The commerce of Calcutta [he said] was in the hands of a very small number of houses before the opening of the present charter; previous to that time the houses were chiefly formed of gentlemen who had been in the civil and military services, who, finding their habits perhaps better adapted for commercial pursuits, obtained permission to resign their situations, and engage in agency and mercantile business. They had of course a great many friends and acquaintances in their respective services, and from those gentlemen they received their accumulations. They lent them to others, or employed them themselves, for purposes of commerce; they were, in fact, at first the distributors of capital rather than the possessors of it. They made their profit in the usual course of trade, and by the difference of interest in lending and in borrowing money, and by commission. In the course of time, carrying on a successful commerce, many became possessors of large capital, and returned to this country, leaving most part of it there; but the persons who succeeded generally came in without capital of their own, the same system being continued, and those houses became the usual depository of a great portion of the savings and accumulations of the military and civil services in India.[39]

Although originally designed to serve as channels for the regular remittance of British treasure to Europe, the agency houses became the depository of the earnings and savings of the British. The savings of the public servants, instead of being regularly remitted to Europe, came to stay in India. They were employed in the development of trade and internal resources. Taking all the three Presidencies together these savings amounted to nearly £4 million sterling per annum.[40] Moreover, the agency houses received deposits from both European and Indian tradesmen, planters, and shipowners. Indeed they ran a business amounting annually to about £5 million sterling, making advances for indigo and sugar cane, cotton and silk, opium and shipbuilding. As bankers they accepted deposits at an interest of 10 per cent. and made advances at 12. As agents and general merchants they charged commission at the rate of $2\frac{1}{2}$ per cent. on most sales and purchases. Thus, like Indian firms, they did a variety of business: agency, mercantile, and banking. But unlike the former, they also issued paper currency. Many of these firms later gave up banking, but the Bank of Hindostan, the earliest of the European banks attached to the house of Alexander & Company, continued.[41]

Free Trade. The main contribution of free trade to the growth of the commercial middle class lay in the gradual removal of every hindrance to the extension of commerce. For a monopoly corporation like the East India Company to remove restrictions on commerce and to introduce free trade seemed obviously anomalous. But in fact it did introduce a principle of free competition that conduced to prosperity and encouraged the extension of trade without much prejudice to the supply of its own 'investment'.

The necessity of such a policy arose from the peculiar nature of the change which the Company's trade with India underwent on the acquisition of the Diwani in 1765. Hitherto its connexion with

---

[39] Mins. of Ev. II, Sel. Com. HC, 1831–2 (735 II), p. 151.

[40] *Sketch of Commercial Resources*, p. 66.

[41] According to Thomas Bracken's statement of 24 Mar. 1832, the house of Alexander had had 'a bank attached to it for 60 or 70 years' (Mins. of Ev. II, Sel. Com. HC, 1831–2, p. 209).

the country had been purely commercial. It was obliged to send out large sums of bullion amounting at times to £400,000 or £500,000 a year to complete its 'investment' for Europe.[42] After 1765 its trade ceased to be a commercial adventure. It became more or less a tribute to conquest. A certain portion of its territorial revenues was set apart and employed in the purchase of goods for exportation to England. This was called the 'investment'. In his *Observations* Charles Grant, an honest civil servant of the Company who retired in 1790, stated that 'in the thirty years following the acquisition of the Bengal provinces, this nation, by public and private channels, derived from them alone, exclusive of its other Eastern dependencies and of the profits of goods remitted, fifty millions sterling'.[43]

On the establishment of its political power the Company, as a monopoly organization, could fix the prices of commodities by the exclusion of all kinds of competition, and could buy Indian goods with Indian money as cheaply as it wished. But that would have impoverished the country and diminished the Company's own return of the annual capital furnished from the public revenues. The Company therefore acted otherwise from motives of both equity and sound policy. By an extension of trade and commerce it increased its revenue resources. By a development of the internal powers of the country it tried to contribute to its prosperity, which was the source that fed the Company's 'investment'. To achieve this object it did two things: first, it granted freedom of trade to all engaged in the country's internal trade; and secondly, it encouraged trade with the foreign companies, who imported bullion to buy Indian goods, and who remained subject to its control. It did not encourage the British free traders who dealt in British manufactures, and brought its governing influence to bear upon their conduct in India. This policy was designed to do more than merely offset the loss caused by the employment of India's revenues in the purchase of its 'investment'.

In the first few years after the victory of the English arms in 1757 the Company's servants and their agents doubtless monopolized most articles of trade, even including those meant for internal consumption. But the Directors initiated a system of restraint as

[42] See Rep. Com. Sel. Com. Court of Directors, 1792–3, p. 12.
[43] Rep. Sel. Com. HC, 1831–2 (734), Gen. App., p. 18.

early as the year 1765 when they vested Clive with full powers to punish the exorbitance of their servants. There were several difficulties impeding the execution of their orders confining their servants to a trade only in the articles of export and import. Among these, distance as well as the absence of a strong local government operated as serious handicaps. None the less their determination to secure the freedom of trade continued unabated.

In a letter of 10 April 1771 the Directors asked the Bengal Government specifically to annul all the passports with which their servants traded without paying duty, and to reduce a number of oppressive tolls which obstructed the flow of trade. They wrote:

From a conviction that a most effectual means to restore and invigorate the Trade of Bengal will be the opening every proper Channel for its extension and giving that General Freedom which is so necessary to encourage the Industry and attract the attention of the Natives we can no longer permit our Servants of any Rank or Station whatever to enjoy the exclusive privilege of Dustucks. And here when we speak of Dustucks you are to understand not only Dustucks but Rowanahs, Perwannahs, Orders, Letters or any other powers or favours which may be conferred and which can in any way yield an influence or superiority in favour of one more than another; and this without the least distinction to Nation or Complexion.*

The speculation that followed the establishment of British influence in Bengal must in itself have caused a considerable rise in the price of commodities. What the Company's servants or their agents did was to try to curb the upward trend by an arbitrary exercise of power. Orders to release inland trade from the barriers of local levies and the imposition of special passports were bound to restore the trade, as they did, to a normal functioning of the principle of supply and demand; the need for this was reflected in the phenomenal increase in prices since 1728, shown in the table on p. 93.

In external trade also the Company made no 'distinction to Nation or Complexion'. Indeed it went out of its way here to encourage foreign companies, even the French—Britain's political enemy who used every opportunity to prejudice British interests. Because of the better terms it offered the bulk of the caste of

* Beng. Desp., 25 Apr. 1771 to 10 Dec. 1773, v. 5, ff. 549–50.

Article	Price at Murshidabad in 1728		Price at Calcutta in 1776	
	Maunds	*Seers*	*Maunds*	*Seers*
Rice (fine)				
First sort per rupee	1	10	0	16
Second do.	1	23	0	18
Third do.	1	35	0	21
Rice (coarse)				
First do.	4	15	0	32
Second do.	4	25	0	37
Third do.	5	25	1	0
Fourth do.	7	20	1	10
Wheat				
First do.	3	0	0	32
Second do.	3	30	0	35
Barley				
Bheont (grain for horses)	4	35	0	22
Oil				
First sort	0	21	0	$6\frac{1}{4}$
Ghee	0	$10\frac{1}{2}$	0	3

Source: 6th Rep. Sel. Com. HC, 1782–3, app. 15.

weavers were found in the East India Company's service. The Company advanced to them the cost of the cloth and enabled them to procure the materials so as to be able to provide cargoes in due time for its ships. But the general terms in which liberty of trade was conceded to the French and others were such that difficulties sometimes arose in procuring the Company's requirements and in securing in due course a fair return on the money so advanced. The reason was that the weavers were 'ever prone to sell and private dealers alike disposed to buy, for ready money and at a higher price, the cloths thus produced, to the manifest injury of the first employer, whose money was thus made a capital for the trade of another'.[44] This was made more likely because of the unrestricted trading of individuals in the Company's service who

[44] Cornwallis to Court, 1 Nov. 1787 (Beng. Let. Rec'd, v. 27, f. 239).

competed, through foreign companies, even for such goods as
formed the proper 'investment' of their own employers.

In a letter of 10 April 1773 the Directors thus complained that
whereas 'the French without money or influence filled their ships
with the prime and valuable manufactures of Bengal', the Company's 'investment' should 'necessarily be loaded with the refuse
and ready-money goods'.[45] In a subsequent letter of 3 March 1775
they traced the manner in which right from 1769 the rising prices
of goods and the extraordinary system of buying them at Calcutta
on the Company's bonds bearing an interest of 8 per cent. prejudiced its own interest to the advantage of others. The total value
of the Company's 'investment' during 1769–73, for instance,
amounted to £2,901,194; and if the average increase in price was
to be estimated at 25 per cent. only, the sum of money paid
because of increased costs amounted to £725,295. And yet the
Company did not deviate from its policy of free trade. It continued
to act on the principle that the capital needed for its 'investment'
should accrue from an increase in trade rather than lower prices or
the obstruction of competition.

After the peace of 1782 several other nationals, such as the
Americans, Tuscans, and Genoese, who had no settlements in
India, brought their ships directly to the Company's ports,
particularly to Calcutta, the seat of its power in the East. These
ports afforded additional opportunities after the French and Dutch
possessions fell into the Company's hands. Of the total bullion to
the value of Rs. 77,20,336 imported into Calcutta during 1795–8,
Rs. 59,29,317 came from countries other than England. Of this
amount, bullion worth Rs. 33,77,203 came from America, 21,08,386
from Lisbon, 3,25,692 from Copenhagen, and the rest from
Hamburg. The value received from London amounted to Rs.
17,91,677 only. Of the total exports from Calcutta amounting in
the same period to Rs. 4,32,38,214, however, goods worth Rs.
2,45,67,473 were received in London, and the balance in other
countries. This shows that while England received Indian goods in
excess of the bullion it exported, the other foreign countries
compensated the loss by a regular supply of their bullion or bills
payable on Europe or America. The result was that even after
deducting the value of transactions made with London, Calcutta

45 9th Rep. Sel. Com. HC, 1782–3, p. 190.

in that period showed a balance of trade in its favour to the amount of Rs.25,09,075.[46]

From a report of the special committee of the Court of Directors dated 27 January 1801, it appears that, as compared with London, foreigners carried more specie than goods to Bengal, that the direct legal private trade to London exceeded all the neutral and clandestine trade to foreign Europe and America, and that the Company's export trade from Bengal amounted to even less than half the total foreign exports of that place to Britain, foreign Europe, and America. During 1795–8, for instance, the annual average of foreign and private exports from Bengal to London direct amounted to Rs. 61,00,000; and to foreign Europe and America, either on neutral or clandestine account, to Rs. 56,00,000, the total being Rs. 1,17,00,000 annually. As against this total, the value of the Company's exports from Bengal amounted annually to Rs. 1,00,00,000.

London [the report added] does not pay a *third* of the amount it receives from Bengal on private account, by the amount it carries thither, the bullion included in which does not exceed a tenth of what it receives. Foreigners pay to Bengal *above half* of the amount they carry away, and of this half, the *greater part* is bullion; that is, *more than a fourth of their exports* is paid in bullion. London, however, carries *more goods* to Bengal, than all Foreign Europe and America; and it carries more *goods* than *specie*. Foreigners carry more specie than goods.[47]

This explains why the Company viewed with disfavour any policy of unrestricted intercourse of British subjects. Besides affecting its monopoly, the Company tended to exhibit impatience about all the rights of colonists, including extensive occupation of land, which might effect the ruin of the people. The foreign traders, on the contrary, remained tractable and brought wealth to the country, which stimulated indigenous manufactures. The Company therefore restrained the activities of the British and encouraged those who engaged to develop the staples. Moreover, the extension of trade with foreigners gave added opportunity to the British, who already possessed by far the greater part of the trade of the Indian seas, to act as agents.

[46] 4th Rep. Sel. Com. HC, 1808–12, app. 47, suppl. p. 14.
[47] Ibid. pp. 15–16.

But this policy operated more to the advantage of Indians than British, for the former transacted the agency business at much cheaper rates. While the English houses charged $2\frac{1}{2}$ per cent., the Indian brokers remained satisfied with a commission of 1 per cent. and at times even $\frac{3}{4}$ per cent.[48] The rise of men like Ram Dulal Day, Ram Chunder Mitter, and a host of Bengal brokers became possible because of this. The Americans, who dominated the foreign group of merchants, employed the agency of Indian firms chiefly from motives of economy. They brought bullion or bills on such of the British firms as engaged in American trade, who honoured these bills and enabled the Americans to procure Indian commodities.

There was yet another disability under which private British firms operated. In the transhipment of their goods they were obliged to use the space assigned to them by the Company in its ships, usually built in India. This had two disadvantages. First, the private traders had to subordinate their interests to those of the Company who gave priority to its own 'investment' in the distribution of space. Secondly, it clashed with the shipping interest of England which had developed in the course of the French revolutionary wars. The British consequently wanted to use their own vessels and send their goods to England without any limitation except that of passing them through the channel of the Company. The grant of this demand signified the end of the Company's monopoly.

Henry Dundas, then President of the Board of Control, realized the danger to which Indian manufactures would be exposed on the complete liberalization of trade to and from India. In a letter to the Directors dated 2 April 1800, he remarked:

The nature of the India manufacture, and the immemorial habits of the manufacturers, exclude the practical application of so indefinite a principle to the Export Trade from India. The manufacture of the finer and more valuable fabrics of India, have always been produced by advances from the Government, or Individuals, for whose behoof those fabrics are manufactured; and if the dealing with those manufacturers was to be laid open to the uncontrolled competition of every individual, the consequence would be a boundless scene of

[48] Mins. of Ev. II, Sel. Com. HC 1831–2 (735 II), p. 151.

confusion and fraud; and, ultimately, the ruin of the manufacturers themselves.[49]

But was there any option? The Company's policy of guided competition contradicted its own monopoly interest. It encouraged a large-scale production of plantation products, especially indigo, which clashed with the limited shipping space available to export the Company's Indian goods. It promoted the culture of Indian cotton to feed, in the absence of an Indian mill industry, the home manufacturers, who were hostile to the importation of Indian cotton goods into Britain. The extension of trade created a class of agents and stockists, a commercial middle class, whose interest it was to bring all the manufactures of the interior to Calcutta, and to force the Company to buy from them with ready money. Anti-monopoly interests had in fact grown among the members of the Company's directors themselves.[50] The opening up of the trade became a historical necessity. A system of large-scale production was bound to alter, as it did, the old pattern of artisan industry, although from its peculiar political connexion with Britain India could not enjoy the full benefit of a gradual change-over to the factory system.

The Charter Act of 1813 opened up the Company's trade to a great extent. Nevertheless its rule continued. In every case individuals had to apply to it for permission to proceed to India. In the period before the complete abolition of its monopoly in 1833, India had the benefit both of its control and of the application of European skill and capital. The new capitalist enterprise affected the artisans adversely but benefited the commercial middle class who later developed industrial interests and supplied industrial finance.

In addition to the prosperity of Calcutta, Milburn noticed a considerable rise in the shipping industry of Bombay, where the Parsis had established a reputation in modern commerce and ship-building. He wrote:

Bombay claims a distinguished rank among our foreign naval arsenals; it has always been famous for shipbuilding, and formerly supplied Bengal and other parts of India with shipping. Many fine

---

[49] 4th Rep. Sel. Com. HC, 1808–12, app. 47, suppl., p. 4.
[50] See C. H. Philips, ed., *The Correspondence of David Scott* (1949).

ships are now built at Bengal, so that this branch of commerce at Bombay has rather diminished. Merchant ships of considerable burthen (from 600 to 1,300 tons) for the country trade, and the service of the Company, have been built here, which, in point of beauty of construction, excellent workmanship, and durability, are superior to any class of merchant ships in the world. . . . Bombay has the peculiar honour of being the first place in the British dominions out of Europe, at which a ship of the line was ever built; it has also added several fine frigates to the Royal Navy: they are all built of Malabar teak, which is esteemed superior to that of any other part of India. The builders are Persees, who are very skilful and assiduous; so that for the skill of its naval architects, the superiority of its timber, and the excellence of its docks, Bombay may be considered of the first importance to the British empire in India.[51]

Milburn noticed many Portuguese and Armenian merchants as well as Hindu and Muhammadan ones, who carried on trade with Gujarat and Bengal, Persia and Arabia. As Bengali merchants, such as Ashutosh Day and Dwarkanath Tagore, the assignees of Palmer & Company and founders of the Union Bank of Calcutta, the Parsis brought prosperity to their community by conducting business in association with the agency houses at Bombay.

The Persees [wrote Milburn] rank next to the Europeans. They are active, industrious, clever, and possess considerable local knowledge. Many of them are very opulent, and each of the European houses of agency has one of the principal Persee merchants concerned with it in most of their foreign speculations. They have become the brokers and banians of the Europeans. The factors belonging to these different houses resident in China, Bengal &c. are generally Persees, and the correspondence is carried on in the country language, so that the British merchant knows no more than they communicate to him. The servants attached to Europeans at this Presidency are Persees, and the best of any in India.[52]

The language factor which gave importance to the Parsis in Bombay likewise operated elsewhere in India, especially in Bengal which had the highest number of Europeans in the country.

The complete opening up of trade in 1833 brought about a radical change in the pattern of India's external commerce. The Company withdrew its annual 'investment', amounting to

<hr>

[51] Milburn, p. 125.   [52] Ibid. p. 124.

about £2 million sterling. This caused the crash of those agency houses whose prosperity depended on the continuance of the Company's monopoly. Their ruin produced a loss to the public amounting to nearly £15 million sterling. As a result there was a great deficiency of working capital, and the shortage of specie was met by a resort to barter trading. Houses were set up both in London and Calcutta, connected with each other as managing agents, designed, in view of limited funds, to obtain goods on consignment. Under this arrangement the London merchants endeavoured to obtain fabrics from their home manufacturers on the basis of long-dated bills to be settled after the disposal of their consignments in India. The Calcutta houses sold these consignments, and with the help of the proceeds, which remained in their hands for some time, they procured similar consignments of Indian goods bound for London. The old pattern of Indian exports being paid for in gold or silver was supplanted by a mere exchange of goods from abroad, and while the Company had used its territorial revenues and the remittances of its servants to supply the cost of its 'investment', the private merchants achieved the same result by introducing a quantity of British manufactures greater in value than India's export goods.

These developments necessitated the separation of the mercantile from the financial branch of commercial transactions. The latter function fell more and more to the sphere of separate banks dealing in finance and foreign exchange. The managerial function also became separated from the proprietary function; for the houses established in London and Calcutta on the collapse of the agency houses acted as managing agents and did not own the fabrics they consigned or sold. Managerial, mercantile, and later industrial functions of business became increasingly subject to the financial control of banks, which pooled the capital resources of the community. It is not within the scope of this work to trace the manner in which this separation and specialization took place, which has been dealt with elsewhere.[53] What is relevant is to note that the new trading arrangement resulting from the shortage of

[53] See C. N. Coote, *Rise, Progress and Present Condition of Banking in India* (1863); G. P. Symes, *History of the Bank of Bengal* (Cal., 1904); H. Sinha, *Early European Banking in India* (1927). The Bank of Bengal was established in 1806 as the Bank of Calcutta. It became known as the Imperial Bank of India in 1921.

specie dictated the expediency of increasing dependence on paper currency and therefore on banks, where more and more people deposited their savings from motives of security and interest. This led to an increase in the number of banks.

Sociologically speaking, too, the new pattern of business was not less significant. It tended to increase the avenues of employment by an extension of specialized services. It brought into being a class of specialists in business administration whose claim for a higher salary and superior status the community had to recognize, regardless of their original standing in society. It dictated the necessity of modifying education so as to facilitate the acquisition of a knowledge of applied skills. It increased the quantity of India's import goods, especially the cheap and fine fabrics of Manchester, which modified the pattern of internal consumption in big cities. It supplanted the demand for the finer products of the Indian artisans, which were both costly and unsuited to the taste of the new middle classes. But since the vast mass of the Indian population consumed its own coarse goods, the extent of the replacement hardly exceeded 6 per cent. in the first few years after 1833.[54]

The expansion of trade and commerce was however remarkable in the period after the complete opening up of the Company's trade. The increased production of the country's staples, including raw cotton, and the facilities for their export kept the balance of trade in favour of India as shown below:

Imports

	Merchandise £	Treasure £	Total £
1834–5	4,261,106	1,893,023	6,154,129
1849–50	10,299,888	3,396,809	13,698,696

Exports

1834–5	7,993,420	194,740	8,188,160
1849–50	17,312,299	971,244	18,283,543

Source: E. Thornton, *Statistical Papers relating to India* (1853), p. 54.

[54] See *Sketch of Commercial Resources*, pp. 25–27.

This expansion of trade arose from the removal of a number of restrictions. The transit or inland duties imposed by each of the Presidencies were abolished, in Bengal by Act XIV of 1836, in Bombay by Act I of 1838, and in Madras by Act VI of 1844. The removal of duties on the export of sugar to British ports was effected by the Tariff Act XIV of 1836, and on cotton by a notification of the Indian Government dated 31 December 1847. Export duty on indigo was however retained, in view of the fact that India produced about five-sixths of the total world supply, and that it could be taxed without interfering with the interest of the Indian producer. A distinction previously existing between British and other ships which discouraged the latter category by an imposition of double duties was abolished under the principle of free trade. All ships were permitted to enter Indian ports on the same terms as their British competitors.[55] Indian lascars or sailors in the Company's service were likewise deemed British seamen.

The abolition of these restrictions enabled Bombay to outstrip Bengal, especially in the export trade of cotton. For example, of the total export of Indian cotton amounting to 165,655,220 lb. in 1849, Bombay contributed 150,754,963 lb., including 94,226,779 lb. supplied by Gujarat.[56]

While studying the effect of the opening up of trade in 1833, one has to bear in mind that India was not exposed to the consequences of unrestricted colonization. The Company's rule acted as a barrier to it. Moreover, the general consensus of opinion expressed before the parliamentary Select Committee of 1831–2 was that indiscriminate colonization must on no account be allowed in India. For example, an able and eminent Bengal civil servant, Holt Mackenzie, declared that what India needed was 'superintendence and direction, with trustworthiness, in the conduct of agricultural and commercial concerns', not a body of uneducated and ordinary Europeans. He therefore recommended that only 'men of good education and steady habits' should be permitted to go out to India for the purpose of superintending agricultural and commercial undertakings.[57] Ram Mohan Rai, a contemporary Indian

[55] Under Act VI of 1848.
[56] E. Thornton, *Statistical Papers rel. to India* (1853), p. 67.
[57] Mins. of Ev. II, Sel. Com. HC, 1831–2 (735 II), Q. 109.

reformer who was in England at the time, supported the same view. He said: 'As the higher and better educated classes of Europeans are known from experience to be less disposed to annoy and insult the natives than persons of a lower class, the European settlers, for the first twenty years at least, should be from among educated persons of character and capital.'[58]

This was precisely the view expressed by experienced officers of Government even before the setting up of the Select Committee on Colonization and Settlement (India) in 1858. They favoured the settlement of Europeans as capitalists and directors, not as common settlers. They too realized the great importance of European skill and capital in the development of India's internal resources, but they suggested that communications must be improved so as to supply a full knowledge of India's agricultural and mineral wealth.

Colonization in India thus remained limited to purposes of superintendence and direction. A parliamentary report of 1852 indicates that the total number of Europeans resident in India not in the service of the Company did not exceed much more than 10,000. It was distributed as follows:

	Male	*Female*	*Total*
Bengal	3,662	3,087	6,749
Madras	1,087	574	1,661
Bombay	980	616	1,596
Total	5,729	4,277	10,006

Source: Rep. Sel. Com. HL, 1852 (P.B. Coll. 117), p. 4.

The population of India about that time being nearly 150 millions, the number of Europeans not in the service of the Company worked out at about one to every 15,000 Indians. Those in the service of the Company, including its non-covenanted branch, did not exceed 2,000. Most of the Europeans lived in the Presidency towns. Those who resided in the interior engaged in agriculture or manufacturing. They were in the main indigo and sugar planters, farmers, landed proprietors, cotton agents, and the like.

[58] Rep. Sel. Com. HC, 1831-2, Gen App (734), p. 341.

This policy of limited colonization operated to the advantage of India. The establishment of Europeans in the various trades and occupations of the country, especially in the capital cities, led to the extension of business and expanded opportunities for employment.[59] Since they engaged Indians in the transaction of most of their business, the Indian middle-class commercial interest increased considerably with an increase in the number of European firms. This is reflected in the following figures applicable to Calcutta:

	Principal Eur. merchants & agents*	Principal Hindu merchants & shroffs	Principal Muslim firms	Beng. commercial traders	Beng. agents or banyans	Paris
1815	23	34	15	29†	—	—
1835	61	29	11	14	24	1
1855	151	41	31	145	45	8
1858	173	52‡	35	159	66	10

* Exclusive of a variety of inferior merchants and brokers. † Including banyans. ‡ Including 8 Madras merchants.

Source: Beng. Directory, 1858, Commercial and *New Cal. Directory*, 1858, Commercial.

Obviously the people who benefited from the growing trade of Europeans in Calcutta were the Bengali Hindus. In the beginning they acted as banyans or brokers to a European firm, learned the tricks of the trade, and then established firms of their own. A leading merchant, Ashutosh Day, the son of Ram Dulal Day, acted as a banyan of Charles Cantor & Company, Ralli Brothers, and Charles Forrester. The *Bengal Directory* of 1835 states that in that year Dwarkanath Tagore was the only Indian member of the committee of management of the Calcutta Chamber of Commerce, Rustumjee Cowasjee being one of the eight members of its committee of correspondence. Again, of the 103 members of the Bengal Chamber of Commerce in 1858, five were Indians; but of these four were Bengalis, namely, Kallydas Rajendra Datt,

[59] Ibid. pp. 476-7.

Ram Gopal Ghose & Company, Shyamchund Mitter, and Hurris Chunder Bose.[60] On the banking side too the Bengalis predominated among India merchants in Calcutta. Of the three trustees of the Union Bank, for instance, Ashutosh Day was one, the remaining two being Europeans. Three of its twelve directors, were Bengalis, one Parsi, and eight Europeans. Of its 202 proprietors in 1835, 73 were Indians and 129 Europeans. Of the Indian proprietors, 70 were Bengali Hindus, 2 Muhammadans, and 1 Parsi. The Bengali Hindus also exercised a virtual monopoly of the several clerical jobs available in the various banks, commercial offices, and warehouses. In 1858, for instance, the Government Savings Bank (established in 1833) maintained on its staff 34 assistants and clerks, with salaries ranging from 350 to 25 rupees. All of them were Bengali Hindus.

Among the Bengali Hindus, however, it was the class of banyans or sarkars, as they were also called, that dominated the whole field of commercial or other appointments. In 1835, for example, the total number of Indians on the petit jury list of the Supreme Court of Judicature at Calcutta was 99. Of these, 96 were Bengali Hindus consisting of 54 banyans or sarkars, 28 writers, 10 zamindars, 4 clerks, and 3 bankers.[61] The Parsis constituted the dominant parallel interest in Bombay and the Brahmans in Madras.

Another remarkable feature of *laissez-faire* noticeable in the period after the liberalization of trade was that the British free traders grew into an organized pressure group designed not only to safeguard commercial rights, but also to influence the policy of Government in the enactment of measures calculated to encourage free enterprise. The establishment of the Calcutta Trade Association in 1830, of the Calcutta Chamber of Commerce in 1834, and of the Indigo Planters' Association in 1854 were all intended to promote the general interests of commerce and to co-ordinate various trades and manufactures.

Of these, the Indigo Planters' Association typified the new development more than the others. It represented the proprietors and managers of the indigo factories, of tea and coffee plantations,

---

[60] See *Beng. Directory*, 1858, Commercial. The figures of employment are generally derived from either the *Beng. Directory* or the *New Cal. Directory*.
[61] Ibid. pp. 470–81.

of silk and sugar factories as well as the landed estates generally. Among others, the duties of the Association were to collect information on 'the state and wants of the various districts' in regard to public works, including roads, canals, navigation, irrigation and bridges; to receive representations on the 'state of the revenue laws', on the 'administration of justice', on the state of the police and its bearing on 'the security of person, capital, and industry'; to receive suggestions for reform on all these subjects; 'to watch the progress of legislation, and to communicate with the higher authorities in India and at home, whenever the interests for the advancement of which the society has been instituted may appear to the committee or Association generally to require it'.[62]

The constitution of the Association suggests that its district committees were established with the object of improving relations between the planters and the peasants as well as of protecting 'the latter from improper and oppressive interference of the zamindars'. In their local relations they were to be guided by a uniform code of bye-laws drawn up with the final approval of the central committee.

The free traders of Britain thus liberated commerce from official bondage and tariff barriers. They obtained from the local governments the introduction of laws the benefits of which extended to the inhabitants of the country generally.[63] They acted as the carriers of liberal traditions and introduced in India a knowledge of European science and technology. They urged the Company to improve India's communications and introduce railways. In short, in the course of time they developed a kind of vested interest in India, which they obliged the Indian Government to preserve, at times, in opposition to the Imperial interest of their home manufacturers. It was this identity of interest between the Europeans in India and the Indian middle class that brought David Yule, the Chairman of the Bengal Chamber of

[62] Ibid. p. 45. The provisions of the Bengal Tenancy Act of 1859, giving occupancy rights to tenants, of the High Court of Judicature Act, and of the Police Act of 1861, providing a uniform and more effective security of person and property, were influenced in large measure by the views of the planting community expressed before the Sel. Com. on Colonization and Settlement (India) in 1858. The representative character of the Indian Councils Act of 1861 was likewise influenced by them.

[63] See 4th Rep. Sel. Com. HC, 1808–12, app. 47, suppl.

Commerce, to preside over the annual session of the Indian National Congress in 1888.

A century of commercial development under the Company thus indicates how the mildness of its government and its regard for the rule of law afforded opportunity to a variety of traditional middlemen and its own employees to grow into the stature of middle-class merchants. Their number grew with the growth of inland and foreign trade. But more important than their quantitative increase was the qualitative change in the character and relationship of the new class of merchants. The beginning of a large-scale commerce and import industry was tending towards a managerial revolution. The emergence of joint-stock companies, which will be discussed in Chapter VIII, had not only begun to separate the managerial and proprietary functions of business, but introduced in India a pattern of commercial organization which, on account of increasing specialization, gave rise to a multiplicity of employment. It called for special education and training without which commerce could not grow into a recognized profession. The new commercial class was in fact taking the lead in English education, especially in Bengal where the superior castes of Brahmans, Kayasths, and Vaishyas were the first to take to new trades arising from the increasing import of foreign manufactures. The traditional gulf between learning and trade had thus gradually begun to narrow. The examples of Ram Dulal Day and Dwarkanath Tagore, of Ashutosh Day and Ram Gopal Ghose illustrated this. They were all Kulins, or members of the superior castes of Bengal, and yet they acted as leaders of modern commerce and education. A proprietor of R. G. Ghose & Company, Ram Gopal became an active member of the Bengal Chamber of Commerce as well as of the Council of Education established in 1845.

Another remarkable change of this period was that the relationship which in England had developed between Government and business as a result of the Industrial Revolution was, under the Company's rule, transplanted into India with certain local modifications. The new Indian commercial class which arose in junior partnership with European firms made use of the trade associations and chambers of commerce which the latter established to safeguard commercial rights. It is true that their use was in the beginning limited to Bengali and Parsi merchants, two of the newly educated business communities of the country. The traditional mercantile houses were slow to change. But it was only a matter of time. The relationship which the Company's rule had established between commerce and politics had come to stay. It marked a radical departure from India's tradition.

IV

The Industrial Middle Class

THE emergence of the Indian industrial middle class took place slowly. As has been seen in Chapter I, the poverty of the industrial workers and their social disabilities operated as serious handicaps to the growth of an industrial society. Although the Company's rule in great measure secured the freedom of the workmen, other handicaps arose from its peculiar connexion with the country.

TECHNOLOGICAL BACKWARDNESS

While England was completing her agricultural revolution and preparing the ground for the emergence of an industrial bourgeoisie in the eighteenth century, India was gradually slipping into the hands of a foreign trading company who from motives of commercial economy and on account of the superiority of Indian fabrics continued the old 'domestic' system of production. Trade and commerce increased, but the basic pattern of industry remained scarcely altered. Delay in the introduction of mechanical and power technology did not call for any radical change in methods of production. In the cloth industry, for instance, a village weaver or his family could complete most of the processes of manufacture which in a factory system separate groups of skilled technicians would have been required to do, each of them as part of a separate ancillary industry.

Until the coming of elaborate machinery in the eighteenth century, the system of production in England too was basically 'domestic'. But the English had already introduced the water-worked fulling mills as early as the fourteenth century. By about 1578 they began the smelting of iron by means of coal, and although coke was not applied to iron until after the beginning of the seventeenth century, they had made a rapid advance in the production of coal, an essential ingredient of the Industrial Revolution.[1]

In his study of the *Culture and Commerce of Cotton in India* Dr. J. F. Royle shows that although up to 1760 the machines employed in England in the manufacture of cloth 'were nearly as simple as those of India', the English had been trying to march ahead and gain a technological superiority over Indian looms. Spinning by rollers came into practice in 1738, and by 1748 carding was being done by cylinders. In 1767 Hargreaves completed the spinning-jenny, and a year later Arkwright perfected the spinning-rollers invented thirty years previously. Manchester, which by 1741 had become a centre of cloth manufacture, started imitating Indian calicoes in the very first decade of the perfecting of these machines. The mechanical process of producing finer qualities of yarn, however, did not succeed until Crompton had invented the mule-jenny in 1779, which came into general use in 1785. It produced both weft and warp sufficiently fine for muslins, which dispelled all fear of competition by Indian cotton goods.

This technological superiority made Manchester the most important of the commercial centres for cotton goods in the world. The aggregate amount of cotton imported into England in 1751 was 2,976,610 lb. only, but it rose to 775,469,008 lb. in 1849, nearly 300 times in about 100 years. The import of Indian cotton into England began in 1783 with 114,133 lb., which increased to 97,368,312 lb. in 1841, more than 800 times in about fifty-eight years.[2] In 1813 only 497,350 lb. was imported. But a year later, in 1814, the first year of the opening up of the Indian trade, the amount rose to 4,725,000 lb. Thenceforward it went on increasing with certain variations.

Britain's technological superiority and her connexion with India were partly responsible for holding up the emergence of an industrial middle class there even in the cotton industry, where the

---

[1] From 210,000 tons during 1551–60 the production of coal rose to 2,982,000 tons during 1681–90. See J. U. Nef, *Rise of the British Coal Industry* (1932), pp. 19–20.

[2] See J. F. Royle, *The Culture and Commerce of Cotton in India* (1851), pp. 80–81. According to Thornton (p. 69) the quantity exported to England in 1841–2 was 118,544 lb., the total including exports to other countries being 194,255,879 lb. The total quantity of cotton exported to England and other countries during 1843–4 amounted to 202,501,768 lb.

excellence of manufacture held its own against any other country. It is true that the Company's Government took several steps to improve the culture and quality of Indian cotton,[3] which prepared the ground for the establishment of cotton mills in India. More and more land came under the cultivation of cotton: Gujarat and Bombay, Malabar and the Central Provinces became rich cotton centres. But though significant and beneficial by themselves, these developments were basically agricultural. The general tendency was to deprive more and more weavers of industrial employment and to force them into exclusive dependence on land.

Unlike the clothiers who heralded the Industrial Revolution in England, the Indian weavers had no marginal savings to subsist on. They were mere wage-earners receiving about two or three rupees (5s. or 6s.) a month, and a man with an income of £48 a year was deemed a middle-class man even in the 1830's.[4] That is why the production of the finer quality of goods depended upon the immemorial custom of advances. Moreover an industrial occupation was not a respectable one. It was low and demeaning in social estimation. Thus both economic and sociological factors precluded the growth of an industrial middle class on European lines.

Writing about the year 1840 Hugh Murray appreciated the quality of Indian handicrafts but deplored the backwardness of the means employed in their production. He said:

> The muslins of Dacca in fineness, the calicoes and other piece-goods of Caromandel in brilliant durable colours, have never been surpassed; and yet they are produced without capital, machinery, division of labour, or any of those means which give such facilities to the manufacturing skill of Europe. The weaver is merely a detached individual, working a web when ordered by a customer, and with a loom of the rudest construction,—consisting sometimes of a few branches or bars of wood roughly put together. . . . That, in an art which such pains have been taken to carry to the highest perfection, no attempt should have been made to improve the machinery, and to remedy the most obvious inconveniences, is a striking example of that blind adherence to ancient usage, which forms so prominent a feature in the Hindoo character.[5]

---

[3] See R. Thornton, *Statistical Papers*, pp. 63–65. The measures ranged from the improvement of seeds in 1788 to the establishment of cotton farms in 1849. See also Royle, pp. 86–90.

[4] *Sketch of the Commercial Resources*, p. 28.　　　　[5] Murray, ii. 442–3.

MIDDLEMEN, COMMERCIAL RATHER THAN INDUSTRIAL

As has been stated, it was customary for merchants to deal either directly with the producers or to employ the agency of middlemen known as paikars and dallals, but in certain areas, especially in Benares, weavers dealt directly with traders. An account of cloth manufacture in Dacca shows that the use of the agency of middlemen was in general practice.[6] They combined against Richard Barwell, the Company's chief at Dacca, who in 1773 appointed two of his superintendents to make advances directly to the weavers. In a representation to Government in 1776 the merchants imputed illicit motives to him and declared that his conduct was contrary to the established mode of business:

Under the Mahometan Government [they said] every possible Encouragement was given to the Cloth Business. . . . And the same Course of Business continued under the Protection of the present Government, transacted through the Channel of a Set of creditable Men, called Dellols; who constantly, in consideration of a small Premium, furnished all Goods by Contract and were answerable for all outstanding Balances.[7]

A representation of Ram Ganga, a former paikar of Dacca, made a similar allegation against Barwell's having dispensed with the agency of middlemen.

From their association with cloth manufacture the middlemen were expected to supervise the producers so as to ensure the quality of goods specified in their contract and to organize their production efficiently and economically. They occupied a position in which they could effect a general improvement in the whole cloth industry as the clothiers did in England. But this did not happen. Unlike the clothiers, the Indian middlemen did not have their own capital. In most cases the merchants beat down their middlemen to the lowest figure. They had scarcely any margin left to work on. What they did therefore was to flourish on illicit gains made from a deterioration in the quality of manufacture rather than from its improvement. The Bengal middlemen were to a large extent responsible for the debasement of the quality of its cotton

[6] 9th Rep. Sel. Com. HC, 1782–3, app. 51, pp. 213–19.
[7] Ibid. p. 213b.

piece-goods. Gujarat later replaced many of its finer products such as *doreas*, *mulmuls*, *baftas*, *romals*, and *saris*.[8]

The Indian middleman thus operated as an agency of commercial supply, not of industrial superintendence and direction, which the Company supplied through the agency of its own servants. The manufacture of saltpetre, a major industry of Bihar and Bengal, represented more or less a similar personnel organization. The Company received a monopoly of its manufacture from the Nawab of Bengal in 1758. But to obviate the inconvenience of direct management it adopted a system of farming for five years, on the same principle as the quinquennial settlement of land, in 1772. Organizationally, this system differed little from the mode of the Company's cloth investment through middlemen. The farmer undertook to supply a specified amount of saltpetre on the same terms and conditions on which a cloth broker engaged to supply cloth. The principle of advance (*dadani*) operated here in the same manner as elsewhere. The saltpetre farmer received an advance amounting to three-fourths of the quantity of saltpetre he stipulated to produce at specified rates ranging from 60 to 75 rupees per 100 maunds of saltpetre. It was expected of him, as of a cloth broker, that he would supervise the process of boiling and extraction, that he would improve its quality, that out of his advance he would regularly pay the molungees or saltpetre gatherers, and that he would provide for a proper storage of the saltpetre until the Company sold it to such merchants as offered the highest price. But here, as in the cloth industry, his profits arose either from a contraband sale or from an irregular payment to saltpetre gatherers. The Indian element of industrial superintendence was ill supplied. The same state of affairs obtained in the manufacture of opium in Bihar and Benares.

In the field of cotton as an agricultural enterprise the element of superintendence and direction was equally wanting. The middlemen or wakarias, as they were called in Cambay, kept the growers in a state of pecuniary bondage from one generation to another. They made advances to the cultivators and purchased their cotton often before it had ripened. They found their interest 'in adulterating the cotton previous to disposing of it to the exporter'.[9]

[8] See 6th Rep. Sel. Com. HC, 1782–3, app. 6, p. 931; also Beng. Pub. Cons., 28 Dec. 1787, r. 3, v. 30.   [9] Royle, p. 30.

Dr. Royle shows that certain European agents also adulterated the produce from motives of illicit gain. He quotes a letter from an American planter addressed to the government of Madras in support of this allegation. In the district of Tinnevelly, the letter says,

the field is occupied by European agents, who instead of encouraging the people to bring clean cotton, give a premium indirectly on the dirtiest trash. A contract is made, usually by the house itself, with the chetties [Madras merchants] for such a quantity of cotton of such a quality, and the very lowest sum is fixed. The chetty, finding he cannot get a price that would justify the delivery of such cotton as he has contracted for, agrees to it, well knowing that they must take such as he chooses to deliver to them at the time.[10]

The broker or gin-house man, whose duty it was to improve the quality, stood between the chetty and the peasant who produced the cotton. He accepted the terms of the chetty as the chetty did of the European agent; and since he had not much margin to go on, he proceeded to mix the good and bad together previous to its being delivered to the chetty. The chetty in turn delivered this to the European agent who lived on the savings of exchange. The manufacturer in England paid a low price, as he did not know what he was buying. This state of affairs continued until 1848, when American saw-gins were first introduced to clean the cotton from the trash.

Though connected with the produce of both the artisan and agricultural industries, the Indian middleman functioned as a commercial agent or broker rather than an industrial manager or supervisor. He was more a receiver of the middleman's profit than an industrial entrepreneur. In the early period of the Company's rule its servants, more particularly its commercial residents, supplied the element of direction. But since that rule tended to extend the life of the old domestic pattern of industrial production, men like Mackenzie and Metcalfe, Bentinck and Ram Mohan Rai, advocated the augmentation of free enterprise under European management. In compliance with one of the provisions of the Charter Act of 1833 legislation was enacted in 1837 to permit Europeans to hold farms of their own in perpetuity. As has been seen, several other measures were also passed to promote European

[10] Ibid. p. 37.

enterprise in India, although it extended mainly to plantation industry.

PUBLIC SERVANTS AS THE FIRST INDUSTRIAL CAPITALISTS

The question of finding capital, more particularly for rural investment, was beset with great difficulty. An indigo or coffee plantation situated in a rural area did not constitute an adequate security for a city banker to advance money except at a high rate of interest. A house or any other property in Calcutta could easily raise a mortgage at 5, 6, or 7 per cent. interest. But no house, indigo factory, or any other form of property situated in the countryside could raise capital to the extent of even one-fourth of its total value, and that too at a rate of interest less than 15 per cent.[11]

Before the year 1837, when Europeans were first permitted to hold farms of their own, it was the Company's civil servants who advanced them capital and guaranteed the security of their enterprise by using their local influence. While deposing before the Select Committee on Colonization and Settlement in 1858, one of the settlers clearly acknowledged the capital contribution of civil servants and declared that 'the root of independent British enterprise in Bengal is to be found in the civil service'. They were the first capitalists to enter the industrial field in India. The European settlers came in virtually as second proprietors and went out into the districts on the personal security of civil servants.

The Company's civil servants in fact took the lead in introducing power-driven industrial plants also. The Gloucester cotton-twist mills were established in Burdwan in the early years of Bentinck's Government.[12] Mr. J. M. Heath, a civil servant connected with the house of Alexander & Company at Calcutta, established an iron foundry at Porto Novo in the Madras Presidency in 1832, where the abundance of wood assured economy and quality in the manufacture of iron. The process of producing a good quality ductile wrought iron was known to Indians in that part of the country. They combined a crucible with their bellows which acted more or less as a miniature blast furnace, but their produce was on a domestic scale only. Heath undertook large-scale production of

[11] Sel. Com. HC on Colonization and Settlement (India), 1858, Mins. of Ev., A. to Q. 1822.
[12] Mins. of Ev. II, Sel. Com. HC, 1831–2 (735 II), pp. 154–5.

cast iron and steel, of which they had no knowledge. He in fact set up a company, including a number of other civil servants, who exercised an exclusive right of mining and procuring fuel in a number of districts on a leasehold basis. The company established two more factories, in Malabar and Salem. It seems that Heath had secured the original monopoly in 1832 in someone else's name; for when the Government became aware of the real situation, 'they issued an order which made it compulsory on all their servants to have nothing to do with the management of the company'.[13] Another company took over the entire undertaking and worked it till 1859, but although the quality of iron was superior to any produced in England, the lack of experienced direction and capital equipment brought about its collapse.

The European agency houses, as has been said, were in the beginning mere distributors of the capital belonging to these public servants. It was only after the opening up of trade in 1813 that independent European capital began to flow into India, and that too not freely until Europeans were permitted to own land in 1837.

PRIVATE EUROPEAN ENTERPRISE

It has been seen that the main field for the investment of private European capital was the country's plantation industry, particularly indigo. Jute, sugar, tea, and coffee came later. Of these, jute became comparatively more important because its export to Britain was greatly increased after the Crimean War had made it impossible to import Russian hemp and flax. In 1855 a European established the first jute mill at Rishra in Bengal to produce jute cloth.

European planters usually advanced loans to growers at a rate of interest lower than that of Indian money-lenders. In Mysore, for instance, the cultivators paid interest to the extent of 36–50 per cent.,[14] but a European settler there charged only 12 per cent. on the mortgage of lands for coffee plantation. The educated and enlightened section of the planting community in fact set examples of industry and perseverance, of philanthropy and integrity of con-

---

[13] Sel. Com. on Colonization and Settlement, 1858, Mins. of Ev., A. to Q. 5332.
[14] Ibid. As. to Qs. 6766–8.

duct. Thanks to this the people were better clothed, housed, and fed.

As regards the use of mechanical power, one of the main difficulties was the undeveloped state of coal mining. It was only in 1820 that a European started a coal mine on a regular basis at Raniganj in Bengal. Its production was low, and it was not accelerated until the opening of the East Indian Railway in 1854, nevertheless the total amount of coal mined in the year 1857–8 was 293,443 tons, less than the average annual production in Britain for 1681–90.[15]

Proposals for the construction of railways in India were initiated by European firms in 1844. The private parties who sought the co-operation of the Company's Government in the formation of railroads included Messrs. White and Borret, Mr. Stephenson, Chairman of the East India and China Association, and some others who prepared a prospectus and report in support of their proposals.[16] It took time before Lord Dalhousie finally overrode the objections of the Directors and laid down a policy on the basis of *laissez-faire*, entrusting the execution of the scheme to private companies on the principle of what was known as the guarantee system. Under the Railway Act of 1854 the Government of India stipulated the terms of contract with a number of companies, such as the East Indian, Great Indian Peninsular, Bombay, Baroda, and Central India, South India, and some others. The railways were in fact the first tangible step towards industrialization. They released considerable capital for circulation, created a variety of new openings for employment, and set into motion a degree of social mobility that the country had never previously experienced. They led to the augmentation of its commercial and agricultural resources, increased the vigour, confidence, and economy with which the Government could carry on its political affairs, and from a military point of view provided important facilities for the movement of troops and stores necessary for defence.

INDIAN INDUSTRIAL FINANCE

The development of an Indian industrial interest was slower still. Industrial investment was fraught with a degree of risk which the

[15] See p. 109 n. above.   [16] P.P. 34(327), 1845; also 76(787), 1852–3.

old Indian bankers did not want to take. A few Bengali and Parsi firms were the first to emerge as industrial entrepreneurs. For instance, Dwarkanath Tagore bought an English colliery at Raniganj in 1836, and later developed a manufacturing interest in sugar and flax. Cavasjee Banajee of Bombay was the first Parsi to attempt to start a spinning and weaving mill in 1845, but the enterprise failed for want of adequate support. For the emergence of a middle-class industrial bourgeoisie Bombay was however more favourable than any other part of India, particularly in the field of cotton industry. Large-scale production of raw cotton in the western part of the country had prepared the ground for it. The introduction of the saw-gin hastened the progress. Following the example of J. Landen, an English cotton merchant of Broach, an Indian established his own saw-gin,[17] and soon afterwards in 1851 Cavasjee Nanabhoy Davar set up his first steam-driven cotton-spinning factory in Bombay. The saw-gin had in fact improved this industry in western India to an extent which made the application of steam a matter of course.

In the ship-building industry too, as has been seen, the Parsis had established a reputation for beauty, strength, and workmanship. They supplied the technical and directional elements which led to the division of labour in that industry. The family of Lowjee Nusserwanjee Wadia were famous master-builders of ships, who also established the dry docks of Bombay.

HANDICAPS

The mechanization of Indian industry was, however, no easy task. It raised a host of problems springing from Indian conditions. Apart from the difficulty of obtaining capital and importing machines, it required engineers and technicians whom India did not possess. It needed mechanical stores and equipment, in the absence of which plants had to remain idle. It demanded a knowledge of industrial statistics which had not yet begun. It dictated the necessity of technical education which formed no part of government policy. On top of all this was the peculiar attitude of British manufacturers, who viewed with disfavour even the estab-

[17] Sel. Com. on Colonization and Settlement, 1858, Mins. of Ev., A. to Q. 8493.

lishment of European-owned Gloucester twist mills under Bentinck, and it was feared lest these should 'compete with the cotton mills in England'. In the course of his statement before the Select Committee of 1832, Thomas Bracken dismissed the fear as groundless; for apart from the difficulties of mechanical repair and technicians, the inhabitants of Bengal did not like the cloths made in the Gloucester mills of Burdwan. They showed 'a prejudice in favour of that which comes from England'.[18] Bracken was therefore doubtful whether the Indian cotton mills would ever be able to compete with those of England.

This backward state of factory industry was responsible for the slow growth of modern towns, which was, however, steady. Reckoning every place with a population of 4,000 as a town, the proportion of the urban to the rural population of the British territories in about 1835 was computed as one to sixteen, or a little over 6 per cent.[19] This figure rose to 8.72 per cent. in 1872, when the first census of India was taken.

While the Company acted as a barrier against the influx of British goods and protected the finer produce of India's rural industries, it gave employment to Indian artisans and realized considerable profit from the proceeds of Indian goods sold in British and European markets. Though commercially sound, this policy tended to retard the growth of urban large-scale factory industry. The emergence in the meantime of the British manufacturing interest in cotton consituted a threat to the Company's dominant commercial interest. The manufacturers began agitating against the continuance of its monopoly; for during six years from 1784 the Company's accounts had registered a net loss of £37,790 in the export trade of woollen goods from Britain.[20] It was alleged that its monopoly commercial interest alone prejudiced the sale of British manufactures in India.

The Court of Directors appointed a Select Committee in 1793 to examine these allegations. The Committee gave a number of reasons for the loss of British export trade: that articles of cotton and silk 'are made better and cheaper in India'; that no reduction in the price of woollens would 'increase the Consumption in a

---

[18] Mins. of Ev. II, Sel. Com. HC, 1831–2 (735 II), Q. 1839, p. 154.
[19] *Sketch of Commercial Resources*, p. 8.
[20] 3rd Rep. Sel. Com. Court of Directors, 1792–3, p. 4.

Country where so many Substitutes for that Article are found better suited to the Climate, and more congenial to the Customs and Prejudices of the Inhabitants'; that it was not possible to increase the sale of British manufactures because India possessed 'raw Materials in the highest Perfection, and Millions of ingenious and industrious Manufacturers who work for One Fifth Part of the Wages given in England'; that the dress of Indians 'is so simple, and little subject to Change, being obliged by the Rules of their Cast [caste] and Sect, to adhere to a particular Mode of Apparel'.[21] But none the less British manufacturers clamoured louder against the Company's importing Indian cotton goods into Britain. The Court's Select Committee tried to justify the Company by citing figures to show that the value of Manchester's cotton manufactures had increased proportionately with the amount of raw cotton imported from India in its own ships, and that there was no reason for Britain's interest being jeopardized by the continuance of the Company's monopoly trade.[22] The Committee's report saved the monopoly in 1793, but one of the provisions of the Charter Act of that year slackened its old restrictions on the residence of European settlers in India.

The Company had to bow before the weight of public opinion in England and to give ground to the free traders who supplanted its commercial economy. But dependent as they were for a long time on home manufacturers for the supply of fabrics and other goods, the growth of factory industry in India did not follow on soon after the decay of handicrafts. It took time for free traders to build up their own industrial capital and to set up factory industries in India, which later competed with the produce of British labour. But even in the beginning, the inflow of foreign capital contributed to the development of India's internal resources, which more than balanced the outflow of wealth from the country.

[21] Ibid. pp. 9–12.
[22] The amount of raw cotton imported into England from India rose from 2,677,042 lb. in 1771 to 31,447,605 lb. in 1790, according to the Court's Select Committee. The value of British cotton manufactures increased proportionately from £3,200,000 in 1783 to £7½ million in 1787.

V

The Landed Middle Class

As has been seen, under the Mughals an intermediate landed interest existed in various parts of the country.[1] It consisted of such landed proprietors as held under-tenures in between a big zamindar or jagirdar and the cultivator. In Bengal these intermediate proprietors were known as taluqdar, a title which in Bihar, Benares, and the North-Western Provinces signified an order of landed interest inferior to a zamindar or jagirdar, but superior to those who held a village or a group of villages (called mahals) in joint proprietorship. This taluqdari tenure existed in other parts of India as well, including Gujarat, Bombay, and Madras. In certain districts of Bengal, for example in Midnapur, there were hardly three or four big zamindars. Most of the proprietors were taluqdars, some so small that they paid a land revenue of Rs. 1,000.[2]

Below the rank of taluqdar were a mass of small proprietors who partly cultivated their own lands and partly let them to others. In Bengal and Bihar they were called mukarraridars or holders of under-tenures on a permanent lease. In Benares and the Upper Provinces the English called them 'village zamindars' or joint proprietors. In most parts of Bombay and Madras they were known as mirasdars or peasant proprietors who could transfer or mortgage their lands independently of their superior overlord.

The rights of under-tenure proprietors existed in the pre-British days, but were not well-defined and recorded. Their exercise depended more on customary regulations than on the force of law. Holders of these under-tenures exercised their rights imperfectly, after struggle and contention, and always risked being reduced or

[1] See above, p. 44.   [2] Rep. Com. HC on Petitions, 1781, p. 29b.

even wiped out by a higher order of landed interest which the Mughal and the Maratha Governments superimposed under various denominations.

Functionally, a farmer of land revenue, though not a proprietor, stood in precisely the same situation as a zamindar in so far as the management of public revenues was concerned. Like the zamindar, he appointed his own collectors, held his own court to settle disputed accounts, and realized all such perquisites as might otherwise have gone into the coffers of the zamindar. In places where there was no zamindar, or where a zamindar declined to accept the terms of settlement, Government usually sent an officer called amil or employed a contractor called farmer who stipulated to pay a fixed sum. Once the general assessment was over, the several zamindars, taluqdars, or farmers made an agreement either with persons of lesser degree or with the resident and hereditary occupants of the land called ryots.

By the time the Company took over the civil administration of the Diwani provinces in 1765 the system of farming the revenue had become by far the most popular of the modes of settlement. Every district was arranged in parganas (fiscal divisions) and farmed to hereditary zamindars or farmers. However, the difference between a zamindar and an ordinary revenue farmer was that while the former engaged to pay his revenue without any security, the latter had to produce security as a necessary condition of his engagement. Moreover, a zamindar, who was treated as a hereditary landholder, was entitled to a pension payable to him at the rate of 10 per cent. in case his zamindari was brought under direct management either through a failure to conform to his agreement or a refusal to accept the terms of Government.

Apart from its being ruinous to the cultivating community, who had ultimately to bear all the burdens, sociologically speaking this system of revenue farming had two main tendencies. First, a revenue farmer whose main sanction was the authority he received from Government, could and did misuse that connexion in expropriating hereditary and lawful owners of land who derived their influence from their being rooted in the community. He thus caused insecurity to private property. Secondly, as the principal motive behind revenue farming was to get the maximum benefit, regardless of how it was collected, the system encouraged extortion and bred a host of illegal imposts called *abwabs* or cesses[3] which obstructed the formation of agricultural capital at intermediate or lower levels. In a letter of 3 November 1772 the Bengal Government informed the Court of Directors that the Mughal governors 'exacted what they could from the Zemindars and the great Farmers of the Revenue, whom they left at Liberty to plunder all below, reserving to themselves the Prerogative of plundering them in their Turn, when they were supposed to have enriched themselves with the Spoils of the Country'.[4]

The security of under-tenures became all the more threatened; for the power to collect the revenues went hand in hand with the responsibility of preserving the peace. Those who made the collections maintained a body of militia which could at any time be used to curb the independence of a holder of under-tenure or to deprive him of his tenure altogether. It is true that under the Mughal Government the zamindar or revenue farmer did the policing in his area

as the subordinate Instrument of a larger System. The Land Servants, or the ancient Militia of the Country, were under his immediate Charge; and being distributed throughout the Zemindarry, enabled the Zemindar both to watch over its internal Quiet, and to obtain Information of whatever passed in any Part of it; and so far the Foujedarry Jurisdiction is inherent in the Zemindar. In the Exercise of it he was subject to a Foujedar, who had the Superintendance of a District comprehending many Zemindarries. . . . It was the Zemindar's Duty to give constant Intelligence . . . and to assist the Foujedar in the Apprehension of Robbers, and in executing the Measures which were required of him for preserving the Peace of the Country; but this Duty first and immediately belonged to the Foujedar, who was the Representative of the Nizam and to him the People looked up for Justice and Protection, even against their Chiefs.[5]

But on the decline of the authority of Government the subordinate instrument dominated the larger system. The zamindars, amils, and farmers arrogated to themselves a variety of judicial, executive, and other functions which of right did not belong to

[3] See Misra, *The Central Administration of the East India Company, 1773–1833* (1959), ch. 4.
[4] 6th Rep. Com. Sec. HC, 1772–3, p. 301a.
[5] Remarks of the Governor-General, Warren Hastings, in Beng. Sec. Cons., 7 Dec. 1775 (ibid. app. 15, p. 939b).

them. It was in this state of affairs that the Company obtained the Diwani of the three provinces in 1765. But for several reasons the old pattern of things continued until Warren Hastings took over the direct responsiblity of civil administration in 1772.

NATURE OF CHANGES UNDER THE BRITISH

The general effect of British rule was to weaken the landed superstructure which throve under the country Governments, Mughal or Maratha. This they did chiefly in two ways: first, by erecting a strong political authority with a network of judicial and executive apparatus which left no room for a zamindar to exercise any public responsibility or function; and secondly, by defining and recognizing the right of under-tenures, which reduced his power to subject them to his observance. Since the second mode was directly responsible for the growth of the landed middle class, we shall confine our discussion to the revenue laws of the British.

Changes in Bengal

The changes which affected the zamindars of Bengal and Bihar did not arise from the formation of records of right. The Company's Government was in fact not in a position in 1765 to form such records. In the words of Clive:

In the infancy of the Acquisition we were under the Necessity of confiding in the old officers of the Government, from whom we were to derive our knowledge, and whom we therefore endeavoured to attach to our Service by the Ties of Interest, until Experience should render their Assistance less necessary. Policy required we should pursue every Step likely to conciliate the Natives to our Government.[6]

The system of revenue farming thus continued in Bengal. What Hastings did in 1772 was to make the system quinquennial and to recognize the rights of taluqdars and smaller zamindars by a settlement of the revenues direct with them. The zamindari of Raja Krishnachand of Nadia was, for instance, parcelled out and settled with a number of farmers. But the taluqdars and smaller zamindars there, as elsewhere, were permitted to bypass their

[6] Clive to Court, 29 Sept. 1765 (I.O. MSS. Eur. E. 12, ff. 76–77).

superior overlords and pay their revenue directly to Government
on terms similar to those offered to farmers. It was the farming
system and the settlement of revenue direct with the under-tenure
holders that Hastings employed as a means to ascertain the revenue
resources of the districts and to bring the zamindars to their
knees.

The farming out of the revenue collection by auction to the
highest bidders was not a sound measure. It introduced a number
of speculators who affected the collections by failing to fulfil their
engagements. It brought discredit to Hastings and weakened his
case against the zamindars. But it was an opportunity for banyans
or commercial brokers to develop a middle-class landed interest
which their English masters also shared with them. The parliamentary Committee of Secrecy reported in 1773 that although
direct evidence to show that the civil and military servants held
land was lacking, the Committee had met with circumstances
which suggested that 'the Company's servants sometimes share
with their *buniyans* in the profits of lands rented by them', and that
in one specific instance this practice was 'directly asserted by the
buniyan, who held the land'.[7]

Further, in a minute recorded in the Bengal Revenue Consultation of 12 May 1775, Philip Francis, a member of the Council,
pointed out that in consequence of the settlement made by the
Committee of Circuit in 1772 'many of the most beneficial Farms
in this Province [Bengal] have fallen into the hands of Banyans'
and that there were reasons to suspect that the various remissions
of rent recommended by the gentlemen in the Company's service
had been 'principally granted in favour of such Farms'.[8]

In a letter of 31 January 1776, the Court of Directors confirmed
the fact of commercial infiltration in land, and noted with regret
that in spite of the regulations of Government to the contrary,
certain district officers held landed interest in the names of their
banyans. This practice had become so general that one Krishna
Kantu Nandi (the well-known 'Cantoo Baboo') a banyan of the
Governor-General, Warren Hastings, held in the name of his son,
Loknath Nandi, a considerable farm in the pargana of Baharband.
Indeed this system of farming seriously injured the prestige of

[7] 4th Rep. Com. Sec. HC, 1772–3, p. 116.
[8] 11th Rep. Sel. Com. HC, 1782–3, app. O, pp. 844b–855a.

the old aristocracy of Bengal and effected dislocation in the ownership of landed property in favour of the rising moneyed class of banyans. But more serious was the famine of 1770, which transformed the relations between landlord and peasant in Bengal. Before this famine the oppressive conduct of farmers and zamindars had forced tenants to quit their houses and go into parts of the country where they could get easier terms of settlement. In a statement before the House of Commons Committee of 1781 James Rennell, the Surveyor-General of the Company, declared that in 1765 he had 'observed Houses uninhabited, and Lands uncultivated' on account of 'the Exactions of the Collectors' of revenue. In the time of Mir Kasim, he added, '30,000 Families quitted the Province of *Rungpore* [Rangpur], a very fertile one, in One Year, and settled in *Coos Bayhar* [Cooch Bihar], the adjoining Province, but then not subject to the Jurisdiction of the Nabob'.[9] A landlord could then oppress his tenants and force them to leave their lands and houses because there were more tillers than lands to till.

But the situation changed when one-third of the population of Bengal and Bihar perished in consequence of the famine of 1770. In the words of G. G. Ducarel, the Supervisor of Purnia in 1771, the ravages of famine caused 'the greatest mortality of the inhabitants, which continued almost twelve months in a degree of severity hardly to be paralleled in the history of any age or country'.[10] More lands were then available than there were tillers to cultivate. In a revenue consultation of 5 November 1776, Philip Francis stated 'In the present State of the Country, the Ryot has in fact the Advantage over the Zemindar. Where so much Land lies waste, and so few Hands are left for Cultivation, the Peasant must be courted to undertake it.'[11]

The scarcity of tillers reduced a number of ancient zamindars to a state of impoverishment. They fell into arrears and could not satisfy the demands of Government. Some of them had to go to prison, while others had to lose the direct management of their zamindaris. The following figures indicate how cheaply the zamindaris were sold for arrears of revenue:

[9] Rep. Com. HC on Petitions, 1781, p. 36a.
[10] Controlling Council of Rev., Murshidabad, Proc., viii. f. 109.
[11] 6th Rep. Sel. Com. HC, 1782-3, p. 943a.

Parganas or Taluqs	Net Rental Rs.	Balance Rs.	Amount for which sold by auction Rs.
Shazadpur	8,957	3,842	4,401
Gosegang	2,377	1,762	900
Muzcoory	1,282	728	800
Shazadpur (a second taluq)	15,719	13,231	4,500
Akbarshahi	6,776	4,183	6,000

Source: Beng. Rev. Cons., 20 Dec. 1776 (in 6th Rep. Sel. Com. 1782–3, app. 15, p. 959).

The non-resident tenants-at-will were in these circumstances the kind of people who dictated the terms on which they would agree to cultivate the lands. Within six years after the famine, wrote W. W. Hunter, the non-resident ryots, who had previously formed an insignificant and degraded order, became the most prominent feature in the rural system of Bengal for thirty years. In former times the non-resident cultivators wandered wearily through the province because they could nowhere find land;

after 1770, the cultivators joined the non-resident class because they could find land everywhere cheaper than the old rates, and a collector, when wishing to imply that an English gentleman had received his land on advantageous terms, briefly describes him as a *paikasht ryot* (non-resident cultivator).[12]

Another group of persons who took advantage of the decline of the old aristocracy of Bengal consisted of the subordinate employees of the Company, especially in its revenue and commercial branches. Even an able and upright district officer such as Jacob Rider, who assisted the Committee of Circuit in the settlement of Nadia in 1772, could only secure with great difficulty the dismissal of his amin who had surreptitiously made out a rent-roll exceeding the assessment already approved by the committee.[13]

It is interesting to note that Jaya Ram, one of the ancestors of the famous Tagore family of Bengal, was an amin who took an active

[12] *Ann. Rural Beng.*, 7th ed. (1897), p. 60.
[13] Committee of Circuit, Proc., 9 July 1772 (I.O. r. 70, v. 14, f. 83). See also 6th Rep. Sel. Com. HC, 1782–3, app. 2, para. 28.

part in the settlement of the Twenty-four Parganas belonging to the Company. He died in 1762. His second son, Darpa Narayan, acquired a knowledge of English and French, and through his service with the French Government at Chandernagore earned a huge fortune with which he bought a large zamindari belonging to the Brahman zamindar of Rajshahi.[14] The celebrated family of Dwarkanath Tagore descended from a junior branch of the family. Born in 1794, Dwarkanath acquired a knowledge of English in Sherbourne's school, and later learnt Persian. He became a law agent, in which capacity he became acquainted with the landed interests of Bengal. But it seems that his fortunes arose from his service as serishtadar (head clerk) to the Salt Agent and Collector of the Twenty-four Parganas, where he later became a Diwan to the same agency. On his resignation from this situation in 1834 he bought part of the assets of Messrs. Palmer & Company. He later developed an industrial interest in the manufacture of sugar and flax, but since the scope of industrial finance was still limited, his interests remained mainly commercial and agricultural.[15]

Towards a Permanent Settlement. A gradual decline in the land-revenue figures brought the system of farming by auction to a dismal end. Hastings appointed an Amini Commission in 1776 to assess the revenue capacity of each district and under the instruction of the Directors decided in the meantime that the land revenue should be settled annually, but not by auction, which they regarded as prejudicial to hereditary proprietors. On the termination of the quinquennial settlement the management of the zamindaris was restored to their respective proprietors in 1777. Hastings constituted a separate Committee of the Revenue in 1781 to improve the collecting, but the net collection made after its establishment fell short of the average annual revenues realized during 1776–9 by £725,238. Hastings's failure to restore the collections to the former level thus brought him discredit. The hostility of the zamindars of Bihar which followed the Chait Singh affair at Benares in 1781[16]

---

[14] Ghose, ii. 160–2.   [15] Ibid. pp. 215–16.

[16] Hastings made exorbitant demands on Chait Singh, Raja of Benares, who had placed himself under the overlordship of the Company, and in 1780 ordered him in addition to supply a substantial body of cavalry. Without his knowledge the Raja's soldiers suddenly rose and massacred a number of English sepoys with three officers. The rising was suppressed, and Chait Singh was banished in spite of the fact that he had no complicity in the massacre.

and the Company's wars with the Marathas and Mysore dictated the expediency of a fixed and equitable land policy which Cornwallis was called upon to execute in 1786.

Following instructions of the Court of Directors, Cornwallis asked the Collectors to report on alleged cases of dispossession and to inquire into the status and position of zamindars. The inquiries continued for two years, but in the meantime, on the basis of a recommendation of John Shore, President of the Board of Revenue, Cornwallis ordered the settlement to be made with the zamindars as hereditary proprietors for a period of ten years from 1790, the settlement to be made perpetual if the home Government approved it. So far the proceedings conformed to the instructions of the Court of Directors.

But as soon as the necessary preliminaries were completed in 1790, Cornwallis decided on an immediate plan of permanent settlement. Shore and Charles Grant, another senior servant of the Company who had made a special study of land revenue, objected that permanence was not justified without a survey, but Cornwallis nevertheless announced on 10 February 1790 that the decennial settlement was to be made permanent if approved by the Court of Directors. Their approval reached Cornwallis in 1793 when what was known as the Permanent Settlement was effected, on the basis of a net revenue amounting to Rs. 26,800,989.[17] The zamindars and other proprietors were deemed to have heritable and transferable property rights subject to the payment of a fixed annual sum to the Government.

CORNWALLIS'S POLICY

In his desire to fix the demand in perpetuity Cornwallis's motive was to restore the confidence of the zamindars in the stability of the new plan of assessment. Suspicious of the intention of the Government in the light of their past experience, they hardly believed that a perpetual settlement would ever follow the decennial one. Cornwallis regarded this feeling of instability as prejudicial to the interest of Government. He therefore took the earliest opportunity to declare the assessment as permanent in order to give the zamindars a sense of security.

[17] See Hunter, *Bengal MS. Records*, 1. 107.

A land-holder who is secured in the quiet enjoyment of a profitable estate [he said] can have no motive in wishing for a change. On the contrary, if the rents of his lands are raised in proportion to their improvement; if he is liable to be dispossessed should he refuse to pay the increase required of him . . . he will readily listen to any offers which are likely to bring about a change that cannot place him in a worse situation, but which holds out to him hopes of a better.[18]

While fixing the demand, Cornwallis was aware that he deprived the Government of a share in any expanding income from the land. He was also not unconscious of the loss which might arise from a gradual depreciation of the country's currency. The question of the rights of zamindars or their legal position did not engage his attention. He regarded such a consideration unnecessary. In some cases the Collectors were in fact 'positively prohibited from resorting to minute local scrutinies for the purpose of ascertaining the resources of the Country'.[19] He considered it immaterial to the Government 'what individual possesses the land provided he cultivates it, protects the ryots, and pays the public revenue.' His policy was simply to have the land revenue settled, with the zamindars or with other proprietors. But he emphasized that landed property should come into the hands of the most frugal and thrifty class of people who might improve their lands, protect their cultivators, and promote the general prosperity of the country.[20]

It is clear that Cornwallis had in view the interests of a new class of zamindars consisting of the Company's regular revenue farmers, its banyans as well as the inferior zamindars and taluqdars who formed a social group different in habits and character from the zamindars descending from ancient families. He had probably been struck by the gradual increase in importance of this new social element; in a letter of 6 March 1793 he stated that there was every ground to expect that: '. . . the large capitals possessed by many of the Natives, which they will have no means of employing when the public debt is discharged, will be applied to the purchase of landed property as soon as the tenure is declared to be secure'.[21]

These considerations led him to ignore the objections of Shore,

---

[18] Forrest, *Selections*, ii. 113 (10 Feb. 1790).
[19] I.O., Desp. to Bengal, 6 Jan. 1815, v. 68, ff. 246-7.
[20] Forrest, *Selections*, ii. 75 (18 Sept. 1789).
[21] 2nd Rep. Sel. Com. HC, 1808-12, app. 9, p. 103.

who feared that far from being able to improve the management of their lands, many of the old zamindars would ruin them through their incapacity and indolence. If there were men who could not improve their lands, Cornwallis categorically retorted, 'the sooner their bad management obliges them to part with their property to the more industrious, the better for the State'.[22]

It is against the background of his regard for the interest of the new landed middle class that some of Cornwallis's other measures, which weakened the old aristocracy of Bengal, can better be explained. Although generally supposed to have been partial to big landholders, he recognized taluqdars and mukarraridars as separate from, and independent of, their overlords. Already under Hastings the class of taluqdars and smaller zamindars had received a distinct status. They were denominated as proprietors of farmed land for two reasons: first, they were originally a class of undertenure holders who farmed their taluqs for Government; and secondly, they subsequently came to include in their rank a considerable number of new entrants, particularly banyans and office employees, who had either farmed out or bought such taluqs or zamindaris when sold by auction, on lease, or otherwise. At the time of the Permanent Settlement their lands were settled with them in perpetuity, and their titles declared absolute.

In a letter of 6 March 1793, addressed to the Court of Directors, the Government of Bengal stated that the principle which had induced it to decide upon the separation of taluqs and mukarrari lands had also prompted it to abolish a custom

introduced under the native government, by which most of the principal Zemindaries in the country were made to descend entire to the eldest son, or next heir of the last incumbent, in opposition both to the Hindoo and Mahomedan law, which admit of no exclusive right of inheritance in favour of primogeniture, but require that the property of a deceased person shall be divided amongst his sons or heirs in certain specified proportions.[23]

---

[22] Forrest, *Selections*, ii. 75.

[23] 2nd Rep. Sel. Com. HC, 1808–12, p. 100. In 1792 an interesting case arose in the Sadr Diwani Adalat at Calcutta disputing the validity of a will which Raja Kishenchund (Krishnachand) of Nadia had made in favour of his eldest surviving son, Sheochund, conferring on him the whole of his zamindar, and making certain pecuniary provisions for the remaining three sons. The Sadr court held that although 'sinful' on the part of the Raja to have done so, the

The abolition of this custom led to the disintegration of estates through partition among heirs.

The abolition of the zamindar's police authority in 1792, and the removal of all kinds of duties previously levied by him on the internal movement of trade, tended further to reduce his influence and resources. While the former measure led ultimately to the transfer of his land militia to the control of the government police, the latter made the mercantile community independent and able to have him prosecuted for any attempted exaction.

The Permanent Settlement and After. The statutory recognition of zamindaris as property transferable without the permission of Government and a simultaneous provision for the partition of estates among heirs led to a great multiplication of the number of estates with a corresponding reduction in the average size of each. The number of landholders, which did not exceed 100 in the beginning of Hastings's administration in 1772, rose in the course of a century to 154,200. The *Bengal Administration Report* of 1872–3 observed (p. 73):

In 38 districts of Bengal proper and Behar, out of a total number of 154,200 estates at present borne on the public books, 533, or ·34 per cent., only are great properties with an area of 20,000 acres and upwards; 15,747, or 10.21 per cent., range from 500 to 20,000 acres in area; while the number of estates which fall short of 500 acres is no less than 137,920, or 89·44 per cent., of the whole.

In Bihar a number of petty estates sprang from the settlement of such rent-free lands as were resumed under Regulations II and III of 1819 and 1828. The number of resumptions in Bihar was much greater than in Bengal, for whereas the total revenue of Bihar rose from Rs. 53,09,181 in 1790–1 to Rs. 97,04,091 (exclusive of Purnia) in 1871–2, the increase in revenue in Bengal proper since the decennial settlement was Rs. 25,80,179 only.[24]

The Mughals took care to preserve the compactness of ancient zamindaris. Although ordinarily heritable, these could not be trans-

father's power to dispose of his property, whether by gift, will, or distribution of shares, even though contrary to the injunctions of the law, was valid (*Reps. of Select Causes, adjudged in appeal before the Sudder Dewanny Adawlut, previous to the year 1805, and to the end of the year 1811* (n.d.)).

[24] The total decennial settlement amounted to Rs. 2,68,00,989 for Bengal and Bihar, the latter being Rs. 53,09,181 only.

ferred without the previous permission of Government. Even a lawful heir to a zamindari had to obtain a certificate of succession which confirmed his claim to it and which secured his loyalty to Government. Moreover, since a zamindar also exercised police jurisdiction, the preservation of the territorial integrity of his zamindari was an administrative necessity. This jurisdiction devolved on whoever inherited the zamindari under a recognized custom of primogeniture. It was more or less an office rather than a property. The preservation of its entirety was conducive to the power and influence of the landed aristocracy on whose support the rule of the Mughals depended.

In search of a more extended support for their rule, the British abolished the customary rule of primogeniture and recognized zamindaris as property transferable without the permission of Government. To secure a timely collection of the revenue, they enacted what is known as 'the sunset law' which required landholders to pay their revenue by a specified date and time. While the saleability of zamindaris tempted landholders to incur loans to meet their social extravagances, the growth of commercial wealth and money-lenders found in land a source of investment and social prestige. The Company's courts provided an element of security and secured the transfers of property either by sale or in satisfaction of judicial decrees.

The sunset law, on the other hand, operated to the great disadvantage of the ancient families of landholders who were constitutionally indolent and exhibited great incapacity in the management of their estates. Zamindaris with more than a fifth of the total revenues of Bengal were put up for sale during 1796–7, and within twenty years after the Permanent Settlement more than one-third of the landed property of Bengal was sold for arrears of rent. The partition suits brought before the Sadr Diwani Adalat at Calcutta showed that the ancient zamindaris, like Nadia, Rajshahi, Cassijura, and others, had by the first decade of the nineteenth century lost most of their original values. Their dismemberment radically altered the distribution and ownership of land. The new moneyed class, especially banyans and brokers, agents and creditors, swooped down with their exorbitant claims arising from compound interest, and exacted their bonds with the help of the newly established courts.

It may be of interest to note that in divesting the Company's revenue officers of all their judicial functions Cornwallis was guided by a desire to ensure complete security of property. His courts were designed so as to enforce the terms agreed to between parties without any extra-judicial consideration. They were to operate as an agency to effect the transformation of society from a basis of status to one of contract. But since the vast majority of the country's population, including the ancient aristocracy, remained uneducated and ill informed about the basic principle underlying the new changes or the working of the new judicial apparatus, the kind of people who took advantage of it were the new middle classes. To the vast majority the working of a contractual relationship proved generally ruinous. A contractual society in Europe was the result of capitalist development which brought about concomitant changes in education and the level of material prosperity. Its growth was internal. In India it was imposed, regardless of the educational and material background. It tended to effect the ruin of the old without shaping the character of the new. Its growth was unnatural.

Growth of Subinfeudation. One of the effects of the Permanent Settlement was the growth of subinfeudation comprising a number of intermediate proprietary layers of under-tenure holders. The device was introduced by the Maharaja of Burdwan to save himself from ruin. He leased out in perpetuity the management of a large part of his estate to several middlemen who paid a fixed sum to him, and settled the lands either with the actual cultivators or with middlemen who paid a higher rental. This arrangement was in violation of the provisions of the Permanent Settlement, under which the period of such leases was not to exceed ten years. Yet the perpetual transfer of estates to middlemen continued until 1812, when the Governor-General in Council abolished the old restriction and authorized the zamindars to grant leases for any period they liked. This led to the development of what is known as patni tenure in Bengal and mukarrari tenure in Bihar. This growth of subinfeudation was recognized by a Regulation of 1819, which tried to secure the interest of patnidars, or holders of under-tenures of a proprietary nature.

The middle-class landed interest thus grew both from the disintegration and partition of ancient estates as well as from the

increase of patni tenure. But in each case the great bulk of purchasers were either townsmen or had some sort of urban connexion.
The general tendency was towards absentee landlordism. The
landed gentry of Bengal, generally speaking, were to become a class
of rent receivers rather than of agricultural entrepreneurs. J. P.
Grant, a member of the Council, pointed out in 1855 that in Bengal
nearly two-thirds of the land was held in taluqdari or under-
tenures.[25]

The interest of the middle-class holders was fully secured by an
Act passed in 1859.[26] This was effected by an improvement of the
law governing the sale of land for arrears of land revenue. Before
this a default of payment made a zamindari peremptorily liable to
sale, and a sale swept away the rights of all sharers. The revenue
law in fact took no notice of the common tenancy in which a
zamindari might be held. Default by any one shareholder rendered
all the other shares liable to sale by auction. The Act of 1859
recognized as separate interests shares of a zamindari, whether held
by several in common tenancy or consisting of distinct and integral
parts of the zamindari, and it allowed a separate account to be
opened in the Collector's books of revenue to be paid by each
sharer. The advantage was that in case of default by any sharer, the
whole zamindari was not put up for sale but only the share of the
defaulter.

The operation of this principle was extended to the protection
of the rights of the holders of under-tenures which existed before
the Permanent Settlement as well as those which were created
after it. The Act provided for the registration of both. While com-
mending these provisions at a Bill stage, the Secretary of the Indigo
Planters' Association made the following comments which eluci-
date the importance of the measure:

The putneedar is a purchaser for a price, or valuable consideration, of
a portion of the zemindari lands in perpetuity, with one condition
attached, namely, payment to the zemindar of a rent, the equivalent,
or supposed to be, of the revenue payable for the lands comprised in the
putnee. It is this condition which constitutes the tenure, connects the
putneedar with the zemindar, and the putnee lands with the zemindari;

---

[25] Rep. Sel. Com. HC, 1858, app. 7, p. 300.
[26] Act XI of 1859, entitled an Act to Improve the Law relating to Sales of
Land for Arrears of Revenue in the Bengal Presidency.

and, except for the obligation which it contains, the putneedar would have an absolute and indefeasible estate, and would be entirely independent of the zemindar. The putnee rent, therefore, is the only interest which the zemindar has in the putnee lands, and therefore non-payment of that rent is the only ground on which the zemindar can claim any power over the putnee tenure, and it is equally clear, that if the putneedar makes no default, he is fully entitled by his contract to be as secure against the zemindar as the latter is against the Government, so long as he pays the Government revenue.[27]

Under the new Act, the patnidar was no longer to be sacrificed. The purchaser of a zamindari at a revenue sale was to take it subject to the patni and all other under-tenures except when the holders of these were themselves defaulters. This principle was extended so as to secure the rights of resident or occupancy tenants.

A legislative measure to secure the rights of tenancy was in fact long overdue because of the serious drawbacks of the Permanent Settlement. In his anxiety to form a uniform system of title from a variety of proprietary and possessory tenures, Cornwallis had neglected to ascertain the rights of under-tenancy, the limits of revenue-paying and waste lands as well as the boundaries of villages. This neglect multiplied litigation to an extent never known before. It tended to sacrifice what might be called the yeomanry by merging all village rights with the zamindar's paramount property in the soil. It is true that regulations guaranteed protection. But since the rates of assessment, which differed from place to place, remained unascertained, it was generally the whim of a zamindar rather than judicial determination that operated in practice. The zamindar would not readily execute *pattas* or leases provided by the regulations. And since these were renewable after every ten years, the cultivators felt apprehensive lest their acceptance of such documents should give a temporary colour to the tenure which they had held from time immemorial.

Changes in the North-Western Provinces

The North-Western Provinces consisted of the districts ceded by the Nawab of Oudh in 1775 and 1801 as well as those conquered from the Marathas in 1803. The ceded districts comprised

[27] Rep. Sel. Com. HC, 1858, app. 2, p. 247.

Gorakhpur, Allahabad, Cawnpore, Farrukhabad, Etawah, Bareilly, and Moradabad. The districts of Agra, Delhi, Aligarh and Saharanpur, including Meerut, were conquered from Sindhia (the Maratha chief), Bundelkhand was taken from the Peshwa (1803), and Cuttack from the Raja of Berar. Cuttack formed part of Orissa, and Delhi was separately administered by a British Resident.

The landed gentry and yeomanry of the North-Western Provinces consisted of taluqdars and village zamindars who held their lands in joint proprietorship. As in Benares they were for the most part Rajputs who had migrated from the west and occupied large tracts of land in co-parcenary tenures. The village zamindars or joint proprietors constituted the great bulk of the resident and cultivating zamindars who employed low-caste men in the cultivation of their lands. Above them was a higher order of landed interest called taluqdars who, as has been said, were subordinate to local chiefs, rajas, or jagirdars.

The first decade of British rule saw the uprooting of a large number of respectable landed proprietors.

In 1802 the Marquess of Wellesley, then Governor-General, introduced in the 'ceded districts' the Bengal pattern of district administration, and without the previous permission of the Court of Directors declared his intention to settle the lands in perpetuity after a period of ten years. In the meantime he decided to farm them out to zamindars, taluqdars, and joint proprietors, and in the absence of these to amils or farmers of revenue. The first two settlements were to be triennial, and the third for a period of four years, before a permanent settlement was to be made. As part of the policy of Government to reduce refractory zamindars, the Collectors were instructed to recognize subordinate taluqdars and to make the settlement with them, permitting them at the same time to make payment directly to Government.

Government thus defined its policy without ascertaining either the respective rights of the various landed interests involved, or the resources of the territories newly acquired. It declared its intention to recognize the rights of all zamindars, taluqdars, and other proprietors, but it made no attempts to ascertain the basis on which their respective rights were founded. All that Government did was to announce a description of the persons with whom the settlement was to be made, either temporarily or permanently, in the character of proprietors. It did nothing to acquire a knowledge of what constituted their property rights.

On the contrary, while the Collectors were ordered to make the settlement with 'the Zemindars and other proprietors', they were likewise asked to recognize the taluqdars as proprietors, 'and proprietors too of that, which if the Zemindar within whose local jurisdiction the Talookdar was comprehended, be a landed Proprietor and his Zemindary his own Estate, must necessarily belong to the Zemindar and not to the Talookdar'.[28] This hasty conduct of Government in fact involved the zamindars, taluqdars, and village proprietors in a triangular conflict for the recognition of their respective rights. In relation to a taluqdar, the village zamindars comprehended in his taluq stood in the same predicament as did the taluqdars in relation to their own superior zamindar. Each group of landed interest thus tried to engulf the other below it. Moreover, 'all sorts of claimants arose, with titles good, bad, and indifferent, and flocked to the Collector's Court at the chief station, urging their proprietary rights'.[29]

In these circumstances, the Collectors usually placed themselves in the hands of kanungos (*qanungos*) and tahsildars, local revenue officers, who exploited the situation to their own advantage and became instrumental in innumerable transfers of landed property fraudulently effected on nominal sums in collusion with the Indian employees of civil courts. 'Nearly one half of the Cawnpore and Allahabad districts thus passed into the hands of the native officials.'[30] And as Government had at that moment no knowledge of villages and estates held jointly by coparceners, they were often sold out through the default of a few principal shareholders in whose names they were exclusively recorded in the government registers. The hereditary proprietors and resident cultivators were thus 'deprived, hastily and absolutely, of their rights, and compelled to sue for leases under some fortunate, perhaps fraudulent, purchaser, whom they hated and despised'.[31]

In a lengthy memorandum dated 1 July 1819 Holt Mackenzie, then Territorial Secretary to Government, deplored this state of affairs and brought to its notice the extent to which fraudulent

[28] James Cumming's Papers, I.O., Home Misc. 529(4), f. 23.
[29] J. W. Kaye, *The Administration of the E. I. Company* (1853), p. 237.
[30] Ibid. p. 241 n.   [31] Ibid. p. 241.

transfers of property had occurred in consequence of the initial error of Government.

In the districts of Goruckpore, Allahabad and Cawnpore [he declared], the public sales appear to have been greatly more extensive than elsewhere; ... and the private transfers by which our Public Officers, the retainers of the Court and the Cutcherry, have gained possession of Estates perhaps equally numerous, have scarcely proved less injurious in their effects on the interests of that great body of the agricultural community, the Village Zemindars.[32]

In certain parganas of Allahabad the Board of Commissioners had stated that the numerous transfers by public or private sale amounted 'nearly to a total permutation of property', following 'immediately upon the introduction of the British Government'. And

as the purchasers in almost all the public sales are the actual Tehsildars, or the sureties for the nominal Tehsildars, the credit of Government is to no small degree affected from these persons having been permitted thus to pervert the influence derived to them by their connection with the Public Service.[33]

The sufferers indeed made no disguise of 'looking forward to the termination of the British Government, for the recovery of their Estates from the consequent termination of the influence through which they had been lost'. The principal and most valuable parts of the district of Allahabad had been engrossed by 'Raja Ooditnarain, Baboo Deokenundun from Benares, and Bauker Ally Khan', a former amil of Kora.[34]

The initial error of policy arose from an impression on the part of the Bengal Government that in the North-Western Provinces, as in Bengal, the dominant proprietary interest was vested in the zamindar. It had little knowledge of the existence of a great body of sturdy proprietors called 'village zamindars', for the most part Rajputs or a class of warriors, who were known for their manly and independent character. Wellesley's declaration of his intention

[32] *Selections from the Revenue Records of the North-West Provinces, 1818–1820* (1866), para. 533, p. 114.
[33] Rev. Cons., 2 July 1811, quoted by Mackenzie, ibid. para. 537, pp. 114–15.
[34] Ibid. p. 115.

in favour of a permanent settlement was the result of ignorance. The Court of Directors, however, rejected this proposal. In 1813 they sent out Lord Moira (better known as the Marquess of Hastings) as Governor-General to carry out their policy, which included the undertaking of a detailed inquiry and land survey as the only effective means of ascertaining the resources of the country as well as the respective rights of agricultural interests. To execute this intention Moira employed an increased number of kanungos, transferred the office of Surveyor-General from the military to the public department, and issued detailed instructions to European Collectors to carry out the most minute survey of every village on the spot for the purposes of settlement, which was to be made not on a permanent basis but for a period that later came to be fixed at thirty years.

To enable the Collectors to carry out the instructions of Government the Governor-General in Council enacted Regulation VII of 1822 which restored to them many of the judicial powers which Cornwallis's Code had deprived them of in 1793, powers which they needed while settling disputed claims in the course of their settlement and survey operations. In the words of a resolution of the Government of India dated 1 August 1822 on the subject, this regulation was to facilitate their

inquiries on the spot, village by village, proceeding upwards from the persons who till the ground to the Government itself, and noticing distinctly all the classes who share in the produce or rent of the land, the extent of the interest of each, and the nature of the title by which it is held.[35]

Lord Hastings had in the meantime taken another measure, the establishment of a Special Commission, under Regulation I of 1821, to restore to the original proprietors the estates which they had lost through the fraudulent conduct of public servants down to 1810. This tended to create a dangerous precedent in that the Special Commissioners were authorized to look into all cases of fraudulent transfers and to reinstate the sufferers notwithstanding the decrees of courts confirming purchases at public auction or private sale. The judges of the Sadr Diwani Adalat, who took a strictly judicial view of things, strongly opposed the measure;

[35] *Sels. from Rev. Rec., N.W.P., 1822–33* (1802), para. 20, p. 5.

but the Governor-General in Council, who took equity and common justice into consideration, nevertheless enacted it.

To impart speed and efficiency to the work of Collectors, Bentinck established a separate Board of Revenue for the North-Western Provinces in 1832, and introduced a superior cadre of non-covenanted Deputy Collectors, able and competent to carry out settlement and survey operations under the immediate supervision of their district officers. Under the direction of James Thomason, who later became the Lieutenant-Governor of the North-Western Provinces, these operations were completed in the 1840's.

The settlement so made is called a village or *mahalwari* settlement. It recognized all possessory and proprietary under-tenures. It provided for the registration of each separate share, so that the *malguzar* (payer of the revenue), or the principal person who previously engaged on behalf of inferior sharers, might not have their shares fraudulently auctioned for arrears of revenue. Another advantage of this mode of settlement was that it brought the rural folk in close contact with the officers of Government who tried and determined all rent suits and other disputes arising between landlord and tenant.

The principle of this mode of settlement was extended to Oudh on its annexation from the Nawab in 1856, but the outbreak of the Indian Mutiny in the following year delayed the settlement, and political considerations influenced the Government to permit the taluqdars of Oudh to retain their hold on under-tenure holders. In the Punjab (Panjab), however, the principle of village settlement was extended and the right of middle-class tenure holders secured in the same manner as in the North-Western Provinces.

Changes in the Bombay Presidency

Before the final defeat of the Marathas and the annexation of their territories by the British a variety of proprietary and occupancy tenures existed, which were comparable to those of the North-Western Provinces. For instance, taluqdari tenure was important in Gujarat. Most of the taluqdars were of a pure Rajput race, descended from the families of ancient chiefs and conscious of a common ancestry; a few of them were of a mixed

Rajput and Koli race, and some were Muhammadans; but as a landed class they were as sturdy and valiant as those of Bihar and the North-Western Provinces. They employed the low-caste people of their villages to cultivate the land.

In the Deccan, which the Nizam of Hyderabad ceded to the British in 1800, the dominant landed interest vested in the mirasdars who were comparable to the village zamindars of the North-Western Provinces. Their lands were heritable. They could transfer them by mortgage, gift, or sale. They were supposed to be the descendants of the original settlers who cleared the jungle and paid a quit-rent for the entire area under their occupation, either cultivated or waste. The payment of a quit-rent was an essential condition of the miras tenure, which carried with it a great degree of respectability. Moreover, a mirasdar could not be dispossessed of his hereditary property unless he was absent for more than thirty years. He represented a class superior to that of a mere resident tenant, who paid annual rent for his lands under cultivation. The mirasdar partly cultivated his own lands and partly let them to others. He dominated the tenants-at-will (called *upri*) whom he employed in the cultivation of his lands.

The 'khots' of the Konkan were a group of leaseholders who held their lands more or less as revenue farmers. On the other hand the district officers, called deshmukhs and deshpandes, held a kind of service tenure known as 'izafat'. Wherever villages were held in joint proprietorship, under what was called bhagdari tenure, the proprietors were jointly responsible for the payment of the government demand. This was comparable to the patnidari tenure of the North-Western Provinces and parts of Bihar.

The holders of these proprietory tenures constituted what might be regarded as the landed gentry and yeomanry of western India, but under the despotic rule of the Marathas their rights were ill defined and they were subject to arbitrary impositions. Besides, the Brahman Government of the Peshwas superimposed on them a higher order of landed interest, the Maratha nobility, who threatened the peaceful enjoyment of these rights.

The Maratha nobility comprised the holders of a politico-military tenure called 'saranjam', which in its nature and content was comparable to a Mughal jagir, a grant made by the state for the performance of civil or military duties or for the maintenance of the personal dignity of nobles and senior officials. The Peshwas also granted a kind of 'zat', or personal saranjam, which was to last for a life or two. The holders of service or political tenures were however not recognized in law as proprietors. The grant of a saranjam was a form of payment for the service rendered to the state.

A personal inam, or gift of land, was, on the contrary, a proprietary tenure. An inamdar was a noble, usually Brahman, who held his lands in fee simple. In a statement before the parliamentary Select Committee on Colonization and Settlement (India) in 1858, John Warden, a Bombay civil servant who had served the Company for over thirty years before his retirement in 1854, stated that the inamdar held his village under a hereditary title, which was better than one could obtain in England:

> The title-deeds of an enamdar are much more copious than any title-deeds in this country; they give a man the land, the trees, the water, the treasure on the surface, and the treasure below; in fact, language is exhausted in its attempt to convey to him the proprietary right in the soil.[36]

The religious and charitable institutions of Hindus and Muhammadans also enjoyed the benefits of inam tenure under the title of devasthan.

When the British took over in 1818, the people who suffered from the dispossession of their lands were the Maratha chiefs and warriors, the holders of military fiefs which lapsed when their service came to an end. The personal inams were however continued. Mountstuart Elphinstone, Governor of Bombay 1819–27, recognized every species of hereditary right, including rent-free inams, established pensions, religious and charitable endowments. Every holder of inam found registered in the Peshwa's records and in actual possession was allowed to continue in the free enjoyment of his gift. Only those who possessed neither an official document nor possessory evidence had to lose their claims; for Regulation XVII of 1827 provided that a continuous possession for thirty years constituted a sufficient title to exemption from the payment of public revenue, and that such possession, for only twelve years before the territory in which the land was situated

36 Sel. Com. HC, 1858, Mins. of Ev., A. to Q. 6062.

came into the possession of the British, was equivalent to possession for thirty years.

Even in respect of service tenure, Elphinstone left the village communities intact. He allowed the village service to be rendered in return for the grant of land or money. The district revenue and police staff of the previous Government was, however, affected by the introduction of the revenue survey and the organization of a stipendiary police. But a concession was made under which those whose assignments ceased could have their lands settled with them on repaying a portion of their emoluments.

In consequence of the discovery of certain unauthorized and fraudulent alienations of inam lands, an inquiry into the validity of titles was begun in 1843 in the south Maratha country. This raised doubts about the creation of fresh inams under the British, and led the Governor-General in Council to enact legislation in 1852 (Act XI of 1852) authorizing the Governor of Bombay to appoint an Inam Commission to investigate the whole question.[37]

However, by the time the Commission was established in 1858, a large number of prescriptive titles had emerged. A list printed on 28 August 1857 indicated that as many as 108,119 titles were questioned, and that of these, decisions had been passed on 6,002 only. By these decisions, 2,948 inams were declared hereditary and permanent, $132\frac{1}{2}$ continuable for two or more generations, 3,135 restricted to present incumbents, $671\frac{1}{2}$ assessable with immediate effect, and 25 treated as saranjam or service tenure.[38] Considering the small number of cases disposed of in the period of forty years since 1818, it is only reasonable to conclude that the great bulk of the inamdars, the landed gentry, and aristocracy of western India, remained in the virtual enjoyment of their property and developed prescriptive titles which could not be alienated without the risk of disaffection. Two Acts were thus passed in 1863, which provided that persons claiming exemption from the payment of full government revenue had the option of avoiding a scrutiny of their title by the payment of a mere quit-rent. This expedited the proceedings of the Commission and saved the interests of the inamdars. By 1873 the bulk of its work was completed.

[37] See Bombay Govt. Sel. no. 132 for an account of the Bombay Inam Commission proceedings.
[38] Sel. Com. HC, 1858, Mins. of Ev., Q. 6153.

Since in the course of the survey and settlement operations the holders of miras tenure were taxed to the extent of about 50 per cent. of the produce, it was generally the first rank of mirasdars, taluqdars, and inamdars whose property attracted capital investment. The areas which abounded in this tenure became rich through the cultivation of cotton for export and were paying to the proprietors, who in time became middle-class landholders by a gradual process of partition.

Changes in the Madras Presidency

The nature of agricultural interests in Madras bore a certain resemblance to those of Bombay. The Madras mirasdars, for instance, also owned villages in heritable shares which they could mortgage or transfer at will. They also traced their title to a common ancestry and held villages either singly or in joint proprietorship. The Nairs of the Malabar side, on the other hand, were comparable to the taluqdars of Gujarat. The Bengal type of zamindari was not a widespread social phenomenon in Madras. Certain local chiefs called poligars occupied half the Northern Sarkars and many of the inaccessible places, where they had never been completely subdued. The poligars retained their feudal character and maintained a partial independence within the limits of their territories. They kept armed retainers and even carried on predatory campaigns, but in most parts of the Presidency there were either mirasdars or village headmen through whom Government collected its revenue.

Wellesley, however, ordered the Madras Government to introduce the Bengal zamindari settlement in 1798. Instead of making a village settlement with mirasdars, or in their absence a ryotwari settlement with individual tenants, Clive, the Governor of Madras and a friend of Wellesley, acted upon the advice received from the Bengal Government and settled the lands in the Northern Sarkars and Baramahal with the poligars and zamindars. In the absence of zamindars or poligars, villages were grouped and formed into estates which were sold by auction to the highest bidders.

The zamindari settlement, however, was not extended to other parts of the Presidency. Its extension was opposed by Thomas Munro, a convinced champion of the ryotwari system, who possessed a profound knowledge of local tenures. He later influenced the views of the Court of Directors, who ordered the introduction of the ryotwari system in 1812. The district judge was divested of his magisterial and police duties, which were transferred to the office of Collector in 1816. The Madras Governor in Council enacted a number of other measures delegating judicial powers to Indian officers called munsifs and to village panchayats.

On account of a high rate of assessment, the ryotwari settlement was however not conducive to the growth of a landed middle class. What favoured its growth, besides taluqdari tenure, was the existence of a large number of inamdars, whose lands were tax-free. The early introduction of survey and settlement operations in Madras brought to light the existence of considerable inams which, as in Bombay, did not pay any rent at all. The Madras Government enacted regulations to test the validity of such titles, although nothing tangible was done to assert the right of Government to resume inams in the case of lapse. In 1845 local officers were directed not to continue inams or any service tenure, but since their immediate resumption, besides causing distress to many, involved detailed and complicated inquiries, their holders continued in possession without much let or hindrance.

Delay in investigating inam titles thus operated to the benefit of their holders. And when the Madras Inam Commission was established in November 1858, it had to take into account the development of prescriptive titles and the possibility of disaffection that might spring from a refusal to recognize them. The Court of Directors had in fact already instructed that, grants or no grants, all inams in the uninterrupted possession of the parties since the introduction of British rule must be confirmed to their holders. They were in favour of resuming fraudulent titles created only since the accession of the British. But even here the Commission was to be lenient in case a holder was not a party to any fraud. This advice was liberally executed by Sir Charles Trevelyan, who took over as the Governor of Madras in 1859.[39]

Speaking generally, the main feature of British land policy during this period was to define and record the rights of agricul-

---

[39] The Madras Inam Commission completed most of its work by 1869, when it was abolished. See Iyengar, p. 287.

tural classes, and to make the enjoyment of these rights subject to enforcement by courts. This led to the formation of land records, proceeding to an extent which covered the interest even of individual sharers of joint property, who became free to dispose of their shares in the manner best suited to their convenience.

An important cumulative effect of such a policy was the rise of individualism among rural societies; for it tended to free the sharers from the bondage of village communities to which they previously remained attached because of the fact that their shares were for all practical purposes inalienable, forming part, as they did, of the total joint property registered exclusively in the name of one of their number, namely their chief proprietor who had a major share. He possessed a corporate character especially because it was through him that the state disbursed and realized the public dues. No alienation of any share was possible except through him. With the registration of separate shares his hold on the local community thus began to wane, especially in the latter half of the nineteenth century, as will be shown in a subsequent chapter. The revenue laws of the British in fact set in motion a process of social mobility. Land became a commodity, and the ease with which it could be transferred afforded opportunity to moneyed people to buy social prestige by purchasing landed estates.

The mobility of land had begun much earlier in Bengal where the corporate character of village property was superseded by the institution of individual zamindars. Transfers were therefore on a much larger scale in Bengal than elsewhere.

The revenue laws of the British effected another change of great social significance. They introduced an element of class consciousness. It arose from legally defined property rights, enforcible by courts rather than by custom. It was on the basis of these rights that the agricultural classes later became divided into tenants and landlords, each class defending its interest against encroachment by the other. A class concept of society in fact began with law and legislative authority.

VI

The Educated Middle Class:
1. Main Objects of Western Education

THE term 'educated middle class' is used here generally to signify the new groups of persons who received higher education through the medium of English and engaged in the various recognized professions that grew in modern times as a result of Western education and capitalist economy. It excludes those versed in Sanskrit, Arabic, or Persian. It is true that the old literary castes of the country were the first to benefit from new developments under the British, but those who did so differed essentially in so far as their mental make-up, morality, and style of living were concerned.

ANCIENT UNIVERSITY EDUCATION

The ancient universities of India were in no way comparable to those that sprang up in modern times. Their emphasis was purely literary and their faculties exclusively Oriental. Taksasila and Nalanda, for instance, taught astrology and astronomy, logic and philosophy, history and law. Vallabhi in Kathiawar and Vikramasila and Odantpuri in Bihar were other centres of higher learning specializing in one or other of the literary branches of ancient learning. Nadia in Bengal and Benares in the Upper Provinces carried the old scholarly traditions down to modern times. William Adam's *Report on the State of Education in Bengal* in 1835 showed that even then Nadia preserved 'its character as a university' and that its rajas 'endowed certain teachers with lands for the instruction and maintenance of scholars'.[1] Tirhut in Bihar

[1] Sect. vii, p. 49. Adam's inquiry was instituted by the Bengal Govt. in 1834.

was a similar seat of higher Oriental learning for which the rajas of Darbhanga had created considerable endowments.[2] The Muhammadans, like the Hindus, viewed education as an act of piety and grace. From religious motives their rulers encouraged the establishment of *madrasas* or colleges of Muhammadan learning.

Another feature of ancient higher education was that the Brahmans possessed the virtual monopoly of Sanskrit. Adam's third report of 1838, for instance, revealed that in the district of Burdwan out of 1,358 students in 190 Sanskrit schools there were 1,296 Brahmans, 45 Vaidyas (medical caste), 11 Daivaynas, and 6 Vaishyas. In the district of South Bihar, on the other hand, all the teachers of Sanskrit schools were Brahmans. Of 56 Sanskrit teachers employed in the district of Tirhut not one was a non-Brahman.[3] Adam was in fact surprised to find that in the two districts of Bihar both teachers and students without a single exception belonged to that caste. There were certain exceptions in Bengal, but these were few and far between.

The families which gave education to children in reading and writing at home included those of landholders and traders, commercial agents and village headmen, pandits and priests. Here too, according to Adam, the Brahmans constituted a much larger proportion than all other classes put together. There were vernacular schools, but few of the Brahmans sent their children to these schools, where accounts were the main subject of instruction. Most of them gave their children a knowledge of reading and writing at home before initiating them in a study of Sanskrit. In Bihar, and more specially in the North-Western Provinces, the Kayasths, a caste of scribes, outnumbered the children of other castes in respect of early schooling in reading, writing, and accounts.[4] The institutions of Muhammadan education were also rather more advanced in these provinces than in Bengal and Bihar where, although Urdu was the current spoken language of the

[2] Sect. vii, p. 116.

[3] *Adam's Reports*, pp. 190 and 194. The total number of scholars in 56 schools in Tirhut was 214, averaging 3.8 to each school. In Burdwan the average was a little over 7. The monthly emolument of a Sanskrit teacher varied from Rs. 5 to Rs. 35.

[4] R. Thornton, *Memoir on Statistics*. It contains useful statistics on education by castes.

educated Muhammadans, it was never used as a medium of written instruction.

MAIN OBJECTS OF WESTERN EDUCATION

Breaking Intellectual Monopolies

The Western concept of middle-class education was national, based on the freedom of opportunity. It was reflected in the economic principle of *laissez-faire*, the antithesis of mercantilism or a monopolist concept of economy and education. Founded basically on the principle of liberalism, the British plan of education was directed against the exercise of any monopoly. In the words of C. E. Trevelyan, its object was 'to promote the extension, not the monopoly of learning; to rouse the mind and elevate the character of the whole people, not to keep them in a state of slavish submission to a particular sect'.[5]

Economy and Utility

A second object of English education was to make the Indian officers of Government intellectually and morally fit to perform their duties with efficiency and probity, especially in the judicial and revenue branches of the public service where their responsibilities and powers were rapidly growing. While the appointment of a higher grade of Indian judicial officer was necessary locally to dispose of the increasing number of civil suits arising from the use of a contractual principle of replacing custom by law, the employment of a superior cadre of revenue officers became indispensable in the execution of a land policy which set out to define and record the rights of the different classes engaged in agriculture through survey and settlement operations. The policy of Indianizing these branches began to be considered more seriously under Moira (1813–23). In Bentinck's time the Governor-General in Council created certain new posts, especially of Principal Sadr Amins and Deputy Collectors, which carried emoluments to the extent of Rs. 600–1,000 a month.

But while their responsibilities were increasing and their tasks becoming more and more specialized, the efforts of Government

[5] *On the Education of the People of India* (1838), pp. 135–6.

to provide for their education still remained limited to a few institutions of Oriental learning. The Bengal Government had, for example, established a *madrasa* at Calcutta in 1781 and a Sanskrit College was established by Cornwallis at Benares in 1792. The Indian officers of justice were in the main recruited from among the scholars of these colleges. A similar college of Sanskrit education was established at Calcutta in 1823. Their utility was, however, restricted to law and their discipline to Oriental learning. The knowledge that they imparted was in no way related to the growing bulk and complexity of the regulations which governed the working and constitution of the Company's courts. Nor was their training relevant to the nature of the professional skill needed in the administration of justice according to the precision of Western principles and methods. Oriental learning had in fact lost most of its utility in the new India. In a dispatch of 1824 the Court of Directors observed that: 'In . . . teaching mere Hindoo or mere Mahomedan literature, you bound yourselves to teach a great deal of what was frivolous, not a little of what was purely mischievous, and a small remainder indeed in which utility was in any way concerned.'[6]

Works on European literature and science could be translated into Oriental languages and made available to Indian scholars. The Committee of Public Instruction which the Bengal Government appointed in 1823 actually tried this, but it proved both expensive and of limited usefulness. Moreover, it had a tendency to perpetuate the traditional monopoly of literary pursuits.

Translation into local vernaculars was beset with similar difficulties. On account of local and cultural variations these too involved heavy cost and restricted use. What the Government wanted was to make the most extensive use of its limited resources. In 1828-9, for example, revenue amounted to £22 million against an annual expenditure of £18 million. But the Indian debt, which had by that time shot up to £40 million, remained to be paid, as well as the payment of the Company's annuity of £630,000 in return for the surrender of its commercial privileges under the Charter Act of 1833.[7] Economy thus constituted a dominant con-

---

[6] H. Sharp, *Sels. from Educational Records*, pt. 1 (1920). p. 92.

[7] The Act allowed the Company to retain, as security, the whole of British territories in India for a period of twenty years.

sideration, and it was in keeping with this that the Act divested provincial governments of their legislative and financial powers which it centralized in the supreme Government of India. It was also to reduce expenses that Bentinck adopted a general plan of uniting the office of magistrate with that of Collector. Indeed it was to meet the rising cost of administration that Government had enacted regulations in 1819 and then again in 1828 to assess all such rent-free lands as were held without sufficient grounds.

Economy and utility were thus two of the main criteria of government policy. A scheme of translation was out of the question. Moreover, the local vernaculars were for the most part undeveloped and poor in content. They could very well be used as media of instruction for the great bulk of rural education, but even here their use presented practical difficulties. Funds were as yet too limited to admit of any vernacular educational scheme being undertaken on a nation-wide scale. The prejudices of caste still remained to be overcome before the benefits of education could be extended to the lower orders of society.

English education was thus considered useful and expedient as well as consistent with the political requirements of British rule in India. But although the basic policy of Government was to widen its scope, practical considerations demanded that it should be limited to the upper and middle classes of urban society. It was believed that these classes, because of their previous monopoly of educational facilities, wealth, and influence, could more easily be trained as teachers, and that once they had received Western education, they might educate their countrymen in their own language. In the words of Trevelyan,

the rich, the learned, the men of business, will first be gained; a new class of teachers will be trained; books in the vernacular language will be multiplied; and with these accumulated means we shall in due time proceed to extend our operations from town to country, from the few to the many, until every hamlet shall be provided with its elementary school. The poor man is not less the object of the committee's solicitude than the rich; but, while the means at their disposal were extremely limited, there were millions of all classes to be educated. It was absolutely necessary to make a selection, and they therefore selected the upper and middle classes as the first object of their attention, because, by educating them first, they would soonest be able to extend the same advantages to the rest of the people.[8]

By a resolution of 7 March 1835 the Governor-General in Council therefore decided on a policy of downward filtration. It was laid down that the object of British educational policy was to promote 'European literature and science among the natives of India', and that consequently all the funds appropriated for the purpose of education would best be employed on English education alone.

Thomas Babington Macaulay, who shaped this policy as the president of the Committee of Public Instruction in 1835, was not unaware of its possible results. He had in fact already expressed his views in the House of Commons before he came out to India as Law Member in 1834. 'It may be', he observed, '. . . that, having become instructed in European knowledge, they may in some future age demand European institutions. Whether such a day will ever come I know not. . . . Whenever it comes, it will be the proudest day in English history.'[9]

The Economic Motive

As has been seen, before British rule there existed both commercial and professional elements capable of growing into a middle class, but the despotic political system of the country, its rigid caste order and monopolist economy were all inimical to its growth. The introduction of Western science and technology thus involved the task of creating through English education a middle class who might act as an agency of imperialist economy and administration. Indeed it formed an integral part of British economic policy that this class should assist the operation of the imperial economy, which signified two main things: encouragement to the import of British manufactures, and incentive to the development of India's internal resources which might pay for its imports and conduce to the prosperity necessary for the purchase and consumption of foreign goods. While the Company's trade monopoly had tended to limit both these objectives, complete freedom of trade was effected by the removal of the Company's monopoly in 1833 and the transfer of the Government to the Crown in 1858. However,

[8] Trevelyan, p. 48.
[9] 10 July 1833, *Hansard*, 3rd ser., vol. 19, col. 536.

another obstacle to the sale of British goods in India was the un-
changing pattern of consumption. The dress of the people and
their mode of living had remained substantially unaltered for ages,
and any attempt to modify these involved a clash with local custom
and caste prejudice. Charles Grant, an evangelical who retired
from the Company's service in 1790, was the first to realize that an
English education would be the best means of changing the old
habits and the values. In his *Observations on the State of Society
among the Asiatic Subjects of Great Britain* (1792)[10] he pointed out
that the communication of European knowledge through the medium of English would be 'honourable and advantageous to us'.
Grant was in fact delighted to note the emergence in his own time
of a group of English-speaking Indians who he believed had at
least in some ways improved by their association with Europeans;
but this effect, he commented, 'is partial, and not discernible in
the bulk of the people; the scope for improvement was prodigious'.
What he meant to suggest was that with the extended use of
English there would come into existence a much larger class of
Indians who might co-operate with the British in the exploitation
of India's resources. This, he believed, would offset the loss arising
from the employment by the Company of its territorial revenues
in the supply of its 'investment', and in addition contribute to its
prosperity.

Three decades later, Bishop Heber noticed discernible changes
in the cultural taste of the wealthy Indians of Calcutta.

Their progress in the imitation of our habits [he wrote in 1823] is
very apparent, though still the difference is great. None of them adopt
our dress. But their houses are adorned with verandahs and Corinthian
pillars; they have very handsome carriages, often built in England;
they speak tolerable English, and they show a considerable liking for
European society. Few of them will however eat with us.[11]

Among other things, the parliamentary Select Committee of
1832 made inquiries about the sale of British goods in India. It
transpired that the upper middle class of Calcutta had developed a
taste not only for imported cotton goods but also for other articles
of luxury. 'Judging from Calcutta', said Holt Mackenzie, 'there

[10] Included in Rep. Sel. Com. HC, 1831–2, Gen. App.
[11] *Narrative*, 3rd ed. (1828), ii. 291.

has been, I think, a very marked tendency among the natives to indulge in English luxuries; they have well-furnished houses, many wear watches, they are fond of carriages, and are understood to drink wines.'[12] When asked to account for an increasing import of European wine into India, Thomas Bracken told the Committee that the natives of Calcutta certainly consumed 'a great quantity of wine', for 'being so much more with Europeans', they were 'divested in a much greater degree of their prejudices and habits than others'. They consumed, 'wines and brandy, and beer', but 'the favourite wine among the natives was champaigne'.[13]

These were the people who constituted the elements of the new middle classes. Though not yet class-conscious, they commanded wealth and influence. Engaged either in government offices or commerce, it was they who supported English education in Bengal. The desire to learn English was found 'in fewer instances in the Behar than in the Bengal districts'. But in both it was 'chiefly learned and wealthy men that sought it for themselves or their children; and with a view to purposes of practical utility' it was to 'those classes in the present condition of native society' that it was 'most suitable'.[14] Macaulay had this class in view when in his minute of 2 February 1835 he declared: 'We must at present do our best to form a class who may be interpreters between us and the millions whom we govern—a class of persons Indian in blood and colour, but English in tastes, in opinions, in morals and in intellect.'[15] Secondary and higher education was intended for this class; and it was with this end in view that Government resolved in 1835 to establish a secondary school at the headquarters of each of the districts.

Sir Charles Wood's famous educational dispatch of 19 July 1854 categorically confirmed this early trend in British educational policy. As President of the Board of Control Wood stressed Western higher education through the English language. He regarded this as necessary for the intellectual and moral improvement of the public servants to 'whose probity' the Company might 'with increased confidence commit offices of trust'. But not less significant was the emphasis on the expediency of creating a class that might

---

[12] Sel. Com. HC, 1831–2, Mins. of Ev. II (735 II), p. 11.
[13] Ibid. As. to Qs. 1934–6.
[14] *Adam's Reports*, p. 219. [15] Sharp, *Sels.*, p. 116.

emulate Europeans in the development of India's resources and increase demand for the consumption of British goods. For, the dispatch clearly said, the advancement of European knowledge

will teach the natives of India the marvellous results of the employment of labour and capital, rouse them *to emulate us in the development of the vast resources of their country*, guide them in their efforts, and gradually, but certainly, confer upon them all the advantages which accompany the healthy increase of wealth and commerce; and, at the same time, *secure to us a large and more certain supply of many articles necessary for our manufactures* and extensively consumed by all classes of our population, *as well as an almost inexhaustible demand for the produce of British labour.*[16]

Conversion to Christianity

While Government wished to introduce and promote English education from motives of economy, administrative expediency, and liberalism, the Christian missions looked to it as an effectual means of evangelization. The Danish Lutheran missionaries were among the earliest of these. They arrived at Tranquebar in 1706, and in 1717 established two charity schools at Madras where they taught English and Christianity. Schwartz was the most distinguished of the later Danish missionaries; he established English schools at Tanjore, Ramnad, and Shivaganga. In Bengal the man who provided the main incentive was Charles Grant, who on his retirement became one of the leading members of the famous Clapham Sect of Evangelicals, to which men like Zachary Macaulay and Wilberforce belonged. While William Carey, J. Marshman, and W. Ward were doing pioneer missionary work in Bengal, Grant had his *Observations* printed in 1813 and got an ecclesiastical clause inserted in the Charter Act of that year which provided for the establishment of bishoprics in India.

From missionary notices it appears that Marshman and Inglis were the first to advocate the use of English as a missionary agency in India. A founder of educational missions, Inglis 'preached a sermon in Edinburgh, in which he urged the adoption of the English language as the means for attracting the Hindus, and bringing them under the influence of the Gospel'.[17] Although

[16] P.P. 47(393), 1854, para. 4. (My italics.)
[17] Rev. J. Johnstone, *Abstract and Analysis of the Rep. of the Ind. Ed. Commission* (1844), p. 11.

English had long been in use in commercial business and its need was increasingly felt by some Indians for employment in government offices, Christian missionaries came to realize its importance in the course of their work among the half-caste Eurasian children, who grew up in ignorance and depravity, neglected by their natural European fathers and 'cast off by the native society to which their mothers belonged'. In both Calcutta and Bombay institutional attempts at English education began for these half-caste children and later extended to others.[18]

But the progress of English education was slow. Indians were generally suspicious and viewed it as a means of proselytizing. This suspicion was not without foundation. Bishop's College, established in 1820 at Calcutta, for instance, did not admit non-Christians. Its object was to produce 'missionaries and catechists' and to engage them 'in evangelizing the heathen'.[19] It was first opened to non-Christian students in 1830; but popular suspicions about it were so strong that the total number admitted did not exceed eleven between the years 1830 to 1845. In a letter of 13 January 1845 addressed to the headquarters of the Society for the Propagation of the Gospel in London, the Rev. Professor A. W. Street of Bishop's College attributed this small number to 'theological odium' which, as he admitted, 'had never been inconsiderable'.[20]

On a representation of the Muhammadans of Calcutta, Bentinck introduced a policy of religious neutrality which declared that in all schools and colleges interference and injudicious tampering with the religious belief of the students, mingling direct or indirect teaching of Christianity with the system of instruction, ought to be positively forbidden. But the attitude of the Christian missions remained more or less unmodified. For in a minute of 12 October 1854 J. P. Grant opposed the extension to mission schools of the grants-in-aid scheme established under the educational dispatch of that year.

[18] Johnstone, *Abstract*, p. 12. Hare, a benevolent watchmaker in Calcutta, ran a free school for Eurasian children. Charity schools for the same purpose were run by the Company's chaplains and by a Christian Society for Promoting the Education of the Poor.

[19] S.P.G. Archives (London), Cal. Let. Rec'd, vol. i, ff. 238–69.

[20] Ibid. f. 241.

I believe [he said] that it will be found a matter of infinite difficulty for the Indian Governments so to distribute and regulate grants in aid to mission schools as not to offend, even in appearance (and here the appearance of the thing is of the essence of the political question), against the still recognised principle of religious neutrality; for one of the acknowledged objects, and the greatest object, of mission schools is proselytism. If private persons spend their own money in endeavouring by legitimate means to convert people of other religious persuasions . . . the people of India are not so intolerant as to question the right of such persons so to spend their money. . . . But the case would be different if the public taxes which are paid by, and are held in trust for the use of the people of India, were, or were believed by the people of India to be, appropriated in aid of such endeavours at conversion. We have only to imagine the same policy adopted at home, to become sensible of what the feelings of Mahomedans and Hindoos under such policy would be in India. . . . I am firmly persuaded that unless in practice . . . all breach, and all appearance of breach, of religious neutrality can be avoided, a blow will be struck at our power in India, which in the course of time may prove fatal.[21]

Grant could not mobilize support in favour of his policy, however. The Directorate established under the dispatch of 1854 favoured interference with the old rules of religious neutrality. The Governor-General himself proposed a revision. The contemporary records of the S.P.G. in London show that the Government was 'well-affected towards it'.[22] But Grant's view proved prophetic. The Indian mutineers at Delhi attacked the church before the barracks, and killed a number of missionaries, including one Chimmun Lall, a doctor convert whose influence the local church had employed in the conversion of a number of Hindus.[23] The Mutiny was suppressed, but it taught a lesson, and a costly one at that. The Government realized the value of Grant's suggestion that religion in India was in essence a political question.

PROGRESS TO 1857

The appendix given on p. 401 below indicates the number of colleges and schools maintained at the public expense in 1845.

[21] *Corresp. with Indian Govt. showing Progress of Measures . . . for carrying out the Ed. Desp. of 19 July 1854* (P.P. 47(72), 1857–8), pp. 80–81.
[22] S.P.G., Cal. Let. Rec'd, 3 Sept. 1856. iii. f. 148; also ff. 71–72.
[23] Ibid. ff. 173–98.

In addition to government colleges, there were those of the Christian missions. In Bengal, for instance, these included Bishop's College, Dr. Duff's English School, the General Assembly Institution, and the Baptist College at Serampur. The Madras Christian College began as a school in 1837. In 1841 Robert Noble established a college at Masulipatam and in 1844 Stephen Hislop founded his college at Nagpur. Christian missions were the first pioneering agency in the field of private English education.

The Vidayala, or Hindu College established in 1816 at Calcutta, in which English was the language of instruction, was an important example of popular initiative, but the Committee of Public Instruction set up in 1823 soon took over its management. Unlike Bengal, where in its early phase higher education was the chief concern of Government, Bombay preserved its Brahmanical control. In 1822 the Hindu upper castes founded an Education Society which established the famous Elphinstone College in 1827. It was modelled on the Calcutta Hindu College, but unlike it was designed principally to educate the upper castes. Mountstuart Elphinstone, who inspired the foundation of the College, was personally a traditionalist. He favoured the preservation of the Brahmanical heritage of the Marathas, since he feared that a policy of widespread education among lower castes ran the risk of causing the disaffection of the upper castes, the ruling force in society.

Considering the number of students by religion, Muhammadans constituted 23 per cent. in Bengal and one-third in the North-Western Provinces. In Bombay Hindu students were by far the largest group, and Muhammadans constituted only 20 per cent. of the total student population. Another significant distinction between Bengal and Bombay was that while the former contained the maximum number of colleges, the latter possessed a far greater number of schools, especially vernacular schools. Higher education in Bengal had from the very beginning a tendency to become top-heavy.

This tendency was, however, limited to Bengal proper. The subordinate province of Bihar showed a special distaste for English. It viewed with suspicion the improved plan of education introduced under the famous dispatch of 1854, and its landholders, for the most part Muslim, tried to oppose it. In a minute recorded on 19 November 1858 the Lieutenant-Governor of Bengal commented that the office of the Inspector of Schools at Patna was no doubt called '*Sheitanka dufter khanah*—the devil's counting house'.[24] It was suspected that the introduction of the 1854 plan had something to do with the outbreak of mutiny in Bihar. Lord Ellenborough, who was conversant with Indian affairs as President of the Board of Control in 1828, and then as Governor-General of India during 1841–4, went so far as to suggest that the English schools in Bihar had perhaps been forced on the people against their will and against the will of the local landholders, who led the revolt against the British in 1857.

While trying to meet this objection, the Lieutenant-Governor of Bengal admitted that the Inspector of Schools at Patna had committed an act of indiscretion by 'ordering people to educate their children' and that the Commissioner of the Patna Division had started an industrial school for which he had raised what was 'little better than a forced contribution'. But this measure was 'unsparingly checked and suppressed by the Government as soon as it came to notice'.[25] English education in Bihar was in fact misconstrued as an attempt on the part of the Government to convert the province to Christianity. In the same minute the Lieutenant-Governor reaffirmed the policy of his Government not to impose English schools against popular will and reassured Ellenborough in the following words:

I am in a position, therefore, to be able to affirm with certainty . . . that, excepting these two instances of error, nothing whatever has been effected towards the spread of education in Behar, or elsewhere within the territories under my authority, in any manner contrary to the absolute volition and spontaneous will of the people, whether of high or low degree.[26]

He made it clear that his Government did not 'desire to assist in the education of a single child not brought to the school with the full voluntary unsolicited consent of its parents', but he did emphasize that attempts to bring education to the province must on no account be given up: 'Are we to stay our healing hand because the patient is ignorant and refractory? The condition of popular

[24] *Ed. in India, Minute of Lt.-Gov. of Beng. on Lord Ellenborough's Letter*, 1860 (P.P. 52(35)), para. 44.
[25] Ibid. para. 19.   [26] Ibid. para. 20.

ignorance is everywhere the condition of political danger; and for that reason alone we ought to persevere in our endeavours to remove it.'[27]

An all-India report for 1859 showed

13 government colleges containing 1,909 students, and 4 aided colleges with 878 students; 74 superior government schools containing 10,989 students, and 209 aided schools of the same or somewhat lower grade with 16,956 scholars; 25 normal schools containing 2,241 students; and 16 colleges for special subjects containing 1,154 students.[28]

Judging from the cost of education in the two years that followed the 1854 plan the rate of progress seemed considerable. Annual expenditure on education increased from Rs. 10 lakhs to Rs. 21 lakhs. The Lieutenant-Governor of Bengal, however, pointed out in his minute of 19 November 1858 that although 'apparently held up as an amazing evidence of extravagance on the part of the Indian Governments, yet after all it was, for all India, much less than a hundredth part of the gross revenue levied from the people; or say, about the cost of two regiments of English infantry'.[29]

NEGLECT OF RURAL EDUCATION

Moreover the benefits of the Anglo-Vernacular schools and colleges were circumstantially restricted to urban centres. In his dispatch of 19 July 1854 Wood was concerned that although the country's rural population contributed the bulk of the public revenues, the efforts of the Government were directed towards 'providing the means of acquiring a very high degree of education for a small number of natives of India drawn, for the most part, from what we should here call the higher classes'.[30]

It is true that James Thomason had laid the foundation for a great advancement in the education of the lower classes in the North-Western Provinces. His object was to enable them to read

[27] P.P. 52 (35), para. 45.
[28] H. Woodrow, *Macaulay's Minutes on Education in India* (1862), p. 2. These were exclusive of missionary schools and colleges. In 1860–1 there were as many as 193 Anglo-Vernacular schools with 23,963 students. See Joseph Mullens, *Ten Years of Missionary Labours in India*, p. 138.
[29] P.P. 52(35), 1860, para. 14.   [30] P.P. 47(393), 1854, para. 39.

and write the vernacular languages, both Hindi and Urdu, so that they might avail themselves of the land tenure rights conceded to them through a regular process of settlement operations.[31] But his newly founded vernacular schools were limited to eight in the districts. The ratio of scholars to population worked out in 1853 at 1 to 327. In the trans-Sutlej territory it was 1 to 301.[32] A missionary notice of 1856 stated that in all other parts of the country 'a school, either Government or Missionary, is as rare as a lighthouse on our coast . . . three or four schools exist among three or four millions of people'.[33]

The Government of Bombay had, of course, paid considerable attention to vernacular education. The educational dispatch of 1854 noted 216 of such schools under the management of the Board of Education, with three Inspectors of Schools, one of whom was an Indian, Mahadeo Govind Sastri. But Bengal and Bihar were found exceptionally lacking in this respect. It was estimated that out of 6·5 million teachable children in these provinces only half a million received any kind or degree of instruction. 'Six millions of children capable of receiving school instruction (remained) wholly uneducated.'[34] Of the two, Bihar was still worse. It was 'proverbially in a state of darkness and very different from Bengal, where indigenous schools abound'.[35]

In these circumstances Wood advised that the education of the lower classes should constitute the direct responsibility of the Government. But the old emphasis on the education of the upper and middle classes by no means suffered any change. On the contrary, Wood directed the establishment of universities to do 'as much as a Government can do to place the benefits of education plainly and practically before the higher classes in India'.[36] A university was accordingly established at the headquarters of each of the three presidencies in 1857.

[31] *Sels. fr. Recs. Beng. Govt.*, 1855, no. 22, pp. 8–13.
[32] P.P. 42 (339), 1857–8, para. 31 (Mcleod's Rep.).
[33] *Christian Ed. for India in the Mother Tongue*, I.O. Tract 633, p. 17.
[34] P.P. 47(393), 1854, para. 94.
[35] *Sels. fr. Recs. Beng. Govt.*, 1855, no. 22, p. 69.
[36] P.P. 47 (393), 1854, para. 40.

VII

The Educated Middle Class:
2. The Learned Professions

AN increasing degree of specialization and a gradual narrowing down of specialized fields has been one of the notable features of professional growth in modern times. Professionalism in fact arose from the advancement of applied skill and knowledge. It necessitated the introduction of a regular system of examination and code of conduct to develop professional efficiency and integrity. While the advancement of specialized skill and education raised the status of those who possessed them without caste considerations, the strength of professional organizations made them free and independent. A common characteristic of all modern professional development has been that money replaced land as the form of payment for the service rendered. Besides, the nature of relationship between the parties concerned became increasingly free and contractual, the enforcement of a contract depending upon the decree of a court rather than the practice of a local custom. In the West these features were the result essentially of economic revolution; in India they proceeded primarily from the operation of British courts. It took time for law to dominate custom. The process is still going on. But a sound beginning had been made by the time the East India Company made over to the Crown in 1858.

THE LEGAL PROFESSION

The most significant of the new professions was the legal profession. It emerged from the Western constitution of courts and legislative enactments in modern India.

An Indian lawyer is called vakil (*waqil*). But the use of this term did not previously signify any specific profession. It was a generic term employed in the sense of an agent or ambassador who represented his principal for varied purposes. A zamindar, for example, would send his vakil to an officer of Government to account for an arrear of revenue or miscellaneous acts of commission and omission. A country Government might likewise appoint a vakil to deputize for it in the court of another ruler or sovereign. The person who represented a party in court was also called a vakil. There was no separate class of legal practitioners under this name.

The early English Government under Warren Hastings did not materially alter the constitution of the country courts beyond adapting them to the requirements of British rule. What Hastings did in 1772 as Governor of Bengal was to reorganize the district administration which had broken down for want of a strong central authority. He constituted in each district a civil and criminal court which functioned under the superintendence of a European Collector. At the seat of his Government at Calcutta he established high courts called Sadr Diwani Adalat and Sadr Nizamat Adalat. The constitution of these courts was slightly modified when Hastings became Governor-General in 1774, but the pattern based on indigenous practice remained more or less unaltered until he had a more elaborate plan drawn up in 1781, with the assistance of the Chief Justice of the Supreme Court established at Calcutta under the Regulating Act of 1773.[1]

Evidence exists to show the manner in which law was practised in the early years of the Company's rule in Bengal. An interesting case, for example, arose in the provincial court of Adalat at Murshidabad in June 1777. One Babun Mohun Dutt sued a person called Shivnath Shoam for the recovery of Rs. 250 on account of ready money and jewels. The Superintendent of that court referred the case to a munsif, a subordinate officer who acted as an umpire with the concurrence of both parties. The final hearing of the case came up on 23 March 1779. Dutt and Shoam were represented by their respective vakils. But while Dutt's vakil was continuing his pleadings, Bhavani Shoam, the father of the defendant, Shivnath Shoam, took the place of his vakil and appeared personally to plead

[1] For the working of the Company's courts see Misra, *Judicial Administration of the East India Company in Bengal, 1765–82* (1952).

the cause of his son, although he was not a party to it. Since the total claim of Rs. 250 included a sum of Rs. 22 on account of wages, Bhavani insisted that the plaintiff's vakil must prove that his principal had been in the service of the defendant, and that in the event of his failure to do so he must give up the whole of his claim. The plaintiff's vakil refused to do this, and the munsif agreed with him that his inability to prove a single count could not with any show of justice invalidate the rest of the claim. Bhavani then lost his temper and broke out in the most reprehensible invectives to the munsif. 'What do you know of justice', he shouted, 'I plead after the Calcutta manner'. He abused the munsif in the most insulting manner and left the court.

The Superintendent of the court sent a summons to arrest Bhavani, but the latter treated the summons with contempt. Bholanath and Gopinath, two of his other sons, together with his local adherents threatened the court peons and put them to flight. However, they seized Gopinath, Bhavani's younger son, and brought him to the court. This obliged Bholanath to present himself before the Superintendent, who ordered his arrest and sentenced him to twenty days' imprisonment. As for the main cause in dispute, he awarded a decree to the plaintiff because the defendant had refused to attend.[2]

The case typifies the manner in which justice was administered and law practised under the judicial reforms of 1772. Under the government regulations the parties were summoned to defend their case either in person or through their vakils. The munsif did not object to Bhavani, though not a party, being accepted as pleader for the defendant. In fact any person could represent a party in court. The vakils themselves hardly possessed a fair knowledge of their cases. In the midst of their pleading the defendants could even ask them to retire and take up the pleading themselves or ask anyone else to do it. The regulations had provided no definite qualifications for a vakil, no precise mode of proceedings, no rules of evidence. The parties or their vakils pleaded cases by a simultaneous exchange of questions and answers. These led to altercations in the open court.

Another interesting point was that the Superintendent ordered the arrest of Bhavani, but the peons brought his son, Gopinath,

[2] I.O., Home Misc., vol. 421, f. 552 (Misra, *Judicial Admin.*, pp. 247–50).

instead. And when his brother, Bholanath, came forward to secure his release, the Superintendent released Gopinath but put Bholanath into prison for twenty days without any trial.

The establishment of the Supreme Court at Calcutta in 1773 and later in the other two Presidency towns was the first effectual step in the growth of the legal profession on modern lines. In the old Mayor's Courts in the Presidency towns the judges were nominated by Government and thus could not assert their independence. Appointed by a charter granted by the king under the Regulating Act of 1773, the judges of the Supreme Court, on the contrary, could force the members of the Government themselves to appear before them to answer to any charge, The court's function was to secure not only the protection of life and property but also the liberty of individuals against arbitrary proceedings, for example of Government or its officers. In the exercise of its power it could issue a writ of *habeas corpus* and might compel the appearance of any offender, and protect individuals against acts of illegal detention. Its procedure had thus to be necessarily complex but well defined, and this made prosecution difficult. Besides British subjects, in the beginning its jurisdiction extended to those employed directly or indirectly in the Company's service. Later, in 1781, this was restricted to the Presidency towns. None the less the Supreme Court operated as a model, and the Company's courts were in time fashioned after it.

At first a series of conflicts developed between the two systems of justice, and it often so happened that any trouble between the Company's court and the King's Court at Calcutta became a subject of contention between the Council and the Supreme Court. The Governor-General, Warren Hastings, and the Chief Justice, Sir Elijah Impey, were however guided by a common desire to build a uniform and efficient judicial system which would unite the benefits of both. The Judicial Code of 1781 was the fruit of their joint effort, although it bore the imprint of the Chief Justice, who drew it up on the basis of his own experience.

What Impey did was not to introduce English law in the Company's courts, or to alter their constitution radically. He realized the need to preserve the law of the land in the administration of civil justice. All that he did was to bring the district courts under the effective control and direction of the Sadr Diwani Adalat at

Calcutta. This he achieved by defining in some detail their respective duties and powers, and by drawing up precise rules governing the mode of procedure and adjudication, record keeping and process serving. On account of the fixed rules of procedure and growing complexity in the scope and size of regulations, it became more and more difficult for plaintiffs and defendants to plead their own cause. Impey indeed laid the foundation for the practice of law to grow into a profession which required a mastery not only of the increasing bulk and variety of legislative enactments, but also of the subtle techniques which courts were called upon to follow under rules. Parties were in these circumstances obliged to engage such persons or vakils as knew both the law and rules of business. It later became obligatory for them to acquire certain professional qualifications before they could be duly registered and allowed to practise in the Company's courts. These qualifications in the beginning included a knowledge of Persian, which was the language of court; a knowledge of Hindu and Muslim law which the Company's courts administered, and of the regulations enacted by the Governor-General in Council and translated into local vernaculars for the use of the vakils and their parties.

The preamble of Regulation VII of 1793 indicated that there were two categories of persons engaged by suitors to represent their case: first, private persons or dependants of the parties specially appointed for the occasion; secondly, men who practised law to obtain a living and who appeared in the courts of justice or wherever the concerns of their clients might require their attendance. The former class, as has been seen, was thoroughly ignorant of the constitution of courts as well as of Hindu or Muhammadan law. They could neither render efficient assistance to their clients nor judge the merits of judicial decisions. Though better acquainted with judicial practice, the regular practitioners were little better substitutes, for they had very little knowledge of the laws and regulations enacted by the Government. And since no regulation existed on the subject of their remuneration, they as well as others had an interest in the prolongation of suits.

The object of Regulation VII of 1793 was to make the pleading of causes a distinct profession. The first thing that it did was to exclude from admission to pleadings the private servants or dependants of suitors. No person except men of character and education having knowledge of laws and regulations was to be admitted to plead in the courts. To make this provision effective the Regulation vested the Sadr Diwani Adalat with exclusive powers to appoint pleaders, for themselves as well as for the provincial and district courts who made the selection of candidates from among such students of the Calcutta Madrasa and the Benares Sanskrit College as were found qualified and desirous of being admitted to the profession. The Sadr Diwani Adalat, however, could appoint any other suitable candidate in case these colleges were not able to supply an adequate number. But in all cases they were necessarily to be either Hindu or Muhammadan by religion, possessing good character and liberal education, preferably bred to the study of Hindu or Muhammadan law. To enable them to acquire a knowledge of regulations, every court had to maintain translated copies and deposit them on a table for inspection by pleaders or any other person who might choose to refer to them.

As for the choice of a pleader, the Regulation declared the parties free to select any they trusted most. But the client was to give him a retaining fee of four annas (6*d*.) along with a *vakalat-nama* or power of attorney. The fees prescribed for pleader in all courts were as follows:

	Rs.	*Per cent.*
On sums not exceeding	1,000	5
„ „ „ „	5,000	4
„ „ „ „	10,000	3
„ „ „ „	25,000	2
„ „ „ „	50,000	1
„ „ „ „	100,000	$\frac{3}{4}$
On sums above	100,000	$\frac{1}{2}$

These fees were payable to a pleader after the judgment had been passed. A principle of free contract was introduced. The client might change his pleader at any time before the passing of judgment. Any breach of contract between a client and his pleader became subject to punishment by court. Contract was thus becoming a legal institution.

Cornwallis introduced another significant principle which contributed to the growth of the legal profession. In his anxiety to effect the security of property he divested revenue authorities of

all their judicial functions, and recognized the right of private
individuals to sue Government or its officers for any act of infringe-
ment. While the separation of powers led to an enormous increase
in litigation,[3] encouraging more and more persons to join the legal
profession, the recognition of the right of individuals to sue the
Government necessitated the appointment of government pleaders
in the several courts to conduct public suits. Under Regulation
VII of 1793 they were appointed by the Governor-General in
Council. They were at liberty to engage in any suit except on
behalf of the opposite party in suits against the Government.
The Cornwallis Code in fact produced a boom in the legal profession, for under the principle of contract recourse to a judicial
decision became the only means to validate private claims of
property.

The profession of law became increasingly conformable to a
pattern. Vakils were authorized to act as arbitrators and to charge
fees for legal consultation. They were enjoined not to file plaints,
answers, or other pleadings without previously ascertaining that
these were in conformity with the regulations. The object was to
avoid irrelevancies and to prevent the use of personal insinuations
and terms of reproach against the opposite party. They were
likewise to see that no irrelevant exhibits were filed or proofs
advanced in support of claims made. Previous to their being
submitted to court the vakils had to examine these as well as the
specific points which their witnesses were expected to prove by
testimony. Any breach of these rules became punishable by censure
or eventual dismissal.[4] Emphasis in the administration of justice
was thus being gradually shifted from justice to law.

The disciplinary provisions intended to ensure the dignity and
uprightness of professional conduct were made more stringent.
The offences cognizable under this head did not remain limited to
demanding or accepting from their clients any money, effects, or
consideration beyond the prescribed fees, or to fraudulent practices or misconduct in the discharge of their professional duty.
They were extended to 'gross profligacy or misbehaviour in their
private conduct'.[5] Irregularity in attendance at courts also became

---

[3] See above, p. 135.   [4] Modified by sect. 1, Act XVIII of 1852.
[5] Sect. 6, Reg. XVII of 1814. This provision was suspended by sect. 7, Act I
of 1846.

an offence. If a pleader failed to attend his court on any day fixed for the transaction of civil business and omitted to notify in writing his inability on a sufficient cause, the court could fine him to the extent of Rs. 50 for the first offence, Rs. 100 for the second, and punish him by dismissal if found guilty of a third offence. Punishment for contempt of court amounted to Rs. 100.

Parties were, on the other hand, authorized to

prosecute their respective pleaders in the Civil Courts of Judicature for any damages or injury which they may have sustained from any breach of the Regulations on the part of their pleaders, or from any fraudulent conduct or malpractices committed by their pleaders regarding the suit.[6]

As has been stated, a knowledge of Persian was one of the essential requirements for a vakil. To supply this demand Persian was introduced as one of the optional subjects at the Benares Hindu College, but although 'correct in theory', the plan was an 'utter failure'.[7] Regulation XI of 1826, therefore, did away with the preference which the candidates of that College previously enjoyed in selection for the office of vakils. It provided that

native students educated in any of the public institutions, who should have received a certificate in a prescribed form, certifying their qualifications as to proficiency in the Hindoo and Mahomedan law, and in the Regulations of the British Government, might be admitted to practise as vakeels in any city or zillah court.[8]

This relaxation proceeded from a shift of emphasis in the qualifications of vakils, who were now to specialize more in the regulations than in Hindu or Muhammadan law. Deposing before the parliamentary Select Committee of 1832, Richard Clarke, an eminent member of the Madras Civil Service, observed:

They have a sunnud or patent, authorizing them to practise; it is one of the duties of the college board to prepare vakeels or native pleaders, who are, however, not required to have so thorough a knowledge of the native law as those who are candidates for the offices of cauzey [*qazi*] or pundit; but they are examined in the native law, and are further required to have a sufficient acquaintance with the regulations passed by the

---

[6] Clause I, sect. 12, Reg. XVII of 1814.
[7] George Nicholls, *Benares Sanskrit College* (1907), p. 19.
[8] Sel. Com. HC, 1831–2, Mins. of Ev. IV (735 IV), app., p. 628.

Government. Individuals of this class, when found duly qualified, receive a certificate from the college board, upon producing which before the sudder adawlut, they receive the sannud or diploma of appointment, in virtue of which they are allowed to practise in any court they may select. The object of these arrangements was as much as possible to assimilate the native to the European bar, leaving it to the clients to make their own selection of their law advisers.[9]

The anglicization of the indigenous legal profession had begun. Many of the vakils, Clarke added, were 'acute reasoners' and some were 'good lawyers'. They discharged their duties well. This was due to better education, for the vakils 'appointed of late' were 'more able than those formerly admitted'.

Describing the contemporary practice of law Clarke said that in the conduct of their suits the vakils drew up all the pleadings and examined witnesses. They did not address the court orally but submitted all their motions and pleadings in writing. The first pleading was the plaint which stated the case of the plaintiff. This was answered by the defendant's vakil stating objections to the plaint. A reply and a rejoinder followed one after another. In the examination of witnesses in Bengal the native serishtadar or munshi, a court assistant, put the usual preliminary questions and carried on until the judge took it up himself and put questions. In ordinary cases it was the serishtadar who conducted most of the case. In civil as well as criminal cases all the proceedings were taken down in writing; for often the European judge could not speak Persian nor the Indian vakil English. In the south as well as in the north the vakils, therefore, had no oral arguments. Whatever they intended to say was reduced to writing in their plaint and answer, reply and rejoinder. The serishtadar who took down the depositions of witnesses in the presence of their vakils had them duly countersigned. Even motions were presented in writing, for it was not customary for vakils to be heard viva voce.

From the evidence of Holt Mackenzie it seems that the legal profession, especially at the district level, had not yet acquired respectability, at least as much as the old profession of law officers, namely qazi and pandit, commanded. Instances occurred where a vakil was promoted to the rank of munsif, qazi, or pandit. But these were exceptions rather than a general rule. Indeed

[9] Sel. Com. HC, 1831–2, Mins. of Ev. IV (735 IV), app., A. to Q. 54.

the situation of pleader [said Mackenzie], has not hitherto been considered a respectable one, except in the highest courts. In the inferior courts, even in that of the district judge, it is not reckoned a desirable profession. In the Sudder Dewanny Adawlut, or chief court at Calcutta, some of the vakeels with whom I was acquainted had large emoluments, and were men of great respectability and talent; and I believe that in the provincial courts the vakeels are frequently very respectable men; but below that they are not generally esteemed at all as they ought to be, considering the importance of a good bar to the administration of justice.[10]

This was due to the fact that in 1832, while English had begun to make its influence felt at the Presidency and provincial headquarters, the districts still remained untouched. Moreover, the vakils at lower levels still employed certain inferior advisers or agents called mukhtars to advise them more or less as solicitors. These were perhaps the successors of a class of legal agents whom Regulation VII of 1793 called 'private servants or dependants of the parties specially appointed for the occasion'. Cornwallis wanted to exclude them from any association with the legal profession, and he did it by an exclusive recognition of a regular class of vakils whose conduct and qualifications became the subject of his and subsequent enactments. In practice, however, the early category of occasional advisers continued to operate in the districts. It seems that on account of increased judicial business, especially on the criminal side, they switched over to criminal courts where they found a rich harvest. For one of the provisions of Regulation XVII of 1814 prohibited all 'authorized pleaders of the zillah and city courts' from 'officiating as agents, or mokhtars in any prosecution', without previously obtaining 'the sanction of the judges of those courts'.

In a statement of 3 April 1832, Mackenzie pointed out to the Select Committee that the vakil did the duties both of counsel and attorney. He was indeed expected 'to do all such acts as may be requisite in the court relatively to the suit until judgment be enforced'. However, most of the attorney's duties, he added, were 'generally done by the mookhtar or private agent of the party, or by the party himself'. The mukhtar was thus not officially recognized and though, as Mackenzie further said, 'there were many who are

[10] Ibid. 16 Mar. 1832, A. to Q. 140, (p. 22).

in fact professional mookhtars in the courts, they are not legally entitled to interfere in the suits, nor is any part of their charges included in the costs adjudged to the successful party'.[11]

In the period after the complete opening up of the East India Company's trade in 1833 law was becoming a secular and separate branch of study. The Charter Act of that year provided for the appointment of a Law Member and a Law Commission to ascertain and codify the laws of India. It was an enormous task, for besides the government regulations there was a body of statute laws applicable to British-born subjects and to all the inhabitants of the Presidency towns. Added to these were the laws and customs of Hindus and Muhammadans which, on account of their variety of interpretations, lent themselves to bribery and corruption.[12]

It is not within the scope of this work to examine in any detail the proceedings of the Law Commission or the history of the Civil and Penal Codes which the work of that Commission produced and which the Indian Government introduced in 1862. What is relevant is to note that the basic principle of its reform was to dissolve the alliance between religion and law. The Commissioners separated law from religion and made it into a civil institution, a fit object of pursuit not limited to a small priestly order but open to all interested persons regardless of caste or creed. In addition to English education, the new legal system caused another movement in society. It cut across caste and struck a blow at the priestly monopoly of legal studies. Before the introduction of the new Codes the laws were indistinguishably mixed up with religious dogmas.

To obtain a moderate acquaintance with either Mohammedan or Hindu law [says Trevelyan], is the work of a whole life, and is therefore the business of a separate profession, with which the bar and bench had nothing in common. The expositors of the law are the muftis and pundits; men, who deeply imbued with the spirit of the ancient learning to which they are devoted, live only in the past ages.[13]

The new legal system removed this old class of legal expositors. It brought the bar and the bench into direct contact with each other. It effected the legal unity of the country and brought into

---

[11] Sel. Com. HC, 1831–2, Mins. of Ev. IV (735 IV), 16 Mar. 1832, Q. 468.
[12] Misra, *Central Administration*, p. 60.   [13] Trevelyan, p. 152.

being a class of legal practitioners patterned alike on a national scale, a class who, on account of the country's expanding economy and growing legislation, was obliged to look forward. The original intention of producing muftis and pandits respectively in the Calcutta Madrasa and the Benares Sanskrit College thus lost most of its force.

Already in 1835 Bentinck's Government had in principle accepted the study of law as a separate faculty. A committee was later appointed to report on how best to introduce it in the colleges of higher education. A professorship was created in 1842 for the Hindu College at Calcutta, although after a first course of lectures by a distinguished Advocate General no appointment was made until 1847, when the post was again sanctioned. A few years later the Council of Education in Bengal decided that law should have a place in the annual examination for senior scholarships and law classes were organized on a permanent footing in the Hindu College in 1855. A professorship of law was at the same time sanctioned at the Madras institution as well as the Elphinstone College in Bombay.

The growing trend of secularization influenced the legal profession in other respects. Act I of 1846, for instance, opened the office of pleader 'to all persons of whatever nation or religion'. The only bar on admission was that one must have a certificate of character and due qualification as laid down by the Sadr Diwani Adalat. The Act also superseded the old rule of pleaders' fees being regulated by law. It declared that they 'shall be at liberty to settle with the parties by private agreement the remuneration to be paid for their professional services, and that it shall not be necessary to specify such agreement in the *vakalatnama*'. Obviously this was the effect of free trade on the practice of law.

Another significant measure in favour of liberalism was the recognition of the prisoner's right of defence by counsel or vakil. Act XXXVIII of 1850, for example, provided that

in all courts and before all magistrates, or persons exercising any of the powers of a magistrate, under the authority of the East-India Company, every person on trial for the commission of any offence shall be admitted to defend himself either personally or by his authorized agent, and after the close of the case for the prosecution, to make full answer and defence thereto either personally or his authorized agent.

An authorized agent could be either an advocate of the Supreme Court of Judicature established by a royal charter, an authorized pleader, or 'by leave of the court, magistrate or other person before whom the prisoner is on trial, any other person who is employed either by the prosecutor or prisoner as his agent'. The class of mukhtars perhaps came to be recognized under this provision as authorized agents to be employed by the parties in their behalf. The regular opening of criminal courts to pleaders who were previously employed exclusively in the conduct of civil suits contributed considerably to the expansion of the legal profession.

Law Officers

The law officers of British courts, including qazis, muftis, and pandits, were members of the old legal profession. Under Mughal rule the qazi and the pandit acted both as judge and law officer, though the mufti exercised an exclusive function of expounding the law. As religion constituted the basis of Hindu and Muhammadan law, the temporal judge

was obliged to call in the assistance of the qazi of the district and even to submit to his authority in the decision of the cause: the gentoo [Hindu] subjects enjoyed a similar privilege with respect to all cases of religious nature in which persons of that persuasion were parties; for in every such case it was necessary that the temporal judge should be assisted by a Brahman of the caste, particularly where the cause was of such a nature as might be attended with the consequence of forfeiture of caste.[14]

The Brahman who presided over the preservation of his caste order had of necessity the support of the king's bureaucracy.

In the early years of British rule the Calcutta Madrasa and the Benares Sanskrit College were designed to ensure a regular supply of Muhammadan and Hindu law officers respectively. The Governor in Council of Bombay formed a separate code which did not administer Muhammadan law. Madras, however, followed the Bengal pattern. In his statement to the Select Committee of 1832 Richard Clarke commented:

[14] 7th Rep. Com. Sec. HC, 1772–3, p. 324. In the famous Patna cause of 1777 the quazi and the mufti made a local investigation and submitted to the Provincial Council at Patna a report covering law as well as fact, a report which the Council acting as court accepted as its decision without trial.

Since the establishment of the college of Fort St. George, there has been a class of native students of Mahomedan law, and another of Hindoo law, under the Sanscrit and Arabic head masters respectively. By a Regulation of the year 1817 it was provided, that no law officer should be appointed excepting after examination by the college board, aided by the native professors of Hindoo and Mahomedan law attached to the college, and by the pundits and cauzeys of the Sudder Adawlut.[15]

The College also admitted private candidates for examination. According to Clarke, the law officers in Madras were generally well informed and 'remarkably acute in applying their knowledge'.

The appointment of a law officer was declared open to all under Act V of 1845. It provided that 'any person may be appointed to be a Hindoo or Mahomedan law officer in any of the courts of justice under the presidency of Fort William in Bengal, who shall have successfully passed through such an examination as the Government of the said presidency shall from time to time prescribe'. This office, however, had outlived its utility. It was abolished on the establishment of the High Courts of Judicature in 1862.

UNCOVENANTED GOVERNMENT SERVANTS

The civil servants of the East India Company were divided into two categories: covenanted and uncovenanted.

The covenanted servants were so called because they had to sign, previous to their appointment, a covenant or agreement designed to ensure the honesty and integrity of their public conduct. They were recruited in England. Until their recruitment was thrown upon to competition under the rules laid down in 1853, the Company continued to exercise patronage under such self-imposed restrictions as tended to improve the quality of its Indian service.[16] In the whole period of its rule no Indian was recruited to its covenanted branch.

The patronage exercised by the local governments of the Company in India applied not to the covenanted service, which belonged exclusively to the Court of Directors, but to its uncovenanted service which included, besides the subordinate Indian agency in the administration of revenue and justice, a considerable

---

[15] Mins. of Ev. IV, Q. 50, p. 6.
[16] Misra, *Central Administration*, pp. 404–14.

establishment of Europeans who, in the early years of its rule, were generally called 'monthly writers'. For they were employed temporarily on a monthly basis to copy papers and to do many odd jobs. The Court usually discouraged such appointments; because, besides tending to reduce the area of their patronage, it made it difficult for the home authorities to subject them to proper control. Considerations of economy, however, willed otherwise, and the local governments usually appointed local hands at cheaper rates to do clerical and other inferior jobs.

The exigencies of war with country powers dictated the necessity of employing a far greater number of uncovenanted servants, largely European. The Court asked the Government specifically to reduce the number of European monthly writers, but its requests remained for the most part unheeded. In 1798, for example, the Company was surprised to note that upwards of 100 of them continued to be employed at Fort William in Bengal.

The uncovenanted Europeans in the Company's service held even higher posts in the Departments of Civil Audit, Salt and Opium. They were employed in considerable numbers even in the Secret and Political Department, where their allowance in many cases exceeded that of covenanted assistants. There was, however, no uncovenanted cadre of civil servants. Europeans or Indians, they were appointed to uncovenanted posts carrying specified salaries. They could not rise in scales, for it was not a graded service.

In the revenue and judicial branch of its service in Bengal the Company continued to employ the Nawab's men without any change until 1769, when European Supervisors were for the first time appointed at the head of its district administration. These covenanted servants came to be designated as Collectors in 1772, because it was through them that the Company took over the collection of its revenue and the administration of civil justice. However, between the years 1774 and 1786 most of the districts remained under the independent charge of Indian officials called Naibs. For the sake of economy the Company preferred them to European Collectors, who were both costly and in the beginning inexperienced. The chief revenue office, called Khalsa, was presided over by a highly paid and experienced Indian called Roy Royan, under whom a large number of Indian assistants operated in its various sections. It was with the establishment of the Board of Revenue in 1786 and the reorganization of the Central Secretariat departments in 1888 and 1889 that Europeans came to occupy not only higher posts but also many of the subordinate ones, such as the offices of serishtadars and accountants, registrars and head assistants.[17]

The Mughal faujdars, who previously presided over the executive administration of a district, had already been supplanted by European magistrates of the covenanted service in 1781. The judges of criminal courts who belonged exclusively to the Muhammadan faith were by a stroke of pen struck off by Cornwallis in 1790. The 'native commissioners', such as amins and munsifs, were the only Indians who continued in the exercise of judicial functions, but not as regular officers of the Government. They were to act merely as referees trying only such cases as were referred to them by European judges, and that up to a maximum limit of Rs. 50. They were paid by commission according to the number of cases.

To meet the financial implications of Europeanization Cornwallis reduced the number of districts, united the magistracy with the office of the district judge, and settled the lands in perpetuity with zamindars. But while the size of the districts became unwieldy, the increase of litigation kept the district officers pinned down to their headquarters. This necessitated the appointment of joint and assistant magistrates, and by the time of Bentinck the magistracy had again to be united in the office of Collector.

In Benares and its adjoining districts of Ghazipur, Jaunpur, and Mirzapur the old subordinate revenue unit of *tahsil* continued to function. The services of the kanungo and tahsildar were retained. In the North-Western Provinces as well as in Bombay and Madras this local unit of revenue administration remained unaffected under its Indian functionary. The Bombay Government maintained even at the district level an Indian official called mamlatdar who under the indigenous rule of the Peshwas had been a collector of revenue. His office under the British was comparable to that of the Deputy Collector instituted under Regulation IX of 1833.

The error of the Bengal system was in fact realized in the very first decade after 1793. In 1803 the Governor-General in Council created a post of Sadr Amin and increased the power of munsif.

[17] Misra, *Central Administration*, pp. 131–8.

Lord Hastings raised the status of both by putting them on the pay-roll of the Government as well as by augmenting their salary and power. Bentinck created a still higher post of sub-judge called Principal Sadr Amin. The Government of Lord Auckland allowed a salary of Rs. 500–600 to a Principal Sadr Amin, Rs. 250–350 to a Sadr Amin, and Rs. 100–150 to a munsif. The first category of these judicial officers was authorized to try suits of any value.

The exigency of survey and settlement operations in the North-Western Provinces led Bentinck to appoint a superior grade of revenue officers called Deputy Collectors. Later, in 1843, the Governor-General in Council made a legislative provision for the appointment of non-covenanted Deputy Magistrates. The increasing requirements of the public service were in fact met by a corresponding extension of the uncovenanted service.

The number of Indians employed in the various civil situations of the Government in India increased from 1,197 in 1828 to 2,813 in 1849. They were distributed as follows.

	1828	1849
Principal Sadr Amins	—	64
Sadr Amins	157	81
Munsifs	86	494
Deputy Magistrates	—	11
Deputy and Assistant Collectors	—	86
Sub-Collectors (Assistants)	—	27
Excise Superintendents	—	15
Tahsildars	356	276
Serishtadars	367	155
Mamlatdars	9	110
Dafterdars	2	19
Kamvisdars	57	—
Adalatis	—	5
Mir Munshi	—	1
Educational services	14	479
Various	149	990
Total	1,197	2,813

Source: P.P. 11 (110C), HL, 1852.

In 1827 no Indian employed in the Judicial or Revenue Departments in Bengal, for instance, received more than Rs. 250 a month or nearly £300 a year. In the twenty years that followed their allowances increased. In 1852 these were as follows:

		£ *per annum*
1	received	1,560
8	,,	840–960
12	,,	720–840
68	,,	600–720
69	,,	480–600
58	,,	360–480
277	,,	240–360
1,173	,,	120–240
1,147	,,	24–120
Total 2,813		

Source: Rep. Sel. Com. HC, 1852–3, app. 3, p. 343.

Besides considerations of policy, the appointment of Indians in the civil administration of the Company was guided by motives of economy. William Wilberforce Bird, a member of the Bengal civil service who had served in the judicial branch of the public service in Benares and later acted as a Special Commissioner at Cawnpore under Regulation I of 1821, clearly pointed out to the parliamentary Select Committee of 1852 that 'the principal objection to any increase in the number of covenanted servants in India is the expense. I am not aware of any other objection'.[18] He added that only 800 of the civil posts were held by covenanted servants. This was in conformity with a statement of Holt Mackenzie who in 1832 had suggested that Indians being 'quite equal to Europeans in intellect', the finances of India 'would be

---

[18] Rep. Sel. Com. HL, 1852, 19(88), Q. 1208. Considerations of economy limited the number of covenanted hands, as shown below:

	1815	*1835*	*1855*
Bengal	460	516	501
Madras	230	224	180
Bombay	98	157	125
	788	897	806

much improved by the employment of natives'.[19] In 1852 Bird went so far as to reaffirm that the British Government had 'derived great advantage from the native uncovenanted service; in fact it would be impossible to administer the affairs of the country without them'.[20]

On political grounds, however, it was considered expedient to maintain the distinction between the covenanted and the un-covenanted branches of the public service. Bird, for example, made no secret of his view that it was essential on the part of Indians to have 'a general impression of the superiority of Europeans'.[21] There was also another consideration. With the establishment of British paramountcy in India a change was coming about in the British attitude towards Indians. According to Bird, 'the Europeans mix very little with the natives'. He thus felt that if Indians were appointed to the covenanted branch of the Company's service, they 'would be exposed to a great deal of personal humiliation'. What he recommended in the circum-stances was 'the extension of the uncovenanted service' rather than 'the destruction of the distinction' which existed 'between cove-nanted and uncovenanted'.[22]

James Stuart Mill also favoured an extension of opportunity for the employment of Indians in the Government. 'I think', he said to the Select Committee of 1852, 'it is of the greatest importance to admit the natives to all situations for which they are fit; and as they are constantly becoming fit for higher situations, I think that they should be admitted to them.' But, like Bird, he did not want to destroy the distinction, although for a different reason.

The covenanted service, from its constitution, [he observed], is a service of gradual rise. A member of that service is not appointed to a particular situation to remain in it during his whole period of service, but looks for promotion after a certain time and hopes to rise to the highest appointments; therefore, as long as the natives are not considered fit for the highest appointments, it would be hardly desirable to admit them to the regular covenanted service, because, if their promotion stopped short while that of others went on, it would be more invidious than keeping them out altogether. . . . If a native . . . is fit for one of the

[19] Sel. Com. HC, 1831–2, Mins. of Ev. II (735 II), Q. 87.
[20] Rep. Sel. Com. HL, 1852 (19(88)), Q. 1146.
[21] Ibid. Q. 1203.   [22] Ibid. Qs. 1197–1200.

higher appointments, let him have it without going through the covenanted service.[23]

It appears from Bird's evidence that before the introduction of English as a regular medium of instruction under the government resolution of 1835, very few of the Indian uncovenanted servants could speak English. For no special qualifications were then looked for in an Indian judge beyond general good character, respectability of family, and in Bengal a competent knowledge of the Persian and Bengali languages. The educational policy decision of 1835 made a great difference: Indians became increasingly fitted for higher situations in the civil service.

DOCTORS

In his two-volume *History of the Indian Medical Service, 1600–1913*, Lt.-Col. D. G. Crawford has traced the history of the uncovenanted and subordinate medical services in India. He has shown how from a very early time the Company's European medical officers called 'Surgeons' employed Indian assistants who later became military or civil assistant or sub-assistant surgeons.

In the Presidency of Bengal the study of indigenous medicine formed part of the curriculum of the Calcutta Madrasa and the Benares Sanskrit College. A separate school for training Indian doctors was opened at Calcutta in 1822. The object was to make them fit for employment under European officers. According to Trevelyan,

there was only one teacher attached to the institution, and he delivered his lectures in Hindusthanee. The only medical books open to the pupils were a few short tracts which had been translated for their use into that language; the only dissection practised was that of the inferior animals. . . . The knowledge communicated by such imperfect means could neither be complete nor practical.[24]

The first tangible advance in the field of medical studies was made by Bentinck's Government. In his desire to extend and improve medical education for Indians Bentinck was guided, as in other fields, by motives of economy. He had before him the advan-

[23] Ibid. Q. 3110.   [24] Trevelyan, p. 27.

tages of the extended employment of Indians in the uncovenanted branch of the Company's judicial and revenue services. He therefore wished to extend the operation of that principle to the Medical Department. He appointed a committee to report on whether Indians would submit to the conditions which higher medical education on European lines entailed. In the light of the committee's recommendations, the Calcutta Medical College was opened in 1835. Its object was to produce sub-assistant surgeons who might take the place of the costly European agency at the subordinate military and civil stations, or who might otherwise be sent out into the country to provide the benefits of enlightened medical attendance. Their promotion to the Indian Medical Service formed no part of Bentinck's original design of 1829, when he undertook to improve the system.[25]

The establishment of a medical school was sanctioned in Madras in 1835. The governors of the school planned to start collegiate classes in 1842. But since the Directors of the Company did not extend their approval, the execution of the plan was postponed until 1852. Bombay took a lead in the meantime, and established in 1845 its Grant Medical College named after Sir Robert Grant, its then Governor.

In all these cases 'the object of educating medical men in India' was, as Bird said in 1852, 'for the purpose of acting in subordination to the medical men educated at home'. This was a view generally applicable to all the branches of the public service.

The higher branches of knowledge and education [Bird added] are supposed to rest with Europeans, and the native medical men are required to serve, under their direction, in the same manner as the uncovenanted civil service in India acts in subordination to the civil servants who are sent out from home.

Bird's opinion was based on his experience of the Europeans who did not like to engage Indian practitioners. 'Some native medical men', he pointed out, 'have been appointed in cases of necessity to the charge of civil stations, which is the position of a covenanted medical officer; but there is this difficulty, that the European society do not like to be attended by native practitioners.' The result was that in spite of their 'eminent qualifications' Indian

[25] Rep. Sel. Com. HL, 1852 (19(88)), Q. 1190, 18 May 1852.

medical graduates remained excluded from appointment to the Indian Medical Service.[26]

Professionally, however, this exclusion had a salutary effect. Young medical graduates educated on European lines found an increasing demand for the use of their talents among 'natives of rank'. 'I know, from my own experience', said Bird, 'that men, after leaving the medical college, have refused appointments under the Government for the purpose of private practice.'[27]

WRITERS, PUBLISHERS, AND PRINTERS

The emergence of a new class of writers, publishers, and printers owed its origin to the establishment of the Indian press.[28] It is not within the scope of this work to deal with this profession. It is however, significant to note a few of the developments that influenced society generally. The first of these was that here too it was originally the Europeans, particularly Christian missionaries, who took the initiative, established their presses, and produced literature in the country's languages, though in the beginning for the exclusive purpose of spreading the Gospel among Indians. This started an Indian cultural renaissance. Secondly, the Indian Press became probably the most effective means of influencing public opinion and government policy. It checked the arbitrary conduct of a despotic administration. Thirdly, the educated class of Indians contributed to the growth of a body of vernacular literature, especially in Bengal where it became an effective agency for the infiltration of European knowledge to the lower levels of society. Here again the process was slow. It first began in Calcutta and later spread out to other parts.

A return made to the Lieutenant-Governor of Bengal in 1855 contained the names of 515 persons connected with Bengali literature in the preceding fifty years. They were either authors or translators of printed books. The list included the names of Raja

---

[26] Rep. Sel. Com. HL, 1852 (19(88)), Qs. 1187–8, 1193, 1192. Four of the Calcutta Medical College graduates went to England in 1844 to acquire further knowledge. In 1861 a Parsi student of the Grant Medical College became a member of the Royal College of Surgeons, but was not admitted to the I.M.S. because of his Indian parentage. See P.P. 42(199) of 1861.

[27] Ibid. Q. 1191.   [28] See Margarita Barns, *The Indian Press* (1940).

Ram Mohan Rai, the great social reformer, and of Pandit Ishwar Chandra Sharma, the Principal of the Calcutta Sanskrit College who became one of the first Senators of the Calcutta University in 1857. Of the total number of 515, as many as 160 were reported dead in 1855, and the remaining 355 consisted of 313 Indians and 42 others, including Europeans and East Indians. Of the Indian total of 313 only 10 were Muhammadans, the remaining 303 being Bengali Hindus.[29]

The report of an inquiry made by the Rev. James Long and submitted to the Bengal Government on 23 June 1854 showed the following results indicating the extent of vernacular printing and publishing between April 1853 and April 1854:

Presses printing Bengali works	46
Books and pamphlets printed	252
Total no. of copies printed	418,275
No. of newspapers and periodicals	19
No. of copies circulated	8,100

Long expressed a sense of satisfaction at the progress made, but it was confined to Calcutta and the areas surrounding it.

I cannot conclude without remarking [he said], that the fact of not less than 200,000 of Bengali books having issued from the Press within the last ten years, is a loud call for effective measures being taken to create a healthy literary taste among the people by a sound vernacular education. These books have their chief circulation in Calcutta and a radius of 20 miles around.[30]

W. Dampier, the Superintendent of Police in the Lower Provinces of Bengal, submitted a report on the same subject on 29 July 1853, which indicated the position in this respect of the various districts of Bengal. It showed that although some of the districts of Bengal proper were emerging in the field of publication, those of Bihar had so far been virtually blank.[31]

ENGINEERS

The profession of engineering remained by far the most backward of the recognized professions, due to the backwardness of technology and factory industry.

---

[29] *Sels. from Recs. Beng. Govt.*, no. 22, 1855.
[30] Ibid. p. 89.   [31] Ibid. pp. 112–19.

A class of engineering was opened at Elphinstone College in 1854, but was discontinued because of the insufficiency of suitable candidates for admission. Dalhousie had in 1848 suggested the establishment of an engineering college in each of the three Presidency towns, but it was not until 1856 that a separate institution for the purpose was opened at the Writers' Building in Calcutta. A school for the improvement of arts and manufactures was separately established in both Madras and Bombay in 1858. The situation was different in the North-Western Provinces. There the Government decided on the construction of the Ganges Canal in 1847, and this decision necessitated the erection of large workshops as well as the establishment of the Thomason College of Civil Engineering in the same year. A few cotton mills came into existence, and the construction of the railways began towards the close of the Company's rule. These created some demand for technical personnel, but they were supplied mostly from England. In India it was the Anglo-Indian community that first entered this profession; Hindus and Muhammadans came much later.

SCHOOL-TEACHERS

Teaching as a profession originated from the government policy of providing for the instruction of the mass of the people, not through English but through the medium of their own language. It initially formed part of vernacular or rural education.

William Adam's mission in 1834 to examine the state of education in Bengal and to suggest the means of improving rural education appears to have been the first step taken by the Government in this regard. His inquiry disclosed a deplorable state of ignorance in spite of an abundance of indigenous institutions, but his report was not adopted for two main reasons: first, money, masters, and books were not available; and secondly, the Government considered it desirable in the first instance to 'raise up a class of educated Bengalees' as 'nurseries for the training of school masters and others'.[32] The original object was thus to produce, through the medium of English, a class of competent persons who stage by stage were to build up a vernacular literature and supplant incom-

---

[32] *Sels. from Recs. Beng. Govt.*, no. 22, 1855, pp. 112–19, Council of Ed. to Beng. Govt., 3 Oct. 1853.

petent teachers, the idea being to improve the quality and content of vernacular education. This the Government proposed to do by securing infiltration of Western literature and science through the agency of the upper and middle classes, whom it put on the priority list. There was no emphasis on methods or techniques; these were not emphasized until the beginning of the present century when the first Education Code was drawn up in 1904.

Normal or training schools existed from an early period, but before the educational dispatch of 1845 Bengal paid little attention to such schools. The Calcutta Sanskrit College also acted as a normal school. There was nothing of the kind in Bihar. By 1859 the number of government-managed normal schools had risen to 25, with 2,241 scholars,[33] but these were mainly in the Punjab, Madras, Bombay, and the North-Western Provinces. The Christian missions ran 30 such schools of their own in 1860.[34]

COMPARATIVE VIEW OF GOVERNMENT EMPLOYMENT

Those who lost heavily with the establishment of British rule, for example in Bengal, were for the most part Muslims. Their main occupations were in government service, especially in the Police and Judicial Departments. They were hard hit by the abolition of the office of faujdar in 1781 and the discharge of the judges of criminal courts in 1790.

On the acquisition of the Diwani in 1765 the English Government agreed to pay an annual sum of £420,000 to the Nawab of Bengal in order to enable him to meet his own expenses and those of his executive government. This for a time served to preserve the Muhammadans of the better class in their jobs for, as the ninth report of the parliamentary Select Committee of 1783 stated, the Muslims had not generally engaged in trade, nor had they disappropriated the ancient Hindu proprietors whom they conquered. Their chief, if not sole, support was a share in the civil and military offices of the Government.[35] But the Nawab's grant was later reduced to £160,000 and the lucrative government posts were taken over by the British. On the military side the position of the Muslims was even worse as the army was another source of employ-

---

[33] Woodrow, p. 2.   [34] Mullins, p. 140.
[35] 9th Rep. Sel. Com. HC, 1782-3, p. 56a.

ment for them and also for certain of the high-caste Hindus. While
the great bulk of the Company's army continued to be Indian in
composition, no Indian held any rank higher than that of Subadar-
Commandant, an officer below the rank of an English subaltern,
who was appointed to each company of the Indian soldiery. The
Select Committee of 1783 thus commented that 'all the lucrative
Situations of the Army, all the Supplies and Contracts of whatever Species that belong to it, are solely in the Hands of the
English'.[36]

The Revenue Department of Government was, even under
Mughal rule, manned almost exclusively by Hindus. They retained much of their hold except under Cornwallis, who Euro-
peanized key positions in Bengal. The district staff of Hastings's
Amini Commission consisted entirely of Hindu officials.[37] The
salary of an Amin or Superintendent ranged from Rs. 50 to Rs. 200
according to the size of his district. He was assisted by a Naib or
Deputy on a monthly pay of Rs. 30–75 with a number of clerks
called muharrirs on Rs. 20–30 a month. From a perusal, for example, of the establishment sanctioned by Hastings for the Central
Amini Commission at Calcutta it seems that the disparity between
the salary of a European and Indian had not yet become so glaring:

Central Amini Commission
European Establishment

		Rs.p.m.
David Anderson ⎫ George Bogle ⎬ Superintendents		1,200
H. Vansittart Persian Translator		200
Writers		300
Indian (upper and middle)		
Ganga Govind Singh Naib Diwan		700
1 Peshkar		250
1 Naib Peshkar		100
1 Serishtadar		250
1 Head Muharrir (Translator)		100
2 Munshis (Clerks)		150
5 Persian Muharrirs at 50 each		250
5 Bengali Muharrirs at 40 each		200

Source: 6th Rep. Sel. Com. HC, 1782–3, app. 15, p. 943.

[36] Ibid. p. 56a.   [37] 6th Rep. Sel. Com. HC, 1782–3, app. 15.

The only senior class of Indian officers whom Cornwallis re-tained were the high-ranking law officers. Of these the Chief Qazi of the Sadr Diwani Adalat received Rs. 600 a month, being the highest paid among all the law officers of the Government. There were two muftis and two pandits, each on Rs. 150 a month. They were assisted by a Persian munshi on Rs. 80 and another clerk on Rs. 40 a month.

The disparity between the pay of a European and an Indian, which was nominal under Hastings, became glaring under Corn-wallis. As against the Chief Qazi's Rs. 600 a month the European Registrar of the Sadr Court received Rs. 40,000 a year, or nearly six times as much. He was assisted by a court reporter on as much as Rs. 18,000 a year. In place of Councillors Wellesley appointed sep-arate judges for the Sadr Court. Their annual salary amounted to Rs. 50,000, which was seven times as much as the salary of the Chief Qazi, a Muhammadan.

The establishment (see opposite) which Cornwallis sanctioned in 1793 for the Provincial Court of Appeal and Circuit at Patna gives an example of the relative situation at the provincial headquarters. Thus of a total monthly disbursement of Rs. 12,562, a sum of Rs. 10,000 was spent on three European judges only. If two of the Portuguese writers are excluded, the European establishment ab-sorbed Rs. 11,400 for five incumbents, leaving only Rs. 1,162 to be distributed among the remaining forty-five. The ratio of difference in pay between an Indian and a European thus worked out at 1:91. But this represented an extreme view of the situation. If the first category of the Indian establishment is regarded as indicating a middle or upper-class pattern of employment and is compared with the European establishment, calculated on the average of Rs. 2,250 for each of the five incumbents, the ratio is 1:20. The ratio between a menial and a middle-class employee, on the other hand, worked out at 1:29, more than the difference between a respectable middle-class employee (Indian) and a European. In the district headquarters, however, the differences were less marked. The average pay of a middle-class Indian employee, for example, in the district court at Chapra, with a minimum of Rs. 30 a month, amounted to Rs. 72 as against a European monthly average of Rs. 1,100, which meant a ratio of 1:15.[38]

[38] 2nd Rep. Sel. Com. HC, 1808-12, p. 145.

European Judges	Rs.	a.	p.	Per month
1st Judge	3,750	—	—	
2nd Judge	3,333	5	4	
3rd Judge	2,916	10	8	
				10,000
European Officers				
1 Registrar	1,000	—	—	
1 Assistant	400	—	—	
2 Writers (Portuguese)	140	—	—	
				1,540
Indian Establishment (Middle)				
1 Qazi	200	—	—	
1 Mufti	200	—	—	
1 Pandit	100	—	—	
1 Serishtadar	100	—	—	
2 Munshis at 50 each	100	—	—	
				700
Indian Establishment (Inferior)				
1 writer	30	—	—	
4 writers at 25 each	100	—	—	
2 writers at 20 each	40	—	—	
1 nazir	20	—	—	
1 naib	10	—	—	
4 oath administrators	28	—	—	
				228
Indian Establishment (Menials)				
20 peons at 4 each	80	—	—	
2 bhishtis at 4 each	8	—	—	
2 scavengers at 3 each	6	—	—	
				94
Total monthly establishment				Rs. 12,562

Source: 2nd Rep. Sel. Com. HC, 1808–12, app. 5.

In the North-Western Provinces Muhammadans held better posts than Hindus, especially in the judicial branch of the Company's service. Bird, who served in this branch for a dozen years in Benares, stated:

The greater portion of those native judicial functionaries are Mahomedans. I do no not think the Hindoos make so good judges as the Mahomedans; the Hindoos are very excellent in the way of keeping accounts, and collecting revenue, and such matters; but for judicial administration I should say the Mahomedans are much better.[39]

In a statement he made before the Select Committee of 1852 he cited the example of one Ibrahim Khan of Benares of whose decisions 'the natives had a very high opinion'. For, as he added, these excelled in quality the judgments of many of the European officers.

Indian Judicial Officers, N.W.P.

P.S.A. = Principal Sadr Amin   H. = Hindu
S.A.   = Sadr Amin   M. = Muslim
        O. = Others

District	P.S.A. H.	M.	O.	S.A. H.	M.	O.	Munsif H.	M.	O.
Delhi	—	1	—	1	—	1	3	3	1
Saharanpur	—	1	1	—	—	—	—	4	2
Meerut	—	1	—	—	2	—	2	5	1
Aligarh	—	2	—	—	2	—	1	4	—
Muradabad	—	2	—	1	2	—	1	10	—
Bareilly	—	1	—	—	2	—	1	10	—
Agra	—	1	—	—	1	—	2	7	1
Farrukhabad	—	—	2	—	—	—	2	5	—
Mainpuri	—	1	—	—	—	—	3	2	—
Cawnpore	—	2	—	—	1	—	—	5	—
Fattehpur	—	1	—	—	—	—	—	3	—
Bundelkand	—	2	—	—	—	—	1	2	—
Allahabad	—	2	—	—	—	—	3	2	—
Gorakhpur	—	2	—	—	2	—	—	9	—
Azamgarh	—	2	—	1	—	—	1	3	—
Jaunpur	—	1	—	—	—	—	—	4	—
Mirzapur	—	—	1	—	—	—	1	1	2
Benares	—	2	—	—	—	—	1	3	—
Ghazipur	—	1	—	1	—	1	1	4	1
Kumaun	—	—	—	2	—	—	2	—	—
Simla	—	—	—	—	—	2	—	—	—
Total	—	25	4	6	11	4	25	86	8

Source: Rep. Sel. Com. HC, 1852 (10 (533)), app. 14.

[39] Rep. Sel. Com. HL, 1852, Q. 1148.

The Muhammadans dominated the subordinate judicial service of the Company not only in Benares but in the whole of the North-Western Provinces. This is clear from the table opposite showing the nature and number of judicial posts held by Hindus, Muslims, and others in 1850.

Hindus constituted nearly 86 per cent. of the total population of the North-Western Provinces, including Benares, against 12 per cent. of Muhammadans. But while the former occupied only 18 per cent. of the total number of judicial situations, the latter held as many as 72 per cent., and at that also most of the senior posts.

The judicial officers in Bombay, however, were more or less all Hindus. In Madras the position was different. There were 40 Muslim officers of a total of 186, much more than their percentage of total population, which did not exceed 8. As the following table shows, Hindu officers held most of the situations in spite of there being a considerable number of Christians in that province:

	Hindus	*Muslims*	*Others*
Principal Sadr Amins	11	2	3
Sadr Amins	15	25	2
Munsifs	102	13	13
Total	128	40	18

Source: As for table opposite.

Thacker's *New Calcutta Directory* for 1858 gives a list of the judicial officers of Bengal, Bihar, and Orissa which shows the following distribution by religion:

Bengal Judicial Service

	Hindus	*Muslims*	*Others*
Principal Sadr Amins	13	12	8
Sadr Amins	15	9	2
Munsifs	112	82	7
Total	140	103	17

There were, however, more Muhammadan judicial officers in Bihar than Bengal. For example, of 42 munsifs in the subordinate province of Bihar, as many as 32 were Muhammadans. Of the 140 Hindu judicial officers only 7 were non-Bengalis, the remaining 133 all being Bengalis. There were fewer Muslims in the executive branch of the service. In 1858, for instance, there were in all 120 Deputy Collectors and Deputy Magistrates. Of these, only 18 were Muhammadans against 48 Hindus. The remaining 54 were either Europeans or East Indians. Of the 48 Hindus, 46 were Bengalis.

The community of Anglo-Indians or Eurasians were excluded from the judicial service of the Government for a long period. In a statement of 18 May 1852 William Wilberforce Bird said that on account of their origin they were despised by both Indians and Europeans and that 'not many persons of mixed blood had been raised in any degree to situations in the administration of justice'. This was due not so much to their incompetence as their being of mixed blood, 'not respected either by the natives or by Europeans, generally speaking'. Though some of them stood high in esteem and had 'good character', they were devoid of social prestige on the whole.[40]

In a petition to Parliament presented in 1849 the Anglo-Indian community presented its case and gave the following figures of the employment of its members, which showed that very few of them held respected positions:

	Approx. No.
Clerks in government offices	759
Clerks in commercial offices	230
Principal Sadr Amins	7
Sadr Amins	4
Munsifs	5
Deputy Magistrates	1
Deputy Collectors	9
Salt Department	2
Excise Department	5
Schoolmasters	110
Coachbuilders	7
Shoemakers	9

[40] Rep. Sel. Com. HL, 1852, Qs. 1152–67.

Undertakers	6
Preventive service	22
Confectioners	3
Engineers and Mechanics	65
Printers	72
Booksellers	1
Auctioneers	1
Civil architects	2
Portrait painters	2
Subordinate medical department	85
Missionaries (Baptist)	3
Indigo planters	30
Brokers	2
Merchants	7
River traders	19
Covenanted Service Military	2
Covenanted Service Medical	2
Uncovenanted medical service	2
Students medical college	13
Drummers, fifers, and bandmaster	73
Veterinary Establishment	1

Source: *Calcutta Review*, Jan.–June 1849, pp. 89–90.

In addition to clerical and ministerial jobs, the Anglo-Indians were preferred as technicians, especially on the railways. In a statement before the Select Committee of 1831–2 it was clearly pointed out that the training of 'the Indo-British, commonly called the half-caste population', as 'mechanics' would be a suitable form of encouragement. The Committee was informed that an Apprenticing Society and a Marine School Society had specifically been formed at Calcutta to train them in mechanical and naval arts.[41] Bentinck sanctioned the establishment of a school of engineering for them, for they showed technical competence and ability equal to Europeans. The Madras Government had established a school of artificers, and while deposing before the Select Committee one of the officers of Government affirmed that 'the half-caste population might be brought forward as mechanics with very great advantage'.[42] The last thirty years of the Company's rule,

[41] Sel. Com. HC, 1831–2, Mins. of Ev. II (735 II), Qs. 1766–7.
[42] Ibid. Q. 1766.

which saw the beginning of mechanical power, were faced with the basic problem of how best to develop technical and skilled labour in India. In the railways, as in other fields, a superior grade of engineers could be imported from England, and they were actually imported. But the great bulk of technical manpower had to be produced in the country for the sake of economy. The East Indians were the first to be initiated. It was they whom the Consulting Engineer of the Government of India in a report of 13 March 1846 recommended should be sent to England to be trained before a general plan for training engine drivers could be established in India.[43]

In the uncovenanted branch of the Company's civil service also the European and Anglo-Indian elements increased considerably in the last decade of its rule. The Indian elements, Hindu and Muslim, remained more or less at a standstill, as shown in the following table:

Uncovenanted Service

Department	1851		1857	
	Europeans and Anglo-Indians	Indians	Europeans and Anglo-Indians	Indians
General	1,131	109	1,398	204
Political	100	39	151	82
Rev. & Judl.	1,523	2,762	1,533	2,560
Total	2,754	2,910	3,082	2,846

Source: Natives Employed in Civil Administration, Return for 1851 and 1857, P.P. 42 (201VI), 1857–8.

Evidently while Europeans and Anglo-Indians increased by about 40 per cent. between 1851 and 1857, the number of Indians in the uncovenanted service decreased from 2,910 to 2,846. In 1849, as has been seen, this figure stood at 2,813.[44] Moreover, Indians figured for the most part in the Revenue and Judicial Departments, not in the General or Political ones.

[43] P.P. 41(68) of 1847.   [44] See above, p. 178.

GOVERNMENT POLICY TOWARDS RELIGION AND
SOCIAL REFORM

A trading corporation in origin, the East India Company generally followed a policy of religious neutrality. The Vellore mutiny of 1806 confirmed its belief in the soundness of such a policy. This mutiny was due to an order of the Madras Government requiring Indian troops, for the sake of uniformity, to wear a new kind of turban and to remove their distinguishing caste marks and earrings when on parade. The sepoys suspected this order as an attempt to convert them to Christianity. They revolted and killed about 200 Europeans at Vellore in Madras. This led the Directors of the Company to issue a dispatch to the Governor in Council on 29 May 1807 which stated:

In the whole course of our Administration of our Indian Territories it has been our known and declared principle to maintain a perfect toleration of the various Religious Systems which prevailed in it, to protect the followers of each in the undisturbed enjoyment of their several opinions and usages; and neither to interfere with them ourselves, nor to suffer them to be molested by others.[45]

This was no mere statement and repetition of policy. The Company acted on it in practice. On the conquest of Cuttack from the Marathas in 1803 the Company's Government took over the entire management of the famous Hindu temple of Jagannath, a celebrated place of worship, and undertook, like its Hindu predecessors, to supply the deficit, if any, from its own treasury. As Governor-General Wellesley, whose Fort William College at Calcutta had become a centre of missionary activity, instructed his officer commanding at Cuttack to 'employ every possible precaution to preserve the respect due to the pagoda and to the religious prejudices of the Brahmins and pilgrims',[46] The Company followed a similar policy in Bombay and Madras, and although missionaries objected, on religious grounds, to the Government and its officers being associated with the financing and management of Hindu and Muhammadan shrines, the Company did not pay much heed to their objections.[47]

[45] I.O., Desp. to Madras (Pol.), vol. 40, ff. 65–66.
[46] P.P. 34(664), 1845.   [47] P.P. 52(31), 1860.

It is true that the Company did from time to time permit missionaries to proceed to India, but they were always cautioned not to associate the Company with their proselytization. In their Madras dispatch (Political) of 29 May 1807, the Directors made this point quite clear. They said:

When we afforded our countenance and sanction to the missionaries who have from time to time proceeded to India for the purpose of propagating the Christian religion, it was far from being in our contemplation to add the influence of our authority to any attempts they might make; for, on the contrary, we were perfectly aware that the progress of real conversion would be gradual and slow, arising more from a conviction of the purity of the principles of our religion itself than from any undue influence or from the exertions of authority, which are never to be resorted to in such cases.[48]

Evidence, however, exists to show that the Company's servants, especially in Madras, and after the complete opening up of trade in 1833, acted in a manner contrary to this declared policy of religious neutrality. Many of them were members of committees of Bible societies in all presidencies.[49] In a minute of 13 July 1847 the Governor-General himself referred to missionary societies 'having met in mess houses and court houses', especially in the Presidency of Madras. This was within the knowledge of the Company, for in a letter of 21 April 1847 the Directors had drawn the attention of the Government of India and impressed upon it the absolute necessity of 'abstaining from all interference with the religion of the natives of India'. They added: 'The Government is known throughout India by its officers, with whom it is identified in the eyes of the native inhabitants, and our servants should therefore be aware that while invested with public authority, their acts cannot be regarded as those of private individuals.'[50] This advice was not published in the *Official Gazette* for fear of what the Government considered would be undue publicity, but the key men in the service were instructed to see that the intention of the Company was duly carried out.[51]

The Company's anxiety was understandable. The entire Hindu

---

[48] I.O., Desp. to Madras (Pol.), vol. 40.   [49] P.P. 42(71), 1857–8, p. 5.
[50] Ibid. p. 3, para. 2.

[51] Violation was again reported in 1859, when civil servants in the Punjab were found attending conversion ceremonies (see P.P. 52(81), 1860).

social system was based on caste. Even local customs and usages were indistinguishably mixed up with religious observances and held as sacred as the Vedas, the Hindu scriptures.[52] Any measure of the Government or action by any of its officials which seemed to outrage established social practices ran the risk of being construed as an act of interference with religion itself. It was one of the duties of Government in the past to maintain the rules of caste, not to change them. Caste was in practice superior to Government. In a statement before the parliamentary Committee on Petitions of 1781 Harry Verelst, who had been Governor of Bengal in 1769, stated:

that they [Hindus] would suffer Death rather than any Indignity to their Cast. That from every Knowledge he had of the Gentoos, he was persuaded, that the Mahomedans, who have usually carried their Conquests by the Edge of the Sword, on all former Occasions, when they arrived in *Indostan*, found it absolutely necessary to sheath the Sword, from a thorough Conviction, that they would deluge the Country with Blood before they could convert one Gentoo to their Laws and Religion; and that they therefore wisely became the Guardians and Protectors of the Hindoo Religion; and that he conceives the Country to have been preserved in that State to the Time he left it in the Year 1770.[53]

Loss of caste meant a total excommunication from society, yet the Company's Government, like its Mughal predecessor, did not interfere. No one held any intercourse with an excommunicated person, not even his wife and children. It became extremely difficult for such a person to engage in any trade or profession. Inferior degrees of pollution, which did not involve a complete loss of caste, required certain forms of expiation, including charities and feeding Brahmans, fines and forfeitures, according to the degree of impurity and capacity for payment. But a gross impurity, such as arose from eating beef, was punishable by total excommunication.

In 1760 there arose an interesting case in which a Hindu had a spoonful of beef broth forced into his mouth.

The Witness, supported by all the Influence of the English Government, used every Means to restore him, without Effect, that on Lord

[52] Rep. Com. HC on Petitions, 1781, p. 37b.   [53] Ibid. p. 37b.

Clive's Arrival in *India* afterwards, they applied to the Bramins and Men of eminent Rank, who were induced to assemble at different Times at Kisnagur [Krishnagar, in the district of Nadia in Bengal], at *Burdwan*, and at *Calcutta*, from the Period of 1760, when he lost his Cast, to 1766, when the last Assembly was held.[54]

But they found no precedent to justify their restoring him to his caste. He never was restored, with the result that he died of a broken heart.

In the course of his evidence before the House of Commons Committee of 1781 George Vansittart quoted a case from the district of Dinajpur in Bengal where he had been a Supervisor. At the time of the famine of 1770, he said 'a poor starving Wretch, of the lower Class of People' happened to eat 'a little of the Flesh of a Cow, that had been killed by Accident'. The Raja of the place took him to the Supervisor and 'demanded his immediate Death'. The customs and manners of the Hindus, he added, 'operate upon them as more than Laws, because they have a religious Attachment to them; that and in fact, they regulate their Conduct'.[55]

A picture of the operation of caste in the Maratha country was presented by one Honwont Row, a Brahman emissary of Peshwa Raghunath Rao, who visited England where he saw the English king and appeared before the Select Committee in 1781. In his deposition he said 'that the inferior Casts of Hindoos pay Respect to the superior; to a Bramin particularly, the highest; that Wealth is nothing in competition with that Degree of Rank; that the low People may drink the Water in which a Superior has washed his Feet'. Honwont Row narrated a series of interesting episodes to illustrate the difficulties he had to experience in travelling to England, and showed how he had to live on his own fruit, sweet-meats, and water that he carried with him on board the ship.[56]

These instances indicate the state of society in the beginning of the Company's rule but, as has been stated, caste ruled supreme until much later, and except in the towns where the influence of English courts and education was tending to weaken its bonds, the attachment of Hindus to old prejudices continued in the main unabated. For example, a serious caste riot broke out in Tinnevelly, a district town in the Presidency of Madras, where the

---

[54] Rep. Com. HC on Petitions, 1781, p. 37b.   [55] Ibid. p. 38b.
[56] Ibid. p. 39a–40b.

police had to open fire on 22 December 1858 resulting in 10 killed and 19 wounded. The trouble arose over the question of carrying the dead body of a member of the Kaikalla or weaver caste through the main street of Tinnevelly. According to an established local custom no dead body of that caste was to be carried through any of the highways. One Mr. Bird, a previous magistrate, had recognized this custom and passed an order to that effect some years before this riot took place. V. A. Levinge, his successor, acted otherwise. In a letter to the Government he reported that shortly before his arrival the Hindus had refused permission for a Christian corpse to pass along the regular street through which dead bodies were taken to the burning or burying ground. The Christian body had therefore to be taken through paddy fields. The cause which led to the Tinnevelly riot was that a Christian witness in Levinge's court got cholera. The magistrate sent him to the government hospital, which was in the heart of the town, where he died on 21 December 1858. The question then arose of his being carried to the burial ground. The police reported to Levinge that crowds of people had gathered at the entrances of all the streets and refused to allow the corpse to pass. The magistrate reinforced the police by more peons and ordered that the corpse must be carried by the high road. But since the deceased person prior to his conversion to Christianity had belonged to the Kaikalla caste, the attitude of the mob hardened. On hearing the orders of the magistrate they armed themselves with stones, and as the police appeared guarding the body, the mob drove them away by the volleys of stones. The magistrate then called in the aid of the military, which opened fire killing ten and wounding nineteen. The accused were tried and sentenced to various terms of imprisonment. Those who absconded had their property attached. But since their offence was different from ordinary crime, the Madras Government extended clemency to them under an order of 22 October 1859.[57]

The Tinnevelly riot case shows that the institution of caste did not under the British receive the recognition it had done under the Mughals. It was being weakened, though not as a result of any deliberate policy of the Company. Two of the important factors that were operating to its disadvantage were the judicial administration of the Company and missionary activity.

[57] P.P. 52(89), 1860, p. 43.

Missionary activity was creating a class of Indian Christians, conscious of a superior status by virtue of education and political influence. Its tendency was to cut across caste and set in motion a process of social mobility. Writing about 1820, the Rev. William Ward hoped that the spread of the Gospel would weaken the bonds of caste.

Let us rejoice [he declared], that the rust of these fetters has nearly eaten them through: there are indications, in the present state of Hindoo society, which evince that, on account of the number of transgressors, these barbarous laws cannot be much longer enforced. The social impulse is evidently felt as strongly by the Hindoos as by other nations; hence, in numerous instances, we find that groups of Hindoos, of different castes, actually meet in secret, to eat and smoke together, rejoicing in this opportunity of indulging their social feeling.[58]

But this was limited to Bengal, where even a number of Brahmans embraced Christianity, which in those days was a paying proposition. Bihar, as has been seen, was suspicious of English education, and so were the North-Western Provinces. In Madras even the Christians were divided on a caste basis. In a representation made as late as 1883 the Christians of Tinnevelly complained to the London office of the S.P.G. that the local Bishop, Caldwell, countenanced the heathen practices of the upper-caste Christians. The representation said that they

for secular help in their education, pretend to embrace Christianity, are received in the Christian seminaries and boarding schools under some private arrangement and are allowed, as they like, to keep all caste distinctions (except that they touch Christians) as if they are in their own houses and in their heathen society. . . . The Christians of one caste behave towards those of another much in the same way as they would do if they were heathens, and not unfrequently quarrels arise between them to the great disgust of the Christian church when they unconsciously say or do anything affecting each other's caste.[59]

From a perusal of the correspondence between the S.P.G. headquarters in London and the Bishop of Madras it seems that from the very beginning it was the poor people who embraced Christian-

---

[58] *A View of the History, Literature, and Mythology of the Hindoos* (1817–20), iii. p. xv.
[59] S.P.G., Madras Let. Rec'd., 5 May 1883, ii. ff. 250–1.

ity from worldly motives, especially under the influence of government officials who aided the progress of conversion. In a letter of 5 May 1883, for instance, the Bishop clearly admitted this.

Christianity from its very commencement [he said] was begun here on a weak foundation. Many of the people who have embraced it have done so from worldly motives. Yet there are some among them who might be called good Christians though most of them are poor. When Christianity was first introduced here it was not particularly the preaching of missionaries that drew the people's attention. It was chiefly the great personal influence which these missionaries acquired among the government civil officials, as there were at that time no settled laws and regulations to rule the people. The government officials who had but an imperfect knowledge of the vernacular and consequently the manners and customs of the country had great regard for the counsel of the missionaries to whom they resorted for advice. The missionaries in return for their advice got such favours as they requested in behalf of those who under the pretext of embracing Christianity sought their help in government affairs, and some of them may have used this influence in making converts. This is plain from the fact of there still being in the several towns and villages rich and influential heathens who needed no help from the missionaries and have therefore remained as such. The accessions during the years 1877 and 1878 were also from among the very poor who professed Christianity on account of certain measures adopted in distributing famine money.[60]

A study of the missionary notices received from the Bishop's College at Calcutta during the Indian Mutiny of 1857 suggests that at Delhi and Agra, as well as at Cawnpore and Lucknow, the mutineers made missionary headquarters their first target of attack, and they turned to barracks after they had avenged themselves on such of the converts as had previously exhibited an air of superiority by virtue of their conversion to the new faith.[61] Instead of advancing the cause of Christianity by an attempt to convince the people of its quality, the missionaries retarded its progress by an endeavour to exploit their poverty, to proselytize them, and to measure the extent of their success by the number of converts so gained.

It seems that the missionaries grew wiser from their experience

[60] S.P.G., Madras Let. Rec'd., 5 May 1883, ii. f. 246.
[61] S.P.G., Cal. Let. Rec'd., 5 June–11 Dec. 1857, iii. ff. 173–98.

of the Mutiny; for when after its suppression it was proposed by a parliamentary act to abolish the institution of caste, the Bishop of Calcutta opposed this. He doubted whether the Government could do it 'beneficially'. The substance of his opposition was that in the absence of a widespread system of education and of a complete hold of Christianity it was caste that had been 'socially and politically the means of keeping India from the utter disorganisation into which its religion would otherwise have long precipitated it'. The Bishop even went to the length of opposing a wide circulation of the New Testament in India. What he emphasized was the need to send out qualified men who might inculcate the love of truth, 'truth among this marvellous race, so proud, so theory ridden, so superstitious, and, when their superstition is uprooted, so sceptical'.[62] In a much later communication received from the Church authorities at Calcutta the great need 'to raise up a ministry, not only zealous and devoted, but learned and able to cope with the intellectual subtleties' of the Hindus, was likewise stressed.[63]

The gradual supersession of custom by law and the operation of British courts produced a much deeper impact on Indian society. The effect in the secularization of law and the legal unity of the country, in the emergence of the legal profession, in the increase in the number of subordinate officers, in the development of a middle-class landed interest, and in the growth of a contractual principle of social relationship (the basis of a class concept in social development) has already been noticed. Here the effects of the rule of law which governed the conduct of justice in British courts will be briefly reviewed.

The principle of the rule of law first began to be administered by the Supreme Court of Judicature established under the Regulating Act of 1773. The original object of its institution was to bring every class of offenders under its jurisdiction. It recognized no caste privilege, no social rank or official position.

An interesting case arose on 6 May 1775 when one Mohan Prasad, the executor of an Indian banker, Bulakidas, brought a charge of forgery against Maharaja Nandkumar, a wealthy and influential Brahman zamindar who had risen to high office in the service of the Nawab of Bengal. During his trial at the Supreme Court in Calcutta he was, like other prisoners, put into the com-

[62] S.P.G., Cal. Let. Rec'd., 23 Jan. 1858, iii. f. 201.   [63] Ibid. ix. f. 19.

mon gaol; and although according to the recognized customs of the country he sought the Court's permission to live in his private house under proper guards, Impey, the Chief Justice, refused this privilege and treated him as an ordinary prisoner, which involved the loss of caste, rank, and position. When his guilt was established, he was executed. Whatever the rights of the case, the Calcutta people viewed it with great dismay and displeasure. They regarded it as an act of sacrilege, for it was a violation of the Code of Manu, an ancient Hindu law-giver opposed to the execution of a Brahman even for a capital offence.

The Company's courts could not long remain unaffected by what happened in the Presidency towns. It is true that its avowed policy was to preserve the country's laws and customs, and in conformity with this its Government in India had Hindu and Muhammadan laws translated into English for the guidance of European judges. A Royal Asiatic Society of Bengal was founded in 1782 to carry on researches in Oriental history and literature. Colleges of Oriental learning were established to train Muhammadan and Hindu law officers. Nevertheless the administration of criminal justice according to Muhammadan law did not fit in with the Western concept of equity, the king's peace, and the rule of law. The British soon realized the impossibility of administering justice within the framework of Islamic institutions. This realization came immediately after the appointment of English Supervisors in 1770.

As Muhammadan law provided for the payment of what was called the blood price as a form of punishment for the crimes committed, it afforded opportunity to the qazi to punish even murderers by fines varying according to the capacity of individuals to pay. A crime against an individual was not an offence against the state. There was no king's peace. Besides, the non-Muslims, who constituted the bulk of the country's population, were in law inferior to Muhammadans; for no Muhammadan could be prosecuted on the evidence of a non-Muslim. The Supervisor of Rajshahi, for instance, reported a case where a Muhammadan woman had murdered a Hindu woman, but since the requisite number of Muslim eye-witnesses was not forthcoming, the qazi could not pass sentence for murder.[64] The Supervisor could not reconcile himself to what he regarded as 'incompatible with equity and the natural

[64] See Misra, *Central Administration*, ch. 6.

laws of society', but he could do nothing beyond recommending the removal of religious bias from the administration of justice. Then again, while under the principle of 'a hand for hand, an eye for an eye, a tooth for a tooth' many offenders had to lose their limbs, serious crimes like murder and homicide escaped punishment if the manner or the object of their commission did not call for a death penalty. No capital punishment was inflicted for a murder unless it was proved to have been committed by a sharp instrument meant for shedding blood. No Muhammadan could be punished for homicide if he could show that he committed it in the course of his attempt to convert the dead man to Islam.

Warren Hastings believed that he could render justice even within the framework of the Muhammadan law. His policy was to effect the supervision of the criminal proceedings of Muhammadan judges, and to interpose the executive authority of the Government where the letter of the law was clearly repugnant to the principle of equity and good government. He tried this experiment. He personally superintended the administration of criminal justice for nearly three years between 1772 and 1775, but in no case did a Muhammadan judge swerve from the provisions of the Quran. To do so was sacrilege to him. Hastings acknowledged his failure and reappointed Muhammad Reza Khan, the Nawab's deputy, at the head of the criminal administration of Bengal.

In 1790 Cornwallis struck off the Muhammadan judges. He was in fact the first Governor-General to reduce the divinely ordained Muhammadan law to a process of civil legislation. In all trials of criminal offences the Muhammadan law officers were now to take into account the intention of the criminal, the nature and circumstances of each crime, and not the manner or instrument of perpetration. He established the principle of the king's peace by divesting relatives of their right to pardon an offender.

The traditional practice of paying a blood price was later completely abolished. Under the new principle of punishment the murder of a person or robbing him of his property was an act committed against the state, not against the individual. That is why under one of Cornwallis's regulations judges were authorized to take cognizance of any offence, independently of the wishes of the aggrieved party to proceed or not to proceed against the offender.

It was later enacted, in keeping with this principle, that fines inflicted by a court could not be appropriated by any party except for the purpose of Government.[65]

Cornwallis effected another significant change. By a regulation of 1792 he revised the law of evidence. It was declared that the 'religious persuasions of witnesses shall not be considered as a bar to the conviction of a prisoner'. Later the force of a decree of Muhammadan law officers became considerably diluted; for a communal riot which broke out at Benares in 1809 necessitated the passing of Regulation I of 1810, authorizing the judge to dispense with the presence in court of Muhammadan law officers whom the Hindus suspected might prejudice the course of their trial for rioting. European judges were later vested with discretion to pass sentences independently of the *fatwa* or decree of a qazi. More radical changes were introduced in 1832. The Governor-General in Council provided for a system of trial by jury which authorized the parties completely to dispense with Muhammadan law if they objected to being tried by it.

The establishment of the principle of the king's peace was of great social significance. It freed the individual from his attachment to family, caste, kin, and community; for it recognized his personal right as distinct from the right of the institution or association to which he might belong. He could seek justice in a court of law independently of his kin. This principle had a tendency to enable an individual to by-pass the local loyalties to which he was immediately attached, and to be directly linked up with the state. It contributed to the growth of citizenship. The kin, which kept its members bound to it by an exercise of discretion in the acceptance of the blood price for an offence committed against them, had to surrender that preferential right in favour of the supreme loyalty, namely to the state.

The abolition of religious discrimination in the administration of criminal justice was a recognition of the rule of law in the Company's courts. This too was a significant step towards the growth of citizenship, based not on religion or caste but on the discharge of certain common civil obligations to the state. The lateral or side-by-side movement and loyalty in society tended more and more to become vertical or up and down, a requisite condition for social

[65] Sect. 3, Reg. XIV of 1797.

mobility which railway and telegraphic communications also encouraged.

The principle of the king's peace was a recognition of the state's fundamental right to interfere, in the interest of the whole community, with the operation of any rule or custom discriminatory or oppressive in effect. Several legislative measures were enacted during this period to abolish a number of inequitable practices founded on religious sanction or superstition. It is true that these measures of reform did not change society to the extent expected of them. A material development of the country's economy and rural education would have made them more sustained in effect. They none the less suggested two things: a desire on the part of early administrators to reform Indian society along liberal principles, and to extend the scope of the state's activity as a means of effecting social reform. This, however, they proceeded to do as part of their administration of law and order.

A regulation of 1797, for example, declared that persons convicted of homicide on the ground of sorcery or anything of that kind would render themselves liable to the death penalty. Further the Muhammadan law provided for *qisas* or retaliation as a form of punishment. But this provision was exclusive in its application; there was to be no retaliation to secure the punishment of parents or other ancestors for the murder of their children, or of masters for the wilful murder of their slaves. A legislative enactment of 1799 prescribed a death sentence in all these cases. Even an accidental homicide became a capital offence subject to the display of mercy or mitigation by the Sadr Adalat.

The social evil of infanticide, particularly of daughters, was another thing which the British tried to suppress as a criminal offence. It was prevalent for the most part among the Rajputs, especially in the Benares Division of the Upper Provinces, and in the Punjab. Arising chiefly from the custom of hypergamy, or marrying females to men of equal, if not superior, caste groups, infanticide had become a general practice to which respectable fathers were driven in an attempt to escape the burden of finding suitable matches for their daughters. It received the attention of Jonathan Duncan, Resident at Benares, who used his influence to suppress the evil. Nevertheless it continued. Wellesley declared infanticide punishable with death under Regulation VI of 1802. Prosecution, however, became difficult in the absence of witnesses, and the practice seems to have continued, for special legislation had to be enacted in 1870 to deal with this crime.

Wellesley took steps to suppress another practice called *sati*, or the immolation of wives on the death of their husbands. On the report received from his district magistrates in 1805 he consulted Brahman pandits on the expediency of declaring *sati* a penal offence, but his recall left that question undecided. Lord Minto took up the matter in 1812, but did not make any progress before he was succeeded by Lord Hastings in the following year. Credit must, however, go to Bentinck who by a regulation of 1829 declared *sati* a criminal offence punishable by law according to the circumstances of each case. Persons convicted of aiding or abetting in the sacrifice of a Hindu widow were to be deemed guilty of culpable homicide, and liable to punishment extending to death at the discretion of the Sadr Court.[66]

Slavery likewise became the subject of legislative action. Already a regulation of 1811 had declared the importation of slaves into British territories a penal offence. An enactment of 1832 extended the area of its operation. It declared it illegal to remove slaves for the purposes of traffic from any province, British or foreign, into any province subject to the Presidency of Fort William, or even internally from one of its provinces to another. Within the limits of a province, however, traffic in slaves continued until 1843, when Act V of that year abolished slavery altogether.

By far the most significant of the social measures enacted under the Company's rule was the one called the Caste Disabilities Removal Act (XXI of 1850). As its title indicated the Act provided that no person should forfeit his or her right to property or inheritance 'by reason of his or her renouncing, or having been excluded from the communion of any religion, or being deprived of caste'. One of its provisions also declared that the old rule of succession to property being dependent on the performance of caste obligations was not to be enforced 'as law in the courts of the East India Company, and in the courts established by royal charter' within the territories 'subject to the Government of the East India Company'.

---

[66] Women convicted of murder or treason in England used to be burnt publicly under a law which remained in force until 1790 (see Lecky's *History of England*, i. 506).

What this Act did was in fact to re-enact the provision of Section IX of Regulation VII of 1832, which had remained inoperative during all these years except for a declaratory *Lex Loci* draft Act of 1845 which had reiterated that the religious belief of a person should not affect the property or succession rights of the person entertaining such belief.

Socially, the Act was pregnant with great danger to Hindu society. It tended to sap the very foundations of its caste system under which a man's right to property or inheritance depended on his remaining a Hindu. That right ceased the moment he or she ceased to be a Hindu. Although otherwise liberal and equitable, it was considered subversive of the basic principle on which the Hindu law of property was founded. Suspicion against the measure grew stronger when it was discovered that a certain missionary organization was interested in its possibilities of stimulating conversion to Christianity.[67] A committee was therefore set up at a meeting held at Calcutta on 14 May 1850 to represent the Hindus of Bengal, Bihar, and Orissa and agitate for the withdrawal of the measure. The committee presented a memorial to the Court of Directors asking them for its immediate repeal.[68] It did not come into force.

The Widows' Remarriage Reform Act of 1856 was another measure of social reform, designed to improve the lot of a child widow and save her from the curse of a perpetual widowhood. It was enacted in response to a humanitarian demand of educated Indians, initiated by Pandit Ishwar Chandra Sharma, the principal of the Sanskrit College at Calcutta and one of the early social reformers of Bengal, who had to face great humiliation at the hands of his co-religionists.

REFORMIST RELIGIOUS MOVEMENTS

From an analysis of the nature of social developments that took place in about 100 years of the Company's rule in India there emerge two main conclusions. First, the intelligentsia, including the public servants and members of the recognized independent professions, though forming by themselves a tiny minority, constituted the dominant strand in the growth of the middle classes.

---

[67] Rep. Sel. Com. HL, 1852, app. A.   [68] Ibid. app. B.

This was chiefly the result of the British educational policy, judicial administration, and political system, not of economic development, except to some extent of the commercialization of agriculture and the slight beginning of the formation of industrial capital. Secondly, the growth of English education and foreign trade had begun to change the traditional pattern of living, social behaviour, and relationship. The members of the higher castes, for example, engaged in a variety of new trades arising from the import of foreign manufactures, and adopted Western styles especially in Bengal where the old gulf between the Brahman and banyan was being thus slowly bridged through increasing occupational mobility. Other operative factors were, besides the increase of imports, the ideological infiltration of Utilitarian liberalism and the progress of Christianity. During 1757–1857, however, these influences remained for the most part limited to the Presidency towns and the neighbouring districts, including a few other capital cities, but particularly Calcutta which, as the headquarters of British commercial and political operations in the East, had the maximum concentration of European population.

Naturally enough, the Hindu society of Bengal was the first to become subject to European influence. The first modern reform movement began in Calcutta. It was led by Ram Mohan Rai (1772–1833), a reformer belonging to a Kulin or superior Brahman family which had been connected with the service of the Muhammadan rulers of Bengal. Educated first at Patna in Muhammadan learning, he became interested in the liberal philosophy of Sufism. He later read Sanskrit at Benares and then began to study English in 1796. On the death of his father in 1803 he moved to Murshidabad, and soon afterwards entered the service of the East India Company where he became a revenue officer under John Digby, who improved his knowledge of English literature. After his retirement from the Company's service in 1814 he settled down in Calcutta where he came into contact with the Serampore missionaries. He developed an admiration for the doctrines of Christianity which he declared as highly rational and conducive to moral principles. He learnt Hebrew and Greek to pursue his researches in Christianity, and in 1820 wrote a book called *The Principles of Jesus; the Guide to Peace and Happiness*. In 1828 he established a theistic society called the Brahma Samaj, and made a serious study of the Upanishads and the Vedanta Sutras which he found comparable to Sufism and Christianity.

Though declaredly founded on the theistic principles of the Upanishads, the Brahma Samaj, as J. N. Farquhar rightly points out, was 'a new creation, finding the sources of its vitality in Christian faith and practice.'[69] Ram Mohan Rai in fact showed no regard for Sanskrit; he actually opposed the establishment of the Sanskrit College at Calcutta in 1823. Like the Anglicists he favoured English education and wanted all public money to be spent on it, not on Sanskrit education. In 1830 he proceeded to England where in giving evidence before the parliamentary Select Committee of 1832 he pleaded for the increasing importation of British capital and skill. One of the leading supporters of his Brahma Samaj was Dwarkanath Tagore,[70] a Brahman commercial magnate of Calcutta, who, like Ram Mohan Rai, had amassed a fortune in the service of the East India Company.

In 1842, nine years after the death of Ram Mohan Rai in England, the leadership of the Samaj came into the hands of Debendranath Tagore, the son of Dwarkanath Tagore. Though a follower of its founder, he was no supporter or admirer of Christianity. He was in fact a Hindu by conviction. He did not favour inter-caste marriages, and published a journal called *Tattvabodhini Patrika* to counteract Christian influences. In the 1860's he was however superseded by the associates of Keshab Chandra Sen, who possessed a sound knowledge of English and became a radical social reformer. In 1864 he made a tour of the country and went to Madras where he founded the Veda Samaj, which later became the Brahma Samaj of South India. Three years later a Prarthana Samaj was established in Bombay on the same lines as the Brahma Samaj of Bengal. Like Ram Mohan Rai, Keshab was an admirer of Christianity and Western culture. He was a strong opponent of caste and favoured the agency of the state to effect social reforms. The Brahma Samaj became the religion of the educated class of Bengali Hindus.

[69] *Modern Religious Movements in India* (1918), p. 29.
[70] See above, p. 103.

Part III

TOWARDS EXPANSION AND MATURITY
1857-1947

VIII

Economic Development

THE expansion of the middle classes depended on an increase in the directional and managerial as well as the supervisory and technical elements of business. It also meant a growth and extension of specialized groups in the public services and the other recognized professions. These in turn depended upon the development of the country's economy, technology, and education.

While, however, the Government of the East India Company had made a sound beginning in the field of education, economy and technology had to all intents and purposes remained neglected. The Company's general policy was to stimulate capitalist enterprise only to the extent consistent with the preservation of indigenous handicrafts; for these fed its 'investment' and on account of their excellence and cheapness brought to it considerable profits in British and European markets. The investment of European capital was, therefore, restricted to the plantation industry, which increased the resources of the country and offset the loss caused by the employment of its territorial revenues in the Company's trade.

The size of free European investment in India grew on the complete abolition of the Company's monopoly in 1833. This weakened the protective influence of the Company's early economic policy and encouraged increased European investment in the plantation industry to counterbalance the increasing imports of finished goods. With this end in view the Charter Act of 1833 permitted Europeans to buy their own land and settle in India. But the Company's rule operated as a check. It was not until 1837 that the Company issued orders to permit grants of land to Europeans. Even so, permission was hedged in by a number of restrictions.

No grant of land, for example, was to be made to any European unless he undertook to reside on it and to cultivate it himself. The granting authority was in addition to be satisfied, before making the grant, that the applicant had 'the means and intention of bringing into cultivation the land applied for'.[1] The result was that even the plantation grew under restraint.

The nature of economic development under the Company's rule was in fact predominantly commercial and agricultural. Land continued as the most secure form of investment. Starting from the position of commercial agents or servants of the Company, as noticed before, Indians built fortunes, especially in Bengal, where they bought landed estates from motives of security and social prestige.

The end of the Company's rule in 1858 marked the real beginning of the era of *laissez-faire*, of free enterprise in commerce and industry. It contributed to the expansion of economic activity and education, of the public services and the learned professions. The exigencies of large-scale production in economic or in other fields caused the emergence of new functional groups as well as the expansion of the existing ones. Together they added to the number of the middle classes. In order to be able to ascertain the size of their growth an attempt will be made to assess the extent of economic and other developments since 1858. For the reasons indicated earlier we shall begin with the economic development.

The first forty-five to fifty years of this period were characterized by an unrestricted operation of the free-trade principle. Lord Curzon's administration (1898–1905) was the first to introduce a measure of state control in opposition to *laissez-faire*. His was simply a recognition of the principle of state participation in the development of India's economy and education, a principle the necessity of which had been realized in the context of Britain's imperialist exploitation, to the prejudice of India's economic interest. After much controversy over Curzon's policy, in the period that followed the end of the First World War in 1918 the policy of state control and participation became increasingly popular, partly because of its protective effect on Indian industry, but more because of the ideological injection of socialism necessary to protect the working class from the evils of capitalism.

[1] I.O., Rev. Desp. to Ind., 24 July 1860, no. 36, para. 3.

Economic development has been chosen as the starting-point of this chapter not because the dominant strand in the Indian middle classes became bourgeois in this period but in order to show how, in spite of the growth of economic activity, the dominant strand continued to be literary and professional. The growth of the economy and technology lagged far behind general education, and never kept pace with the growth of population.

It is not the aim of this study to estimate with any degree of accuracy the extent of India's economic development. All that is attempted here is to use certain criteria roughly to indicate the expansion of the economy in terms of its magnitude. These relate to foreign trade and the rise of joint-stock companies, to certain manufacturing industries and banks.

The figures quoted to show the gradual increase of economic activity must not, however, be taken to represent a corresponding increase in the size of the new classes arising from it; for right up to the first decade of the present century these enterprises were for the most part held by foreign Europeans, except in the cotton textile industry where Indians played a major part from an early period. But even there the managerial and technical hands were for a long period either European or Anglo-Indian. The expanding economy none the less signified on the whole an added opportunity for employment, and although Indians long remained in subordinate posts, the rise of a working class with men from different castes contributed to occupational mobility, which weakened the bonds of caste to an unprecedented degree. The increase of imports, on the other hand, modified the traditional way of living and created additional avenues of employment in such new trades as engineering, medicine, drugs and chemicals, scientific instruments and appliances, printing and paper, wines, cigars and cigarettes, haberdashery and millinery, drapery and hairdressing, furnishing and decorating; and in recent decades, bicycles and motor cars, luxuries and cosmetics, mechanical and electronic goods.

FOREIGN TRADE

The following table gives an idea of the rate of progress in the external trade of British India in the five decades between 1842 and

1892, including merchandise and treasure, both private and on government account:

Year	Total Imports and Exports Rs. crores
1842	24·81
1852	38·42
1862	92·11
1872	92·97
1882	150·07

Source: *Moral & Material Progress Report, 1882–3*, p. 215.
Exchange is calculated at 2*s.* to a rupee for 1882.

It is obvious that the value of foreign trade showed a steep rise at the period when the East India Company handed over to the Crown in 1858. It was followed by a stabilizing tendency and a steep rise again towards the close of the 1870's. In subsequent years too India's foreign trade figures showed a steady rise throughout, as indicated below:

Year	Total Imports and Exports Rs. crores
1891	195·61
1901	245·70
1912	485·31
1921	581·62

Source: *Statistical Abstract, 1883–92*, vi. 202; *1912–21*, No. 57, p. 402.
For 1901, Cd. 1801 (1904), p. 466. Exchange is calculated at Rs. 15 = £1 for 1901.

This rise in the value of foreign trade continued until it reached a peak of Rs. 646.19 crores in 1928–9, when on account of the world depression the figure began to decline. The downward trend continued, as shown below:

Year	Imports and Exports (Rs. crores)
1928	646·19
1929	601·67
1937	362·99
1940	355·66

Source: *Statistical Abstract for relevant years.*

The total fell as low as Rs. 321.57 crores in 1938, which meant a decline of nearly 100 per cent. in ten years and caused unemployment and political unrest. It was during this period that a great deal of European capital was repatriated from India because of political insecurity. The peak figure of 1928 was not achieved again even as late as 1948, when the total value of imports and exports amounted to Rs. 425 crores only.[2] It rose to Rs. 1,077 crores in 1956, but then total imports exceeded exports to the amount of Rs. 174 crores, a departure from the traditional excess of exports over imports under British rule.

Export Surplus

The outstanding feature of India's external trade under the British was the export surplus, not of treasure but of merchandise. Taking a period of ten years from 1873, the net surplus, including treasure and merchandise, amounted to £16,382,411, or over Rs. 16 crores a year.[3] The surplus of merchandise exported during 1842–82 averaged nearly £16,170,000 annually. In the same period the value of treasure imported into India exceeded the export of treasure by an annual average of more than £8 million sterling, as shown below for five decades:

Surplus of Bullion Imports into India
(£ million)

Year	Imports of treasure	Exports of treasure	Excess of imports over exports
1842	3·44	0·22	3·22
1852	6·83	1·06	5·77
1862	20·51	1·11	19·40
1872	4·56	1·30	3·26
1882	13·45	1·04	12·41

Annual average of excess £8·86 million.

Source: Statistical Abstract for relevant years.

---

[2] See U.N., *Economic Survey of Asia and the Far East, 1956*, p. 202.
[3] *Moral & Material Progress Rep., 1882–3*, including figures on the import of treasure.

The surplus of exports continued even in subsequent years. Inclusive of merchandise and treasure on private and government account, the amount rose from Rs. 27.31 crores in 1891 to Rs. 49.76 crores in 1919.[4] For two subsequent years there was a temporary increase of imports. But the traditional trend was restored again, and the value of exports increased. For example, the net excess of exports over imports, rose from Rs. 44.81 crores in 1928 to Rs. 46.59 in 1929 and to Rs. 89.46 crores in 1936. But, as will be seen, this rise was due to the export of treasure, especially in the 1930's, not merchandise. The year 1919–20 was the peak year in respect of the export of merchandise.

As has been said, excess of treasure or bullion imported into India constituted another feature of her external trade. The net value of treasure imported between 1871–2 and 1892–3 amounted to Rs. 220.90 crores, and the net export of merchandise and treasure on both private and government account amounted to Rs. 386.43 crores in the same period.[5] The table given below establishes beyond doubt the fact that the import of treasure was in excess of its export even until recent years:

Net Import of Treasure
(*Rs. crores*)

Year	Net import
1890	19·81
1900	10·34
1912	51·20
1920	8·59
1930	22·86

Source: *Statistical Abstract* for relevant years;
1900 figures from Cd. 1801 (1904), p. 466.

The capital so imported was, however, for the most part foreign, especially British. The possibility of its repatriation constituted a real threat to India's economy and to the prosperity of the classes who enjoyed the benefit of its employment in Indian trade and industry. This threat actually came about in the period after 1930

---

[4] See *Statistical Abstract* for relevant years.
[5] Ibid. *1883–4* to *1892–3*, p. 203.

when the political instability of the country led to the repatriation of a good deal of foreign capital. The net export of treasure from India during 1931-7, for instance, amounted to as much as Rs. 371.30 crores.[6] The withdrawals of treasure were for the most part private. Out of a net withdrawal of Rs. 371.30 crores, the amount withdrawn privately came to as much as Rs. 338.52 crores or a little over 90 per cent. of the total. The withdrawal on government account amounted to nearly Rs. 32.80 crores only.[7]

The increase in India's foreign sea-borne trade from Rs. 24 crores in 1842 to Rs. 646 crores in 1929 was due in large measure to three factors: free trade, improved communications, and the opening of the Suez Canal in 1869. The *Moral & Material Progress Report, 1882-3* (p. 215) commented:

With the single exception of a Customs duty on rice of 6*d.* per cwt., the export trade is now entirely free. The Customs tariff on imports is confined to arms and ammunition, liquors, salt and opium, upon all of which (except arms and ammunition) corresponding Excise duty is levied. No transit duties are levied within the boundaries of British India, though several Native States still retain this form of taxation. . . . The extension of railways throughout the country and the opening of a short sea route to Europe through the Suez Canal have combined with the abolition of Customs duties to augment greatly the foreign trade of India in recent years.

Trade Surplus Appropriated to Development and Home Charges

The regular annual surplus of India's foreign trade was employed in the remittances which the country had to make towards the Secretary of State's bill drawn on account of (1) payment of interest on loans contracted by the Government of India for its ordinary purposes as well as for the construction of productive works such as railways and irrigation, and (2) payment for services of a political and non-commercial character rendered by England to India. In a period of ten years from 1873, for instance, the net excess of total exports ran at the rate of £16,382,411 a year, but the amount of the Secretary of State's bill drawn averaged £16,070,208.[8] The following table shows how even in subsequent

---

[6] Ibid. *1928-9* to *1937-8*, pp. 628-9.   [7] Ibid. pp. 628-9.
[8] Ibid. p. 215.

periods the payment of the Secretary of State's bill more than exhausted the savings from India's external trade:

Year	Net surplus of exports by sea	India Council's bill paid in India
	£	£
1898	20,142,670	18,883,879
1899	13,841,029	18,703,761
1900	10,983,073	12,824,491
1901	17,989,510	18,535,842
1902	18,611,169	18,724,021
Ann. average:	16,313,490	17,532,398

Source: *Moral & Material Progress Rep., 1901.*

In addition to the payment of the India Council's bills, there were other remittances on account of private capital invested in commercial and industrial undertakings by Europeans temporarily resident in India, as well as of savings made by them in the various professions.

These remittances to England constituted a perpetual drain on the revenue resources of the Government of India. Sometimes the Secretary of State for India forced the Government of India to part with whatever savings the latter made towards the payment of the debt the former incurred on government account. General Sir Richard Strachey, the famous Bengal civil servant and Finance and Military Member of the Viceroy's Council in 1878, described the relation of the Secretary of State with the Government of India as 'that of the Wolf and the Lamb in the fable'.[9] The reason was that the Indian Government had with difficulty effected a saving of £1½ million to stave off borrowing for productive public works. But, as Strachey observed, 'the Wolf' came down and said 'By no means, that 1½ millions is my cake, not yours. I will take it and pay off my debts'.[10]

Added to the Secretary of State's dominance was the lack of unity in the financial policy of his India Office in London. Strachey compared that office with

a Deity like some of those adored by the Hindoos with many heads and many hands. One mouth blows fiery hot, & another icy cold at the

[9] I.O., MSS. Eur. E. 218, vol. 519 (VIII), Lytton's Correspondence in India, no. 81, 6 Aug. 1878, f. 1.   [10] Ibid. f. 2.

same moment. One hand drives us on, & the other curbs us in. Of course we must accept our Gods, such as they are, & make the most of them. But it is as well to understand their attributes if we can.[11]

Strachey in fact deplored what he considered the high-handedness of the Secretary of State and added: 'India is roughly treated & never taken into the confidence of London & is afraid to say what it thinks for fear of being snubbed. It is a very mischievous condition of things.'[12] This was not an isolated comment. The helpless state of the Government of India was, as will be seen, admitted by a number of Viceroys, including even an exceptionally powerful one like Curzon.

For a poor country like India to maintain a costly administration in England, willing and able to direct and control finances even for extra-Indian purposes, was doubtless wasteful. It adversely affected India's economic development, but it did not constitute an absolute drain on her resources since, in order to avoid a great divergence of prices which remittances in money might cause by a diminution and augmentation respectively of the volume of currency in the remitting and receiving countries, they were made in commodities. This mode of payment in kind contributed of necessity to the development of India's internal resources, especially her agricultural produce, such as raw cotton and jute, indigo and sugar cane, tea and coffee, rice and wheat, oilseeds and pulses. The removal of duties gave incentive to export and enabled Indian goods to compete in world markets, especially in British spheres of influence in the East.[13] For example, the value of raw cotton exported was £2.39 million in 1842. It rose to a little over £5½ million in 1860, and then again to £37½ million in 1865.[14] This sudden rise was, however, due to the American Civil War during which England had to depend more or less exclusively on the supply of Indian cotton. Later on, it declined. But in spite of the increasing demands made on it by Indian cotton mills, the value of raw cotton exported amounted to nearly £23 million in 1934.

Similarly, the value of jute and jute manufactures together was only £623,995 in 1860, but exports of raw jute alone amounted to

[11] Ibid. ff. 4–5.   [12] Ibid. f. 5.
[13] See *Moral & Material Progress Rep. 1882–3*, p. 216.
[14] *Statistical Abstract* for relevant years.

Rs. 10.87 crores or £7,246,666 in 1934.[15] The export of grains affords yet another indication of the extent of agricultural development. The value of grain exports was £·63 million in 1842. It rose to £3·58 million in 1860, and then again to £27·26 million in 1880. In 1912 exports of rice alone amounted to more than Rs. 32·5 crores or 21·7 million sterling. Under the Company's rule wheat never figured as an article of foreign trade. It developed later when exports rose from a little over £2 million in 1879 to £22 million in 1886. The growth of trade in such staples not only contributed to the revenue resources of the Government, but also to the industrial development of the country.[16]

The Import Pattern

India's export trade was no less significant from the point of view of paying for imports of finished goods and bullion. Of the import of foreign merchandise, British cotton manufactures were by far the most important. As the following table shows, these amounted to nearly half the total value of the articles imported into India in the five decades from 1842–3:

Imports into India
(£ million)

Year	Cotton manufactures	Other articles	Total
1842	3·13	4·47	7·63
1852	4·80	5·27	10·07
1862	9·63	13·00	22·63
1872	17·23	14·64	31·87
1882	24·80	27·29	52·09

Source: *Moral & Material Progress Rep., 1882–3.*

The proportion of cotton manufactures to the total value of the merchandise imported declined in the present century. The development of the mill industry in India and changes in the pattern

[15] *Statistical Abstract 1928–9* to *1937–8*, pp. 1095–6.
[16] See S. Srinivasa Raghvaiyanger, *Memorandum on the Progress of the Madras Presidency*, 1892, in I.O., P.B. Coll. 220, paras. 34–38, pp. 43–52. This is an excellent report which throws useful light on the economic condition of India with special reference to the Madras Presidency during a period of forty years preceding 1892.

of living brought other import goods into prominence. These included building and engineering materials, machinery and mill-work, metals and hardware, drugs and chemicals, bicycles and motor cars, paper and paints, luxuries and cosmetics. This decline had begun to be appreciable towards the 1890's. In 1901, for example, the import of cotton manufactures, including yarn and twist, amounted to Rs. 21.92 crores against Rs. 32.38 crores of other articles. But in 1921 the difference became exceedingly marked. The total value of private merchandise imported into India amounted to Rs. 266.34 crores. Of this, cotton goods accounted for Rs. 56.93 crores only.[17]

JOINT-STOCK COMPANIES

The increase in the number of joint-stock companies may be another yardstick to measure the progress of economic development. Their social significance lies not only in the separation of the proprietary and the managerial elements of business, but also in the extension of the area of capital circulation.

The emergence of private joint-stock business enterprise is to be traced from the decline of the houses of agency which began in 1828, and from the complete opening up of the trade of the East India Company in 1834. As has been stated, these events produced a state of commercial crisis. While the opening of the Company's trade made way for the increase of private European business in India, the collapse of the leading houses of agency withdrew from the market considerable sums of hard currency as the basis of external trade. The extension of business and the shortage of specie dictated the expediency of seeking the co-operation of the community in the supply of finance capital and of the manufacturers in the supply of goods on the basis of commodity exchange. That necessitated the organization of joint-stock insurance companies and banks on the one hand and of managing agency firms on the other.

The size of business exceeded the limits of what was called partnership, under which a partner was a proprietor and manager rolled into one, severally and jointly responsible for loss and profit.

[17] *Statistical Abstract, 1912–21*, pp. 414–17. The figure for 1901 is from Cd. 1801 (1904), pp. 470–1.

A firm run on the principle of partnership was not a corporation. Prior to its being recognized as a corporation under Act XLIII of 1850, the shareholders of a joint-stock enterprise were also essentially partners, and although an increase in the number of such partners in a joint-stock establishment had brought into being a separate group of business executives, the executive element so brought into being formed an integral part of the shareholders themselves. The executives became a separate entity only when joint-stock business assumed a corporate character in law.

Early Development

One of the early examples of joint-stock business was the Union Insurance Company established in Calcutta in 1828, with Rustomjee Cowasjee as one of the four members of its Committee of Management, and with its agency offices spread over the whole of Bengal, Bihar, Assam, and the North-Western Provinces.[18] On the transport and steam navigation side the following table gives an idea of some of the early joint-stock companies:

Companies	Established	Capital	Shares
Calcutta Steam Tug Assn.	1836	Rs. 5,00,000	—
Steam Navigation Co.	1840	£1,000,000	20,000
India Genl. Steam Nav. Co.	1844	Rs. 20,00,000	2,000
Ganges Steam Nav. Co.	1847	Rs. 9,00,000	600

In addition to these, the Assam Company, established in 1840 with a capital of Rs. 50 lakhs, and the Bengal Coal Company established in 1843 with a subscribed capital of Rs. 11,68,000 were important among joint-stock business establishments. The former was incorporated under a separate Act XIX of 1845, while the latter was registered under Act XLIII of 1850.

Joint-stock business, however, made its influence felt more in banking than in other fields. The banks in fact were the first to exercise an effective pressure for a general act of incorporation to enable themselves to sue and be sued by one of their recognized officers. In addition to the government banks of Bengal, Madras,

[18] See *Beng. Directory, 1835*, Commercial. Besides the district headquarters in these provinces, its branches included even small places like Revilganj and Allyganj (Siwan), which were important from a commercial point of view.

and Bombay, established under royal charters, there had come into existence a number of private joint-stock banks in the period following the opening up of the Company's trade. These, for example, included the Agra and United Service Bank established in 1833; the Union Bank of Calcutta, 1835; the North-Western Bank of India, 1841; the Oriental Bank, Bombay, 1842; the Commercial Bank of India, Bombay, 1845; the Dacca Bank, 1846, Simla Bank, Cawnpore Bank, and Delhi Bank. The memorials which some of these private banks presented to the Governor-General in Council, with requests to pass a legislative Act to recognize them as corporate bodies, show that before 1850 they had been constituted under their own separate deeds of agreement. Each such deed defined the amount of subscribed capital, with the value of each of the shares, the scope of business and constitution.[19] Excepting the Union Bank of Calcutta, which had been incorporated under a specific Indian Act (XXIII of 1845), all other banks were governed by the existing law of partnership under which all their shareholders had to join in any action brought before a court of law.

While pointing out the inconvenience arising from the operation of the law of partnership, the Managing Director of the Oriental Bank, Bombay, in a memorial of 2 August 1848, referred to an action brought by the Trustees of the Bank against one Summermul-Adamul to recover Rs. 500. The case came up for trial in the Court for Small Causes in Bombay on 27 July 1848. The judge was convinced that the Bank had given a loan of Rs. 500 to Summermul-Adamul, but since all the shareholders had not joined the action severally as plaintiffs, the Bank lost the case.

A second serious impediment to the growth of banking was the absence of the principle of limited liability. Under the law of partnership all the shareholders of a joint-stock enterprise were its partners, severally and jointly responsible for any act of their directors as well as liable to the public not only to the extent of their shares in the common stock, but of the whole of their private property for any outstanding engagements of their concern. This caused the ruin of the Union Bank of Calcutta. It is true that under Act XXIII of 1845 the Bank had been permitted to sue and be sued in the name of its Secretary or Treasurer. It was also required to

[19] See Encl. to I.O. Legis. Proc., 27 Dec. 1850, r. 207, vol. 64.

publish its accounts periodically for the information of the public. But the mismanagement of the directors, who fabricated their accounts to deceive depositors and shareholders, led to the ruin of the Bank which had a capital of £1 million sterling. The proprietors suffered for the misdeeds of directors who were also co-partners.

Memorialists from the North-Western Provinces desired that the responsibility of shareholders should cease to be unlimited. They pointed out that

unlimited responsibility has been found in India in a high degree illusory to creditors, and not to involve the advantage it imports, namely a real & unviolable power over the collective wealth of the Proprietary body; on the other hand it is found liable to be abused, and recent Experience in India has shown that it may be applied by the managing body against their Co-partners oppressively, and in a manner extremely alarming, and contrary to equity.[20]

What the memorialists wanted was to limit the liability of shareholders to the extent of double the amount of their paid-up capital in the total stock. To secure the interest of creditors they recommended that every shareholder should give a promissory note equivalent to the stock he held in the bank payable and redeemable in part or full as required by the directors or managing committee for the time being. Notes of this description, it was suggested, might give far greater protection to creditors than unlimited liability which a managing body could use against its own shareholders. Though conducive to the interest of shareholders, the Government regarded this suggestion as limiting the power of the public which under the existing law extended beyond the shares they held in the stock. Act XLIII of 1850 thus provided for the incorporation of joint-stock companies without limiting the liability of shareholders.

Under the rule of the East India Company few joint-stock companies were formed. The Company was concerned more with lending and borrowing than trade and agriculture. From a letter of 27 May 1848 which the Finance Department of the Government of India wrote to the Company it appears that the development of banking was slow, especially in the North-Western Provinces and

[20] Encl. 34 to ibid.

Madras, where it had produced little or no effect on trade and agriculture.[21] 'All these banks', the letter said, 'issued Notes, but experience had shown as regarded private Estabts., that the issue had been entirely unsuccessful and that as the Notes were excluded from the Government Treasuries, they obtained no credit or circulation with the public.'[22] Thus although the Company's monopoly had been abolished, its rule operated as a serious check on the growth of free enterprise.

The growth of the modern banks tended to affect the interests of India's traditional mercantile houses adversely, especially those of the shroffs who dealt in credit and the bullion trade. This development did not affect the rising class of Indian agents, variously known as banyans or gomastahs, who carried on the business of Europeans. They on the contrary prospered, for they acted both as middlemen and junior partners. Their numbers grew with the growth of the European houses of agency.

The business of the houses of agency was, however, concentrated for the most part in the Presidency towns, and even so, not all carried on banking business. The influence of shroffs and indigenous banking houses continued more or less unabated, particularly in the rural districts and provincial headquarters where, as has been stated, even some Europeans dealt with them or their agents. It is true that the supply of indigenous manufactures through Indian or European agents was gradually becoming popular, and tended to replace the traditional system of *dadni* or advance, which impeded the freedom of bargaining. Instead of allowing the manufactures of the interior to remain locally scattered, European firms and their agents moved them increasingly to the Presidency town for central large-scale buying and selling. The movement of inland trade was becoming more and more vertical. But this process was very slow because the East India Company preferred to maintain its commercial establishments in the districts, to continue the system of advance, and to buy locally in the interior rather than at the Presidency headquarters.

In the absence of banks in the interior, therefore, many of the European traders also borrowed from shroffs. Even the civil and military servants of the Company could not dispense with them. The commercial crisis of the year 1828–9 and the following years

[21] See paras. 4 to 16.   [22] See para. 19.

in fact threw the public servants almost wholly upon indigenous bankers.[23] In a memorial of 19 September 1849 the directors of the North-Western, Delhi, and Cawnpore Banks clearly pointed out to the Government that it was to save the Company's European servants from an exclusive recourse to Indian bankers that had led them to establish the North-Western Bank of India in 1833. They admitted that such of the public servants as required assistance on the collapse of the important houses of agency 'were compelled to have recourse to the native shroff to whom 24 per cent. was the common rule of interest'. In spite of the high rate of interest, it was not without difficulty that they could get money from the shroffs. The thoughtless and the extravagant in both services were in such circumstances 'induced to accept aid from their subordinates in breach of regulations and to the great detriment of the service. The establishment of Banks therefore became both expedient and necessary.'[24]

The Lieutenant-Governor of the North-Western Provinces reported that he appreciated the fact that although the banks of those provinces had been of little benefit to trade and agriculture, they were beneficial to the members of the services, for they had tried to extricate them from pecuniary embarrassments and to take 'both lenders and borrowers out of the hands of natives'.[25] While encouraging the establishment of more and more of these banks, therefore, he had at the back of his mind the exclusion of shroffs from the field of public service, and there too from superior levels. 'Civilians and specially those of higher standing and in respectable situations', he suggested, 'should have open deposit accounts with the Banks rather than with natives'. He preferred a 'Bank' to 'a native merchant' because the latter 'was liable to give an air of undue importance to such a transaction'.[26]

A perusal of the several memorials which led to Act XLIII of 1850 shows that although by the end of the Company's rule modern banking industry had begun to affect the interest of indigenous bankers, the effect remained none the less peripheral, limited more to lending and borrowing by public servants than to matters of trade and agriculture. As will be seen later, the joint-

---

[23] See Encl. 34 to ibid.   [24] See Encl. 34 to ibid.
[25] G.O.I. to Court of Directors, Finance Dept., 27 May 1848 para. 4.
[26] Ibid. para. 5.

stock banks were limited in number, and even this limited number remained concentrated in the Presidency towns for a long period.

Another significant point that one notices in the early development of modern joint-stock business relates to its managerial aspect, especially to the managing agency system which, like the banks, grew out of the ashes of the houses of agency. It is significant because the growth and expansion of joint-stock companies proceeded under managing agents who in the early records of the East India Company were called variously 'Secretary', 'Manager', or 'Managing Director'. Functionally, the new system differed but little from the houses of agency; for both were in principle the organs of a free-trade economy. But while the agency houses had traded with rupee capital, the managing agents, owing to the scarcity of specie, started as commercial media for the exchange of goods, representing for the most part such companies as were established in England with sterling capital. Basically they began as traders, and later became organizers and managers of industry. It was mainly through their agency that European capital and skill found their way into India. They used these in the organization of industrial undertakings and the development of India's resources which paid for the increasing import of foreign manufactures. The success of their industrial enterprise depended on the size of their commercial profit which they employed in the establishment of more and more plants. The whole system was in fact integrated with the imperialist economy. Whatever its other effects may have been, it doubtless supplied a pattern of industrial organization. It differed in this respect fundamentally from the houses of agency whose control did not extend beyond securing a due return of interest on loans made to an individual or a firm. The managing agency system introduced a degree of administrative control and financial integration in business which had never existed before. It preserved the legal and functional independence of each of the concerns opened by a pioneering managing agency firm, and yet the firm exercised an overall control by putting up most of the capital in the concerns so floated. The example of Mackinnon-Mackenzie & Company, a managing agency firm established in 1847, may be quoted to illustrate the point. It is still one of the leading firms in India.

A resident of Campbeltown in Scotland, William Mackinnon was a failure in an early venture to maintain a shop there. He went to Glasgow where he ultimately entered the office of a Portuguese merchant. But dissatisfied with the lot of an office assistant, he left for India where he arrived in 1847. He got a job in the Cossipur Sugar Mill near Calcutta in which his friend, Robert Mackenzie, who was a flourishing merchant at Ghazipur near Benares, held a major interest. Mackinnon became the manager of the sugar mill, and in December of the same year Mackinnon and Mackenzie formed a partnership, establishing the firm named after them. Their business flourished, and they soon realized that they might do better to carry their own goods, with those of other merchants, in their own ships. They thus started chartering vessels on their own account, which plied from Glasgow to Liverpool and Calcutta, and from Calcutta to Australia and China. An opportunity presented itself to the firm in 1854, when the Government of the East India Company invited tenders for a mail contract between Calcutta and Rangoon. Mackinnon got the contract. He came home and raised money in London and Glasgow to set up a regular shipping line. He thus established the Calcutta & Burma Steam Navigation Company, Ltd., registered on 24 September 1856 with a small capital of £35,000 in 700 shares. He soon visualized the possibility of a new trade route through the Suez Canal, which might increase the importance of Bombay. The firm augmented the strength of its merchant fleet, and successfully negotiated a contract with the Government of Bombay to run the mails twice a month from Bombay to Karachi, and eight times a year up and down the Persian Gulf. The original name of the shipping company, a separate establishment controlled by the pioneering firm, was changed into the British India Steam Navigation Company, Ltd., the famous B.I. with its headquarters in London, which still rules the eastern waters.[27]

Andrew Yule of Calcutta was another famous example of a managing agency firm which established a wide variety of industrial units which it managed and controlled. Some of the other leading firms in India include McLeod, Martin, Bird, Jardine and Henderson, Duncan, Octavius Steel, Gillanders, British India Corporation, Shaw Wallace, and others. The managing agency system, although it contributed to the horizontal expansion of new industrial plants, led from motives of economy and a desire to

[27] See George Blacke, *B.I. Centenary, 1856–1956.*

Economic Development 231

eliminate wasteful expenditure arising from unhealthy competition, to the vertical integration of their finances, direction, and management. A managing firm pooled the capital resources of each of the separate companies floated by it, and these companies operated under a unified control. This became a model of industrial organization which Indian capitalists adopted to their advantage. Its basic feature was the employment of trade surpluses in the extension of industrial enterprise under the centralized control and management of the pioneering firm, which acted as a catalytic agent in the fusion of commercial and industrial capital.

An interesting point that arises in connexion with the managing agency system is that the executive element in joint-stock companies in India did not grow internally from below. The rise of the managerial group in business was not so much the result of a qualitative change arising from a quantitative increase in the bulk of stockholders; it was imported from Britain as an artifact. The managerial element so imported contributed, through the expansion of business, to increase the size of proprietary bodies.

Later growth. The number of joint-stock companies increased after the Crown had taken over from the Company in 1858. The total number registered up to March 1881 was 1,069, but many of these had been wound up or had otherwise discontinued their business. The actual number of the companies working in 1881 was 474 only. The following table shows their distribution:

Joint-Stock Companies in 1881

Companies	Bengal	Bombay	Madras	Mysore	U.P.	Punj.	C.P.
Banking	15	2	72	51	8	3	—
Insurance	—	5	—	—	—	—	—
Mills & presses	21	59	2	—	1	1	1
Mining & quarrying	7	4	4	—	—	1	—
Planting	103	1	3	—	3	1	—
Trading	27	23	11	3	12	5	1
Misc.	4	6	4	—	—	1	—
Total	177	100	96	54	24	12	2

Source: I. O. Records, no. (48) 1606 (Statistics on British India).

I.M.C.—16

Thus most of the joint-stock companies were concentrated in Calcutta and Bombay; Madras and Mysore commanded 96 and 54 respectively, but these were for the most part credit associations. The North-Western Provinces and Oudh, which formed the United Provinces of Agra and Oudh in 1902, had begun to emerge as a centre of joint-stock business, especially in banking and trading. Another interesting feature of the regional distribution was that while Bombay led in mills and presses, Bengal, which then included Bihar, had the virtual monopoly of planting companies.

The period following 1881 showed a considerable increase in the number of joint-stock companies and their capital. The *Moral & Material Progress Report, 1902–3* pointed out (p. 47) that in a span of fifteen years from 1888–9 the number of joint-stock companies rose from 895 to 1,440, and that their paid-up capital increased from a little over £15 million to £26 million. As in 1881, most of these companies operated in Bengal and Bombay which possessed

43 and 40 per cent. respectively of all the paid-up capital; in Madras the number of companies (424) was larger than in either of the former provinces, but the paid-up capital constituted only about 7 per cent. of the whole; in the United Provinces the paid-up capital of the 86 companies aggregated £1,268,000 or 5 per cent. of the whole.

In point of paid-up capital, Bombay in fact stood first as indicated in the following table:

Paid-up Capital of Joint-Stock Companies, 1902–3

Province	No. of companies	Average paid-up capital
Bombay	329	£31,600
Bengal	407	£27,900
Madras	424	£ 4,300
U.P.	86	£14,700

Source: *Moral and Material Progress Rep., 1902–3*, p. 47.

By the turn of this century the joint-stock companies of the United Provinces, though small in number, had thus built up a sound foundation. The distribution among industries of paid-up capital of registered companies for the year 1902–3 was as follows:

Paid-up Capital, 1902–3

(£ '000)

Banking and insurance	3,308
Trading and shipping	4,861
Mining and quarrying	1,671
Mills and presses	12,714
Tea and planting	2,438

Source: As for table above.

It is clear that the largest aggregate capital of over £12 million or nearly 49 per cent. of the total was for weaving, spinning, and pressing of cotton, jute, wool, and silk. Of this nearly 59 per cent. belonged to the Bombay Presidency. This meant that in the economic field the growth of the middle classes was concentrated in Bombay and Bengal, and there too in the textile industry, banking, and insurance.

In the first twenty-five years of the present century, while the number of the registered joint-stock companies increased from 1,405 in 1901 to 5,311 in 1925, or nearly four times, the amount of their paid-up capital showed an increase of more than seven times, i.e. from Rs. 37.39 crores to Rs. 277.28 crores.[28] Of the 5,311 registered companies, 4,926 were in British India, and only 385 in Indian states. Of the total for British India, 2,451 or nearly 50 per cent. were in Bengal. But in point of their average paid-up capital Bombay preserved the lead with an average of Rs. 12.71 lakhs against Rs. 4.34 lakhs for Bengal. In Northern India the United Provinces had by 1925 forged their way up with 228 registered companies with an average capital of Rs. 5.61 lakhs against Bengal's average of Rs. 4.34 lakhs. The number of registered companies in Madras was 679 against Bombay's 804, but the former's average paid-up capital amounted to Rs. 1.82 lakhs against the latter's Rs. 12.71 lakhs. Another peculiar feature of this period was that joint-stock companies spread to new industrial fields, such as rice and flour mills, oil and sugar mills, breweries and distilleries, landed estates and buildings, hotels and restaur-

[28] See Rep. on Joint-Stock Companies, 1925–6, table 1, p. 3.

ants. In addition, there was a considerable increase in banking and insurance, transit and transport, trading and manufacturing companies.

In about another ten years the number of joint-stock companies doubled, increasing from 5,311 in 1925–6 to 10,061 in 1936–7,[29] and then again to 22,675 in 1947–8.[30] The following table gives an idea of the increase in the different spheres of joint-stock enterprise:

Companies	1928–9	1936–7	1947–8*
1. Banking, including investment trust	1,358	1,981	1,776
2. Insurance	85	778	357
3. Transit & transport	219	418	1,245
4. Trading & manufacturing	2,061	4,193	13,646
5. Mills & presses	506	634	1,875
6. Tea & other plantation products	537	559	788
7. Mining & quarrying	274	338	667
8. Estate, land, building	96	187	666
9. Breweries & distilleries	—	—	38
10. Sugar	33	196	182
11. Hotels, theatres, &c.	—	—	1,147
12. Others	331	777	288
Total	5,500	10,061	22,675

* Exclusive of Pakistan.

Sources: Statistical Abstract (excl. Burma), *1936–7*; Min. of Commerce, *Progress of Joint Stock Companies in India* (1955), pp. 11–12.

The figures for 1947–8 are for divided India. Nevertheless joint-stock companies registered a remarkable increase everywhere, especially in sugar, transit and transport, trading and manufacturing companies, mills and presses—including rice and flour mills—breweries, hotels, theatres, and entertainments. They indicate the development of new tastes and a rise in the standards of comfort and civilization.

However, the amount of paid-up capital registered a decline.

[29] See *Statistical Abstract* (excl. Burma), *1936–7*.
[30] See G.O.I., Min. of Commerce, *Progress of Joint Stock Companies in India* (1955), pp. 11–12.

While before 1925 there was a greater increase in capital than in the number of registered companies, this trend was reversed after 1925. In three years paid-up capital declined from Rs. 277.28 crores in 1925–6 to Rs. 243.44 crores in 1928–9. It rose to Rs. 272.24 crores in 1936–7, and again to Rs. 596.56 crores in 1947–8. But while the number of registered companies increased fourfold, the amount of paid-up capital only more or less doubled, and that too in the 1940's, not in the 1930's when, as has been stated, there was considerable repatriation of foreign capital from the country.

In most of the companies the increase in their paid-up capital in the decade 1936–7 to 1947–8 was nearly 100 per cent., except in the case of sugar companies where the amount of paid-up capital rose from Rs. 9.25 crores in 1936–7 to Rs. 19.26 crores in 1947–8, although the number of companies declined in the same period from 196 to 182. The trading and manufacturing companies increased from 4,193 in 1936–7 to 13,646 in 1947–8 with a corresponding increase in their paid-up capital from Rs. 95.42 crores to Rs. 229.85 crores in the same period. They included a variety of trading occupations which tended to transform India's traditional pattern of living.[31]

FACTORY INDUSTRY

The growth of factory or organized industry is another index of India's economic development. It may be illustrated here by considering only a few specific industries. For example, because of its traditional excellence the cotton textile industry was the first to be organized on a large scale, worked by steam. The first mill for the spinning of cotton was established in 1851 on the island of Bombay. Weaving was mechanized soon afterwards. By 1876 the number of cotton mills was 47, and in 1882 it was 62.[32] The first phenomenal growth of the industry took place in the twenty years ending 1902–3 when the number of mills rose to 201 and, as the following table shows, India had by the second decade of this century developed

---

[31] In 1947–8 these included trading associations and companies dealing with printing and publishing, chemicals, engineering, iron, steel, and ship-building managing agencies (2,482), public service, cement, gas, water, ice, canvas, rubber, tobacco, &c.

[32] *Moral & Material Progress Rep., 1882–3*, pp. 208–9.

a considerable export trade in cotton manufactures, including twist and yarn.

Cotton Exports, 1862–1919

Year	Total value (£ million)
1862	0·74
1872	1·19
1882	2·17
1902	5·58
1912	8·13
1919	18·27

Source: Statistical Abstract for relevant years.

Cotton mills were for the most part joint-stock concerns, concentrated in the Bombay Presidency. Of the total number of 62 mills in 1882, for example, 46 were in that Presidency, 29 of these being in the island of Bombay itself. In about twenty years the number of cotton mills rose from 201 in 1902 to 237 in 1921–2, but their paid-up capital increased at a faster rate still, rising from nearly £12 million to £26 million in the same period. Calculated at Rs. 15 to £1, £26 million sterling meant Rs. 39 crores. However, this rate of capital formation soon declined. By 1937–8 the number of cotton mills had increased to 403 in British India and the Indian states, but the total amount of paid-up capital had fallen to nearly Rs. 38 crores, less than the total for 1921–2.[33]

The growth of the industry was due not to any protection, favour, or advantage accruing from the policy of the Government, but to the cheapness of Indian labour and the local production of the raw materials, and to the extension of railways, the technical service of Europeans, the freedom from competition, and the expansion of Britain's imperial market in the East where Indian business operated freely in association with the British.

These factors applied equally to the jute industry. It belonged almost exclusively to Bengal where it constituted a European monopoly in the same way as tea and coal. In 1828 jute exports amounted to 364 cwt. valued at Rs. 62 or nearly £6. In 1850 exports of raw jute amounted to about Rs. 2 lakhs, and of manu-

[33] See *Statistical Abstract, 1928–9 to 1937–8*, pp. 518–19.

factured jute to Rs. 2.15 lakhs.[34] In forty years these values increased respectively to Rs. 6.84 crores and Rs. 2.51 crores, taken together an increase of 225 times.[35] Exports of jute manufactures rose steadily in value until they reached Rs. 52.65 crores in 1918–19.

In addition to cotton and jute mills, other mills and factories using mechanical power sprang up, especially in the 1880's; for in the previous decade most parts of the country were in the grip of recurrent famines, with the result that a number of collieries—a barometer of industrial progress—had to be closed owing to the impossibility of finding markets for the coal already raised.[36] At the end of 1889–90, however, there were

114 cotton mills and 27 jute mills worked by steam, 315 cotton and jute presses, 51 rice mills, 60 saw mills, 21 breweries, 2 woollen mills, 6 silk mills, 3 soap factories, 6 large tanneries, 48 iron and brass foundries, 14 large sugar factories, 23 coffee works, 66 cutch and lac factories, 61 oil mills, 44 flour mills, 24 ice factories, 23 pottery and tile factories, 15 bone-crushing factories, and 34 tobacco and cigar factories, besides a large number of indigo and tea factories worked on indigo and tea plantations.[37]

Towards the closing decade of the nineteenth century India was thus emancipating herself from a state of economic chaos and entering on a new era of industrial development. But this was only a beginning; speaking of the state of industrial development the *Moral & Material Progress Report* for the year 1902–3 observed (p. 173):

Nothing illustrates better the present state of industrial development in India than the fact, that after the cotton and jute industries, ... there was only one of the manufacturing industries ... namely the iron and brass foundries, in which as many as 20,000 persons are returned as having been employed during the year. In the preparation of agricultural staples for the market, employment is found for larger numbers; indigo factories ... employed over 81,000 workers; cotton ginning, cleaning, and pressing mills over 65,000; jute presses 22,000. But of manufacturing industries, properly so called, ... the most important, after

[34] Raghvaiyanger, *Memo. on Madras* (P.B. Coll. 220), para. 43, p. 56.
[35] Cd. 1801 (1904), p. 476, giving figures for jute exports for 1891–2.
[36] *Beng. Admin. Rep.*, 1872–3. The Report said: 'In England, where 100,000,000 tons of coal are annually raised, it is difficult to meet the demand; in Bengal, where the outturn [annual] has been reduced to 322,000 tons, it is difficult to find demand for the small quantity that is raised' (p. 228).
[37] *Memo. on Madras*, para. 43.

cotton and jute mills, are the iron and brass foundries (20,674), silk filatures (10,652), tanneries (8,626), and others of still less importance.

The first two decades of the present century witnessed not only the expansion and multiplication of existing industries but also the establishment of new industrial plants. Two of the most important of these were the hydro-electric power station in Bombay and the Iron and Steel Works at Jamshedpur in Bihar, the latter being the first of its kind in the whole of the British Empire. Both belonged to the Tatas, the famous industrialists of Bombay.

It is true that India could not take full advantage of the war-time opportunities during 1914–18. The difficulty of importing machinery and skill made it practically impossible to start new enterprises. But the capital accumulated during the war led to huge floatations on its termination. The magnitude of this development may be realized from the fact that while the number of companies registered in 1918–19 was 198, with a capital of £4½ million, the number for the year 1919–20 totalled 906, with an aggregate capital of £183 million.[38] The results of the industrial censuses of 1911 and 1921 showed that the number of industrial establishments, both registered and unregistered, with twenty persons or more employed in each increased from 7,113 in 1911 to a little over 15,000 in 1921.[39]

The increasing import of machinery and mill-work lend additional support to the view that India had by the second decade of this century entered on a new era of industrial progress. This is clear from the table given below:

Imports of Machinery and Mill-work
(Rs. crores)

Year	Value of machinery and mill-work	Value of railway plant and rolling stock
1873	1·00	0·43
1882	1·34	1·11
1892	2·11	1·48
1912	5·41	6·40
1921	34·25	18·91

Source: *Statistical Abstract* for relevant years.

[38] *Moral & Material Progress Rep.*, *1919–20*, p. 78.
[39] See *Census of India: 1911*, vol. i, pt. 2, p. 332; *1921*, i. 292.

But considering the size of the country and of its population the decade before 1921 was still 'the beginning of an industrial renaissance'.[40]

The first Indian Industrial Commission was appointed by the Government of India under a resolution of 19 May 1916. While asking the Commission to report on the expediency of government participation and direction in India's industrial development, the Government clearly admitted that in spite of satisfactory progress made in the cotton, jute, and iron and steel industries, the fact remained that 'she [India] is still in the main a producer of raw materials'.[41] The report which the Commission presented in 1918 showed how little the rise of modern industry had influenced the great bulk of the country's population, which remained engrossed in agriculture, which afforded them a bare subsistence because they used the most antiquated methods of cultivation. The Commission regretted that although India was a country rich in raw materials, it remained poor in manufacturing accomplishments. The exponents of *laissez-faire* had in the past considered Government ill qualified to further industrial development by any direct action. The Government had also laboured under an erroneous theory that tropical countries, with their fertile lands and trying climate, were more suited to the production of raw materials than manufactured goods. The progress of the textile and iron and steel industries had to some extent dispelled this mistaken view, but it was the war and the exigencies of defence that dictated the necessity of creating in India the manufactures necessary for industrial self-sufficiency and military defence, since it was no longer possible to rely on the importation of essential goods. It was therefore to accelerate the pace of economic development that commerce and industry became transferred subjects to be administered by Indian ministers under the Government of India Act, 1919.

This Act was in its economic aspect designed to harmonize India's industrial interests with the imperial interests of Britain. With this end in view it introduced a system of provincial autonomy to speed up the progress of commerce, industry, and education on the one hand, and provided constitutional safeguards to protect British interests on the other. Consistently with this aim the

---

[40] *Moral & Material Progress Rep., 1919–20*, p. 77.
[41] Ind. Indust. Commission, 1916, *Rep.*, p. 301.

Government of India appointed in 1921 a Fiscal Commission to review its tariff structure in keeping with the principle of imperial preference. Among other things, the Commission desired the appointment of a Tariff Board to administer the policy of protection recommended by it. Its object was to see that India should attain the position of the foremost industrial nations of the world, able not only to supply 'her own needs' but also to export 'her surplus manufactured goods'.[42] The Commission suggested a revision of existing tariffs so as to enable the Government directly to aid the country's industrial development by the supply of subsidies, technical knowledge, and information.

But this policy did not materialize since, as will be seen, there ensued a prolonged period of political unrest which clouded thinking and prevented economic issues from being examined on their own merits. Whatever the other results of the non-cooperation and civil-disobedience movement directed against British rule, it delayed India's economic development on modern capitalist lines. While the civil service was geared to the preservation of law and order, incentive to capital investment was reduced by political insecurity. This explains why the average paid-up capital of joint-stock companies declined towards the 1930's. The British, who possessed the bulk of capital, knowledge, and skill, preferred withdrawal rather than the extension of their business. The Indian capitalists, who were just emerging as an independent industrial force in the country, were confronted with the growing demand for socialism, a post-war development. Consequently the earlier favourable trend of economic development received a positive setback. This is shown by the fact that the value of imports of machinery and other capital goods, which had by 1921 reached a total of a little over Rs. 53 crores, fell to nearly Rs. 10 crores in 1929–30.[43] Although this might in part be attributed to the trade depression, which had just begun, even after it the figure remained low. For instance, the import of capital goods amounted only to Rs. 19 crores in 1938.[44] It reached Rs. 78 crores in 1948–9, when the politics of the country had become stabilized and a sense of security in business had begun to emerge. Even so, a statement

[42] Indian Fiscal Commission, 1921–2, *Rep.*, p. 117.
[43] *Statistical Abstract, 1929–30.*
[44] G.O.I., *Prog. of Joint Stock Companies* (1955), p. v, table 4.

made on 16 June 1952 by Mr. C. D. Deshmukh, then Minister of Finance, revealed that the repatriation of foreign capital had continued, though not as heavily as in the 1930's. The total amount repatriated between July 1947 and December 1951 was Rs. 52.6 crores. This constituted only a fraction of the total foreign capital investment which, according to a report of the Census of India on foreign liabilities and assets in 1950, amounted to Rs. 596 crores or nearly 44.7 per cent. of India's total capital investment in 1949.[45] However, continued repatriation was significant in that it reflected a want of full confidence in the industrial policy of free India.

The main factor conducing to the progress of manufacturing industries in India in recent decades was the policy of protection introduced in 1923. The expansion of Indian-owned banks, the establishment of the Reserve Bank of India in 1936, and the development of investment trusts about the same period were among other factors which helped the growth of trade and industry in recent years. The outbreak of the Second World War in 1939 afforded additional opportunity for industrial expansion.

It was during this period [says a government report] that such industries as manufacture of hydrogenated oil, transport and electrical equipments, machine tools, basic chemicals, power alcohol, synthetic resins and plastic etc. which until then had been almost non-existent in the country, were started. This trend has continued with an ever widening range in recent years.[46]

UNEVEN CHARACTER OF ECONOMIC DEVELOPMENT

India's considerable development in about a century was most uneven in that the circulation of wealth remained concentrated in large cities, especially in the Presidency towns of Bombay and Calcutta. This early lopsidedness in economic development not only widened the gulf between urban and rural standards of living and culture, but also produced a wide range of regional variations in economic prosperity. Three yardsticks will be used to ascertain the degree of unevenness, namely the concentration of foreign trade, the unbalanced structure of income-tax, and the segregation of banks.

[45] *Statistical Abstract, 1940–50.*   [46] *Prog. of Joint Stock Companies,* p. v.

Concentration of Foreign Trade

The following table, which shows the proportionate share of each province in India's sea-borne trade with foreign countries, gives a clear indication of the concentration of external trade in Bengal and Bombay:

Province	Percentage of imports 1872	1902	Percentage of exports 1872	1902
Bengal	50·9	41·7	43·2	41·8
Bombay	34·7	41·6	41·4	36·0
Madras	9·8	9·1	11·1	12·0

*Source: Statistical Abstract, 1863–72, vol. i, no. 7, pp. 16 f., 124 f.;
1902 figs. from Moral & Material Progress Rep., p. 170.*

In point of bullion imports Bombay stole a march over Calcutta. Together they exercised a virtual monopoly over the bullion trade during the whole of the nineteenth century. The following table gives an idea of the proportionate share of each province in respect of bullion imported into India from 1861 to 1901:

(Rs. crores)

Province	1861	1881	1901
Bengal	3·52	1·92	3·41
Bombay	5·96	9·01	8·87
Madras	1·18	0·32	0·67

Note: Early figures given in sterling are converted @ 2s. = Rs. 1.

*Source: Statistical Abstract, 1861, i. 13; 1881, v. 208; for 1902,
Cd. 1801, p. 488.*

Bombay thus dominated India's bullion trade commanding, as it did, between 60 and 80 per cent. of the entire bullion imported.

The great bulk of all the country's foreign trade passed through Bombay and Calcutta, two of its bottle-necks. The figures given below indicate the proportionate share of the chief ports of British India (excluding Burma) in private trade with foreign countries in merchandise:

Imports and Exports, 1901–2

Chief ports	Percentage of imports			Percentage of exports		
	1900	1901	1902	1900	1901	1902
Calcutta	41·7	40·1	41·5	50·5	43·1	40·4
Bombay	34·5	34·7	35·0	25·3	30·4	29·8
Madras	7·4	7·4	7·7	5·0	3·6	3·7
Karachi	6·0	5·2	6·6	3·1	7·6	6·2

Source: Moral & Material Progress Rep., 1902–3, p. 170.

From 70 to 80 per cent. of private foreign trade in merchandise thus passed through two only of the chief ports of India. This naturally effected the concentration of commercial wealth in Calcutta and Bombay, a trend which continued even in subsequent years,[47] and explains why these two capital cities produced by far the largest number of the Indian middle classes, both educated and commercial. Madras lagged behind in business enterprise; its economy remained dominantly agricultural. Other provincial capitals too showed a marked difference in the content of economic development. The uneven growth of the economy produced a correspondingly uneven social structure, representing varying standards of comfort and civilization, social thought and relationship. It produced a cultural crisis where new ideas and institutions came to clash with the old. It led to movements for religious and social reform which emphasized the need for readjustment or coexistence. The crisis none the less still continues; for the bulk of the country still remains industrially undeveloped and educationally backward.

Unbalanced Taxation of Incomes

The unbalanced character of income taxation may be a second criterion to measure the unevenness of economic development. Though highly significant, it is not possible to examine this in any detail, and this inquiry will be limited to an examination of some of the results of a confidential investigation which the Government of India instituted in 1888 to report on the economic conditions, with special reference to the lower orders of society.[48] In the Bengal districts the scope of the investigation was also extended to income

[47] *Statistical Abstract, 1912–13 to 1921–2.*
[48] The results of the investigation are contained in P.B. Coll. nos. 220 and 221.

taxation. The following table based on the results of that inquiry is specially significant, for it gives the proportion of assessees to the total population of the various Bengal divisions:

Income-Tax, Bengal, 1891–2

Division	Current demand & penalties (Rs. lakhs)	No. of assessees	Demand per assessee Rs. a. p.			Proportion of assessees to population, i.e. one in:
Chittagong	0·91	5,129	17	12	4	816
Dacca	2·83	10,677	28	8	0	922
Presidency, excl. Calcutta	2·56	12,634	20	4	3	675
Calcutta	18·05	21,902	82	11	3	31
Rajshahi	2·90	12,472	23	5	0	645
Burdwan	1·95	8,896	21	15	0	864
Chota Nagpur	0·94	4,311	21	5	10	1,073
Orissa	0·51	2,576	19	15	4	1,570
Bhagalpur	2·31	10,604	21	13	1	809
Patna	3·83	13,972	27	7	1	1,131
Total:	36·83	103,176	28	8	0*	853*

* Average.   *Source: Skrine Mem.* (P.B. Coll. 220), p. 57, table 6.

This table shows the incidence of income-tax for the year when the report on the condition of the lower classes was presented to the Government of India. It establishes beyond doubt the existence of a wide gulf in the distribution of wealth and the consequent standard of living; for while the proportion of assessees to population was 1 to 1,570 in the Orissa Division, the corresponding figure for Calcutta proper was 1 to 31 only. It also shows how Calcutta was able to pay and actually paid half the total amount of income-tax payable in the three provinces of Bengal, Bihar, and Orissa. The divisions of Bengal proper were on the whole much better off than those in Bihar or Orissa. The first six of the divisions which formed part of Bengal proper contained 70 per cent. of the total number of assessees, with an average demand per assessee of Rs. 32 or nearly £3 a year against nearly £2 in Bihar and Orissa. It represented an exceedingly low rate of taxation, but the reason was that the bulk of taxation was paid, as will be seen, by persons in lower income groups.

Segregation of Banks

Banks are by far the most important indicators of the extent of capital circulation and the volume of business at different levels. The following table, showing the number of banking establishments in Bengal, shows clearly how in spite of a considerable increase in the number of banks in recent decades their traditional concentration in Calcutta continued:

Banking Offices in Bengal

Year	Stations served	Total no. of offices	No. in Calcutta	Outside Calcutta
1861	2	12	11	1
1881	3	13	11	2
1901	5	15	12	3
1917	13	46	27	19
1947	..	243	166	77

Note: The banking offices of Bengal were exclusive of Assam, Bihar, and Orissa.

Source: Thacker's *Beng. Directory.*

After the second decade of the present century banking establishments spread out to district and subdivisional levels. The figures nevertheless indicate how slow was the rate at which banking capital filtered down to local stations. They are also significant because they suggest that the development of banking proceeded at more or less the same rate as that of commerce and industry.

The pattern of Bombay conformed nearly to that of Calcutta, as indicated below:

Banking Offices in Bombay

Year	Stations served	Total no. of offices	In Bombay proper
1881	7	16	10
1901	9	22	11
1917	20	59	28

Source: Thacker's *Ind. Directory.*

In the Madras Presidency, the North-Western Provinces, and the Punjab banking offices were relatively scattered. Progress was slow everywhere except in the second decade of the present century, when numbers began to grow rapidly, as in Calcutta and Bombay. In the Punjab and the North-Western Provinces, however, the 1880's registered a noticeable change in the rate of increase: numbers more than doubled, as shown below:

Banking Offices in the Punjab and U.P.

Year	Punjab		U.P.	
	Stations served	*No. of offices*	*Stations served*	*No. of offices*
1861	5	5	4	6
1881	6	10	9	20
1901	11	25	11	26
1917	28	68	23	44

In industrial development and the progress of banking that went with it, the North-Western Provinces and Oudh were forging ahead with Cawnpore as their nucleus. But since the old cities of Agra, Allahabad, and Lucknow retained their administrative importance, the distribution of banks in these provinces was more diffused in spite of their concentration at Cawnpore. The Punjab followed a more or less similar pattern. The number of purely Indian-owned and managed banks in this part of the country had risen to six before 1902, and as many as thirty-eight came into existence in about fifteen years thereafter.[49]

Capital Circulation

The figures of capital circulation confirm the fact of the country's increasing wealth but of its inequitable distribution For example, the value of government currency notes in

---

[49] The Indian owned and managed banks established before 1902 were (1) Oudh Commercial Bank, 1881; (2) Kashmir Bank, 1882; (3) Allahabad Trading and Banking Corporation, 1883; (4) Bhargava Commercial Bank, 1893; (5) The Punjab National Bank, 1895; (6) Ajodhia Bank, Fyzabad.

circulation[50] increased at the following rate (in Rs. crores):

1862	4·41	1921	166·15
1881	13·50	1941	421·05

Source: Statistical Abstract for relevant years.

But the proportional volume of currency notes domiciled in the various regional circles indicates beyond doubt the element of great disparity in the circulatory capacity of each circle, an important factor responsible for the slight growth of business classes in circles other than Bombay and Calcutta. This is clear from the table given below.

Average Value of Govt. Currency Notes in Circulation

(Rs. crores)

Circles	1862	1871	1881	1891	1901	1921
Calcutta	2·42	4·30	6·43	9·71	12·75	50·06
Bombay	1·58	4·14	3·49	8·90	7·71	51·25
Madras	0·41	1·03	1·26	2·76	3·01	15·62
Lahore	—	0·52	0·81	1·34	2·04	14·78
Allahabad	—	0·36	0·72	1·22	1·43	—
Cawnpore	—	—	—	—	—	8·98
Karachi	—	0·22	0·33	0·67	0·80	7·74
Rangoon	—	—	—	0·58	0·95	18·85

Source: Statistical Abstract for relevant years.

These figures confirm that Bombay and Calcutta together dominated the capital market of the whole country commanding, as they did, nearly 70 per cent. of the total circulation of government currency notes. They also indicate the speed at which the circulation of capital proceeded, especially in the first two decades

[50] The currency notes were duly backed up by reserves. In 1921, for example, the reserves were as follows (Rs. crores):

	Reserves held in India	Reserves held in England	Currency notes in govt. treasuries
Gold	24·37	8·34	3·95
Silver	65·56		
Govt. securities	68·07		

of the present century which registered a sudden increase in the volume of circulation. A peculiar feature of this period was the gradual narrowing of the gap which had previously existed between Calcutta and Bombay on the one hand and the rest of India's capital cities on the other. The proportionate share, for example, of Lahore and Calcutta in 1871 was 1 to 8. Fifty years later this difference was reduced, and in 1921 the corresponding figure stood at 1 to 3.4. The gradual infiltration of capital at provincial and local levels effected corresponding changes in the people's habits of spending and saving through banks. It meant increasing capital formation and the growth of the money-based classes in society. Doubtless this growth was slow. But even when it increased in speed, it could not keep pace with the rise in population, especially in the period after 1921.

INDIAN INDUSTRIAL INTEREST

Indian capitalist interest in modern industry developed more rapidly in Bombay than in Calcutta where because of European dominance Bengali business men operated more or less as brokers and junior partners rather than independent financiers and industrialists. Accounting for the industrial superiority of Bombay the *Report* of the Indian Industrial Commission, 1916–18, commented:

If the cause be sought, some indication may be found in the fact that Indians have held a large and important share in the trade of Bombay since the city first came into English hands. The Mahomedans of the west coast, especially, traded by sea with the Persian Gulf, Arabia and East Africa from much earlier times. The Parsees and Hindus from the northern Bombay coast districts are recorded at the beginning of the British occupation, as taking, with the Mahomedan sects of Khojas, Memons and Bohras a most important share in the trade of the port as contractors, merchants, financiers and shipbuilders, and have throughout shown themselves little, if at all, inferior to the English in enterprise, and usually in command of more capital.[51]

When, after the introduction of the first factory in Bombay in 1851,[52] the number of cotton mills increased, the Bombay Presi-

---

[51] Para 102; see also para. 135.   [52] See above, p. 117.

dency, and especially the island of Bombay and Ahmedabad, maintained the lead. Cawnpore in the United Provinces came next in order of importance. There Indians dominated the industry in the same way as they did in Bombay.

In his *Structure of Indian Industries* (p. 281) Dr. M. M. Mehta has made a statistical study of certain Indian business communities in relation to specific industries. He shows that right up to 1911 the British played a major part in India's industrial activity, except in its western sector where the Parsis, Jews, and Gujarati Hindus held the ground successfully:

A group of 15 Managing Agents controlled and managed 189 industrial units in 1911, 93 of which were controlled and managed by the 'Big Five' Managing Agency Houses of Calcutta, viz., Messrs. Andrew Yule, Bird, Shaw Wallace, Duncan and Begg, Dunlop and Company, all of which were foreign owned and operated. With the exception of Tatas, there was no Indian Managing house which controlled or managed more than 5 industrial units. In the Eastern Sector, the only Indian firm which deserves mention was that of Messrs. N. C. Sirkar and Company which managed five big collieries and which had on its Board of Directors a large number of foreign directors. In the Western Sector, however, a large number of Indian Managing Agents mostly belonging to the Jewish, Parsee and Gujarati community were just budding in. Prominent among these enterprising Indian industrialists were Sassoons, Khataus, Cowasjis, Thackerseys, Jeejeebhoys and Wadias.

Foreign interest was not less strong in the western sector, but it is significant to note that it held a virtual monopoly of eastern trade and industry, especially of Bengal, where British and Scottish interests had an almost exclusive control of tea, jute, and coal. Of the 40 jute mills in 1911, Messrs. Bird and Andrew Yule managed and controlled as many as 13; and together with Shaw Wallace they held as many as 37 of the 75 collieries, commanding Rs. 2.31 crores of the total paid-up capital of Rs. 5.01 crores. In the tea industry 10 managing agents controlled and managed 74 companies holding a total paid-up capital of Rs. 255.68 lakhs. Of the 10, only 4 managed 42 companies owning Rs. 148.46 lakhs. The following table, based on Mehta's study, gives an idea of how business came to be increasingly controlled and managed by Indians since 1911, and especially since the repatriation of British capital from the 1930's on:

Industrial Control by Community

	No. of companies			No. of directors		
	1911	*1931*	*1951*	*1911*	*1931*	*1951*
British	282	416	382	652	1,335	865
Parsis	15	25	19	96	261	149
Gujaratis	3	11	17	71	166	232
Jews	5	9	3	17	13	—
Muslims	—	10	3	24	70	66
Bengalis	8	5	20	48	170	320
Marwaris	—	6	96	6	146	618
Mixed control	28	28	79	102	121	372
Total	341	510	619	1,016	2,282	2,622

An analysis of this table reveals that of the Indian communities the outstanding rise in recent decades was that of the Marwaris. The Parsis, Gujaratis, and Bengalis were ahead of them in 1911 and as late as 1931. The Parsis dominated the cotton textile industry, and one of their number, the Tatas, started the Iron and Steel Works at Jamshedpur in 1907 and the hydro-electric works in Bombay in 1910. The Gujaratis and the Marwaris, however, overtook the Parsis in the cotton industry in the 1930's. The most important of these were the Birlas, Juggilal Kamlapat, Ruia, Ambalal Sarabhai, Kasturbhai Lalbhai, and some others. Of these, the Birlas, who had just begun to emerge in the early part of the 1920's, rose to prominence a decade later. As Dr. Mehta states (p. 311):

The Marwari Group, which came last of all, is now occupying a most dominant position, their most recent acquisition[s] have been the outright purchase of E. D. Sassoon United Mills (total assets: Rs.8 crores) by Messrs. Agarwal and Company; Century Spinning and Manufacturing Company (total assets: Rs.5 crores) by Messrs. Birla Bros., Ltd.; Svadeshi Cotton Mills Company, Ltd. (total assets: 5½ crores) by Messrs. Jaipuria Brothers, Limited; and Sir Shapurji Broacha Mills, Limited, and Madhouji Cotton Mills Limited by Dalmia-Jain Group.

He shows that 'about four-fifths of the productive capacity in the Cotton-Mill Industry of Ahmedabad and over half of the productive capacity in the Cotton-Mill Industry of Bombay is now controlled by Gujrati and Marwari Managing Agency firms'.

The Marwari group came to predominate in the sugar mill industry as well. Before the protective tariff of 1931 the only managing agency firm interested in sugar was that of Messrs. Begg Sutherland and Company. The Marwaris entered it after the grant of protection, and so did the Punjabis. The most important of the new groups included the Narangs, the Birlas, the Dalmia-Jains, and the Karamchand Thappars. The British have in recent years extended their activity in such new fields as rubber and oil, electricity and engineering, branches of industry which require a high degree of technical knowledge and skill.

INCREASING SIZE OF INDUSTRIAL EMPLOYMENT

This rough indication of the manner and extent of India's economic development has shown that although it was slow and uneven, it was steady and sizeable. But socially speaking, it did not bring about a corresponding increase in the size of industrial employment, especially at the directional level. The reason, as has been said, was that modern capital and skill, which were for so long foreign, were controlled and managed in a highly integrated manner; and even when Indians took over the system from the British, they needed to effect little or no change. Historically, the expansion of business in India had proceeded from the top downwards, not from the bottom upwards. An Indian plutocracy had even earlier formed a separate caste by itself, and those who carried on business under them did so as their subordinate and servile agents, not as free merchants. The managing agency system fitted in with this background of Indian development. A managing agency firm, Indian or European, similarly held the bulk interest in the several industrial units whose administration it controlled by a system of multiple directorship. Capital remained concentrated under both. Indeed the directors of Indian industries were persons who must generally be classified as members of the upper rather than the middle classes; for the industrial power of the country was in the hands of a few persons only. On the basis of certain specific industries Mehta (p. ix), for example, shows that about 100 persons held as many as 1,700 directorships of important concerns; 860 of these were held by 30 persons, and of these 30 10 only held between them as many as 400 directorships.

The managing-agency system, however, must also be viewed from a different angle. Its financial and administrative integration made for economy, which created an ever-increasing surplus employed in the expansion of industry. Instead of clogging, the system contributed to the formation and flow of capital by establishing more and more companies and expanding those already in existence. These increased the avenues and scope of industrial employment. Every industrial unit, with its legal and functional independence, maintained a separate staff. What did not increase proportionately with the increase in the number of separate companies was the number of directors; but the supervisory, technical, and other subordinate staffs grew with the growth of industrial units. The system checked the growth of directors who were in most cases proprietors themselves, not of the managers of separate establishments. However, even the number of directors was, by Mehta's own computation, greater than that of the companies; while the former increased from 1,016 in 1911 to 2,622 in 1951, the latter rose in the same period from 341 to 619.

The industrial census of India first held in 1911 recorded the number of persons employed in direction, supervision, and clerical work in all industrial establishments with 20 or more persons using mechanical power or otherwise. The industrial census of 1921 also recorded the increase that had occurred in the previous decade in the size of industrial employment covering directional, supervisory, and clerical elements. This increase is evident from the table given below.

Nos. Employed in Direction, Supervision, and Clerical Work

	1911	*1921*
European and Anglo Indians	9,437	14,671
Indians	60,794	108,573
Total	70,231	123,244

Source: Census of India: 1911, vol. i., pt. 2, table 15 (p. 332); 1921, vol. i., subsidiary table 8 (p. 292).

Although the number is infinitesimally small when compared with the total population of the country, the European and Anglo-Indian elements held most of the superior positions in Indian industry, especially in the manufacturing and constructional fields. Indians in the main occupied subordinate and clerical situations, Europeans and Anglo-Indians managerial and technical ones. The following table gives an idea of their relative distribution in certain specific industries:

Nos. Employed in Direction, Supervision, and Clerical Work
(in manufactures and construction)

	1911		*1921*	
	Europeans and Anglo-Indians	*Indians*	*Europeans and Anglo-Indians*	*Indians*
Manufacture of spec. products like tea, coffee, indigo, and rubber	1,627	10,346	3,160	10,044
Textiles and connected industries	1,426	18,597	2,184	28,033
Metal industries	1,243	3,886	2,054	9,183
Transport and communications	1,302	4,155	1,814	12,675

Source: As for previous table.

The table clearly shows that Europeans and Anglo-Indians were predominant in the manufacture of special products; in the metal industries, including arms factories, iron foundries, iron and steel works, machinery and engineering works, mints and public works; and in the construction of means of transport and communications, such as bicycle and motor-car works, railway workshops and shipyards, telegraph and postal workshops, coach-building factories and tramway workshops. By 1921, except in the manufacture of special products, which declined in so far as indigo was concerned, Indians (Hindus and Muhammadans) had begun to make steady progress, and their proportionate share in metal industries as well as in transport and communications indicated a rising trend. The following table, however, shows that Europeans and Anglo-Indians continued to exercise a virtual monopoly of the higher posts in the Railway Department:

Railway Employment by Community

	Europeans and Anglo-Indians		Indians	
	1921	*1931*	*1921*	*1931*
Officers	1,315	1,423	262	776
Subordinates above Rs. 75 p.m.	12,056	6,598	19,985	13,571
Subordinates between Rs. 20–75 p.m.	3,678	9,347*	233,416	242,073
Subordinates under Rs. 20 p.m.	741	632	411,176	497,639
Total	17,790	18,000	664,839	754,059

* Subordinates in this year were between Rs. 30–75 and under Rs. 30.

Source: Census of India: 1921, vol. i, pt. 1, subsid. table 8, p. 288; *1931*, vol. i, pt. 1, subsid. table 6, p. 316.

Thus the upper and middle-class appointments in the railways were held for the most part by Europeans and Anglo-Indians who had a monopoly of all posts of officers' rank in 1921. Ten years later the Indian element in that rank more or less trebled. Even so, Europeans and Anglo-Indians held 65 per cent. of these higher posts although they constituted only 0.05 per cent. of the total population of India in that year.[52] They also occupied nearly one-third of the subordinate posts carrying Rs. 75–250 a month.

The Irrigation Department ranked next to the railways in

[52] See *Census of India, 1931*, vol. i, pt. 1, p. 625. It included Armenians and other foreigners besides European British subjects. The Anglo-Indians were returned as Europeans (ibid. p. 426). The European British subjects in India, according to census returns, were as follows:

	M.	F.		M.	F.
1901	112,687	42,004	1921	119,149	46,336
1911	134,950	50,484	1931	110,137	45,418

point of European and Anglo-Indian predominance, as shown below:

Lower and Upper Middle-Class Appointments
(in the Irrigation Dept.)

	Europeans and Anglo-Indians		Indians	
	1921	*1931*	*1921*	*1931*
Officers	229	263	535	841
Upper Subord.	12	25	12,000	1,428
Lower Subord.	11	8	5,542	2,528
Clerks	36	21	5,086	6,703
Total	288	317	12,363	11,500

Source: *Census of India: 1921,* vol. i, pt. 1, subsid. table 7; *1931,* vol. i, pt. 1, p. 317.

In the Posts and Telegraphs Department, Europeans and Anglo-Indians figured dominantly in the telegraphs and the scientific and technical section of the department. They were prominent in the higher posts such as those of superintendent, deputy, and assistant superintendent, holding nearly one-third of the total number of such posts. Indians were in the main predominant as postmasters and deputy postmasters, stationmasters and clerks.[53]

In transport or communications Europeans and Anglo-Indians predominated in such higher posts as required applied knowledge and technical skill, for they were the first to enter these fields. Hindus or Muhammadans came in later. Until late in the 1880's even lower and upper subordinate posts in the Public Works Department were for the most part occupied by Europeans and Anglo-Indians. Indians, however, entered the railways and public works as contractors. The total number of European and Anglo-Indian contractors in the Railway and Irrigation Departments was in 1921 only 38 against the total of 11,603 Indian contractors.[54] The rise of Indian elements in the field of applied sciences and

[53] *Census of India, 1921,* vol. i, pt. 1, subsid. table 7, pp. 290–1; *1931,* vol. i, pt. 1, subsid. table 6, pp. 318–19.

[54] Ibid. p. 228.

technology in fact belongs to recent decades, except in Bombay where the development of the cotton mill industry necessitated an early advancement of technical education.

Summary

Modern capitalism in India thus emerged from the import of foreign capital and skill. It began as part of the imperialist economy in that its early aim was to produce raw materials in India to feed Britain's industry. But the development of agricultural produce did two things: it created out of the export of agricultural produce a trade surplus which paid for the construction of railways and other reproductive public works; and secondly, it paid for the import of capital goods and machinery which began locally to manufacture the raw materials so developed. This pattern of things continued until after the experience of the First World War there began a new era in which the Government introduced a policy of protection and direct participation in the industrial development of the country.

IX

Land Policy and Changes

THE policy of the East India Company in securing the interests of the middle-class resident proprietors and cultivators and in recording property rights and protecting them by the rule of law has been described in Chapter V. Its effect was prejudicial to the interests of European settlers as well as big Indian landholders. On the termination of the Company's rule in 1858, however, there came a change in favour of both. The motive was in the main economic and political.

LAND POLICY LINKED WITH *LAISSEZ-FAIRE*

The economic objective of the new land policy was to remove the old fetters on European settlement and to introduce such easy conditions of land tenure as might stimulate 'the employment of British capital, skill and enterprise in the development of the material resources of India'.[1] Land policy became part of the total imperial policy designed to develop agricultural produce to feed Britain's industry. In a dispatch of 31 December 1858, the Secretary of State for India stressed this object and advised the Government of India favourably to consider the several applications of persons 'who, either on behalf of themselves or of Companies' they proposed to establish were 'desirous of obtaining grants of unoccupied land for the purpose of carrying on the cultivation of Cotton and of other exportable products for the supply of manufacturers in this Country'.[2]

On the basis of the waste as well as cultivable lands available at the disposal of the Government, the Secretary of State for India in Council adopted by a resolution of 17 October 1871 rules govern-

[1] I.O. Rev. Desp. to Ind., no. 2 of 31 Dec. 1858, para. 8. [2] Ibid. para. 1.

ing the disposal of such lands. In drawing up these rules the Council was guided by a desire to promote the attainment in India of 'a complete ownership in the soil free of all demand by the State on account of Land Revenue, so far as this may be done without injury to the interests of the State and without detriment to the rights of third parties'.[3] Under this principle applications for the sale of unassessed government lands were to be granted in perpetuity, subject to no enhancement of land revenue. The waste lands so granted were to be redeemable at the grantee's option by a payment in one sum equal in value to the revenue redeemed, so that the land might thenceforward be permanently free of all demand for land revenue.[4] The old rule obliging the grantee to cultivate or clear any specific portion of land within any specific time was done away with. The disposal or development of a grant was left 'entirely to the owner's judgment and self interest'. A maximum limit of 3,000 acres was fixed to the size of all grants, and it was further laid down that 'the price to be paid for unassessed land should not exceed Rupees $2\frac{1}{2}$ per acre for uncleared land, or Rupees 5 per acre for land unencumbered with jungle, subject to deduction of area for swamps or unculturable land'.[5]

These rules were drawn up in conformity with the desire of the settlers who wanted land in fee simple, with a grant of land in perpetuity 'either gratuitously or in consideration of an immediate payment under which the land should be for ever discharged from all demands on account of land revenue'.[6] The settlers got what they wanted. Nevertheless the effect of the Company's policy remained. The lands granted to the settlers were not the lands occupied by Indian proprietors or cultivators. They were un-

[3] Coll. to Rev. Desp., 9 July 1862, para 4.

[4] In their Despatch no. 6 of 6 May 1857 (para. 14) the Court of Directors for the first time waived their objection to settlement in perpetuity and sanctioned 'as an experiment the alienation in perpetuity, to any person of substance and respectability, of land belonging to the government upon condition of the application of a certain amount of capital to the cultivation of the most valuable products of the soil'. But even here the Court 'expressed an opinion that easy terms of long lease, such as for a period of twenty or thirty years, might be sufficient at present to attract British capitalists' (Rev. Desp. 31 Dec. 1858, para. 5). The Company had in principle been opposed to a permanent settlement which the India Council now advocated.

[5] Resol. on subject of Waste Lands, no. 3264, 17 Oct. 1861, encl. in Coll. to Rev. Desp., no. 10, 1862.

[6] Rev. Desp., 31 Dec. 1858, para 3.

assessed waste lands in which no right of proprietorship or of exclusive occupancy was known to exist at the time of their grant or in former times. They were situated for the most part in the hilly and forest tracts of Assam, Sunderban, Dehra Dun, Kumaun, and Garhwal in the north, and in Mysore and Nilgiri in the south. The growth of the plantation industry in these areas benefited both India and Britain. The application of European capital, skill, and enterprise effected considerable improvement in the agriculture, communications, and commerce of the surrounding country.

POLITICAL ASPECT OF LAND POLICY

The political aspect of British land policy aimed at creating a landed middle class in India who from motives of self-interest might support the British in the development of the country's material resources. The grant of waste lands in perpetuity, redeemable at the discretion of a grantee, was therefore not confined to European settlers. In his Revenue Dispatch of 31 December 1858 the Secretary of State, Lord Stanley, made it clear that in any recommendations for the grant of waste lands or for the redemption of land revenue the Government of India was to be 'especially careful not to confine them to such as may be calculated for the exclusive advantage of European Settlers, and which cannot be equally participated in by the Agricultural community generally'.[7]

The redemption of the land revenue signified an absolute right in the property redeemed. When applied to the grant of waste lands, it gave encouragement to agricultural development, but when extended generally to the estates of Indian landholders, it involved serious loss to the public finances. Stanley was not unaware of this.

But the political results of such a change [he observed], cannot be overlooked. The fortunes of the Zemindar who has been allowed to extinguish his fixed annual liabilities by a single payment are from thenceforth still more intimately connected than they are at present with those of the British Government. The immunity from taxation ... renders his loyalty a matter of prudence and self-interest.[8]

This obviously clashed with the trend of the past fifty years of the Company's rule which had in effect reduced the power of big

[7] Ibid. para 8.   [8] Ibid. para 7.

landholders by recognizing the rights of the middle-class landed gentry, including also a body of joint proprietors and resident peasants, many of whom belonged to upper castes and possessed intelligence, public spirit, and enterprise. But since its system of periodical settlement of the land revenue led to the increase of demand from time to time, Stanley considered it responsible for breeding poverty. He believed that if the public demand were to be limited and the zamindar allowed to redeem the land tax on the basis of the existing rate of assessment, this might encourage the accumulation of agricultural capital.

Sir Charles Wood agreed with his predecessor, Stanley, but he preferred a general permanent settlement to the proposed redemption of the land revenue, which in effect also meant a settlement of land in perpetuity. In his Revenue Dispatch of 9 July 1862 he affirmed that 'Her Majesty's Government entertain no doubt of the political advantages which would attend a permanent settlement'. He added:

The security, and, it may almost be said, the absolute creation of property in the soil which will flow from limitation in perpetuity of the demands of the State on the owners of land, cannot fail to stimulate or confirm their sentiments of attachment and loyalty to the Government by whom so great a boon has been conceded, and upon whose existence its permanency will depend.[9]

This political stress in British land policy was understandable. The industrial basis of support in society was still lacking; and even if that element emerged at a future date, it might be an eventual competitor rather than a friendly co-operator. As for the new educated professions, including even the public services, they were far too limited in number and were not rooted in the people. Although not exclusive of landed interest, they did not command the respect commanded by the ownership of a big landed estate. It was not unnatural, therefore, to seek a basis of support in the class which had the virtual monopoly of land. 'It is most desirable', Wood observed, 'that facilities should be given for the gradual growth of a middle class connected with the land.'[10] By these facilities he meant permission to be extended to landholders for the redemption of land revenue in the areas already settled perman-

[9] I.O. Coll. to Rev. Desp., no. 14 of 9 July 1862, para 47.   [10] Ibid. para 48.

ently, and the introduction of a permanent settlement in those where no such settlement already existed. The increased

security of fixed property and comparative freedom from the interference of the fiscal officers of the Government [he pointed out], will tend to create that class which although composed of various races and creeds will be peculiarly bound to the British rule; whilst under proper regulations, the measure will conduce to the improvement of the general resources of the empire.[11]

This renewal of emphasis on the creation of a landed middle class differed in its approach from Cornwallis's partiality to zamindars. Then as now, it is true, the zamindars were to be a landed middle class in the sense that they were situated between the ruling class and the peasants and that they would act as rural capitalists by assisting the British in the development of material resources. The recognition in the intervening period of the separate rights of subordinate proprietors and resident cultivators as well as the development of free trade made all the difference. While the necessity of securing indigenous support in the commercialization of agriculture was felt with much greater intensity, the interest of the subordinate agricultural classes could not be overlooked in any attempt to make zamindars a junior ally of the British. The Crown could not undo the work of the Company. Stanley and Wood desired the growth of a landed middle class, but 'without dispossessing the peasant proprietors and occupiers'.[12] The latter clearly pointed out that in spite of their comparative poverty many of the peasant proprietors and resident cultivators possessed 'great intelligence, public spirit, and social influence',[13] which they could best use in the improvement of their condition if the public demands on their land were limited.

The post-Mutiny concept of a landed middle class was thus richer in its economic content and broader in social basis. Wood's declared policy was to base British rule broadly 'on the contentment of the agricultural classes' who formed 'the great bulk of the population'. Its very security, he emphasized, depended on these classes. 'If they are prosperous', he argued, 'any casual outbreak on the part of other classes or bodies of men is much less likely to become an element of danger, and the military force, and its conse-

[11] Ibid. para 7.   [12] Ibid. para 48.   [13] Ibid. para 48.

quent expense, may be regulated accordingly.'[14] The Secretary of State therefore wished to limit the public demand, so that the proprietors of land might be induced to invest capital in agricultural development, beneficial both to India and to Britain.

In a minute recorded separately, Sir John Lawrence, who later became Governor-General and Viceroy, supported the case for a general permanent settlement for much the same reason.

I recommend a perpetual settlement [he declared], because I am persuaded that however much the country has of late years improved, its resources will be still more rapidly developed by the limitation of the Government demand. Such a measure will still further encourage the investment of money in the land, and will give still greater security to the land revenue itself, which, in years of great calamity, occurring every now and then, has suffered largely, though the loss has been more or less of a temporary character. It is also very desirable that facilities should exist for the gradual growth of a middle class in India, connected with the land, without dispossessing the present yeomen and peasant proprietors. There are many men of much intelligence, spirit, and social influence among those classes, who are yet so poor that they find it difficult to maintain a decent appearance. . . . What is really wanted is, to give the intelligent, the thrifty, and the enterprising among them, the opportunity of improving their own condition by the exercise of such qualities, and this can be best done by limiting the public demand on the land. When such men acquire property, and are in a thriving state, they are almost certain to be well affected to the Government.

Like Wood, Lawrence stressed that 'it is on the contentment of the agriculturists, who form the real physical power in the country, that the security of British rule, to a large extent, depends. If they are prosperous the military force may be small, but not otherwise.'[15]

The concept of an Indian middle class connected with the land was thus not exclusive. It included the intelligent, public-spirited, and enterprising section of all such classes as engaged in agriculture. The superior class of zamindars was, of course, uppermost in the minds of the new policy makers. The proposed permanent settlement was to benefit that class most. But the benefit that might

[14] I.O. Coll. to Rev. Desp., no. 14 of 9 July 1862, para. 48.
[15] *Dissents . . . placed on record by members of the Council of India on . . . sale of Waste Lands, &c.*, p. 14 (in I.O. Rev. Desp., vol. 10, 1862).

arise from the limitation of the public demand was to be extended to the other agricultural classes also under proper regulations. It would be erroneous therefore to suppose that the India Council favoured what might be called a feudal-imperialist alliance. The judicial administration and revenue laws of the East India Company had already weakened the aristocracy and been to some extent responsible for the Mutiny of 1857, which was an expression of feudal revolt though national in magnitude. A permanent settlement, it was believed, might go a long way to restore the confidence of the agricultural classes, a measure which the Council of India considered expedient from both economic and political points of view. But to assume that it was intended to leave the determination of subordinate agricultural interests to the mercy of their overlord would be far from the truth. The new land policy formed an integral part of the policy of *laissez-faire*. Its object was to create, by conferring free property rights, a composite landed middle class who might participate in the development of the imperialist economy and form a contented and stable social element to support British rule in India.

The proposal, however, did not materialize. It fell through on financial grounds. The Indian economy had become seriously strained by the Mutiny and a radical change in the tax structure of the country was called for. The Government of India introduced income-tax, but big business and the professions were both loath to pay anything towards the relief of the public exchequer and it was soon abolished. The abnormal necessities of the Government had forced it to levy an import duty of 10 per cent. *ad valorem* upon the cotton manufactures of Britain. The opposition of the Lancashire manufacturers was understandable, but even the urban classes in India opposed it since they resented the rise in prices which it naturally caused. Who was then to pay for the increasing cost of administration in India? The only reply was that the agricultural classes must continue to bear the burden. Speaking against the proposal for a permanent settlement, one of the members of the Council of India said: 'Can it be the part of wisdom to cut off with our own hand a stream of revenue flowing, as it may be said, spontaneously into the Exchequer with the sanction of immemorial usage?'[16] He preferred the established periodical settlement under

[16] Ibid. p. 5 (Dissent by R. D. Mangles).

which the rate of assessment was increased not only with the increase of productivity but also in keeping with rising prices.

The proposal for a permanent settlement was thus killed before being put into effect. In his Revenue Despatch of 9 July 1862 the Secretary of State added a proviso that 80 per cent. of the cultivable area must be brought under cultivation before a permanent settlement could be introduced. This shelved the issue for a time. Then came the success of canal irrigation in the North-Western Provinces, which set the current against the expediency of a permanent settlement in those provinces. In a dispatch of 17 March 1866 the Secretary of State, Lord De Grey, proposed that a rule be laid down

excluding from permanent settlement all estates the assets of which would when canal irrigation shall have been carried to the extent at present contemplated, exceed, in the opinion of the officers of the settlement and the Irrigation Department, the existing assets in a proportion exceeding 20 per cent.[17]

Since the general tendency among civil servants was opposed to the extension of the Bengal pattern of revenue settlement, the Board of Revenue at Allahabad generalized the terms of this rule so as to exclude from the permanent settlement all estates 'the assets of which have not reached 80 per cent. of the amount which they are susceptible of attaining under a full development of the available means of cultivation and irrigation'.[18] This generalization in effect excluded all estates which had not reached the potential limits of exploitation and which might do so by canal irrigation, wells, water-courses, embankments, manuring, and similar means.

The fulfilment of these preliminary conditions led to the creation of a separate Department of Revenue, Agriculture, and Commerce, with A. O. Hume as Secretary in 1872. This turned the tide in favour of the cultivating classes. A friend of the peasants, Hume realized the necessity of collecting enough agricultural statistics before a permanent settlement could be justified. Lord Lytton abolished this separate department, but the findings of the Famine Commission of 1881 strengthened the case of the cultivating classes. A. P. MacDonnell, an able Bengal civil servant, pointed

---

[17] I.O. Rev. Desp. to India, no. 15 of 1867, para 1.   [18] Ibid. para. 3.

out in a memorandum he produced in 1883 the necessity of agricultural statistics as the basis of a sound land policy. The Government of India accordingly established a regular system of statistics
in 1884 which it has maintained ever since. The issue of a permanent settlement became for all practical purposes a dead letter.

LAND POLICY IN OUDH

The intermediate proprietary classes in Oudh, however, stood in
a different predicament. The position of the great bulk of resident
cultivators was even worse. There was no fixity of their tenures.
The big landholders, known locally as taluqdars, maintained a
regular band of armed retainers who kept the peasantry in a state
of servility. Before the annexation of Oudh in 1856, 'no tenure was a
fixity, and a Taluqdar who possessed himself of a county to-day,
might be driven from every village to-morrow. Such was not the
case, however, under the British. A title once declared and recognised
was as immutable as the Government itself.'[19] Indeed the rule of
might operated in Oudh where no person, not even a weak taluqdar,
could be sure of his position against a superior overlord.

As for the low-caste tenants-at-will, they were no better than
chattels. 'The Chamár, Lodh, Kurmi, and all inferior castes',
wrote a military officer, 'are the prey of all, caught at every hour of
the day or night, made use of as beasts of burthen, beaten and
abused, treated as if incapable of feeling pain or humiliation, never
remunerated, but often deprived of the scanty clothing they may
possess.'[20]

Indeed the Governor-General, Dalhousie, viewed the annexation of Oudh as an act of liberation. The instructions which his
Government issued in a letter of 4 February 1856[21] about land
settlement in the annexed province was imbued with a spirit of
liberalism. The province was formed into a chief commissioner-
ship under Sir James Outram, who was advised to proceed with a

[19] Gubbins, quoted in H. C. Irwin, *The Garden of India* (1880), pp. 182–3.
Martin Gubbins was Financial Commissioner appointed on the annexation of
Oudh in 1856.
[20] Ibid. p. 153.
[21] Dalhousie to Outram, 4 Feb. 1856, in *Papers regarding Oudh Proprietary
Rights &c.* (Cal. 1865), pp. 1–2.

summary settlement to be made village by village with the parties in actual possession. As in the North-Western Provinces, the Government instructed settlement officers to deal with resident cultivators and village zamindars rather than with absentee taluqdars and farmers of revenue. The object was not to exclude the taluqdars, but to safeguard the rights of occupancy tenants and village zamindars who constituted the bulk of the middle-class agricultural interest. The Government wanted to protect them against the tyrannical conduct of a taluqdar or an interloper who reduced them to subjection. Of 23,543 villages included in taluqs at the close of the Nawab's rule in 1855, 13,640 with a revenue of Rs. 35,06,519 were settled with the taluqdars themselves. Only 9,903 villages with a revenue of Rs. 32,08,319 were settled with persons other than taluqdars. What the settlement officers did was to make the settlement with village proprietors and resident cultivators in the first instance; but where there were no such proprietors, they settled with the taluqdars.

The taluqdars, however, resented the recognition of the occupancy rights of tenants and the proprietary rights of village zamindars, a class of subordinate proprietors who held villages in joint proprietorship. They did not scruple, therefore, to exploit in their favour any disaffection against the Government arising from its measures of social reform which, though liberal in principle, offended the religious susceptibilities of the people. The abolition of the Religious Disability Act of 1850, the Widows' Remarriage Reform Act of 1856, and the suspicion aroused in Bihar against the misunderstood object of English education, especially by its dominant landed interest which belonged for the most part to Muhammadans from pre-British times, have already been referred to. The village settlement of Oudh followed in the context of these measures which caused disaffection. The taluqdars of Oudh consequently joined the Mutiny which broke out in Lucknow on 30 May 1857,[22] and even petty zamindars and village folk make common cause with their taluqdars against what they characterized as the Christian Government of the country.

The Mutiny was essentially a feudal revolt, but the participation of under-proprietors and common folk, though arising from religi-

---

[22] See Forrest, *History of the Indian Mutiny*, i. 261, indicating the bearing of the revenue policy of Government on the Mutiny.

ous considerations, gave it a false colouring and it appeared to be a national revolt, with the taluqdars at the head of a large following of what looked like their own men. This influenced the Governor-General, Lord Canning, in the formulation of a pro-taluqdar land policy as a surer means of re-establishing British authority as well as preventing the occurrence of another mutiny. The aim of this policy was to put an end to the system of village settlement; to make the subordinate tenures contingent upon the performance of certain specific services to an overlord, and to recognize the taluqdars as of ancient origin, cherished and rooted in the soil of the country. It was a restoration of the principle of personal service on the part of under-tenure holders, a feudal institution which the British had long since abolished in the North-Western Provinces by a recognition of their separate rights and the transfer of their loyalty from their overlord to the state.

The experience of the Mutiny therefore emphasized the political aspect of land policy. It suggested the expediency of encouraging European settlement as pockets of local influence, and of limiting the public demands by an extension of the Permanent Settlement to other parts of the country, especially in the North-Western Provinces and Oudh where the mutineers had caused heavy losses to British lives and property. The proposal to create a middle class connected with the land was to a large extent the result of this experience. The benefit of this policy, if executed, would have gone essentially to the class of large landholders. But since the separate rights of village zamindars and occupancy tenants had become well-established in law under the Company's rule, these remained intact, except in Oudh where the taluqdars regained their old powers over subordinate proprietors and occupants.

Under the arrangement made in Oudh after the restoration of peace in the winter of 1858, however, it was provided that the taluqdars in the exercise of their powers would in future be subject to any measure which the Government might think proper to take for the purpose of protecting the inferior zamindars or occupants from extortion. When he became Viceroy in 1864 Lawrence directed an inquiry into the occupancy rights of tenants. But while reporting the results of his investigation the Chief Commissioner of Oudh concluded 'that no length of occupancy maintained by a ryot under the Native Government gave him a right to hold his land against the will of his zamindar'.[23] The Government of India nevertheless intervened, and its intervention led to the Oudh Rent Act XIX of 1868. This Act benefited the village zamindars more than occupancy tenants. The former became in effect a class of peasant proprietors, but so far as occupancy tenants were concerned, the Act placed on formal and legal footing the taluqdar's power to evict them at will. This power to obliterate occupancy rights became an instrument which the taluqdars used in the arbitrary raising of rents.[24]

The Oudh Rent Act XII of 1886 was designed to protect statutory tenants against arbitrary eviction, but did not give them the privileged rights which the village zamindars and occupancy tenants exercised in the North-Western Provinces under the old laws of the East India Company. The difference persisted. In 1891, for example, while the privileged occupancy tenants held 33.1 per cent. of the total area in the North-Western Provinces, their counterpart in Oudh held only 1.4 per cent. Proprietary tenures, on the other hand, occupied 22.9 per cent. of the total area in the North-Western Provinces against 10.8 per cent. in Oudh, where the percentage of tenants-at-will amounted to 82 against 34 in the North-Western Provinces.[25]

PLIGHT OF THE PEASANTRY IN BIHAR

The reopening of the question of a permanent settlement affected the peasantry in Bihar more seriously than elsewhere. Though it made no progress beyond the stage of correspondence and exchange of views, it lent support and added strength to the claims of the zamindars in a province where, in the absence of education among the lower orders of society, they could indulge in rapacity without fear of punishment or public opinion. The report of the Indian Famine Commission of 1881, for instance, pointed out that the people who ploughed and sowed in Bihar had no assurance of reaping the fruits of their industry. The rent law did impose

---

[23] Miller, *Condition of Agric. and Labouring Classes* (P.B. Coll. 220), para. 82.
[24] The notices of ejectment filed in Oudh increased from 23,600 in 1876, to 91,200 in 1882, when it was feared that the Government might take steps to protect tenants' rights (ibid. para. 83).
[25] Ibid. para. 85.

certain restrictions on proprietors, but it had practically been a dead letter.

Local officers too were of little or no help. They left proprietors free to commit illegal acts, for they did not want to run the risk of alienating them. That was the effect of reopening the question of permanent settlement, even though at the top level. One of the authors of a paper brought before the Commission commented:

When, as in Behar, the relations of landlord and tenant are those of a high-handed, unscrupulous proprietary class, breaking the law to increase their own illegal gains, on the one hand; and a tenantry, robbed of its rights through the negligence of their rulers and ground down under every form of oppression, on the other, it is absurd to talk about 'embittering' them. . . . The administration in Behar stands in the discreditable position of countenancing, and so abetting, notorious abuses for fear of the commotion which would ensue if the people knew their rights and were encouraged to assert them.[26]

What the Commission would have liked the local officers to do was to acquaint the people with their rights and encourage them to resist the illegal acts of proprietors.

This comment applied chiefly to the districts of Darbhanga and Muzaffarpur, but the district of Saran was no better. According to a report of its Subdivisional Officer, quoted in the same paper, about 600,000 of the poorer people of that district subsisted on only a rupee and four annas (about 2s. 6d.) each a month. More than half of this number had to remain satisfied with even less.[27]

The European indigo planters of Bihar were not less oppressive. The system of indigo plantation 'involved an amount of lawlessness and oppression, principally in the shape of illegal seizure and retention of land, and to a minor degree, in the shape of extorted agreements to cultivate, and of seizure of ploughs and cattle'.[28] The oppressive conduct of the Bihar planters attracted the notice of Sir Ashley Eden, the Lieutenant-Governor of Bengal, who ordered an inquiry but took no further action on an assurance

[26] App. 1, para. 9, p. 189. [27] Ibid. para 13 pp. 189–90.
[28] I.O. Coll. 14 to Rev. Desp. fr. Ind., no. 43 of 21 Dec. 1877, para. 4. This collection is significant in that it contains all the judicial and police papers connected with the oppressive proceedings of Bihar planters. These were produced in the course of the inquiry which Eden had ordered.

given to him by the Bihar Planters' Association formed in 1877 to regulate their internal affairs. Eden, however, prepared a scheme to modify the rent law which ultimately led to the introduction of the Bengal Tenancy Bill in 1882.

The immediate necessity for modifying the rent law of Bengal arose, as has been stated, from the state of extreme depression to which the tenants of the Darbhanga estate had been reduced. In Eden's words, they were 'tenants of the richest province in Bengal, yet the poorest and most wretched class that we find in the country'.[29] Darbhanga in fact formed part of the worst famine tract in Bihar. The income of the estate arose from the arbitrary raising of rent, which had increased considerably from the time of the Permanent Settlement. The Famine Commissioners ascertained that the subdivisions of Madhubani, Supaul, and Sitamarhi had been by far the worst sufferers in the famines of 1770, 1866, and 1874. A common cause was, of course, the cessation of monsoon rains, but more serious than that was their poverty which arose from the oppressive demands of the estate.

The Famine Commissioners were struck by the poor and helpless condition of the tenants of the Darbhanga estate, especially in the Alapur pargana of the Madhubani subdivision. A paper laid before the Commission stated:

The gross rental of that part of the Darbhanga estate that lies in the Alapur Pargana is four lakhs, the revenue is Rs. 1,810, i.e. less than 1/200th part of the rental. The Government outlay, apart from what was spent out of the estate, then under the Court of Wards, on the pargana in famine relief in 1874, was more than 2½ lakhs, or considerably more than the State has received from the pargana from the date of the permanent settlement up to the present day.

The author deplored the fact that the Raja of Darbhanga, who was allowed to enjoy all the proceeds of this estate except a tiny fraction (less than 1/200th), should have kept his people 'in a condition of such miserable poverty that a single crop failure plunges them into destitution, and that then the destitution, so occasioned, has to be relieved, in part at least, ... on a scale which swallows up

[29] See Collins's *Rep. Cadast. Survey Muzaffarpur*, 18 July 1887, para. 3 (in P.B. Coll. 268).

all the revenue which the State has received from the land for eighty years'.[30]

PRO-TENANT TRENDS

The helpless condition of the peasantry in Bihar thus called for interference on the part of the Government. Eden recommended in 1878 the introduction of an effective procedure to enable a tenant

to maintain his right of occupancy when acquired to hold his land subject to fixed condition of tenure, to be certified exactly of the amount which he would have to pay on it annually, to resist illegal distraint, illegal cesses, and illegal enhancements, and to have at hand a trustworthy record of demands and payments.[31]

This led to the appointment of a rent law commission in 1880 and the introduction of the Bengal Rent Bill in 1882.

In its original form the Bill provided that if a tenant had held any land continuously for twelve years, he would become a settled ryot with powers to transfer his land by sale. Any person holding land was in fact to be treated as a settled ryot unless otherwise proved. The Bill also provided against arbitrary rent increases, and went so far as to recommend that all rents should be limited to one-fifth of the gross produce of land. This gave rise to determined opposition and it became watered down as a result of compromise. It resulted in the Bengal Tenancy Act of 1885 which even in a diluted form became the first effective landmark in the history of tenancy legislation in Bengal.[32] Under one of its provisions the Act recommended the introduction of survey and settlement operations to form trustworthy records of rights, something which Eden had recommended in 1878. The first cadastral survey under this provision began in the district of Muzaffarpur in 1887.

The landholders as a class were solidly opposed to any extension of tenant rights, especially to the formation of land records through survey operations. Organized locally in associations of their own, they presented several memorials to the Government of Bengal, but these had no effect. Far from limiting the scope of inquiry and the

[30] Ind. Fam. Commission, 1881, *Report*, app. I, para. 4, p. 188.
[31] *Rep. Cadast. Survey Muzaffarpur*, para. 3, p. 15.
[32] See Northbrook Coll., I.O. MSS. Eur. C 144, v, no. 3.

formation of records to certain parts of Muzaffarpur, the Government of Bengal by a resolution of 9 November 1891 allowed the extension of cadastral survey to the districts of Darbhanga, Saran, Champaran, and such other parts of Muzaffarpur as yet remained to be surveyed. In a memorial of 15 September 1892, therefore, the British Indian Association of Bengal, the Bihar Landholders' Association, the Bhagalpur Landholders' Association, the Zamindars' Panchayat, and the Indian Property Association all joined together to represent their case to the Secretary of State for India in Council.[33]

But the scheme had already received the Secretary of State's approbation. In a letter of 24 December 1891 he had already advised the Government of India to go ahead with its execution. 'After a careful consideration of the subject', he wrote, 'I cordially concur with your Government in accepting the decision of the Bengal Government that a survey should be made and a record-of-rights should be prepared in North Bihar'.[34] The landholders failed to put the clock back. The operation of this plan was later extended to the whole of Bihar as well as to the districts of Bengal. The officer who tenaciously fought for tenant rights was Sir A. P. MacDonnell who was Lieutenant-Governor of Bengal at the time when the controversy was still going on. In a remarkable note of 20 September 1893 he traced the history of zamindari tenure from before the Permanent Settlement of 1793 and showed how in about three generations the income of the zamindars of North Bihar had increased more than eightfold, and that at the cost of the tenants. Macdonnell was in fact a tenants' man. But the zamindars lost because there was no justice in their case. They had more than discredited themselves in the past hundred years.

All that the Bihar Landholders' Association could do after this failure was to refuse to co-operate in the execution of the scheme by withholding the services of their *patwaris*, or village accountants, who kept the records and possessed the knowledge of local tenures. The Government withdrew its orders for the registration of *patwaris* and introduced a plan for training its own men; and when by a resolution of 21 August 1893, moved by Parmeshwar Narayen

<hr />

[33] See Bihar Cadast. Survey Corresp. (P.B. Coll. 268), pp. 135–42.
[34] Ibid. para. 9, p. 191. Sir A. P. Macdonnell's note on zamindars is in the second part of this correspondence.

Mahtha and Babu Ramdhari Sahai, the Tirhut Landholders' Association thanked the Bengal Government for the withdrawal of its orders, the Lieutenant-Governor replied saying that the work of the Government would go on in spite of the zamindars' *patwaris*.[35]

The landholders' case was however taken up by the Indian National Congress, a political body established in 1885 to represent the interests of educated Indians. It reopened the question of a permanent settlement and agitated for its extension to all parts of the country. The matter came up for reconsideration by Curzon, who after a detailed study of the papers connected with it came to the conclusion that the Permanent Settlement had done more harm than good to the economy of the country. By a resolution of his Government in 1902, therefore, he settled the question for all time.

Curzon in fact regarded the peasantry as the real people of India, silent and unable to voice its interest but possessed none the less of feelings and opinions which it was the duty of the Government to respect. In a farewell address to the Byculla Club in Bombay on 16 November 1905 he said of the peasant that he

should be the first and the final object of every Viceroy's regard. It is for him that we have twice reduced the salt-tax, that we remitted land revenue in two years amounting to nearly 2½ millions sterling; for him that we are assessing the land revenue at a progressively lower pitch and making its collection elastic. It is to improve his credit that we have created co-operative credit societies, so that he may acquire capital at easy rates, and be saved from the usury of the money-lender. . . . When I am vituperated by those who claim to speak for the Indian people, I feel no resentment and no pain. For I search my conscience, and I ask myself, who and what are the real Indian people; and I rejoice that it has fallen to my lot to do something to alleviate theirs, and that I leave them better than I found them.[36]

This trend continued in subsequent years. It led to peasant movements and finally to the abolition of zamindaris in free India, movements which were led by Indian socialists and peasant leaders. The officers of Government who had in the past represented the interests of tenants later found themselves handicapped by the success of the Indian middle classes in mobilizing peasants and workers against the British.

[35] Ibid. pp. 133–4.
[36] Curzon of Kedleston, *Lord Curzon in India* (1906), pp. 584–5.

MIDDLE-CLASS PROPRIETORS AND MONEY-LENDERS

Middle-Class Proprietors

The creation by law of property rights tended to liberate the peasant from his traditional dependence on the landlord. But owing to the neglect of rural education and the virtual absence of any organized rural credit system, the institution of free property benefited middle proprietors and money-lenders more than the tenants. The traditional landholders were a decaying class and the revenue laws of Government reduced them more and more. But the new moneyed classes, commercial or professional, with economic interests in land were proving themselves more oppressive to cultivators than the old zamindars, especially in Bengal where the literary or professional classes were interwoven with landed interests to a degree never attained in other provinces.

The kinds of tenancy which promoted the growth of middle proprietors and other middle-class landed interests in the North-Western Provinces were in the main four. The first category, recognized under Act XVIII of 1873, consisted of persons who in the permanently settled districts possessed a permanent transferable interest in land, intermediate between the proprietor of a *mahal* and the occupants, and at a fixed rent which had not changed from the time of the Permanent Settlement. The second type of tenancy related to a corresponding interest in the periodically settled districts of the North-Western Provinces, the holders of what was known as *si'r* land at a rate 25 per cent. less than the prevailing rent.[37] It was a category of what previously constituted joint proprietors or co-sharers who parted with their proprietary rights in *mahals* but held their *si'r* lands in such *mahals*, cultivating such lands themselves with their own stock or by means of hired labour. The third category included tenants with privileged rights. These had held their land at the same rate since Cornwallis's Permanent Settlement of the eastern districts. They were granted

---

[37] Act XVIII of 1873 defined *si'r* land as land continuously cultivated for twelve years by the proprietor himself with his own stock, or by his servants, or by hired labour. It also included land recognized by village custom as the special holding of a co-sharer, and treated as such in the distribution of profits or charges among co-sharers.

hereditary right of occupancy, and since such tenants were allowed to transfer their rights by sale, they were practically in the position of under-proprietors. They held their land at fixed rates of rent with sub-proprietary rights. The fourth kind consisted of occupancy tenants who enjoyed a hereditary right of occupancy on the condition of twelve years of continuous occupancy.[38]

In point of both income and social status the occupancy tenants were inferior to any of the first three categories of tenancy which formed peasant proprietorship. To the class of peasant proprietors must be added another class of petty zamindars or malguzars, as they were called in the Central Provinces. Together they constituted a landed middle class, engaged in the cultivation of their land, either with the help of their own stock and servants or by using the hired labour of low-caste men to whom they rented or otherwise let some portion of their land. Despite certain nominal differences this class of proprietors was 'virtually the same throughout the Madras and Bombay Presidencies and Berar, throughout almost all the Punjab, throughout perhaps the larger part of the North-West Provinces, and in a portion of Oudh'.[39] The patni and mukarrari tenures of Bengal and Bihar fell more or less into the same category. The only notable difference was that while in the permanently settled areas, especially in Bengal, increasing subinfeudation created a graduated layer of proprietary tenancy conducive to absentee landlordism, the general tendency elsewhere was to discourage such a phenomenon by limiting the power of transfer and mortgage.

The Famine Commissioners of 1881 reported that the classes of peasant proprietors and ordinary zamindars were by far the most prosperous of the agricultural classes. They were generally known for their thrift, and it was among their ranks that capital accumulated to some extent in the rural areas, although indebtedness existed among some of them. In some degree they were also involved in the Deccan agrarian riots of 1873. But the report of the

---

[38] In the *Directions to the Settlement Officers* drawn up by James Thomason, Lieut.-Governor of N.W.P. in 1849, he first expressed an opinion that a civil court should recognize a term of twelve years' proved occupancy as establishing a presumption in favour of a hereditary right. This view was incorporated by sect. 6 of Act X of 1859 under which a tenant with twelve years of proved occupancy was to be a statutory tenant.

[39] Ind. Fam. Commission, 1881, *Rep.*, app. 2, Q. 9, p. 30b.

Special Commission on these riots showed that indebtedness extended to only a third of the whole number in the Deccan.

Relatively speaking, however, the landed middle class of Bengal was better off; for according to a paper submitted to the Famine Commission the land revenue per square mile in Bengal amounted to £17 14s. as against £22 in Bombay, £29 in Madras, and £45 4s. in the North-Western Provinces. In the Punjab the corresponding figure was £17 0s. 6d. But the land revenue per head of the population was 2s. in the Punjab as against 1s. 1½d. in Bengal, 3s. 6d. in Bombay, 2s. 6d. in Madras, and 2s. in the North-Western Provinces.[40] With the gradual fragmentation of landed property, however, the upper and middle-class landed interests in Bengal were increasingly reduced to the status of lower middle classes. Their position grew worse when with the growth of education and provincial autonomy they were slowly excluded from the public services in other parts of the country.

Indeed the increasing fragmentation of holdings, which proceeded from partition suits as well as from the freedom with which property could be transferred by sale, produced results of great social significance. The bulk of middle-class proprietors, as has been seen, were respectable Hindus, persons belonging to upper castes in society, particularly in Bengal. In the Madras and Bombay Presidencies too the old literary classes held considerable interests in land. The Rajputs, with some Brahmans and Muhammadans, constituted the bulk of under-proprietors, including proprietors of *mahals* in the North-Western Provinces. Decline in their prosperity arising from the division of property, therefore, drove them increasingly to resort to English education as a means of improving their lot. This was particularly so in Bengal because of the absence of any legal restriction on the subinfeudation or transfer of property.

A confidential report on the economic condition of Bengal in 1891, for example, showed that the landed middle class had begun to decline, especially in the Dacca Division where it consisted of priestly and literate castes. Speaking of this division, the report said:

They are very numerous in this Division, and generally have a minute share in a landed estate, on which it would be impossible to support

[40] Ind. Fam. Commission, 1881, *Rep.*, app. 1, Minute by Sir L. Mallet, p. 143.

life. Hence they throng our high schools, and gain a smattering of English, in the hope . . . of obtaining some Governmental post. . . . This process is at work in the central and western districts and in Western Bihar; and its outcome is a yearly swelling class of hungry malcontents. Their disappointed hopes find an echo in the utterances of the native press and of the professional agitators who are constantly representing the richest and happiest peasantry in the world as a down-trodden and starving people.[41]

This report is significant in that it suggests the beginning of attempts on the part of the lower middle classes to enlist the peasantry on their side to strengthen their demand for increased employment in Government.

The division of landed property signified an increasing number of sharing proprietors and a corresponding increase in the number of Collectors and rent suits. In the combined districts of Muzaffarpur and Darbhanga, to give one example, there were in 1840 a little more than 4,000 estates. This figure rose to nearly 15,000 in 1887, and that for Muzaffarpur alone.[42] The creation and rise of separate proprietary interests with powers to collect rents separately destroyed the corporate character of villages, which had in the past depended on the collective mode of disbursing and realizing public dues. As indicated in the Introduction, the effect of this disintegration was to obscure the local loyalties which the heads of villages commanded by virtue of their economic superiority and exclusive recognition by the state. In the course of about 100 years of British rule these loyalties were being slowly transferred to the officers of Government. But one of the results of educational and economic change was 'to bring new men to the surface'. These were what a report of 1891 called 'professional agitators'—a class of politicians who vied with the bureaucracy for the loyalties lost by the once powerful class of chief proprietors known as lambar-dars or zamindars. The rivalry of politicians and public servants for the loyalty of the people which began in the 1880's still continues.

Money-lenders

Modern banks affected the Indian shroffs, but since the rise of these banks was initially slow, they continued to carry on their

---

[41] Skrine Mem. on Lower Orders in Beng. (P.B. Coll. 220), para. 53, p. 15.
[42] *Rep. Cadast. Survey Muzaffarpur*, 18 July 1887, para. 9, p. 17.

business. However, in modern times money-lenders came to be a heterogeneous class. They included all castes and professions—banyans and Brahmans, landed proprietors and salaried employees, any group of persons who had money to lend. The class grew considerably under the British because, while the expansion of commerce and opportunities of employment were favourable to the accumulation of money, the security of land tenures attracted that money as the best form of investment. Shrewd and thrifty, the class of money-lenders preyed alike upon the ignorant tenantry and the indolent aristocracy. While the former incurred loans for seeds, cattle, and food grains, the latter did likewise for reasons of family prestige and social extravagance. Both suffered privation at the hands of money-lenders.

The Marwaris were specially extortionate. In a statement of 1879 Sir Richard Temple, then Governor of Bombay, declared that in about fifty years of British administration the powerful and largely ramified class of Marwaris had increased considerably in the Deccan as money-lenders. They, as well as the Brahmans, absorbed proprietary rights in the Deccan villages, which led to the Deccan agrarian riots of 1873.

The findings of the Famine Commission of 1881 brought to light several cases of injustice on the part of money-lenders, especially in Jhansi, Central India, where they took dishonest advantage of the ignorance and necessitousness of zamindars. In one case a man had borrowed at 36 per cent. and pledged the whole of his landed property for the amount. In another case the man had not only pledged his property, but had agreed that the mortgage would become an absolute transfer on his failure to repay the principal with interest at 24 per cent. per year. In yet a third case a proprietor owed a debt of Rs. 500 in return for which he had given over his estate to the creditor for a period of ten years, himself paying the rent as a cultivator. At the end of ten years he was to repay the principal and interest at 6 per cent., or the estate would become the creditor's. In about ten years the money-lenders realized from this estate a profit of a little over Rs. 7,000, and yet the debt ran up to Rs. 10,000.[43] The Famine Commission reported that to a greater or lesser extent the same sort of thing went on all over India.

[43] Ind. Fam. Commission, 1881, *Rep.*, app. 1, p. 186.

To check the rapacity of money-lenders the supreme Legislative Council in India passed the Jhansi Encumbered Estate Act (Act XVI of 1882) which obliged civil courts, in adjudicating on contracts, to inquire into their character, and to enforce the payment of only so much as might be found consistent with the principles of equity and justice. The operation of this Act was restricted to Jhansi. Elsewhere the courts intensified the evil by giving usurious contracts a force which custom and the weight of local opinion would have denied them before. The Jhansi Encumbered Estates Act was, however, not without effect even elsewhere. It influenced an important case between *Lalli* vs. *Ram Parshad* in which an original debt of Rs. 97 due by an agriculturist to a money-lender had in a period of ten years grown to Rs. 991 after the deduction of Rs. 157 already paid. The case finally came up for a decision before Mr. Justice Mahmood and the Chief Justice of Allahabad. Their judgment was important in that it indicated how lands were being transferred from the cultivating community into the hands of money-lenders all over the country. But more important than that was their enforcement of an equitable principle in spite of the inequitable nature of the contract. The Chief Justice thus concluded his judgment:

It is bargains of this description between the small village proprietors and money-lenders that are gradually working the extinction of the former class in many of the country districts and producing results which are not only a serious scandal but a positive mischief. For it is to be borne in mind that the pecuniary difficulties of the persons I have mentioned are as often as not the results of misfortune rather than improvidence and that bad seasons have as much to do with causing them as waste or extravagance. Whichever way it be, this is certain that money lenders, as any one who sits in this Court must see, are to an alarming extent absorbing proprietary interests in the village communities and that the body of ex-proprietors is enormously on the increase. It is of course not my business to discuss the policy that should govern the action of the State in dealing with this state of things, but as a Judge having power to enforce equitable principles, I am resolutely determined, until I am set right by higher authority, to give effect in cases of this kind to the principles propounded by the eminent lawyers to whose utterances I have referred, and to see that justice is done. It may be that the repeal of the usury laws prohibits me from adopting the course I propose to take. As to this it is enough to say that Lord Sel-

borne, Lord Hatherley and Sir George Jessel in the judgments to which
I refer, remarked in the clearest and most emphatic language that the
repeal of the usury laws in England had in no way touched or affected
the power claimed by the Court of Chancery to grant relief in such
matters.[44]

It was in these circumstances that Curzon effected a shift of
emphasis from university to rural education, and had a measure
enacted to establish co-operative credit societies for the first time
in 1904. Other Acts were passed in subsequent years to establish
a sound co-operative credit system for agricultural and other rural
purposes, but for a variety of reasons which it is not possible to
examine here, no sound rural credit system has yet been evolved.

The development of British land policy thus lends itself to a few
interesting conclusions. The class which gained most was that of
peasant proprietors and middle-class zamindars, especially money-
lenders, who came to grab a large proportion of proprietary interests in most villages. The superior class of proprietors, old or new,
remained for the most part a class of rent receivers, and since no
rule of primogeniture governed the succession of property, they
became in time reduced to middling and later to lower income
groups. But since the proprietary classes were in the main those
who held respectable and superior rank in society by virtue of their
caste or by conquest, a reduction in the size of their property drove
them to resort to education to improve their lot. It was only when
the number of educated persons exceeded the employment available that political conflicts arose. The aim of British policy to
create a middle class of rural entrepreneurs did not generally succeed. The commercialization of agriculture remained more or less
a European enterprise. To Indians heavy interest on agricultural
loans and the security of property were more attractive than
capitalist undertakings.

[44] Sec. to Chief Comiss., C.P. to Sec. to G.O.I., Rev. & Agric., 25 July 1888,
quoted in *Condition of the Poorer Classes in the C.P.*, para. 10, pp. 6–7 (in P.B.
Coll. 221).

X

Educational Policy

THIS chapter will deal with the members of the Indian educated classes who received some form of higher education and not with the merchants, bankers, managers, and directors of firms, who have been dealt with elsewhere; but before examining the growth of some of the more important professions, it is appropriate to discuss the educational policy of the Government and the nature of the education it imparted. These naturally moulded the character of educated Indians.

THE EDUCATIONAL DISPATCH, 1854

The famous dispatch of 1854,[1] by stressing the principle of popularizing Western education, made the first departure from the earlier policy of 'downward filtration' as the means of educating the mass of the people. Its aim was not to check the progress of higher education; on the contrary, it recommended the establishment of universities, the expansion of secondary education, and encouragement to missionary and other educational institutions by introducing a system of grants in aid. Its policy was the expansion of education, but it introduced a new principle, affirming the responsibility of the state to educate those who possessed no means to educate themselves.

This was, however, difficult of achievement. The population was not only as large as that of all the European states together, but it varied widely in creed, language, race, and custom. The old literary classes, who had the virtual monopoly of education, were opposed to its being extended to inferior castes. Then there was the financial consideration, which ruled out anything like compul-

[1] See above, p. 154.

sory education. Besides the risk it ran of incurring the disaffection of higher castes, a system of compulsory education might also disrupt the economy of the poor people whose children performed various tasks of manual labour to support the family. The dispatch was in fact a challenge to India's tradition based on caste order and rural economy; its aim, as has been stated, was to change both. But this was an impossible task. The upper and middle classes continued to enjoy an almost exclusive privilege of education. And since a demand for higher education was at the time limited to the few, the Government did not find it difficult, even with its limited resources, to educate them.

BEGINNING OF STRESS ON RURAL EDUCATION, 1870

In 1870 a remarkable change of emphasis in favour of rural education occurred. The home authorities issued orders that 'Government expenditure should be mainly directed to the provision of elementary education for the mass of the people'.[2] In the same year the Government of Lord Mayo made additional provision for primary education. It introduced a policy of gradually transferring primary education to the local bodies provided by an Act of 1870. It is of interest, however, to note that this shift in emphasis followed immediately after four Indians had successfully competed in the Civil Service Examination in 1869. If the Government spent the bulk of its educational allocations on university education, this might enable many more Indians to enter the Indian Civil Service, a European preserve from a political point of view.

EDUCATION LEFT TO FREE ENTERPRISE, 1882

An Education Commission appointed in 1882 was specifically directed to report on the best means of giving effect to the Act of 1870 as well as to a plan then being proposed to entrust the Indian representatives of the local bodies with the charge of all but the higher educational institutitions.[3] The Commission appreciated the need to educate the mass of the people, but so far as the question of agency was concerned, recommended a shift in emphasis from a

[2] *Moral & Material Progress Rep., 1881–2*, p. 145.   [3] Ibid.

system of public control to private enterprise as the best means of executing the intention of the dispatch of 1854. The Government of India in a resolution of 3 February 1862 clearly pointed out that it was 'not possible ... to find funds sufficient to meet the full requirements of the country in the matter of primary education, if those requirements are to be judged by any European standard' and advised that if progress was to be made 'every available private agency must be called into action'.[4] The new policy was to hand over even some of the government colleges and schools 'to bodies of Native gentlemen who will undertake to manage them satisfactorily as aided institutions'.[5]

The Government thus adopted a policy of *laissez-faire* in education. As a result, educational expenditure, especially on government secondary and primary schools, registered a marked decline. In about three years local taxation and popular endowments took over nearly three-fourths of the burden.[6] Encouraged by this result, the Government reaffirmed its policy 'to avoid entering into competition with private enterprise'. It declared that its duty was to pioneer the way; 'but, having shown the way, it recognizes no responsibility to do for the people what the people can and ought to do for themselves'.[7]

Far from checking it, this policy accelerated the growth of higher education. As the following table shows, the number of colleges increased considerably in spite of the partial withdrawal of government support:

Colleges and Students

Year	No. of Colleges	No. of students
1873	55	4,499
1881	85	7,582
1886	110	10,538
1893	156	18,571

Sources: For 1873 and 1893, *Statistical Abstract*; for 1881 and 1886, as for n.6 below.

[4] Quoted in Ind. Ed. Com., 1882, *Rep.*, para. 5.   [5] Ibid. para. 6.
[6] India, Educ. Dept., Education in Ind., *Quinquennial Review, 1886–1904.*
[7] Ibid. para. 17, p. 6.

Increase in Colleges as Compared with Schools

While in a period of twenty years the number of colleges trebled, that of college students approximately quadrupled. The number of secondary schools also rose, but not to the same extent. It rose, for example, from 4,122 in 1881 to 5,097 in 1893, nearly 25 per cent. in twelve years. The number of students, on the other hand, increased from 2.22 lakhs to 5.11 lakhs during the same period. The position of primary schools was even worse. Between 1881 and 1893 the number rose from nearly 92,000 to 97,000, and scholars increased from 2.28 to 2.95 million. This shows that while the number of primary schools increased by 5 per cent. in twelve years, the number of scholars rose by only 25 per cent.

The reason for a slower rate of growth in primary education is not far to seek. While the upper and middle classes in the urban areas possessed both the means and the will to educate their children, the great bulk of the rural folk had neither. Only government support and encouragement could have awakened interest and enabled them to make progress. The policy of private enterprise, however, left them to help themselves.

It seems that a certain section of British administrators realized that the earlier policy of creating a middle class of educated Indians had been a mistake; for once that class began to grow in stature, a demand for an equal share in the administration of the country began. Refusal to recognize their claims caused bitterness and disaffection. Perhaps to rectify that error attempts were made to retard the progress of higher education partly by an emphasis on primary education but more by limiting the responsibility of the state in the advancement of education as a whole. This sense flows from the presidential address delivered by Curzon at an educational conference held at Simla on 6 September 1901.

There exists [he said], a powerful school of opinion which does not hide its conviction that the experiment [of English education] was a mistake, and that its result has been disaster. When Erasmus was reproached with having laid the egg from which came forth the Reformation, 'Yes', he replied; 'but I laid a hen's egg, and Luther has hatched a fighting cock'. This, I believe, is pretty much the view of a good many of the critics of English education in India. They think that it has given birth to a tone of mind and to a type of character that is ill-regulated, averse from discipline, discontented, and in some cases actually disloyal.[8]

APPROACH TO TECHNICAL EDUCATION, 1888

The question of technical education also appears to have been approached to some extent from a political angle; for example, even Bihar, which had in the past strongly opposed English education, registered an increasing demand for it and this led one of its district officers to remark that 'unless technical schools are provided as outlets, the mere scholastic element will breed political discontent'.[9] The remedy was to create outlets through industrial development. But the Education Commission of 1882 had instead recommended vaguely that a secondary school course should be introduced to fit boys for industrial or commercial careers. To make the recommendation precise the Government of India stated that drawing and rudiments of science should be taught in all but the most elementary schools. This the Government considered a step forward.

Basically, technical education was connected with the expansion of industrial employment for a population outgrowing the resources of a backward and conservative agricultural economy. It was concerned with the need to develop India's material resources through scientific methods and to improve agriculture and manufactures for the world market. But since industrial establishments were far too limited in number, there was little demand for technicians. The establishment of technical schools on a large scale was thus considered undesirable because it might tend to increase unemployment. The Government clarified this policy in a resolution of 18 June 1888 which said:

Technical education proper is the preparation of a man to take part in producing efficiently some special article of commercial demand. It is the cultivation of the intelligence, ingenuity, taste, observation, and manipulative skill, of those employed in industrial production, so that they may produce more efficiently. And thus technical education of the special, as contradistinguished from the preparatory, kind is an auxiliary of manufacture and industrial capital. In India at the present time the

[8] *Curzon in India*, pp. 315–16.
[9] *Moral & Material Progress Rep., 1882–3*, p. 148.

application of capital to industry has not been developed to the extent which in European countries has rendered the establishment of technical schools on a large scale an essential requisite of success. But the extension of railways, the introduction of mills and factories, the exploration of mineral and other products, the expansion of external trade, and the enlarged intercourse with foreign markets, ought in time to lead to the same results in India as in other countries, and create a demand for skilled labour and for educated foremen, supervisors and managers. It may be conceded that the effect of these various influences on an Asiatic people is very gradual, and that it would be premature to establish technical schools on such a scale as in European countries, and thereby aggravate the present difficulties by adding to the educated unemployed a new class of professional men for whom there is no commercial demand.[10]

Even in the few existing Indian industries—cotton and jute mills, certain coal mines and iron foundries—senior technical and managerial staffs were recruited from England. Technical education in India thus suffered from want of opportunity to aid scientific research and higher manipulative skill. It grew mainly as part of general education, concerned more with theory than practice.

BEGINNING OF AN ERA OF CONTROL, 1899-1905

Curzon's Government was the first to apply a check to free enterprise in education. He introduced a system of control which extended to all grades of institutions, from the universities to primary schools. Discussion began after the publication of Sir Henry Cotton's *Quinquennial Review* in 1899; and the Simla Conference over which Curzon himself presided in September 1901 laid down the main principles of the educational policy he later adopted.

In keeping with his policy of control Curzon reduced the number of colleges and the Government's expenditure on university education. Before 1904 there were some 175 colleges; these were geographically distributed at the rate of not even one to a large town, city, or defined area but were clustered in the large cities, with 22 in Calcutta and 14 in Madras, while places like Allahabad, Nagpur, Benares, Poona, Trichinopoly, and Dacca had two or three apiece. He abolished a number of intermediate colleges, and

[10] *Papers relating to Technical Ed. in India, 1886-1904* (Cal., 1906), p. 36.

Educational Policy

1904, which redefined the duties and powers of universities.

Before the passage of this Act the business of a university was
limited to the affiliation of colleges and the examination of students.
It had little to do with the control of studies, professors, and students. The Act declared a university to be incorporated for the
purpose, among others, of making provision for the instruction of
students, with power to

appoint University Professors and Lecturers, to hold and manage
educational endowments, to erect, equip and maintain University
laboratories and museums, to make regulations relating to the residence
and conduct of students, and to do all acts . . . which tend to the
promotion of study and research.[11]

It made the connexion of college and university closer, and defined
the conditions for the affiliation or disaffiliation of a college. The
Act in fact provided for a systematic inspection of colleges, and
introduced official control to an extent shown in the following
table:

Constitution of University Senates, 1904

University	Previous total no. of senators	Total reduced under 1904 Act	Elected	Nominated	Eur.	Ind
Calcutta	181	84	20	64	41	43
Bombay	296	100	20	80	41	59
Madras	198	70	20	50	36	34
Punjab	136	75	15	60	35	40
Allahabad	112	75	15	60	39	36

Source: Orange, Prog. of Ed. in Ind., 1902–7.

On top of the University Act came the Education Code of 1904
designed to regulate all kinds of educational institutions. The combined effect was to reduce the rate of increase in the number of
colleges, which rose from 175 in 1902 to only 186 in 1911 and 195
in 1916, an increase of 20 in about 14 years. But control of affilia-

[11] Educ. in Ind., Quinquennial Rev., 1902–7, vol. i, para. 12, p. 6.

tion by no means limited the admission of students, especially to aided and recognized colleges. The number of students increased from nearly 36,000 in 1911 to over 58,000 in 1916.[12]

Primary education made rapid progress. Between 1887 and 1902, for example, the number of pupils in all primary schools, government and private, had risen from 3.02 to 3.88 million, an increase of nearly 0.86 million in fifteen years. This number rose to 4.77 million during 1902–7, an increase of 0.98 million in only five years. Obviously the rate of progress in primary education trebled in consequence of Curzon's policy.

Curzon in fact shifted the emphasis from the education of the few to that of the many. In his presidential address to the Simla Conference he thus clearly explained this new emphasis. He said:

> Primary education, by which I understand the teaching of the masses in the vernacular, opens a wider and a more contested field of study. I am one of those who think that Government has not fulfilled its duty in this respect. . . . This, I think, has been a mistake, and I say so for two principal reasons. In the first place, the vernaculars are the living languages of this great continent. English is the vehicle of learning and of advancement to the small minority; but for the vast bulk it is a foreign tongue which they do not speak and rarely hear. . . . My second reason is even wider in its application. What is the greatest danger in India? What is the source of suspicion, superstition, outbreaks, crimes—yes, and also of the agrarian discontent and suffering among the masses? It is ignorance. And what is the only antidote to ignorance? Knowledge. In proportion as we teach the masses so we shall make their lot happier, and in proportion as they are happier so they will become more useful members of the body politic.[13]

In regard to technical education, Curzon realized the necessity and importance of co-ordinating it with industrial development. In the sense of specialized training for commercial or industrial employment, technical education raised the problem of three grades of institutions: technical colleges at the top, craft schools at the bottom, and technical schools in between them. The object of technical colleges was to provide instruction and training in the principles of science and their application to industrial arts; the

[12] See *Statistical Abstract, 1912–13 to 1921–2*, p. 244.
[13] *Curzon in India*, p. 330.

object of craft schools was to train artisans to follow their calling; the aim of technical schools was to produce overseers and foremen to supervise artisans and to execute the instructions of executives. These last needed some training in scientific principles and the working of machines; but unlike engineers, they were not to receive complete instruction and training in the sciences.

In Curzon's time there were four engineering colleges in existence, namely, the Civil Engineering College at Sibpur in Bengal, the College of Science at Poona, the College of Engineering in Madras, and the Thomason College of Civil Engineering at Rurki.[14] There were also four government engineering schools, one each at Patna, Lahore, Dacca, and Jubbalpur, and four aided schools of engineering. They had all arisen from the necessity of satisfying the requirements of the Public Works Department for the construction and maintenance of public buildings and installations, roads, and canals. They trained Indians for the subordinate and upper subordinate situations of Government; superintendents and executive engineers were recruited from Cooper's Hill College in England.

There was no advanced technical college in Curzon's time. Madras, Sibpur, and Poona had after 1880 started apprenticeship classes in mechanical and electrical engineering only. The Victoria Jubilee Technical Institute, established in Bombay in 1887, trained only licentiates in electrical, mechanical, and textile engineering. What Curzon did was to institute state technical scholarships to enable Indians to receive higher technical education in foreign countries and 'to assist in promoting the improvement of existing native industries and the development of new industries wherever possible'.[15] He made a start by assigning four scholarships to Bengal for mining and two to Bombay for the textile industry. As for other provinces, he set on foot inquiries into their individual requirements. He believed that qualified engineers of Indian origin would in time replace such Europeans as held senior positions in the industries specially operated by Indian capital.

---

[14] Sibpur, Poona, and Madras all had licentiate courses in civil engineering until 1880 when they organized degree classes in this branch. To satisfy increasing demand for electrical and mechanical engineers they opened apprenticeship classes.

[15] Educ. in Ind., *Quinquennial Rev., 1902–7*, para. 586.

The replacement of Europeans by Indians was, however, far from easy. For example, the Madras Chamber of Commerce declared that

practically all manufacturing industries in India are at present run by Europeans, and they, when requiring men with expert knowledge for responsible posts (such as an ex-scholarship holder would naturally aspire to) would almost certainly prefer to employ a European, whose capacity and general reliability they could better form an opinion of.[16]

The Upper India Chamber of Commerce also held a pessimistic view of Curzon's scheme of state scholarships.

So far as the organised industries of these provinces are concerned [a committee of the Chamber said], it is not thought that specially trained scholars, who have undergone such a course of studies as is contemplated by the Government of India's scheme, would be of any material value. These students would presumably expect to be installed in positions of trust and importance, and as it is not considered that it would be possible for them in the time at their disposal to gain more than a limited and circumscribed acquaintance with the practical details of the particular industries they had selected for their studies, it would be extremely doubtful that the heads of important concerns would regard them as qualified to replace European experts, possessing years of practical experience, in the more responsible appointments.[17]

The committee did not comment on the value of such students as instructors for technical schools. But so far as the major industries were concerned, they affirmed that 'the knowledge gained by a thorough training in a factory working under Eastern conditions would seem to provide a very much more useful preparatory course than the superficial instruction which a scholar would be likely to receive in foreign countries'.[18]

Curzon's plan to fit Indians for higher technical posts in Indian industries was in fact a restatement of an earlier policy to secure extended employment for them in the engineering branch of the Public Works Department, which the home authorities viewed as an alternative to the increasing demand for the Indianization of the covenanted civil service. For no kind of education seemed better

[16] *Quinquennial Rev.*, *1902–7*, para. 590.   [17] Ibid, para. 591.   [18] Ibid.

adapted to pave the way for 'multiplied employment in independent careers than that which qualifies for engineering and kindred occupations'.[19] In a letter of 10 August 1876, for example, the Secretary of State, Lord Salisbury, advised the Government of India that the colleges of engineering in India should be limited 'to meeting the wants of natives of India', not of 'persons of European parentage' who had till then exercised a virtual monopoly of admissions to higher classes.[20] The Government of India however took no immediate action. Of 22 appointments made to upper subordinate posts in 1878, only 4 were 'natives' of pure Indian origin, the remaining 18 being Europeans or Eurasians. Though forming a tiny percentage in the total population of the country, they held more than half the upper subordinate posts, as the following table shows:

Upper Subordinate Establishment, 1879

	Natives	*Europeans & Eurasians*
India	344	485
Madras	125	119
Bombay	158	59
Total	627	663

Source: I.O., Sels. from Desp. to India, P.W.D., no. 32 of 17 July 1879 para. 3.

A dispatch by the Secretary of State of 17 July 1879 further pointed out that the disproportion between the numbers of Europeans and Indians in the upper subordinate branch of the Public Works Department arose also from 'the frequent importation from Europe of mechanics of various descriptions for service on State Railways', although, as the same dispatch affirmed, 'intelligent natives are in many respects better suited than Europeans of the class employed in this branch of the public works establishment'.[21] It may be noted that these importations were in addition to the

---

[19] Ibid. para. 591.
[20] I.O., Sels. fr. Desp. to Ind., P.W.D., no. 74 of 20 Dec. 1883, para. 23.
[21] Referred to in ibid. para. 5.

regular supply of British engineers from the Engineering College at Cooper's Hill.

The predominance of Eurasians in the Public Works Department arose from a doubt about the exact meaning of the term 'Natives'. Act 33 Vict. cap. 3 defined this term as 'persons born and domiciled within the dominions of Her Majesty in India of parents habitually resident in India, and not established there for temporary purposes only'. This definition included persons of European or mixed descent for whom the Government of India was desirous of providing every opportunity for education and employment. The Secretary of State, however, advised the Government of India to interpret the term 'Natives' as persons of 'pure Asiatic origin', and the latter did this by a resolution of 11 November 1882.[22] It may be of interest to note that the Government of India had previously recommended the closing of the Cooper's Hill College and the establishment of a college of similar character 'for the training of natives in India'.[23] The Secretary of State, however, did not agree to this. He insisted that employment in the upper subordinate situation be guaranteed to Indians of pure Asiatic origin and that Europeans or Eurasians be taken on only when Indian candidates were not forthcoming. This change of policy came into effect under Lord Ripon (1882–5), when degree classes were first started in the existing colleges of civil engineering in India.

The Eurasian or Anglo-Indian community regarded this change as highly prejudicial to its interest. In a memorial presented to the Government, the president of their 'Railway and Government Servants' Association complained that they had been excluded from certain privileges which they had previously enjoyed in the same way as European British subjects in India. The Secretary of State agreed with the Government of India in rejecting their memorial, and observed 'that the law cannot be altered so as to extend the range of the exceptional privileges enjoyed by any particular class'.[24]

Attempts had thus been made to encourage Indians to take up technical careers the scope of which extended beyond the salaried services of the state. What Curzon tried to do was to effect a further extension of this principle to such industries as were run by Indian

[22] I.O., Sels. fr. Desp. to Ind., P.W.D., no. 74, paras. 12 and 16.
[23] Ibid. para. 8.   [24] Ibid. 30 Sept. 1886, para. 6.

capital. His object was to limit the importation even of senior grades of engineers, not only for the traditional purpose of the Public Works Department but also for industrial purposes. But since Indians had in the past been excluded from responsible posts, the industries had reason to doubt their ability to handle technological problems efficiently, especially when trained abroad independently of the needs of India.

However, it was Indian business and political leadership that took the initiative in advancing the study of science and technology. J. N. Tata, a leading industrialist of Bombay, was the first to meet Curzon on his arrival in India and co-operated with him in the establishment of what soon became the Indian Institute of Science at Bangalore. The Mysore Government lent the site and the Government of India made an initial non-recurring grant of Rs. 2,50,000 in addition to an annual grant of Rs. 87,750. The leaders of the Swadeshi movement in Bengal started a college of engineering and technology at Jadaopur in 1907, at present one of the important centres of technical education in India. The credit for establishing a degree college in mechanical and electrical engineering, belongs to Pandit Madan Mohan Malviya, a member of the Indian Industrial Commission of 1916 and founder of the Benares Hindu University, who in response to the needs of Indian industries opened that college in 1918.

In spite of his failure to do anything tangible in the field of technical education, Curzon's efforts constituted a landmark in the development of educational policy. His Education Code and the University Act of 1904 laid the foundations of a unitary and centralized system of education. His reforms paved the way for the transformation of Indian universities from mere affiliating and examining bodies into residential and teaching institutions. The Sadler Commission of 1917 took its cue from Curzon's reforms. It recommended a unitary system of university education for India and that all formal instruction should be given by the officers of the university under the immediate direction of its authorities. Practical considerations, however, made it impossible to dispense with all the affiliating universities. What was possible in the peculiar circumstances of Indian development was to limit their area and to open new universities as residential and teaching institutions. The universities of Dacca, Aligarh, Benares, and Lucknow, were established on unitary principles. The whole idea was to regulate and control university education centrally through university bodies.

Curzon also emphasized the study of vernaculars at a university level. Before this the modern languages of India had no place in university curricula except in Madras. Calcutta and Madras universities now made vernaculars one of the compulsory subjects of study. The establishment of a Department of Archaeology and measures to protect historical monuments in India were further steps to revive the study of Indian culture as a means to counteract anglicization.

Curzon introduced two more important changes. He made science a separate study and teaching a specialized profession. It was realized that Indian thought and literature suffered generally from a lack of precision, and that the teaching of science was exactly the tonic needed. This was therefore the period when students began moving away from the study of arts and the universities began to permit candidates to read for a separate degree in science. The process was, however, slow; even by the close of the first decade of this century, 85 per cent. of students graduating in the four main faculties of the Indian universities were arts graduates, 2 per cent. science, 9 per cent. medicine, and 4 per cent. engineering. In some of the universities a degree in arts was granted for science subjects. Of every 100 graduates in arts, for example, the percentage of those who took one or two science subjects was 36 in the Calcutta university, 46 in Madras, 34 in Bombay, and 25 in Allahabad.[25] Most of these graduates proceeded to the study of law or to the M.A. degree. The number who studied for doctoral degrees was negligible.

The emphasis on the training of teachers was intended to make teaching into a separate specialized profession conducive to the maintenance of control and discipline in schools. This will be dealt with elsewhere. It is sufficient to say here that the number of training colleges was increased and the Education Code of 1904 for the first time made the appointment of a certain minimum number of trained teachers a necessary condition for the recognition of schools. Quantitatively speaking, the number of trained teachers remained inadequate; the *Moral and Material Progress Report* even for the year 1919–20 found it inconsiderable. It stated (p. 164):

[25] Educ. in Ind., *Quinquennial Rev.*, 1902–7, para. 99.

'Out of total of 204,000 teachers of vernacular in India only 70,000 [34 per cent.] were trained at the end of the official year 1919–20. In Anglo-Vernacular schools, out of a total of 100,000 Anglo-Vernacular teachers only 35,000 [35 per cent.] were trained, and only 11,000 [11 per cent.] possessed a degree.' What Curzon did in fact was to institutionalize future trends of policy the main features of which were central control, promotion of vernaculars, and a search for a broad-based system of education.

The demand for responsible government led to the transfer of education to the charge of Indian ministers in the provinces under the Act of 1919. But the necessity of co-ordination could not long be ignored. A conference of Indian universities set up in 1924 an Inter-University Board to facilitate, among other things, the exchange of professors, the standardization of academic qualifications by a recognition of each others' degrees and diplomas, and the co-ordination of university work as a whole. However its recommendations were for the most part inoperative. The Government of India constituted in 1935 a Central Advisory Board of Education whose function it was to formulate an integrated policy to cover in a general way all grades of educational institutions in the country and to correlate them with the questions of employment.

Educated unemployment was among the most serious of the educational problems which the British had to face in their time. Since they had introduced English education primarily to satisfy the needs of the public services, and since success in examinations constituted the only passport for admission to these and other services, the main task of the universities was to fit students for the purposes of these examinations, so that they might share in the administration of the country or enter the independent professions. Ideologically the functions of the universities changed from time to time. From mere examining and affiliating bodies they grew into unitary centres of teaching burdened with the ideal of working for intellectual freedom and spiritual emancipation. But as the auxiliary committee of the Indian Statutory Commission reported in 1929, the old theory 'that a university exists mainly, if not solely, to pass students through examinations still finds too large acceptance in India'. The desire that it should produce broad-minded, tolerant, and self-reliant citizens remained more or less a pious wish.

The problem related not so much to the unemployment of those who passed as of those who failed at these examinations. The following table gives an index of the very high degree of wastage which involved problems of a social and political nature:

Results of Examinations

	1864		1873		1907	
	Candidates	Passes	Candidates	Passes	Candidates	Passes
Matricula-tion	2,203	1,034	5,273	1,829	24,000	11,000
First Arts	510	217	970	478	7,000	2,800
Bachelor	126	64	362	165	4,750	1,935

Source: Statistical Abstract for relevant years.

The situation created by an increasing degree of wastage as well as by an excess of passes over the number of available jobs dictated a shift of emphasis from a purely literary and top-heavy university education to technical, vocational, and rural education. The object was to develop, with the aid of technical and vocational knowledge, new opportunities and avenues of employment, and to widen the educational base by means of such rural education as might fit in with the requirements and conditions of village life. This led to a two-pronged attack on the problem: to start agricultural and other vocational classes as part of the general education courses at all levels, and to establish separate vocational schools to which students might proceed when they had reached the appropriate level.

This arrangement was in large measure consistent with the suggestion made in 1881 before the Indian Famine Commission by Sir Richard Temple. He desired not only that agricultural classes should be started in all grades of schools, but also that civil servants should be equipped with a knowledge of agricultural science. Curzon's reorientation of educational policy also had a similar objective, although nothing tangible was done to achieve it as part of an educational programme. In a meeting in December 1935 the Central Advisory Board of Education, while expressing concern over the growing size of educated unemployment, emphasized the need, among other things, of practical training for those who possessed little or no aptitude for literary pursuits. Provision for such training was to form part of the scheme of general education, where intending candidates could receive it as a preliminary qualification for specializing at appropriate institutions. In addition, the Board expressed a desire to introduce a system of rural education under which boys and girls in rural areas should be given 'such training as would develop in them a capacity and desire for the work of rural reconstruction'.

In conformity with these recommendations the Government of India invited Mr. S. H. Wood, Director of Intelligence to the Board of Education in England, and Mr. A. Abbott, formerly Chief Inspector of Technical Schools, to visit India. They made a survey of the United Provinces, the Punjab, and Delhi. Their *Report on Vocational Education in India* appeared in 1937, when the Congress Party came to power in the several provinces, and it influenced the views of Dr. Zakir Husain's Committee appointed soon afterwards by the Congress to examine the question of educational reconstruction.

Abbott and Wood both agreed that primary schools should become centres of rural uplift, an agency for the propagation of health, good habits, and enlightened outlook on rural economy. As regards high schools they commented that these had become too 'examination-ridden'. They pointed out that the Higher Secondary Schools should 'not only instruct boys but also train them how to study, in the hope that they may remain mentally alert and continue the pursuit of intellectual interests after they leave school'. In the first part of the report, dealing with general education and organization, the authors recommended, among other things, the introduction of manual work of various kinds as forming part of the curriculum of every school.

On the main question of vocational education, dealt with in the second part of the report, the authors tried to dispel the idea that vocational training stood essentially on a lower plane than literary or general education. They pointed out that general and vocational education must not be treated as distinct branches of education but emphasized their unity and suggested that they were rather the earlier and later phases of a continuous process fostered by a single coherent society. While they stressed 'the importance of regarding vocational education as being an extension of general education', they pointed out 'the necessity of looking upon it as a specific preparation for work in industry, commerce and the professions'. They viewed the progress of vocational education as inseparably connected with the progress of industry and commerce. Their report reiterated that the mere multiplication of vocational institutions was no solution to the problem of educated unemployment. The real solution lay in the creation of more employment through industrial development. 'The existence of skilled workers', said Abbott, though essential, is not in itself enough to create organised industries. Capital, means of transport, and reasonably assured markets are also needed'.[26] What was furthermore urgently needed was a planned and phased scheme of industrialization on a scale commensurate with the requirements of the people and the extent of the available raw materials.

Indeed industrial development alone could create demands for more and more of technicians and skilled labour.

Large-scale industries [Abbott said], require an adequate supply of men specially trained for the responsible posts in them. It cannot be expected, however, that men will undergo training for work in these industries unless they see a reasonable prospect of suitable employment. The expansion of vocational education should therefore not greatly outstrip the development of industry.[27]

The basic education scheme of the Indian National Congress, especially in Bihar, tried to put the cart before the horse. It did something more than that. The principle underlying earlier developments was to have vocational classes attached to general education courses, so that those who possessed no aptitude for purely literary pursuits might acquire a preliminary knowledge and practice of crafts before being able to specialize in separate technical institutions. Obviously vocational classes in general educational institutions ought to be of a preparatory and optional nature. What the basic and post-basic schools in Bihar did was to make crafts compulsory for all as well as to vocationalize even general education at different levels. As a result these institutions remained neither fully general nor fully vocational. Committed to the charge of intellectually ill equipped and professionally ill trained teachers, with hardly any appreciation of the nature of educational develop-

---

[26] Abbott and Wood, ii. 41–42.   [27] Ibid. p. 110.

ment in the past, these institutions became a drain on the public revenues. They imparted neither a scientific discipline nor an efficient literary education, for they allowed an overlapping of the general and vocational processes so distinctly pointed out in the report by Abbott and Wood.

The Secondary Education Commission of 1953, however, adopted a fairly sound approach to educational reconstruction. Providing, as it did, for a diversification of the secondary education courses separately from purely vocational and technical schools, it met the requirements of general education and also opened out fields for subsequent specialization. The post-basic schools have been integrated with diversified secondary schools. But the danger of the present mode of diversification is that the period of general education is shortened by an early introduction of specialized groupings. This may affect the liberal quality of modern education.

Certain idiosyncrasies of basic education still persist, especially in the Rural Institutes which the Government of India established following the recommendations of the Committee for Higher Rural Education set up by it in 1954. They are supposed to impart instruction equivalent to a three-year degree course in such subjects as may be of special relevance to the rural services of the Government. But in actual practice they confuse education with craft, and the academic content of the instruction they impart is necessarily of an inferior order. They exist on government grants, and attract students because the Government undertakes to absorb their products in the community development projects and the national extension services. They work on the general belief that what is needed for a rural officer is devotion to duty, not necessarily an intelligent grasp of rural problems. They retain their bias for basic education; for the original object of their institution was to absorb the products of post-basic schools not recognized by any university as equivalent to secondary schools.

INCREASING GROWTH OF HIGHER EDUCATION

Before discussing the various professions adopted by the educated middle classes, it is pertinent to examine the increasing growth of higher education, which was the basis of recruitment to the professions. The yardstick employed to measure this growth is the number of scholars, of candidates, and passes at the various university examinations from the matriculation onwards. The matriculation examination is included since it was of great significance in the earlier periods and success in it constituted a passport for admission to the professions themselves. In the University of Madras, for example, in 1860 a candidate with matriculation could proceed to study for a B.L. (Bachelor of Law) degree, and in special cases the university even admitted certain candidates to a degree course in law provided that they passed the matriculation examination.[28]

Passes during 1864–73

Examination	Calcutta University	Madras University	Bombay University
Matriculation	8,025	3,974	1,970
First Arts	2,055	1,127	321
B.A.	860	296	168
Honours & M.A.	216	9	34
Law	704	78	33
Medicine	496	10	94
Civil Engineering	36	8	83
	12,392	5,502	2,703

Source: Statistical Abstract for relevant years.

The table above gives the number of passes in a period of ten years during 1864–73. Of the total annual average of nearly 2,000 passes, more than 1,200 or 61 per cent. belonged to Calcutta University. With 704 out of a total of 815 in law, Calcutta was by far the most important of the three universities turning out law graduates. In civil engineering, however, its achievement was poor in comparison with that of Bombay, and still poorer when it is made clear that not all the Calcutta students belonged to Bengal.

If matriculation results are excluded, the total number of passes would be reduced from 20,597 to 6,628, giving an annual average of 662.8. Estimating the average percentage of passes at 45, this annual average would give an average number of candidates of

[28] P.B. Coll. 150, para. 61, p. 27. A B.A. degree was necessary for B.L. in Calcutta.

nearly 1,500 and an average number of students, including those of the previous classes, of nearly 3,000. This roughly corresponds with the actual number of college students of all kinds, which at the close of the decade amounted to 4,499 on 31 December 1874.[29] Assuming the population of British India to be nearly 200 million, there were thus 2.25 college students to every 100,000 of the population.[30]

In the decade 1879 to 1888 the number of passes increased from 20,597 to 54,035; and the annual average, which was nearly 2,000 during 1864–73, rose to 5,403. The rate of progress, including matriculation passes, thus increased by 2.5 times.[31] Exclusive of matriculation passes, the annual average of passes rose from 662.8 to 1,936. The quinquennium following 1888 maintained a rate of progress more or less equivalent to that of the preceding decade, as the following table shows:

No. of Passes During Five Years, 1889–94

Examination	Calcutta	Madras	Bombay	Allahabad	Punjab
Matriculation	11,340	6,936	4,100	3,322	2,659
First Arts	4,356	3,260	1,329	1,059	671
B.A.	1,695	1,464	747	533	275
Honours & M.A.	276	32	23	76	25
Law	642	244	316	108	7
Medicine	560	172	386	—	111
Civil Engineering	76	24	332	669	3
Total	18,945	12,132	7,233	5,767	3,751

Annual Average of Passes

	1864–73 (10 yrs.)	1879–88 (10 yrs.)	1889–94 (5 yrs.)
Ann. average of passes, incl. matric.	2,059	5,403	9,165
Ann. average of passes excl. matric., First Arts, and above	662	1,936	1,947

[29] *Statistical Abstract, 1840–72*, no. 9, p. 81.
[30] The *Census of India, 1872*, underestimated the population at 206 millions for the whole of India.
[31] *Statistical Abstract, 1887–8 to 1890–1*, no. 24, p. 189.

These figures clearly indicate that the rate of progress in higher education began to increase considerably in the 1880's and more still in the following decade. This was the beginning of resurgence for the educated middle classes. Education became a free enterprise in 1882. The expansion of the local bodies came in 1885. Discussion on the expansion of the Indian Legislative Councils on a principle other than that of nomination began in 1886. In the same year the Secretary of State appointed an Indian Public Service Commission to examine the whole question of how best to secure the extensive employment of Indians in the civil service. The recognition of an elective principle of representation in the Legislative Councils was in fact the first triumph of the Indian middle classes. The Indian Councils Act of 1892, which recognized this principle for the first time, marked the beginning of the end of British rule. This was again the period which witnessed the rise of Indian capitalism and of a cultural revolt against the West.

Judging from the number of students in all the arts and professional colleges, there was a fourfold increase in twenty years. Numbers increased from 4,499 in 1874 to 18,571 in 1894.[32] With a population in British India of nearly 230 million in 1891, there were nearly 8 college students to every 100,000 of the population. The rate of increase in college students was thus multiplied by about 3.5 times in spite of the growth of the total population in the two decades beginning in 1874.

In the decade beginning in 1893–4, India suffered from outbreaks of famine. Moreover in this period the effect of Curzon's policy of control began to be felt. Consequently there was no phenomenal growth in higher education. The annual average of passes in this decade nevertheless rose to 4,700, excluding matriculation results.[33] The *Quinquennial Review* of the progress of education for 1902–7 showed that in the three closing years of the preceding quinquennium the annual output of graduates alone averaged 1,935, exceeding 2,000 only once. These numbers included 'all the Bachelors of Arts, of Science, of Engineering, of Oriental Learning and of Medicine, and in addition thereto the Licentiates of Medicine and Surgery and of Engineering'.[34] It is interesting to note that the

---

[32] *Statistical Abstract* for relevant years.
[33] Educ. in Ind., *Quinquennial Rev.*, *1902–7*, para. 8.   [34] Ibid. para. 97.

1902–7 Quinquennial Review found that the number of university graduates was still inadequate to staff colleges and secondary schools, and refuted the general belief that the output of graduates was in excess of the number for whom there was employment stating that:

Of 1,935 graduates of the Universities, 540 become Bachelors of Law, and in most cases proceed to the Bar. This leaves a yearly supply of nearly 1,400 graduates available for the other professions, for the branches of the public service in which graduates are employed, for teaching in colleges and schools, and for service in Native States.[35]

In 1903, it stated, Curzon caused a return to be made on the subject of Indians employed in the public services at salaries exceeding Rs. 75. The return did not show the full extent of the demand for graduates in government service, but only revealed that Indians were employed in more than 16,000 posts at salaries higher than Rs. 75. It did not take into account the new avenues of employment created by the opening of new departments, by the reconstitution of the Secretariat, by the increase in foreign trade and joint-stock companies, and by the efforts Curzon had made to encourage Indian industry to meet the possibility of a future war. Although steady, the supply of graduates was thus considered still insufficient. What caused political disorders was not the number of successful candidates, but the huge wastage arising from the failure of 55–60 per cent. of the candidates taking the various examinations.

In the context of the total population the number of graduates was almost insignificant at the turn of this century. An annual average output of 312 graduates in 1874 rose to about 2,000 in Curzon's time. Assuming 1,000 as the annual average over a period of thirty years, the number of graduates in 1903 would be nearly 30,000, employed mainly in the public services and the professions. The total population of India in 1901 was 294 million. If we estimate it as 300 million for the year 1903–4, there was 1 graduate to every 10,000 of the population.

The following table illustrates the growth of higher education in the first four decades of the present century.

[35] Educ. in Ind., *Quinquennial Rev.*, *1902–7*, para. 97.

Growth of Higher Education, 1911–39

Year	Colleges	Scholars	Graduates	Under-graduates	Total of Grad. & Undergr.
1911	186	36,284	4,232	9,319	13,551
1916	195	58,639	8,371	46,722	55,093
1921	231	59,595	9,097	49,782	58,879
1931	317	99,493	14,766	76,534	91,300
1939	385	144,904	22,647	115,446	138,093

Source: Statistical Abstract for relevant years.

The accuracy of these figures cannot be fully guaranteed. They are nevertheless significant in that they indicate the trend of progress in higher education. In a period of thirty years while the number of colleges doubled, and of scholars quadrupled, graduates increased by more than five times, and undergraduates by more than twelve times. The table establishes beyond doubt the increasing demand for higher education, but it also makes clear that while more and more students proceeded to college education, the bulk gave up before completing a degree.

The early 1940's witnessed a phenomenal increase in the number of colleges and students. The former rose from 425 in 1940–1 to 593 in 1945–6.[36] This was for undivided India. By 1949–50 this number had risen to 796, exclusive of Pakistan. The *Statistical Abstract, 1952–3* (pp. 105, 111) shows that the number of men and women graduates of all faculties amounted in 1949–50 to 181,134, of whom 77,890, or nearly 42 per cent., belonged to professional colleges, and the remainder to colleges of arts and science. The number of undergraduates, on the other hand, totalled 199,703. Together they formed a total of 380,837 in 1949–50. If this figure is reduced to 360,000 to avoid overstatement, there was 1 college student to every 1,000 of the population, which was 360 millions in 1951. The proportionate increase in the number of graduates was much greater than ever before. In 1949–50, for example, the number of graduates in colleges was 50 to every 100,000 of the population. While the number of college students increased from 48 to 100 to every 100,000 of the population, that of graduates

[36] *Statistical Abstract, 1952–3,* p. 81.

rose from 8 to 50 in about ten years after 1939. The comparison, it is true, is defective, for the figures for 1939 were for the whole of India while those for 1949 were exclusive of Pakistan. But the error would be on the side of understatement, not of exaggeration.

The Lag in School Education

School education, however, did not keep pace with higher education. The relative position prior to 1919 has already been discussed.[37] The rate of progress increased when education became a provincial 'transferred' subject, but neither secondary nor primary education increased to the same extent as higher education. For instance, the number of scholars in all kinds of colleges in 1921 was 59,595. It rose to 144,904 in 1939, nearly 2.4 times as much. The number of pupils in schools of all kinds during the same period increased from 8.32 to 14.55 million, only 1.7 times as much.[38] The difference in the pace of college and school education was accentuated in the decade following 1939. In 1949–50, for example, the number of all kinds of college students rose to 380,837, that is, 2.7 times as much in ten years. The corresponding figure for pupils in all kinds of schools rose from 14.55 to 23.66 million, an increase of only 1.6 times as much.[39] Higher education was thus becoming increasingly top-heavy, especially after British influence had waned.

Uneven Distribution of Colleges

Higher education was not only top-heavy, but unevenly distributed. In the beginning, colleges, like joint-stock companies, were established in the Presidency towns, especially in Calcutta which had the maximum degree of concentration. Later they were started in other provinces, but remained for a long time limited to provincial headquarters or chief towns. The provinces which later became significant in college education were the United Provinces of Agra and Oudh, the Punjab, and Bihar. Of the 231 colleges in 1921, for example, 61 were in Madras, 46 in Bengal, 17 in Bombay, 42 in the U.P., 26 in the Punjab, and 14 in Bihar. The remaining 25 were situated in other parts of the country, including Burma. Of the total number of 59,595 college students in 1921, on the

[37] See above, p. 284.
[38] *Statistical Abstract, 1912–13 to 1921–2*, p. 225; *1930–1 to 1939–40*, pp. 139 f.
[39] Ibid. *1952–3*, tables 37 and 38, pp. 105 and 111.

other hand, 21,595 or nearly 36 per cent. belonged to Bengal, and 10,491 or about 17 per cent. to Madras. Although the U.P. had more than twice the number of colleges than Bombay, the number of college students in the U.P. was only 7,128 as against Bombay's 7,424. Bihar and Orissa had 2,470 scholars in 14 of its colleges, which gave an average of 175 students to a college as against the U.P.'s 169.[40] Many of the district colleges in Bihar now have more than 2,000 students each.

The rate of progress in Bihar was slow until 1939 when the total number of colleges in the province was 17 only. The 1940's, however, recorded a phenomenal rise. While colleges increased from 14 in 1921 to 45 in 1949, students rose from 2,470 to 23,529 in the same period. The following table gives the relative position of six Indian province in respect of the proportion which the number of students in colleges of all kinds bore to their total population in 1949–50:

Proportion of College Students to Population, 1949–50

Province	Population (millions)	No. of scholars to every 100,000 of population
Madras	57·01	88
Bombay	35·95	137
West Bengal	24·81	272
U.P.	63·21	52
Punjab (India)	12·64	157
Bihar	40·22	58

Source: Statistical Abstract, 1852–3, p. 21.

Of the Indian states in 1949–50, Mysore and Travancore-Cochin (now Kerala) were far ahead of the others, as shown below:

State	Population (millions)	No. of scholars to every 100,000 of population
Mysore	9·07	174
Travancore-Cochin	9·28	193
Hyderabad	18·65	53
Rajasthan	15·20	82

[40] *Statistical Abstract, 1912–13 to 1921–2*, tables 144 and 145, pp. 242 f.

XI

The Professional Classes

EXCEPT for the educated and salaried employees in business, the bulk of the Indian professional classes excluded those engaged in trade and industry, who in England constituted powerful groups among the educated classes. Moreover, except during the three most recent decades, the increase in the number of Indian lawyers and public servants, doctors and teachers, writers, scholars, and members of other recognized professions was due to educational, judicial, and administrative development rather than to technological or industrial progress. In fact, from the peculiar circumstances of their growth the professional classes in India continued to comprise those who also ranked high in the hierarchy of caste.

These groups became the spearhead of the Indian middle classes. Though composed of different castes, they developed a common interest and outlook, a common language and behaviour pattern, and these features contributed to the growth of Indian nationalism. Class-consciousness spread among the ranks of the landholder and the cultivator, the trader and the industrialist, but their outlook continued to be parochial rather than national. The professional classes were the first to break through caste or regional barriers and to develop a sense of unity and solidarity which made possible the development of nationhood in India. By the middle of the nineteenth century there were very few members of the new professions, which started growing with the establishment of the universities in 1857. As has been seen, this growth was accelerated in the 1880's. Of the various professions law became by far the most important, and it was not until 1920 that this profession began to give way to science and technology, trade and industry.

Since considerations of space do not permit the inclusion of all the professional groups, this discussion will be confined to government servants and lawyers, teachers and technicians; and even in respect of these it may be possible to do no more than touch the fringe.

The discussion of government servants here will be limited to judicial and executive officers, including the officers of the police.

The officers of Government under the British possessed a professional character not only because their jobs became more and more specialized but also because the tenure of their office and conditions of service were such that they made them impersonal in the performance of their public duties. Under Mughal rule the service of an amir or mansabdar was personal and his appointment or dismissal a matter of imperial whim. Under the British recruitment to the public service was determined by fixed rules, contractual in nature and mild in operation. Unlike service under a Mughal king, it was no adventure. It depended on a candidate's ability to pass a prescribed test or examination as the condition of his admission to the service. It became a learned and recognized profession.

Causes of Increase

The first cause of increase in the number of government servants was the centralization of public functions. Under the country Government, Mughal or Maratha, the community exercised a great many of these functions. The head of a joint family, or of a caste or village community, settled local disputes and kept the local peace. A village headman or chief proprietor undertook collectively to pay the public dues, except perhaps in Bengal where individual zamindars had superseded the village community and brought under their immediate control the local militia employed for the purposes of defence and revenue collection. Even so, the zamindars were rooted in the soil; and since their chaukidars (watchmen) were paid in kind by the community, they looked upon it as their master.

What the English Government did was to divest the community of these functions and transfer them to an official apparatus, either reconstituted or newly created. For example, when Cornwallis, abolished the police authority of zamindars in 1792 he appointed in their place Indian darogas who later came to be designated as sub-inspectors of police, responsible immediately to a magistrate who was a civil servant. Though for some time they continued to be paid by the village community, the old militia of village chauki-dars gradually came under the immediate charge of sub-inspectors of police. It was then proposed in 1815 to make them paid servants of Government. Lord Hastings opposed this proposal. His conten-tion was that chaukidars must remain subservient to the society, for he feared that if they became paid servants of Government, they would behave as 'masters' of the people, and that an 'authority would be established, pregnant with the most odious tyranny'.[1] The change was delayed only for a time. By 1856 the entire chaukidari system had come to be integrated with the Government police force. Instead of remaining as the servants of the people, they became its masters, representing the might and authority of Government in villages. The integration of what had once been village militia did not help to reduce crime which, on the contrary, increased to an extent necessitating the increase and reform of the whole police force.

Under Act VI of 1870 an attempt was made to associate pan-chayats (town or village councils) with the conduct of the chauki-dari system. The provisions of this Act were extended in the 1890's to rural unions to seek the co-operation of villages. But they were mere agencies for the assessment and collection of chaukidari tax without any control over chaukidars at all. Schemes were also proposed in 1903–4 to make village panchayats popular and attrac-tive by giving them certain functions of a judicial, municipal, and educational nature. But these never were put into practice.

The report of the Royal Commission on Decentralization (1909) recommended a reconstitution of village panchayats with powers to try petty civil and criminal cases, to look after minor village works, to control primary schools, and to manage fuel and fodder reserves. It also suggested a certain allocation of funds out of the land cess levied for the purposes of local boards, of special grants for particular objects, of receipts from village cattle-pounds, and out of small fees on civil suits filed before them. The report of the Bengal District Administration Committee (1915) which the

[1]Minutes of the G.G. (Lord Moira) and of members of his Council on poli-tical state of India. I.O., Home Mis., 603–4, 1815–17.

Government of India had appointed to suggest means to improve the administration of the districts, went a step further. It recommended that village panchayats should be reinvested with the supervision and control of the chaukidars operating within their local jurisdiction. Two chapters of this report were devoted to the reconstitution of villages and suggested plans for reforming local bodies on the principle of indirect elections beginning from the village upwards. One of its recommendations was to entrust local defence to village panchayats with powers of taxation to meet local needs. However, they all remained inoperative because the period of political unrest which followed the non-cooperation movement in the beginning of the 1920's gave them no chance of being tried out.

The Panchayat Raj Acts of the Congress Government partially conform to these recommendations. For example, the 'mukhiya' appointed under these Acts in Bihar corresponds in most respects to the 'President' of the scheme proposed in 1904, representing the executive authority of the panchayat which extends to the arrest of any person committing an offence in his presence, to the dispersal of unlawful assemblies, and to the discharge of miscellaneous executive duties relating to the affairs of his village. These Acts, however, do not cover all the recommendations either of the Decentralization Commission or of the District Administration Committee.

The panchayats reconstituted under the Panchayat Raj Acts suffer from two main limitations. The first of these is of a sociological nature. The ancient and original basis of their authority was not law. It was custom under which they recognized hereditary privileges and punished offences, not according to the degree of criminality but to caste considerations. Offences were limited, and their punishment varied from caste to caste, according to the capacity of the accused to bear it or the power of a panchayat to enforce it. There was no uniformity in the principle of punishment, no rule of law, no legislative enactment, no civil or penal code, no criminal procedure, no law of evidence. All these developed in the course of about 200 years of British rule in India. The recent Panchayat Raj Acts came in the context of these developments. Modern panchayats are thus constituted under legislative enactments and are required to administer justice within the framework of the law, of which they have little or no knowledge. They have to act on the principle of legal equality, which the elders of the village community consider repugnant to caste privileges. They have to follow a certain measure of legal and procedural technicality to which they had never been accustomed in the past. Indeed the officers of village panchayats have necessarily to reckon with the legacies of British rule, and those whose duty it is to administer these Acts immediately in villages, have to be aware, even though in a general way, of what that rule stood for especially in the administration of justice. This is a task which raises an educational issue of great magnitude. Independently of an educational programme equal to the task, any attempt to extend village panchayats as a measure of decentralization may intensify caste rivalry and group jealousy which, instead of reducing the burden of superior courts, may add to the load of their business.

The second limitation is of an economic character. The panchayats of the pre-British days operated under the influence of village headmen who were also, generally speaking, chief proprietors holding, in addition, a respectable position in the caste hierarchy or official nobility. They formed a class of peasant proprietors variously known as lambardar, malguzar, or mirasdar. An individual zamindar of a *mahal* containing a number of villages represented a superior landed interest. He was looked upon as a source of protection in the same way as the chief proprietor of a village.

Villages in the past acted corporately because village lands in practice remained communal. This does not mean that there were no individual shares or plots separately cultivated and held. What imparted corporateness to village property was the recognition by Government of the exclusive right of the chief sharer to pay for all others in the village. Since minor sharers and cultivators possessed no separate record of rights of their own, transfer of property outside the community became a rarity; for it fell ultimately to the chief sharer or headman to allow or reject a transfer. Transfers, if any, took place within the community.

The revenue and rent laws of the British altered the situation radically. What they did was to define all kinds of landed interest and to prepare separate records of right which enabled individuals to transfer their interest in land freely and independently of chief proprietors. A village community had in the past preserved its corporateness because of the collective responsibility of its head-man and the immobile nature of its land. The revenue laws of the British destroyed both.

Whether . . . it be *lambardar* or landholder [said a report of 1891], the influences which have hitherto held and controlled the masses are gradually being weakened under the levelling influence of British rule. Where there is a strong Government giving protection equally to all, where there are impartial courts of justice and carefully prepared records of agricultural right and holdings, the protecting arm of the more powerful individual is no longer needed by the once helpless many.[2]

British rule thus disintegrated both the social and economic basis of village panchayats. In these circumstances, any attempt to decentralize the administrative and judicial functions of Govern-ment has to be accompanied by an extension of the state machinery of supervision and control, which means the appointment of an increasing number of public servants. The extension of the state's functions and the consequent increase in the number of govern-ment servants proceeded likewise from the gradual supersession of custom by law. Its necessity arose immediately from the inability of the British to understand the country's varied customs and usages which they found irreducible to any fixed principle.

Difficulties arising from the operation of custom were experi-enced especially in the administration of justice. Even an able and honest civil servant like C. W. B. Rous, President of the Calcutta Committee of Revenue in 1776, was perplexed by the contradic-tory legal opinions delivered in writing by ten Brahmans who, in the case of a Hindu widow against her grandson, had declared her as entitled to half the share of a disputed estate. To Rous's great surprise, the grandson subsequently obtained from the same set of Brahmans another legal verdict which strengthened his claim to the entire estate, the widow being considered entitled to a bare maintenance.

To prevent the miscarriage of justice, therefore, the British pro-ceeded to codify Hindu and Muhammadan laws. From the very

[2] N.W.P. *Admin. Rep., 1890–1*, quoted in Miller, *Condition of Agric. & Labouring Classes* (P.B. Coll. 220), para. 92.

beginning of their direct rule in Bengal they also endeavoured to introduce uniformity in process and record-keeping so as to facilitate inspection as well as to make judicial officers conform to a given standard. Cornwallis carried this principle further than had ever been attained before. A fundamental principle of his judicial reforms was to supplant custom by court-made justice. From ordinary civil suits the operation of this principle extended to the regulation of the control which a father exercised over his son, a husband over his wife and a master over his slave.[3] The abolition of infanticide, sati, and a number of other practices were some of the forms in which law was penetrating the Indian social system. The later civil and penal codes of India were examples of further inroads of law on custom.

Not less important than justice was the administration of revenue where, as has been shown, law began to revolutionize social relationship by the attempt to define and record agricultural rights. This necessitated the extensive employment of Indians in the Revenue Department. It called for the reorganization of provinces into divisions, increasing the number of districts and subdivisions and introducing wherever necessary still smaller units of civil administration to enable officers of Government to come into close contact with the people. The exigencies of famine and relief, of survey and rural credit, of forestry and agricultural statistics increased the load of public business and led not only to the appointment of additional deputies and assistants, but also to the creation of separate cadres of forest and agricultural officers, co-operative registrars, inspectors, and a host of other officials.

The land and famine policy of the British in fact suggested the expediency of state interference as the best means to secure relief; and once the principle of state action ws recognized here, it was a matter of course to extend its operation to other economic fields, such as industry and commerce, tariff and taxation. This extension in the scope of the state's activity naturally signified a corresponding expansion in the bulk of the public service, a tendency that was reinforced by considerations of specialized service. The object of specialization was to simplify administration so as to secure efficiency and to facilitate control. Basically arising from a large-

[3] See Misra, *Central Administration*, p. 358.

scale productive system, specialization signified functional stratification, a hierarchy of specialists and experts.

It was not long after the Crown had taken over in 1858 that
simplification in the administration of justice began. The Civil
Procedure Code was passed in 1859, the Criminal Procedure Code
and the Indian Penal Code in 1861. In the same year a parliamentary statute (24 & 25 Vict. c. 104) empowered the Crown to
establish by letters patent, High Courts at Calcutta, Bombay, and
Madras in which the Supreme Courts and the Sadr Diwani and
Nizamat Adalats were merged in 1862. The High Courts were
vested with both original and appellate jurisdictions, but at first
their jurisdiction was limited to the Presidency towns, which dated
back from the Charter of 1726 establishing the Mayor's Court.
By their extraordinary original jurisdiction and by their appellate
jurisdiction these High Courts came to control all the other courts
of justice, civil or criminal. The same Act permitted the creation
of a separate High Court for the North-Western Provinces, established in 1866. The High Courts of other provinces were established later by Acts of the Indian Legislature. In 1868 the office of
Sadr Amin, created in 1803, was abolished. The office of Principal
Sadr Amin, created in 1831, was designated as Subordinate Judge.
The system so established effected the legal unity and integration
of the country.

The result of specialization on the police side was to divest the
magistracy of such duties as were of purely police concern. Starting
originally as an executive and police officer, the successor of the
Mughal functionary called faujdar in 1781, the magistrate came
also to exercise a measure of judicial authority that never belonged
to his predecessor. In 1786 he also became Judge and Collector. In
1793 Cornwallis separated revenue from justice and vested the
former function in the Collector. But civil justice and the magistracy remained united in a single officer called Judge-Magistrate.
This system did not work well. In 1810 separate magistrates were
appointed in certain districts in the interests of law and order.
Their number increased and the office came to combine revenue
functions in 1831, when the magistrates became Collectors and
District Magistrates.[4] The Civil Judge became a separate officer
exercising the powers of sessions judge as well. The combination

[4] See Misra, *Central Administration*, ch. 6.

of powers in practice continued from motives of economy. The Divisional Commissioners appointed under Regulation I of 1829 also exercised revenue authority and powers of criminal justice. This, however, affected efficiency, especially at higher levels of control. In 1837, therefore, the Bengal Government appointed a committee to recommend plans for a separate police organization. But nothing remarkable came of it since after the abolition of its monopoly in 1833 the East India Company was guided more by considerations of economy. Its immediate concern was to realize from the Indian revenues the value of its assets, not to allow any increase in the cost of administration which provision for specialized services would involve. It was not until 1860 that the Government of India appointed a Police Commission to suggest suitable reforms, and on the basis of its recommendations the Council of India passed an Act (Act V of 1861) which provided for a hierarchy of police officers separately from the magistracy.

The police reform of 1861 took its cue from an experiment made in Sind by Sir Charles Napier, its Commissioner. He had organized a police force which differed from the police of the rest of the country in that it was a separate and self-contained organization, its officers having no other functions. Bombay followed this example and in 1853 appointed a Superintendent of Police for every district. Though subordinate to the District Magistrate, the Superintendent had exclusive control over the police force of his district.

Act V of 1861 entrusted the general management of the police force in every province to an Inspector-General of Police. The district police were placed under Superintendents who were aided by assistant Superintendents. The Commission made no reference to any police officer of the rank of Deputy Inspector-General, but as they recommended that Divisional Commissioners of Revenue should cease to be Superintendents of Police, the Inspector-General came to be assisted by one or more Deputies. In some cases the Divisional Commissioners themselves were given authority for appointment, promotion, and internal discipline, and were thus to act as Deputy Inspector-General. The District Magistrates were in most provinces similarly vested with a general control over the disciplinary arrangements of the district police, including punishment of subordinate police officers. The exercise of such control was however limited to the District Officer. The magistracy in general ceased to discharge the purely police function of thief-catching. The Divisional Commissioners were also subsequently divested of the authority given to them in some places under Act V of 1861.

Nature and Extent of the Increase

In 1857 there were nearly 900 covenanted civil servants in India, of whom not a single one was Indian, and, as has been stated,[5] the total number of uncovenanted servants in the same year was 5,928, of whom 3,082 were either Europeans or Anglo-Indians, and the remaining 2,846 Indians.

On 31 December 1901 the number of judicial and executive officers of all races exercising jurisdiction in British India, including the courts of appeal, amounted to 10,249. Of these 315 belonged to the units superior to districts, and the remaining 9,934 to the districts and their subordinate units.[6] According to Curzon's inquiry of 1903, the number of posts held by Indians alone at salaries exceeding Rs. 75 totalled more than 16,000, about 6,000 more than the 1901 total for all races. It is probable that both these totals did not take into account the number of police officers, who in 1901 totalled 7,125, of whom more than 6,000 were sub-inspectors drawing pay below Rs. 75 per month.[7] If, taking matriculation as the lowest qualification for appointment, the number of police and other officers on a minimum of Rs. 50 a month is added to these 16,000, the total number of Indians in government employment in 1901 might be taken at a figure approaching 25,000. The number of Indians employed in government service on Rs. 100 and over a month in 1873 totalled 4,039.[8]

In later years, it seems, the number of regular paid members of the judicial and executive service of the Government did not increase; for honorary judges and magistrates were appointed from among the educated classes of Indians who relieved the regular cadres in the discharge of ordinary judicial and executive business. The following table, which does not include police officers, gives an idea of the relative strength of paid and honorary judicial and executive officers in the present century.

[5] See above, p. 194. [6] Cd. 1801, p. 340. [7] Ibid. p. 352.
[8] See I.O., MSS. Eur. E. 218, 23/1, f. 65.

Judges and Magistrates in Civil and Criminal Departments

Year	Stipendiary	Honorary
1931	8,271	18,609
1940	6,480	21,485
1945	7,020	18,706
1950*	9,034	11,668

* Figures relate to India alone, prior to the merger of Indian states, and excluding Pakistan.

Source: Statistical Abstract for relevant years.

The table given below indicates the rate of increase in the number of police officers from sub-inspectors upwards:

Year	Number
1901	7,125
1931	14,654
1939	12,565
1946	9,078
1950	19,566*

* Excluding Pakistan.

The figures for the judicial, executive, and police officers in the present century lend themselves to certain interesting conclusions. They clearly show that there was a gradual decline in the number of judges and magistrates belonging to the regular salaried cadres. This effected an economy without a sacrifice in speed or efficiency; for the honorary judges and magistrates, who were men of education, substance, and social prestige, generally performed their duties with credit. The enlightened members of the community had in addition the satisfaction of being associated with the administration of the country. After the transfer of power in 1947 the number of salaried judges and magistrates increased from 7,020 in 1945 for united India to 9,034 in 1950 for divided India, while the number of honorary officers decreased in the same period from 18,706 to 11,668. The number of police officers, on the other hand, increased from 9,078 to 19,566 in about five years. The total strength of the police rose from 141,542 in 1946 to 322,123 in 1950.[9]

A decrease of honorary officers signified an increased cost of administration under Congress Government in free India. It might be argued that the increase of the official machinery of administration resulted from a partial separation of the judiciary from the executive, but apparently it resulted from the growth of crime which, with the decrease of honorary officers, necessitated an enormous increase in the cost of police administration. This might be justified as an expedient to meet the problem of educated unemployment, but it is done at the cost of the tax-payers who receive no return in the form of social security.

The following table gives the strength of the civil police force for British India, and shows how much it increased after the transfer of power in 1947.

Police Force

	1881	*1901*	*1921*	*1931*	*1939*	*1950*
Commissioners of Police, I.G., D.I.G.	26	34	64	63	57	67
District S.P., Deputy & Assistant	330	477	985	972	863	1,499
Inspectors & sub-inspectors*	14,582	6,614	13,121	13,619	11,645	18,000
Sergeants & head constables	..	17,611	28,066	25,825	24,457	40,415
Mounted constables	3,156	2,589	2,767	2,236	1,376	1,499
Foot incl. water police	105,072	117,819	157,855	158,972	150,533	260,643
Total	..	145,110	202,858	201,687	188,931	322,123

* The *Statistical Abstract, 1881*, shows inspectors and sub-inspectors under the headings subordinate officers with Rs. 100 and over and those with less than Rs. 100 a month. With sergeants and head constables they totalled 21,782.

Source: Statistical Abstract for relevant years

These figures clearly suggest that by 1901 law and order was such that it did not call for any considerable increase in the police force,

[9] *Statistical Abstract, 1952–3*, table 59, p. 176.

which remained more or less on the same level as that of 1881. Internal disorders and external dangers in the course of the First World War combined to raise the number of controlling officers from 34 in 1901 to 74 in 1918–19. It fell to 64 in 1921. But in the first two decades of the present century the total strength of the police force increased considerably. The mounting demand for freedom made the task of keeping law and order increasingly difficult in spite of the modern means of communication at the command of the Government. The position began to improve after 1931 and showed considerable improvement by 1939 when political violence seemed to have lost its force. After independence in 1947, however, the problem of law and order became far more serious than before and the size of the police registered an unusual increase, as shown by the figures for divided India in 1950. Of the total police force of 322,123, Part 'A' States, which did not cover all the previous British 'Provinces', had 292,085. The conclusion that the Congress Government needed a relatively much greater police force to maintain law and order is therefore entirely justified. It cannot be argued that this increase proceeded from the merger of what were previously called 'native states'.

The table given below gives the relative costs of police administration in British India and independent India. The figures up to 1939 are for united India, while the figure for 1950 is for divided India.

Cost of Civil Police

Year	Rs. crores	Year	Rs. crores
1881	2·33	1921	10·69
1892	2·71	1931	12·17
1901	2·91	1939	10·85
1912	5·75	1950	39·24

Sources: For 1892 and 1901: Cd. 1801 (£ converted @ 1s. 6d.=Rs. 1); for 1939: Cmd. 6441; for all other years, *Statistical Abstract.*

Another interesting conclusion emerging from the police figures is that in a period of twenty years ending in 1921, while the force increased by only 1.4 times, the cost of its maintenance more than trebled.

One reason for this was the increase in the number of officers. If sub-inspectors and higher posts are treated as officers and those below as men, the proportion of officers to men will be found to have increased from 1:15 in 1901 to 1:13 in 1931. In other words, there was 1 officer to every 13 men in 1931 as against 1 officer to every 15 men in 1901. As regards officers themselves, the proportion of those in senior ranks increased more than that of subordinates, as is clear from the following table:

Year	(a) Inspectors-Gen. down to Deputy and Asst. Supt.	(b) Inspectors and sub-inspectors	Proportion of (a) to (b)
1901	511	6,614	1:13
1921	1,049	13,121	1:13
1931	1,035	13,619	1:13
1939	920	11,645	1:12
1950	1,566	18,000	1:11

Source: Statistical Abstract.

These figures are significant in that they agree with the nature and extent of educational development in recent decades. Like higher education, civil administration too was becoming more and more top-heavy. Considerations of space prohibit the examination of this important question in any detail. This must be left to future research. But the conclusion that the cost of administration grew especially on account of a proportionate increase in higher posts seems irresistible; it is also supported by the following table indicating the number of persons and class of personnel employed in the central Government during 1950–2:

Central Government Appointments, 1950–2

Year	Admin. and Executive	Clerical	Skilled and Semi-skilled
1950	51,860	142,003	147,956
1951	54,814	142,850	145,304
1952	58,555	150,870	145,455

Source: Statistical Abstract, 1952–3.

Thus while in one year, from 1950 to 1951, the administrative and executive personnel registered an increase of 2,954, the clerical staff increased by 847 only. This meant an increase of 3.5 officers to one clerk. Taking all three years together, the number of clerks appointed exceeded that of administrative and executive personnel, but still indicated no more than 1 officer to 1.5 clerks. The figures for skilled and semi-skilled personnel speak for themselves.

GROWING POWER OF THE BUREAUCRACY

Under the British from 1799 the central Government was vested in the Chief Secretary and Secretary to Government. The Chief Secretary's powers were those of general control and authority so to distribute the establishments of different departments as might appear to him best calculated for the proper conduct of business. The execution of details formed no part of his responsibility; individual Secretaries of the respective departments were solely responsible for these. The operation of this principle extended to other departmental chiefs at provincial and district levels and was a recognition of the gradual separation of controlling and executive functions at various levels. The rise of bureaucracy in fact originated from the opening of more and more departments, with specific and increased powers assigned to departmental chiefs.[10] It was a cumulative result of increased business, paper work, and regard for the rule of law. It grew more and more rigid with the progressive increase in the volume of legislation which clogged the movement of files and delayed the formation of decisions, since a departmental chief had to be sure of the legality or otherwise of a decision before he took it.

The high salaries of covenanted civil servants was another factor in the growth of their influence and prestige. The scale of salaries under Hastings and Cornwallis[11] was raised again under Wellesley. For example, the annual salary of his Chief Secretary amounted to Rs. 55,000 and of his Secretary to Government Rs. 50,000. Wellesley set an example which subsequent Governments

---

[10] This question is examined in some detail in Misra, *Central Admin.*, which shows the manner in which departmentalization proceeded, especially under Cornwallis and Wellesley.

[11] See above, pp. 187–8.

followed. The extended functions of the state, which now covered a wide range of duties connected with the administration of land, was another factor contributing to the enhanced power and authority of the bureaucracy. The Government owned and managed forests and huge commercial undertakings like roads and bridges, railways and irrigation works, salt and opium factories, water-supplies and hydro-electric works, all run and managed by civil servants.

To this must also be added the influence stemming from superiority of rank in the hierarchy of caste, for most of the Hindus in the service of the Government were upper-caste men, especially Brahmans and Kayasths, who dominated the field. The Indian Public Service Commission reported in 1887 that of 1,866 Hindu members of the judicial and executive services as many as 904, or nearly half, were Brahmans, and 454, or nearly a quarter were Kayasths, who were called Prabhus in Bombay. The number of Kshatriyas or Rajputs was 147; of Vaishyas 113; of Shudras 146; and of others 102.[12] The Brahmans were especially dominant in Madras, with 202 of a total of 297, and in Bombay, with 211 out of 328.

Caste prejudices were particularly strong in South India where Brahmans held most of the government posts. For example, the *Census of India, 1901* reported that the higher castes exhibited strong prejudice against allowing their children to sit in the same building with children of low origin. 'Cases are by no means rare', the report stated, 'where the efforts made to enforce an equality of treatment for the depressed castes have led to large schools remaining closed for years and to disturbances of the peace and the destruction by fire of the crops and huts of the people belonging to these castes.'[13] The indirect effect of Brahmanical dominance was especially prejudicial to the lower orders of society; for decisions as to the location of new schools and grants-in-aid lay with the officers of the Education Department who were for the most part Brahmans or members of other higher castes.

Speaking of employment in Government by caste, the 1901 Census reported that the Brahmans were dominant in spite of their small percentage in the population: 'The Brahmans, though forming less than one-thirteenth of the total number of Hindus, hold 8

---

[12] Ind. Public Service Com., 1887–90, *Rep.*, p. 33.   [13] *Report*, i. 163.

appointments out of 11, and the Prabhus, Baniyas, and "Sindhi Hindus", many of whom doubtless belong to the above castes, all but 4 of the remainder.' The return contained no entry for lower castes.[14] The figures for education, even for 1921 and subsequent years, show the dominance of upper castes, especially of Brahmans. It is only under the constitution of free India that, for political reasons, depressed castes have been guaranteed reserve seats in the public services.

The brown bureaucracy of the British in India remained largely Brahmanical and definitely dominated by the members of a few upper castes.

Historically speaking, therefore, the bureaucracy of British India had developed many of the characteristics which go to the making of totalitarian rule. Among forces militating against it were the rule of law and a free judiciary, the growth of parliamentary institutions, and the rise of Indian capitalism and free industrial enterprise. Of these three, the first had taken some root, but the remaining two, parliamentary government and industrial capitalism, had just begun to emerge as an independent force in the 1920's when, under a Western ideological obsession, there arose demands for the public ownership of the means of production and distribution. These grew in strength in the following two decades.

But what did public control mean in the peculiar context of India's historical development. It necessarily meant a further increase in the power of its bureaucracy. It meant control of nationalized industries by government servants, an extension of 'red tape' to commercial and industrial undertakings where progress depends upon quick decisions, and both delay and increase in cost. The exercise by the state of its regulatory function controlling productive relations is one thing, but to extend that function to the actual operation and management of industries is quite another. It means state capitalism, which in the West arose from an economy of plenty. In the underdeveloped state of the Indian economy it not only means killing the already weak and limited entrepreneurial ability of the nation, but also depriving labour of its bargaining capacity. The only safety valve is a resort to the parliamentary machinery of government, but since this is still not rooted in society, it may be dispensed with in favour of totalitarian

[14] *Report*, i. para. 367, p. 220.

rule. The advocates of nationalization, therefore, have in actual practice been playing a bureaucratic game.

Bureaucracy in itself, however, is not to blame. It is after all a mode of conducting business, a mode that springs from a peculiar system of government and political philosophy. As Professor Ludwig von Mises rightly says:

Those who criticize bureaucracy make the mistake of directing their attacks against a symptom only and not against the seat of the evil. . . . It is true that the officeholders are no longer the servants of the citizenry but irresponsible and arbitrary masters and tyrants. But this is not the fault of bureaucracy. It is the outcome of the new system of government which restricts the individual's freedom to manage his own affairs and assigns more and more tasks to the government. The culprit is not the bureaucrat but the political system.[15]

THE LEGAL PROFESSION

The development and diversification of the sources of wealth and the corresponding extension in the operational area of law necessitated specialization in the legal profession. It is true that as yet the extent to which this has taken place is limited, since the economy is still mainly agricultural and law cases most commonly arise from land disputes. There are few cases relating to civil liberties or to a violation of constitutional provisions; nevertheless, they are on the increase, and there is ample material to discuss the nature and extent of specialization. Such a discussion could include a study of legislative trends and judicial developments, of legal education and professional practice, but considerations of space permit only a quantitative review of the profession from a historical point of view.

More Litigation in Zamindari Areas

It has been seen how the setting up of the Supreme Court in Bengal enabled that province to take the lead in establishing the new legal profession, and how Cornwallis's Permanent Settlement compelled recourse to judicial action as the only means of enforcing rights. Litigation consequently developed earlier in Bengal than

[15] *Bureaucracy* (1945), pp. 7 and 9.

elsewhere; for example, the *Statistical Abstract, 1881,* shows that the total number of original and appellate civil suits there amounted to 0.5 million out of 1.6 million for the whole of British India in that year. The total value of the suits was Rs. 16.54 crores for British India, of which Rs. 5.18 crores, or nearly a third again, came from Bengal.[16] The number of civil suits in India increased to 2.2 million in 1901, and their value to Rs. 28.71 crores in the same period. Bengal's share was nearly one-third of the number of suits and 38 per cent. of their value.[17] Together with the United Provinces, Bengal claimed 1.2 million of the total number of suits. Obviously the zamindari tenure, especially in the permanently settled areas, produced more ligitation than the ryotwari system. The zamindars as a class served to feed the courts, and the rent laws designed to protect tenancy rights brought the tenants to contest cases.

The period of twenty years after 1881 seems to have been a prosperous one for the legal profession; in the present century civil suits showed a general tendency to decline, especially after 1933 when the maximum recorded was 2.7 million. This number declined to 1.8 million in 1939. Of the Indian provinces, however, Bihar was an exception. There the general tendency was for civil suits to register a steady rise. The number of civil suits in Bihar and Orissa together in 1921 totalled 1.6 lakhs against 2.18 lakhs for Bihar alone in 1937, rising to 2.46 in 1940. This may perhaps be attributed to the peasant movement there which was at this period by far the most powerful in the country. The tenants had the backing of their leaders, especially Swami Sahjanand and Jadunandan Sharma, who assisted them in their judicial actions against zamindars.

In the production of law graduates the difference between Bengal and other provinces was still more marked. While in the decade 1864–73 Calcutta University produced 704 Bachelors of Law, Madras produced only 78 and Bombay 33. In the decade 1879–88 Madras and Bombay tried to catch up, but the difference was still considerable. In eight out of those ten years, for example, Calcutta produced 924 graduates, while Madras and Bombay turned out only 232 and 156 respectively in ten full years. There was one law graduate to every two B.A.s in Calcutta, but the corre-

---

[16] *Statistical Abstract, 1879–80 to 1888–9,* p. 48.
[17] Ibid. *1892–3 to 1901–2,* p. 343.

sponding proportion was one to eleven in Madras, and one to nine in Bombay.

A Period of Prosperity, 1870–1920

Like the number of civil suits, the number of law graduates also increased especially in the twenty years following 1881, as is clear from the following table.

Law Graduates

1864–73 (10 yrs.)	815
1879–88 (10 yrs.)	1,312
1889–93 (5 yrs.)	1,317

Of this total, as many as 642, or nearly half, graduated from Calcutta University; 316, or nearly a quarter, from Bombay; and the remainder from Madras, Allahabad, and the Punjab. Though far behind in the first decade, Bombay thus soon caught up and ranked next to Calcutta in the production of law graduates by the 1890's.

Decline

The following table gives the number of law students which may serve as an index of the growing size of the profession, for most of the law graduates became lawyers:

Law Students

1912–13	3,036
1921–22	5,234
1939–40	6,749
1949–50	9,464*

* Divided India.

Of the total number in 1921–2, as many as 1,946 were graduates, including 11 holding Masters' degrees in law. For 1939–40 the number of graduates was 2,758. If 45 is assumed to be the average percentage of passes on the basis of 9,464 students, the number of law graduates would come to 4,275 for divided India. If against this is set the total number of 540 Bachelors of Law produced in 1901, it is clear that the output of law graduates in about five decades increased by eight times. This means that the number of lawyers increased far more than the number of civil suits which, on the contrary, showed a general tendency to decrease, especially after 1933. These figures thus establish beyond doubt the fact of growing unemployment in the legal profession. The Sapru Committee on Educated Unemployment brought this fact to light in 1935.

Comparative View of Increase in Number of Lawyers

Thacker's *Indian Directory*, which gives the names of lawyers, shows that in 1861 there were 32 advocates in the Supreme Court at Calcutta. They were all Europeans. Among 80 of the attorneys, proctors, and solicitors who practised in that court, only 4 were Indians. One of them was Woomesh Chunder Bonnerjea, who in 1885 became first President of the Indian National Congress. There were not many Indians among managing and articled clerks either—only 5 out of 26. It was at the small cause court that Indians constituted the majority of pleaders: 28 out of 51 of them. Of these 26 were Hindus and 2 Muhammadans. The remaining 23 were either Europeans, Anglo-Indians, or Christians.

The establishment of the Calcutta High Court in 1862 and the growth of university education soon afterwards led to an increase in the number of Indian advocates and vakils of the High Court. The following table indicates the rate of increase:

Advocates and Vakils of the Calcutta High Court

Date of call or admission	No. Advocates	No. Vakils
Up to 1870	19	31
1871–80	64	30
1881–90	60	45
1891–1900	126	86
Total	269	192

Source: Thacker's *Ind. Directory, 1901*, pp. 239–43.

Of the total number of advocates, 167 were Indians, but the proportion of Indian vakils was much higher: 189 of a total of 192. By 1900 the legal profession became Indian in composition even in

I.M.C.—22

the highest ranks, with a fair sprinkling of Muhammadans who counted for little in the years previous to 1880. Some of the advocates and vakils were employed in the public service, especially in the judicial branch of the Government. The bulk of them, however, practised law in the various courts of Bengal and Bihar. As their names suggest, they were largely Bengali Hindus. Among attorneys, proctors, and solicitors too Indians increased considerably, their number in 1900 being 135 out of 235. They also were for the most part Bengali Hindus. The number of pleaders at the small cause courts in Calcutta rose from 51 in 1861 to 152 in 1900; with few exceptions, they were all Bengali Hindus. Muhammadans were found only at the highest level of the legal profession.

Bombay and Madras presented a more or less similar picture except that the number of the vakils of High Courts was proportionately much greater than in Calcutta where on account of a relatively higher population of Europeans the number of Indian advocates was by far the largest.

Advocates and Vakils of the High Court in Bombay and Madras

Date of call or admission	Bombay		Madras	
	Advocates	Vakils	Advocates	Vakils
Up to 1870	9	18	13	6
1871–80	25	76	28	35
1881–90	42	82	24	140
1891–1900	100	198	21	210
Total	176	374	86	491

Source: Thacker's *Ind. Directory, 1901*, pp. 1172–3 and 1284–90.

Of 176 advocates in Bombay, 108 were Indians, of whom 54 were Parsis. The remaining 68 were Europeans, Anglo-Indians, and others. Prominent among the Indians in the list for 1901 were Phirozshah Mehta, admitted in 1868, Mohandas Karamchand Gandhi in 1892, Muhammad Ali Jinnah in 1896, and Vallabbhai Patel in 1899. They were all barristers and advocates of the Bombay High Court. The vakils of this court were for the most part Hindus, with a fair sprinkling of Parsis. Below them came attorneys and solicitors who were largely Anglo-Indians and Parsis. Then came the pleaders who were mainly Hindus who practised in district and subordinate courts.

Not all the vakils of the High Court practised law, although most of them did. Of 491 vakils of the Madras High Court, for instance, 54 were in the public service, mainly in the judicial branch of the Government as munsifs and sub-judges; some served as professors and assistant professors of law, and some as Deputy Collectors and Statutory Magistrates.

Like Bengal, Bombay, and Madras, the United Provinces of Agra and Oudh also registered a marked increase in the number of lawyers during 1890–1900, as is clear from the following table:

Advocates and Vakils of the High Court in U.P.

Enrolment	Advocates	Vakils
Up to 1870	4	30
1871–80	36	53
1881–90	70	51
1891–1900	100	235

Source: Thacker's *Ind. Directory, 1901*, pp. 243–6.

The Muhammadans, who constituted the bulk of the landed aristocracy in the U.P., especially in Oudh, were dominant among Indians who were barristers. For instance, of the 18 advocates of the Allahabad High Court in 1901, 10 were Europeans or Anglo-Indians, 6 Muhammadans, 1 Hindu, and 1 other. In other courts Muhammadan advocates were by far the largest in number, although Muhammadans formed hardly 15 per cent. of the U.P. population. In government service they enjoyed, in proportion to their numerical strength, nearly four times as many high appointments.[18] The vakils of the High Court, however, were for the most part Hindus. Prominent among them in 1901 were Munshi Jwala Prasad, President of the Vakils' Association established in 1875, and Pandit Motilal Nehru, father of Pandit Jawaharlal Nehru. Among other important vakils who practised at Allahabad in 1901 were Pandit Madan Mohan Malviya, a founder member of the Indian National Congress and later Vice-Chancellor of the Benares

[18] *Census of India, 1901*, vol. i, para. 366, p. 220.

Hindu University, and Sir T. B. Sapru, a leading moderate and leader of the Liberal Federation of India established in 1918. Of the total number of 369 vakils of the High Court, only 33 were Muslims. The vakils represented a middle-class economic interest in society and were the products of Indian universities, but since a middle-class element was generally wanting among Muhammadans, the number of Muslim vakils was in proportion to nearly half their numerical strength in the population. There were even fewer Muhammadan pleaders as these were high government officials and advocates educated in England. The class so educated represented the landed aristocracy in society.

In 1901 a comparable situation existed in Bihar where Muhammadans held considerable upper-class zamindari interests. Their proportion to the total population of the province was even less than that in the U.P.; yet of the 17 barristers practising at Patna 12 were Muhammadans. Of the remaining 5, only 1 was a Hindu, the number of Europeans being 4. Prominent among Muhammadan barristers were Syed Ali Imam, Syed Hasan Imam, and Syed M. Haque, who later joined Congress and supported Gandhi's non-cooperation movement in Bihar. On the other hand of the 12 vakils of the High Court there was not a single Muhammadan. All were Hindus.

The following table gives a comparative view of the increase in the number of advocates and vakils of the High Court in the first two decades of the present century.

Advocates and Vakils of the High Court

	1901		1921	
	Advocates	*Vakils*	*Advocates*	*Vakils*
Bengal	269	192	646	443
Bombay	176	374	275	1,033
Madras	86	491	63	300

Source: Thacker's *Ind. Directory.*

Besides the advocates and vakils of the High Court, there were, as has been seen, attorneys, solicitors, pleaders, and mukhtars. In later years barristers were distinguished from advocates, and High

Court vakils from ordinary vakils who generally practised in subordinate courts. In subsequent years there was a greater increase in the number of these ordinary vakils, pleaders, and mukhtars. The number of barristers and advocates showed a general tendency to decline, though not appreciably until 1940.

The legal profession in India did not develop a tradition of scholarship as it did in Europe or America where, as the *Report* of the University Education Commission of 1948-9 (p. 257) stated,

legal education has long occupied a high niche among the learned curricula. Products of the study of law have frequently risen to positions of distinction in public service or have amassed fortunes in the private practice of law or have acquired wide reputation as scholars without even entering practice. Legal education is on an elevated plane and teachers of law enjoy a high respect, perhaps as high or higher than those of any other field of education. The names of Dicey, Pollock, Anson, Maine, and Holdsworth of Oxford, as examples, are known wherever there is knowledge of law and jurisprudence. The same might be said of men like Roscoe Pound of Harvard University in America.

In India, however,

we have many eminent practitioners and excellent judges. The law has also given us great leaders and men consecrated to public service. Most conspicuous of these is Gandhiji. Here the comparison ends. We have no internationally known expounders of jurisprudence and legal studies. Our colleges of law do not hold a place of high esteem either at home or abroad, nor has law become an area of profound scholarship and enlightened research.

The Commission attributes this want of scholarship and research to 'conditions inherent in our position as a dependent nation'. But this is an over-simplification; if it were true, how could India have produced such eminent and internationally known scientists as Raman, Bose, and Bhabha, or such a great man of letters as Tagore. A more likely explanation is that the modern legal and judicial system was imported from Britain, where the study of law and jurisprudence had become a secular institution, but the secularization of law in India was a task fraught with enormous risk since it involved interference with religion, which formed part of the institution and administration of property.

Another consideration is that it is difficult for Indian practitioners to think independently of the influence of India's traditional learning by rote, of the joint family system, and of a society based on the rigid principle of caste and an agricultural economy. Indian jurists could not possibly grasp the complexity of legal concepts which in the West had grown correspondingly with the diversification of the economy and the growth of civil liberty and constitutional conventions, the main object of which was to secure the freedom of individuals and classes and to protect property rights under a social system becoming more and more subject to control by the apparatus of the state. They simply could not cast loose from their moorings and think independently in Western terms. To do so required an education and training in the science of methodology where Indian universities, because of their traditional literary emphasis, remain even now poorly equipped.

OTHER PROFESSIONS

This section will deal mainly with medicine, teaching, and engineering. Of the three, medicine remained by far the most important, second only to law. The following table gives a comparative view of the trends in each of them:

Medicine, Teaching, and Engineering

Year	Medicine		Teaching		Engineering	
	Colleges	Students	Colleges	Students	Colleges	Students
1911–12	4	1,396	12	552	4	1,187
1916–17	8	2,511	15	765	4	1,319
1921–2	8	4,065	20	1,247	5	1,443
1931–2	11	4,201	23	1,582	7	2,171
1939–40	12	5,640	25	2,229	7	2,509
1949–50	45	14,097	71	4,742	29	12,331*

* Includes students of technology also; there were 2,515 students of engineering alone in 1948 (see Univ. Ed. Com., *Rep.*, p. 232).

Source: *Statistical Abstract*, no. 57, table 147, pp. 244–5; no. 66, table 139, p. 404; *1939–40*, table 56, p. 131 and table 36, p. 92; *1952–3*, table 34, p. 82. The figures for 1949–50 are for divided India, including Indian States; prior to that, for British India.

The slowest growth in each was of students at teachers' training colleges. The number of engineering students began to increase in the 1930's, but more rapidly in the next decade. Comparing the number of law students with that of these three professions taken together, the following table brings out the continued dominance of law.

Year	Law students	Students of medicine, engineering, & teacher training
1911–12	3,036	3,135
1916–17	5,426	4,595
1921–2	5,234	6,755
1931–2	7,151	7,954
1939–40	6,749	10,378
1949–50	9,464	31,170

These figures lead to interesting conclusions. Until 1932 the number of law students was more or less equal to the total number of students of the other three professions. In 1940 numbers of law students showed a decline, but increased again in 1950. Nevertheless the rate of increase lagged far behind that of medical and engineering students. In a period of twenty years after 1931, while students in medical and engineering colleges increased respectively by nearly 3.5 and 6 times, the corresponding figure for law students was 1.3 only. The teaching profession on the other hand remained for the most part in the hands of untrained teachers. Doubtless the number of training colleges increased considerably, but not the number of students, who remained far behind the other professions, since teaching was ill paid and students were not attracted to it.

Engineering and Technology

As late as the 1930's engineering and technology remained far behind medicine. Both made progress in the early 1940's, engineering and technology more than medicine and surgery. The *Report* of the University Education Commission of 1948–9 points out that in a period of fifteen years from 1930 the Engineering College of the Benares Hindu University admitted 1,996 students, of whom 910 (i.e. 45 per cent.) graduated in engineering. If the same percentage of results is assumed for the other universities over a longer period, the following table indicates the approximate number of graduate engineers produced:

Students and Graduates in Engineering and Technology

Year	Students	Graduates
1911–12	1,187*	534
1921–2	1,443*	649
1931–2	2,171*	947
1941–2	3,009†	1,354
1949–50	12,331†	5,549

* Pure engineering.   † Includes technology.

On an average, the number of graduate engineers and technologists can be assumed to be about 1,800 a year. The intake of the various branches of engineering alone, however, was not considerable. The University Education Commission calculated it as 2,515 only for the year 1948. On the basis of 45 per cent., India was thus producing at the time nearly 1,130 graduate engineers. This was a poor rate; at about the same period Britain produced nearly 3,000 a year. The Commission pointed out that in America the average annual output of graduate engineers was nearly 50,000 in the 1940's. This was about 17 times the number produced in Britain and 40 times that in India.

Qualitatively speaking too the position was far from satisfactory. The Indian universities were not able to undertake any detailed study of India's technological problems; nor did they carry out research to build up a body of scientist engineers. The *Statistical Abstract* shows that right up to 1921–2 no students attained a Master's degree in any branch of engineering. In 1931–2 Bombay alone had to its credit one holder of a Master's degree in electrical engineering. The figures for subsequent years also indicate that little or nothing was done in the field of technological research. The ordinary graduates were mainly civil engineers. The output of mechanical and electrical engineers became noticeable towards the third decade of this century when mining and metallurgy graduates were still rare, there being only three in 1931–2, and that exclusively in the U.P.

Backwardness in the study of engineering and technology in India was to some extent due to the traditional preference for purely literary pursuits, but mainly to the industrial backwardness of the country and the British policy of excluding Indians from the engineering branches of the Railways, Telegraphs, and Public Works Departments for such a long time.

Medicine and Surgery

In medical education India was relatively advanced, having a long tradition of its own.[19] Besides the medical colleges in the three principal cities of Calcutta, Madras, and Bombay medical schools were established in the different parts of the country, and in 1911–12 there were 24 such schools with 3,800 scholars. In 1939–40 there were no more than 30, since some of them had in the meanwhile been converted into medical colleges. The number of students in medical schools rose from 3,800 in 1911–12 to 6,737 in 1939–40. In fact before the 1930's the bulk of medical practitioners were trained in these schools. They were maintained either by the Government or private agencies, especially missionaries.

The number of higher degrees awarded for medicine, as compared with engineering, was much greater than that of licentiates. The following table gives a comparative view, on the basis of the university results of 1921–2 for the whole of British India:

University Passes in Medicine and Engineering, 1921–2

	Medicine and Surgery	Engineering
Master's & Doctoral degree	5	*nil*
Bachelor's degree	406	62
Licentiates	43	51

The results of examinations not conducted by universities registered a total of 68 graduate engineers against 190 licentiates, equivalent to upper and lower subordinates.

[19] See above, p. 59.

The general tendency in medical education was to drop the licentiate examination and to develop research and specialized studies in such fields as surgery and opthalmology, gynaecology and cardiology, children's diseases and social therapy. The study of engineering, on the contrary, remained for all practical purposes limited to three of its main branches, civil, mechanical, and electrical, with a heavy bias on the side of traditional civil engineering. The number of licentiates continued to be prominent in the examination results, as shown below for the year 1939-40:

University Passes in Medicine and Engineering, 1939-40

	Medicine	Engineering
Doctoral degree	10	nil
Master's	24	nil
Bachelor's	752	323*
Specialized†	81	nil
Licentiates	nil	119

*Civil eng., 165; electrical, 94; mechanical, 49; mining & metalurgy, 15 (in U.P. only).

†Incl. hygiene, sanitary science, public health, opthalmology, surgery &c.

Source: Cmd. 6441, table 62, pp. 146-7.

Apart from the incentive to go in for medicine which was provided by the Government for military and other reasons from an early period, medicine enjoyed a peculiar advantage which was denied to engineering. The medical degrees of Indian universities were recognized by the British General Medical Council, and the holders of such degrees were entitled to be entered in the British General Medical Register. This qualified them for practice throughout the British Commonwealth.

During the First World War the size of the medical profession increased considerably. The immediate object was to meet military contingencies, but this expansion impaired the quality of medical education. Thus in 1921 the General Medical Council decided that medical degrees should not automatically be recognized and that a system of inspection should be instituted to see that Indian universities conformed to the minimum standard required for recognition by that Council. Indian universities, however, resented the plan of periodic inspection. The result was the establishment of the Indian Medical Council in 1931. Its object was to lay down and to maintain a requisite standard of medical education in these universities. As part of their policy to conform to these standards most of the provinces undertook to abolish the diploma or licentiate hitherto given by separate provincial examination boards.

While considering this a welcome step in the right direction, the University Education Commission of 1948–9 expressed some concern over the increasing number of medical colleges which, in the absence of adequate equipment and of duly trained and experienced staff tended to affect the standard and quality of medical education. It stated that

some of the provinces have increased the number of students admitted to medical colleges to sometimes double the number, with the result the training that is imparted to such *alumni* with inadequate staff can hardly be said to meet the minimum standard required. The Commission is not aware of any positive steps taken by the Indian Medical Council to rectify these serious defects.[20]

Teacher-Training

The question of ensuring the professional efficiency of teachers has been neglected. There is nothing comparable to the Indian Medical Council to set and maintain teaching standards. As has been seen, the number of schools and pupils increased far more rapidly than the number of training colleges, and especially than the number of scholars in such colleges. Until quite recently some teacher-training colleges in India were found to have on their staff young instructors who lectured to students on methods, psychology, and similar subjects without having any qualifications or experience. This was particularly the case in colleges said to have a strong bias in favour of basic education, where examinations were conducted through the agency of Government.

Business Administration

Commercial education and business administration has emerged as one of the rising professions in India in recent decades, as the result of the advancement of commerce and industry. Commerce,

[20] *Report*, p. 266.

previously looked upon as a means to promote private gain, developed into an intellectual activity, drawing upon all departments of knowledge. It became a separate discipline requiring research and ability of a high order. In fact with the growth of joint-stock concerns and financial trusts, business became the concern of the community, influencing public interests and policies. Its administration naturally partook of the character of public administration, requiring a knowledge not only of the laws governing economic institutions but of the principles and methods applicable to them. Business administrators came to be members of recognized professions, possessing not only skills but also a knowledge of general principles and natural laws.

CUMULATIVE SOCIAL CHANGES

In the light of what has been said, we can sum up the cumulative changes that modern education and capitalism brought about in the traditional social system of the Hindus who constituted, and still constitute, the bulk of India's population.

The most remarkable change is that the foundations of the old mutually exclusive and hereditary status groups of caste, which recognized no natural equality of man, have been shaken. They have been shaken not so much by the religious renaissance of the nineteenth century, for this was a reorientation of India's liberal tradition and gave a new interpretation to the philosophical liberalism of Indian social thought; it put the old wine into a new bottle. The new forces which weakened the traditional social order were those of Western education and a capitalist economy, a free judiciary and parliamentary institutions.

The contribution of Western education lay mainly in three things. First, it broke the intellectual monopoly of the Brahmans by opening the doors to all classes. Secondly, it created an educated class of Indians comprising members of the various learned professions who cut across caste and became supporters of liberal reforms, whereby liberalism became increasingly institutionalized. Thirdly, it set in motion an unprecedented degree of occupational mobility which helped to increase social mobility. Whereas under the traditional caste order learning remained with the Brahman and craft with the artisan, what Western education tried to do was to cross-fertilize the two. Equality of educational opportunity left the artisan free to acquire learning and the Brahman free to become a technician. Since modern business and technology demand both skill and a knowledge of principle, those who pursued them became entitled to the respect that attaches to education and learning. Indeed, Western education not only supplied the ideological principle of liberalism but created new social classes to champion that principle. In the past religious movements had also preached the ideal of equality and fraternity, but since education had been a monopoly institution, not diversified but literary in character, no new classes had emerged to support that ideal or put it into practice.

The influence of the modern legal and judicial system went deeper still. Hinduism first began to be modified not in schools and colleges but in the law courts. They acted as levellers of social distinction based on caste. From mere protectors of person and property they grew into the watchdogs of civil liberty. The professional duty of the new class of legal practitioners demanded conformity with the rule of law. The professional discipline which regulated their conduct became contractual in nature. It made them liable to prosecution in the event of failure properly to serve their clients regardless of caste or religious persuasion. The institution of British courts in India thus brought into being a class of persons who could not refuse legal assistance to anybody who needed it.

It was a consequence of the British economic order of *laissez-faire* and of the British educational and legal systems that the state was in duty bound not only to uphold a free economic system but also to protect and promote the interest of individuals in the pursuit of that system. With certain modifications, the British transplanted to India the relationship which had come to subsist between business and government at home. The various chambers of commerce, trades associations, and bodies of millowners obliged the Government of India to remove trade barriers, to improve communications, and to effect land, police, and judicial reforms so as to ensure the security of property. The introduction of a free press and representative government was also to some extent motivated by the consideration of reducing the authority of the executive in the interests of free trade. To these must be added the professionalization of modern business and the influence exercised by financial trusts, the directors of industry and their technical personnel, all resulting from the growth of capitalism.

But, as has been seen, these changes were for the most part limited to certain big cities and large towns. Their influence on India's bureaucracy did not extend to the rural areas commanding nearly 80 per cent. of the total population. It was only partially felt even in district and subdivisional towns, unless these happened to be industrially developed. While the operation of the imperialist economy limited the growth of Indian capitalism, it was in Britain's interest to maintain the myth of superiority of its Indian bureaucracy, dominantly European at the higher levels. And since India's tradition of caste authoritarianism fitted in well with the imperial scheme of things, Indian bureaucrats, who usually belonged to higher castes, were quick to step into the shoes of the British who left India in 1947.

Bureaucracy thus continued to retain its hold over business in India and is increasing its hold with the extension of the state's economic function. This may be beneficial to the educated middle classes, since as officers of Government they step in as controllers of nationalized industries without any personal stake in them. But it is no gain to the country as a whole. The system of state control in fact stifles the growth of entrepreneurial elements which India has in past badly needed to speed up production. Traditionally recruited from the literary classes, with no business acumen, civil servants are most unsuited to accelerate production in Indian conditions, especially within the framework of law and legislative authority. Only private enterprise and international co-operation could increase the rate of progress without endangering freedom and parliamentary democracy.

Part IV

CHARACTER AND ROLE OF THE INDIAN
MIDDLE CLASSES

XII

The Period Before 1905

By the circumstances of their growth the bulk of the Indian middle classes came to consist of the intelligentsia—public servants, other salaried employees, and members of the learned professions. As a consequence of the traditional social system and the dependent economy of the country, social stratification first proceeded from legal, educational, and administrative changes, not economic diversification. Of the professions, law became by far the most important and powerful; and it was not until after the first two decades of the present century that the technical and business professions slowly began to rise to importance.

The period before 1905 may be divided into two parts. The first was that of the Company's rule which witnessed the rise of the new middle classes. They consisted of Indian agents and employees of the East India Company and private merchants. They built large fortunes with which they bought considerable landed estates. They were the people who in Bengal largely supplanted the old aristocracy and commercial monopolists. They and their descendants were the first recipients and patrons of English education. The Brahman family of the Tagores is an admirable illustration of the manner in which the descendants of a servant and agent of the Company rose into a new aristocracy, combining wealth and education. The first Indian to compete successfully in the Indian Civil Service Examination in 1864 was Satyendranath Tagore, a grandson of Dwarkanath and elder brother of the poet Rabindranath.

The second part of this period began with the spread of English education among ordinarily well-to-do and lower middle-class families, especially after 1870. Although the influence of the educated aristocracy continued, the growth of education and the professions created conditions in which the middle classes came to challenge that influence by demanding representative institutions; for few of the great zamindars would 'consent to submit to the indignities of a canvass'.[1]

UPPER-CLASS DOMINANCE TO 1892

Before the introduction of an elective principle under the Indian Councils Act of 1892, the aristocracy was dominant in politics. Its interests were represented by the British Indian Association, established in 1851. This was the first organized body of Indians known for their wealth, social position, and education. Though basically a landholders' organization, the Association included among its members 'the representatives of the most important interests, whether territorial, commercial or professional'.[2] Of it Sir Alexander Mackenzie, Lieutenant-Governor of Bengal in 1895, said:

I have always regarded the British Indian Association as the premier Association in India expressing the views of what I may call *raises* [aristocracy] and leading classes of Bengal, the leading Province. I always knew in bygone years that when they were applied to by Government for advice on any matter, we were sure to have an opinion given by men who felt the responsibility of their position as leaders of the people. There is no country in the world where modern democratic notions find a less congenial soil than in India, or where they may, if pushed to extremes, afford more dangerous mischief. Hence the importance of a body like [the British Indian Association] and men with a solid stake in the country.[3]

Indeed the members of the British Indian Association were generally invited to serve on the Legislative Councils. Between 1862 and 1892 as many as thirty-five of them became members of the Bengal Legislative Council. They represented agricultural, commercial, and professional interests of a superior order. In the first decade following the introduction of constitutional reform under the Indian Councils Act of 1861, members of the Tagore family were by far the most influential of them. Maharaja Rama-

---

[1] Let. from British Ind. Ass., 30 Apr. 1898, in I.O., Home Proc. (Public), Nov. 1898, vol. 5414, para. 5, f. 2324.
[2] Memo. fr. Sec., Brit. Ind. Ass., to Chief Sec., Govt. of Beng., ibid. para. 13.
[3] Ibid. para. 18, f. 2331.

nath Tagore (1800–77), who became a member of the Bengal
Legislative Council in 1866 and of the Central Legislative Council
in 1873, was a brother of Dwarkanath. A Brahma Samajist and
member of the Calcutta Corporation, he helped to found the
Association of which he remained President for ten years. Another
founder member was Prasanna Kumar Tagore (1801–68). Educated
at the Hindu College at Calcutta, he became a government pleader.
In 1854 he was appointed a clerk assistant to the Legislative
Council and in 1863 became a member of the Bengal Legislative
Council. Another founder member was Maharaja Bahadur Sir
Jotindra Mohan Tagore, a third member of the same family and
nephew of Prasanna Kumar who was educated at the Hindu College
and by a European tutor. He inherited extensive landed property
and made endowments for religious, charitable, and educational
purposes. He became a member of the Bengal Legislative Council
in 1870 and of the Central Legislative Council in 1877.

On the business side of the British Indian Association Ram
Gopal Ghose (1815–68) was one of the leading members. The son
of an ordinary shopkeeper, Ghose became a big merchant. Like
most of his contemporaries he was educated at the Hindu College.
An active member of the Bengal Chamber of Commerce, he was
one of the earliest leaders of education and social reform. He
became a member of the Bengal Education Council established in
1845, and in 1862 of the Bengal Legislative Council.

Of thirty-five members of the British Indian Association who
had served on the Bengal Legislative Council before 1892, nearly
one-third belonged to the legal profession, especially to the High
Court in Calcutta. Since their chief economic stake in society was
land, these lawyer members fought for the preservation of zamindari rights in the same way as did the Maharaja of Darbhanga, a big
landholder of Bihar who was also a member of the Central Legislative Council.

An interesting test case arose in 1885 on the question of the
Bengal Rent Bill. Introduced in 1882 on the recommendation of
the Famine Commission of the previous year, the Bill proposed to
concede certain tenancy rights which the zamindar party considered highly prejudicial to its interest. Under the Bengal Tenancy Act X of 1859, for example, an occupancy right accrued to a
tenant who had legally held his land for twelve years, but if he was

transferred from one plot to another, even in the same village, he ceased to be entitled to that right. This gave rise to great uncertainty and it was the tenant who stood to suffer. The proposed Bill therefore provided that if a tenant had held land continuously for twelve years, he would become a settled ryot with full occupancy rights, transferable by sale. It even went so far as to declare that any person holding land as a tenant was to be regarded as having held it for twelve years unless otherwise proved. One of its clauses nullified all contracts previously entered into between zamindar and tenant during the last twelve years. Another provision obliged zamindars to give compensation for any disturbance caused by eviction. The Bill was also intended to protect non-occupancy tenants against arbitrary ejection. It included provisions to restrict the power of zamindars to raise the rent. One of these, for example, limited all rent to one-fifth of the gross produce of land, a provision which landholders opposed with all the strength and influence they commanded.

After lengthy debates in the Council the Bill was referred to a Select Committee which discussed it in as many as sixty-four meetings, each lasting for nearly four hours. *The Englishman* of 14 February 1885 wrote:

There has probably never been a document laid on the Council table subject to so many dissents as the Report of the Select Committee on the Bengal Tenancy Bill presented yesterday. The Select Committee was exceptionally large, its deliberations have been protracted over an almost unprecedented number of sittings, and each member seems to have been quite determined to have his own way. . . . The main interest which attaches to the dissents is not, however, a personal one. It consists rather in the revelation which they afford as to the diametrical opposition of the two parties in the Council on the great issues involved; and as to a conflict on general principles as strongly waged within the Select Committee as it has been waged outside in the Press.[4]

The composition and character of the two parties involved in the Bill may be ascertained by reference to a letter dated Calcutta, 17 March 1885, which the Viceroy, Lord Dufferin, addressed to Lord Northbrook, one of his predecessors, describing the Council proceedings on the Bill. It shows how the Central Legislative

[4] Encl. to let. no. 3 in Northbrook Coll., I.O. MSS. Eur. C. 144, vol. v, 16 Feb. 1885.

Council was sharply divided into two groups. The zamindar party consisted of the Maharaja of Darbhanga, Babu Peari Mohan Mukerji, Rao Sahib Visvanath Narayan Mandlik, and Syed Amir Ali. Except for the Maharaja of Darbhanga, all the three Indian Councillors were lawyers by profession. Mukerjee and Ali, both members of the British Indian Association, were from Calcutta, and Mandlik from Bombay. There was no Indian tenant representative in the Council: government officials defended the tenants. Besides the Lieutenant-Governor of Bengal, they included Sir Steuart Bayley, Reynolds, Hunter, and Gibbon. However, through the intercession of the Viceroy, the Council made a number of concessions which watered down the effects of the original Bill. In his presidential address the Viceroy clearly admitted this, saying:

I fear that the enumeration I have made of these modifications which have told so largely in favour of the zamindars, will have renewed the pang felt by those of my honourable colleagues who were opposed to their being made, and who, so far from admitting that the zamindars have been hardly dealt with, contend, on the contrary, that this Bill still falls short in giving adequate protection to the raiyat.[5]

Still dissatisfied with the concessions made to the zamindars, the Maharaja of Darbhanga and Babu Peari Mohan Mukerji first moved a postponement of the Bill, but when that fell through, they opposed it. The Bill was passed by an official majority of votes. It is interesting to note that Ashutosh Mukerjee, a leading vakil of the Calcutta High Court and later Vice-Chancellor of Calcutta University and an influential man in the public life of Bengal, also opposed the Bill. He declared that it was contrary to what he called the absolute rights of the Bengal proprietors conferred upon them under Regulation I of 1793. At the request of the Central Committee of Landholders he prepared a pamphlet—*An Examination of the Principles and Policy of the Bengal Tenancy Bill*—and agitated against the passage of the Bill which, as has been said, was passed by the mere weight of the official majority.

THE RISING INFLUENCE OF THE MIDDLE CLASSES

In the twenty years preceding 1892 the middle classes had begun to make their influence felt. That influence, as has been seen, arose

[5] Ibid. encl. to no. 4, 17 Mar. 1885, ff. 14–15.

from the growth of English education after 1870 and especially in the 1880's. The establishment of the Punjab and Allahabad Universities in this period was a consequence of the efforts of private Indian agencies, especially of the educated professions.

The rapid expansion of English education, especially in Bengal, proceeded immediately from economic motives. The increase in the population and progressive fragmentation of land was reducing the once respectable class of proprietors to increasing dependence on education as a means of livelihood. The North-Western Provinces *Administration Report* for 1890–1 has already been referred to,[6] and it has been seen how the priestly and literary castes, who in Bengal had some small shares in landed estates, thronged English high schools to get just enough education to fit them for clerical jobs. The class called by this report 'the professional agitators' sprang from among the 'hungry' but educated 'malcontents' whose number swelled annually.

In one of his private and confidential letters to Northbrook, Dufferin also bore testimony to the rising influence of what he called 'Babu politicians', who arose from among the ranks of middle or small proprietors. He said:

In conclusion, however, I think I can safely say that however annoying may be the violence, childishness and perversity of the Bengalee press and of young Babu politicians, their influence at present is neither extensive nor dangerous. The mass meetings and all the paraphernalia of the Indian Caucus, though they make a noise and may appear effective and formidable in the telegrams which the Associations transmit to England, do not really amount to much for the present, but it does not follow that some years hence what is now in the germ may not grow into a very formidable product.[7]

This establishes beyond doubt the fact that by the 1880's the educated middle classes had begun to exercise a palpable degree of political influence. They were in the formative stage with the promise of becoming formidable.

The social and political pretensions of the educated middle classes had no chance of recognition except on a democratic principle of representation. Nomination as the basis of appointment

[6] See above, p. 312.
[7] MSS. Eur. C. 144, no. 16, f. 3, 23 June 1886.

to the Legislative Councils or recruitment to the civil service tended to prejudice their claims and favoured only men of considerable property and social position. It was thus understandable that they should demand representative institutions. Their English education and professional training made them specially ready to make this demand. The professional elements even of landholders' associations advocated the introduction of parliamentary institutions in India. For example, many of them seceded from the British Indian Association and in 1876 formed a separate organization called the Indian Association. Surendranath Banerjea, a dismissed member of the I.C.S., was the most prominent of its leaders. The Indian Association paved the way for the establishment of the Indian National Congress in 1885.

MIDDLE-CLASS OPPOSITION TO TENANT RIGHTS

It has been seen how the educated classes, who before 1905 were for the most part upper-caste men and landed proprietors, especially in Bengal, opposed the extension of any tenant rights, although tenants were the people who constituted the bulk of population. Determined to go ahead with tenancy reforms and thereby to win the support of the mass of the people, the Government feared that an expansion of Legislative Councils might result in the blocking of progressive legislation in the interests of the country as a whole. Writing to Northbrook on the subject of extended representation, Dufferin said in a letter of 16 October 1886:

If it could be done, of course it would be an excellent thing; but the more I see of these people the less sanguine I am of reaching a conclusion which will both work advantageously for the country at large and satisfy native aspirations. There would be great difficulty in getting hold of the best men, and then, when we have got them, they represent after all only an infinitesimal section of the people and the interests of a minute minority in reference to a great proportion of the subjects with which legislation deals. All the efforts of the Government of India are principally directed towards the improvement of the condition of the masses. We should be very apt to find ourselves thwarted and opposed by constituencies whose qualifications are simply wealth and education. For instance, all our recent legislation would have been carried with infinitely more difficulty, and against a heavier dead weight of opposition, if more natives had been present in the Council.[8]

Dufferin was thus not in favour of expanding the Legislative Councils in spite of the growth in English education since 1861, when the first Indian Councils Act had been passed. He obviously feared that representation of the educated classes, besides being prejudicial to British interests, would impede legislation beneficial to the country at large.

We have recently relaxed the law in relation to debtor and creditor [he added], and contemplate a still further relaxation of the penalties of imprisonment for debt. On such a point probably we should not receive much help from Members who would naturally be connected with the money-lending classes. On the education question the Brahmins would do everything they could to prevent the lower castes sharing in its advantages, whereas we should wish to do the very opposite.[9]

The apprehension of the Government arose not only from the anti-tenant role of the Indian members of the Council, but also from the nature of the demands made by the Indian National Congress, the political organization of the educated classes. For example, since 1866 the country had been faced with famine conditions resulting in a general state of agricultural distress. By one of its resolutions the Congress session of 1886 expressed a deep sense of concern over what it regarded as the growing poverty of the Indian people. But the remedy it suggested was not to interfere with the oppressive conduct of zamindars or the usurious operation of money-lenders, but to introduce representative institutions in Government. The Congress believed that the introduction of a representative Government 'will prove one of the most important practical steps towards the amelioration of the condition of the people'.[10] A second measure urged by Congress in a resolution in 1888 was the introduction of the Bengal pattern of the Permanent Settlement in all parts of the country, a measure which, as has been seen, operated to the great hardship and disadvantage of tenants.

[8] Ibid. no. 17, f. 2.
[9] Ibid.
[10] Resol. 2 of 1886 in encl. to ibid. no. 20.

DOMINANCE OF EDUCATED MIDDLE CLASSES IN BENGAL

The Indian Councils Act of 1892 turned the balance of power and influence in favour of the educated middle classes, especially of the legal practitioners. By its provisions the Legislative Council of Bengal was to consist of 20 members of whom not more than 10 were to be officials. Of the 10 seats reserved for non-officials, nominations to as many as 7 were to be made by the Lieutenant-Governor from panels recommended by the Calcutta Corporation, municipal and district boards, the Bengal Chamber of Commerce, the Trades Association, and the Senate of Calcutta University. Only one of the remaining three seats was 'ordinarily' to be held by the great landholders of the province. In other words, no seat was specifically reserved for the landholders, and since few of them consented to being returned on popular votes, they remained deprived of any representation in the Council, although 95 per cent. of the population of Bengal was rural.[11]

In a memorandum of 30 April 1898, the Secretary of the British Indian Association complained that on account of the peculiar constitution of municipal corporations and district boards it was the professional classes that got elected, not the great landholders.

A cursory glance at the reports [it pointed out], will show that these bodies are mainly composed of small land-holders and traders, vakils, mukhtears, school-masters and medical practitioners. Rightly or wrongly, men of property and position, with their oriental notions of propriety, as a rule, keep themselves aloof from meddling in the Municipal and the District Board elections. If by chance any of the large land-holders offer themselves as candidates for election to a seat in the Council, they are sure to be defeated by a combination of vakils, mukh-tears, small traders, money-lenders and school-masters. The District Boards and Mufassil Municipalities, and even the Calcutta Corporation and the University, have as a rule elected pleaders and members of the other branches of the legal profession. They have occasionally elected representatives of that section of the educated middle class which, too strongly imbued with western radical ideas, has necessarily no sympathy with either landowners or ryots, and which is out of touch with the bulk of what is after all a purely agricultural community.[12]

[11] In Bombay the landholders had two seats although its rural population constituted 81 per cent.
[12] I.O. Home Proc. (Public), Nov. 1898, vol. 5414, ff. 2327–8.

Thus by the end of the nineteenth century the educated middle classes had emerged as an interest distinct from both the great landholders and tenants. Besides legal and medical practitioners, they comprised schoolmasters, traders, and money-lenders.

DOMINANCE OF EDUCATED MIDDLE CLASSES IN CONGRESS

The educated middle classes dominated the Indian National Congress and entered Legislative Councils as Congressmen. In a report of 18 June 1899 the 'General Superintendent of Operations for the Suppression of Thagi and Dakaiti', C. S. Bayley, informed the Government of India that in the 1893 elections to the Bengal Council the *Indian Mirror* stated that

five out of the six members elected were Congress men. In 1895 the Police Inspector of Tirupati in Madras discovered a Telugu pamphlet in which, among other results of the Congress agitation, the fact was mentioned that Government had appointed four representatives of the Congress and had given them seats on the Legislative Council. As lately as the sixth of the current month the 'Advocate' (Lucknow) drew the attention of its readers to the fact that six prominent Congressmen are or have been Judges of different High Courts and that several others have received decorations or Native Titles.[13]

CONGRESSMEN AS GOVERNMENT SERVANTS

The appointment of Congressmen to Legislative Councils or to government posts was thus regarded in those days as a matter of credit or achievement. In a footnote of his report of 18 June 1899 Bayley indicated that the appointment of six of the Congressmen as judges 'was exclusively upon their professional merits and had nothing to do with their Congress associations'. An interesting case which arose in 1901, however, suggests that the Government was also guided by other motives. It related to the appointment as Judge of the Bombay High Court of N. G. Chandarvarkar who, prior to this appointment, had been President of the Lahore session of the Indian National Congress held in 1900. The case throws light on the character of early Congressmen, especially of the 'moderates' who formed their dominant group. Replying to an

[13] Hamilton Coll., I.O. MSS. Eur. D. 510/2, xiv. 67.

objection of Lord George Hamilton, the Secretary of State for India who viewed this deal as contrary to principle, the Viceroy, Lord Curzon, wrote:

I think that it would be a great mistake not to appoint this man, and that it might be a great advantage to appoint him. Although a politician in his earlier days, he had, for 10 years, stood entirely outside of the Congress movement, and had not attended a single one of their meetings. He was selected as President of the last meeting to the disgust of the extreme faction ... because the bulk of the party felt it most desirable in existing circumstances to have a temperate man, and because they wanted to hold out the olive branch to me in the hope that I may take it. Chandarvarkar, as you know, then made a very moderate and milk-and-water speech. Now, if his abilities warrant his being placed upon the Bench, which I believe they do ... you might more or less disarm him in the future and get him on your side. If you fail to appoint him, you infuriate the man himself, and you throw back the moderate party in the Congress into an attitude of hostility and revenge. I should be sorry to see this done, because, as I have often told you, the Congress is, in my opinion, rapidly sinking into insignificance. Any tactics that might savour of persecution would at once revive it as a fighting force, and give us much trouble in the future.[14]

The Early Supporters of Congress

A confidential report of the Chief Secretary to the Government of Bengal, dated 18 July 1899, showed that 'the principal subscribers of the Congress now are the members of the legal profession and their clients'.[15] In fact of the total of 13,839 delegates who attended the various annual sessions between 1892 and 1909, as many as 5,442, or nearly 40 per cent., were members of the legal profession. The other important groups were those of the landed gentry with 2,629 delegates, and of the commercial classes with 2,091. The rest of the total was made up of journalists, doctors, and teachers, with a very small number representing other professions.[16]

The predominance of the legal profession in Congress was to a large extent limited to Bengal, where the middle classes had

[14] Ibid. 510/7, ff. 160–1. In a previous letter of 3 Jan. 1901, Curzon referred to the compliments made to him by the moderates 'expressing pious aspirations' which, he said, 'it will be my duty to shatter' (ibid. f. 6).

[15] Ibid. 510/2, xiv. 229.

[16] P. C. Ghosh, 'The Development of the Indian National Congress, 1892–1901' (Lond. Univ. Ph.D. thesis, 1948), chart C.

become relatively more powerful. Those who subscribed to Congress in other parts of the country included zamindars and certain chiefs. According to the Chief Secretary's confidential report, for example, 'the late Maharaja of Darbhanga gave Rs. 10,000 annually to the Congress fund'. Commenting on the attitude of the ruling Maharaja he said:

It is not known whether the present Maharaja will continue the subscription. I gathered from a conversation which I had with him that he is not inclined to give any assistance to the Congress, but it is quite possible that he will yield to pressure. He informed me that an endeavour had already been made to obtain a contribution from him.[17]

Maharaja Sir Jotindranath Tagore and his brother Sir Surendranath Tagore of Bengal were believed to be subscribers to the Congress, 'not from active sympathy with the movement, but from fear of newspaper attacks'.[18] Obviously, the educated middle classes had by the end of the nineteenth century emerged as a force to be reckoned with even by the landed aristocracy of the country.

C. S. Bayley's report[19] pointed out that among the leading early supporters of the Congress were the Maharaja of Darbhanga, the Raja of Vizianagram, the Maharaja of Bhaunagar, the Gaekwar of Baroda, the Raja of Ramnad in Madras, and the Tatas of Bombay. In 1890, for instance, the Maharaja of Darbhanga and the Raja of Vizianagram 'each subscribed Rs. 5,000 towards the cost of Babu Surendranath Banaji's deputation to England to lecture on behalf of the Congress'. At a meeting held on 2 February 1894 Banerji mentioned that in the previous year the Maharaja had contributed Rs. 20,000. 'In 1893 and 1895 an "Indian Friend", who was supposed to be the Maharaja of Darbhanga, gave Rs. 15,000 to the Permanent Fund of the Congress and Rs. 8,000 to the Special Fund for "India" ', a journal of the British Committee in London whose Secretary was A. O. Hume, a retired Civilian and friend of the Congress.[20] Similarly the Gaekwar of Baroda financed the Parsi Congress leader, Dadabhai Naoroji. Colonel Biddulph, Agent to the Governor-General in 1899, reported that 'over a lakh

[17] I.O., Hamilton Coll., MSS. Eur. D. 510/2, xiv. 230. Though helping 'the Congress Party', the Maharaja was 'at heart thoroughly loyal' to the British (see ibid. 509/5, Curzon's letter no. 103).
[18] Ibid. 510/2, xiv. 229. [19] See above, p. 352.
[20] I.O. MSS. Eur. D. 510/2, xiv. 65.

of rupees had been taken out of the Treasury by His Highness (the Gaekwar of Baroda) without the knowledge of the Minister presumably for some secret purpose'.[21]

Congress Opposition to Tenant Rights

Supported by such classes as had proprietary interests in land, the Congress and its representatives in Legislative Councils opposed the passage of any measure calculated to protect the peasantry. An interesting test case arose in 1899 when the Punjab Land Alienation Bill was introduced in the Central Legislative Council. The object of the Bill was to restrict the sale and mortgage of lands in the Punjab, so that money-lenders might not easily have them transferred in satisfaction of their decrees. The agricultural debtor had to pledge his harvest or land, and the judicial system afforded the money-lender the means of rapidly realizing his dues. The pleader, who was himself a creation of this system, offered his services to both parties and encouraged litigation to his own professional advantage. The proposed Bill thus affected the interests of both the pleader and the money-lender. It prohibited sales except to a resident of the same village or to agnates of the two parties concerned. It also limited mortgages to fifteen years at the end of which the land was to revert free from encumbrance to the mortgager.

By a resolution of 1899, however, the Congress opposed the passage of the Bill. It stated that instead of giving relief to the people by restricting the freedom of sale or mortgage, the Government, wherever it was a rent receiver, should prohibit 'any enhancement' of its own rent, and that where private landlords were rent receivers, it could make 'some provision to prohibit undue enhancement of rent'. The opposition to the Bill in the Council was led by Sir Harnam Singh, who represented the interest of landowners and money-lenders. He was, however, guided by certain interested pleaders at Lahore who wrote his speeches.[22] Referring to him in a private letter to the Secretary of State, Curzon, commented:

Sir Harnam Singh has made himself the mouthpiece of those classes in the Punjab who are opposed to the Bill, and I need hardly tell you that neither his speech some weeks ago, nor the Note of Dissent, was

[21] Ibid. 510/2, f. 65.　　　[22] Ibid. 510/6, 24 Oct. 1900.

written by himself. He is a mere figurehead, who has been put up by the discontented parties, and his materials are provided, and his speeches written, by some interested pleader at Lahore.[23]

None the less, the bill was passed.

MIDDLE-CLASS OPPOSITION TO FACTORY REFORMS

Though advocating the cause of Indian industry, the middle classes were no friends of industrial workers. The general tone of the vernacular press which represented their views was opposed to any factory reform designed to improve the condition of labour. What they agitated for was the imposition of countervailing duties on foreign imports into India, not the alleviation of the distress of the working class. In 1889, for example, Curzon passed a measure imposing duty on the import of sugar. The *Hitvadi* in its issue of 24 March described the enactment in the following words: 'This is the first law of its kind in this country, which has for its object the protection of indigenous commerce and industry. Never before did we see the Government passing a law of this nature—a law so welcome to the people of India.'[24] Other Indian newspapers made similar comments. Nevertheless the same issue of *Hitvadi* opposed the Mining Bill whose object it was to improve the living conditions of women and children and to restrict their employment under a certain age.

The Bill under notice [it commented] proposes to do what the Factories Act has done and will impose harassing restrictions upon mining labour. . . . The Indian labourer is very poor, and even with the earnings of his entire family cannot make his two ends meet. He does not want the uncalled for generosity of the Government.[25]

MIDDLE-CLASS SUPPORT OF INDIGENOUS CAPITALISM

Though opposed to the extension of tenant rights and labour reform, the middle classes in general advocated indigenous capitalist development. As a consequence of occupational mobilization many of the Kulins or members of higher castes, including Brahmans, developed interests in modern trade and industry. Some of

[23] I.O. MSS. Eur. D. 510/5, 15 Aug. 1900, f. 326.
[24] Curzon to Hamilton, 13 Apr. 1899, ibid. 510/1, para. 18 of no. 17.
[25] Ibid. para. 19.

them, as has been seen, became the leaders of education and business. This occupational mobilization was of great social significance.
It tended to effect a radical change in the traditional relationship of
the literary and the business classes. The intellectual and the pluto-
crat, who had in the past pulled in opposite directions, were under
the British being drawn close together. Their coming together was
also due to political reasons; for while British rule thwarted the
aspirations of educated Indians by excluding them from higher
posts in the civil service, it prejudiced the interest of Indian
capitalists by denying them their right to protection. Both sociologically and politically, therefore, the growth of an alliance between the intellectual and the business man was of considerable
importance.

The National Congress naturally became the rallying ground for
the educated as well as the business classes. Of the total number of
1,584 delegates who attended its Poona session in 1895, as many as
437 were members of the commercial classes. The number of
business representatives who attended the Calcutta session in 1896
was 88 only, but at the 1906 Calcutta session it was 230.[26]

Men like Naoroji, Dutt, and Gokhale were not business men,
but they agitated for the development of indigenous capitalist
enterprise. They believed that the operation of the imperialist
economy hindered the pace of India's industrial progress; for
although it encouraged agricultural and commercial development,
the dominance of the import industry had the effect of destroying
the country's artisan production without promoting a corresponding increase in the output of mill-made goods. The paucity of
indigenous capital, technical skill, and enterprise partly accounted
for the state of industrial backwardness. But imperialism was not
free from its own responsibility. It constituted a serious strain on
India's financial resources, and much of the trade balance which
might otherwise have contributed to industrial advancement went
towards the payment of the 'home charges'.

MIDDLE-CLASS OPPOSITION TO IMPERIAL POLICY

The Indian middle classes were as a rule opposed to the military
and financial policy of the British Government in India. On

[26] Ghosh, chart C.

account of the gradual extension of territories and the enhanced proportion of European troops to Indian, the regular military expenditures of the Government had risen from nearly £3 million in 1793 to £14 million in 1856. The military and naval resources of the East India Company were employed not only in India's interest, but also in the general interest of the British empire in the East. For example, the expenditures involved in the two wars with China in 1839 and 1856 as well as in the expeditions to Persia were borne largely from Indian revenues. The Afghan war as well as the Burmese wars which swelled the public debt of India were undertaken either in the interest of Britain or the commercial interest of the Company. But their cost was met from the territorial revenues of India. The Company's commercial expeditions to the different parts of Africa, China, and the Straits Settlements were likewise carried on at the cost of the Indian revenues.

The principal head of expenditure prior to 1858 was defence. In 1856–7 it amounted to nearly £15 million out of a total revenue of £31.9 million. During the Indian Mutiny of 1857–8 defence expenditure rose to £21 million and then again to £25.5 million in the next year. Added to this were the military charges incurred in England for the payment of salaries when on leave and pensions of British troops serving in India, for the expenses of the military college in England, charges of recruitment, passage outfits of the officers, and other similar expenses.[27]

The civil charges of the Government increased no less rapidly, from £400,000 in 1765 to £23 million in 1857. This was mainly due to the increase of territories, the Europeanization of the public services, and the expansion of the administrative machinery, especially of revenue and justice. The cost of civil and military administration increased considerably after 1858. The Government of India protested against the diversion of India's revenues to extra-Indian purposes, but, as will presently be seen, the imperial authorities paid little attention to this.

Added to the increasing cost of civil and military administration was the dislocation caused to the Indian finances by recurrent famines in the decades following 1860. Nevertheless the import duty on cotton twist and yarn was reduced from 10 to 5 per cent. in 1861, causing a loss of £40,000 annually to the Indian reven-

[27] See P. J. Thomas, *The Growth of Federal Finance in India* (1939).

ues. The import duty on yarn was further reduced to $3\frac{1}{2}$ per cent. and on cotton-piece goods to 5 per cent. in 1862. One of the main objects of this was to stimulate the import of British cotton goods into India. To achieve that object fully the whole of the customs duties on cotton goods was swept away in 1878, resulting in a sacrifice of £250,000 annually to the revenues of the Government of India. This was followed in 1882 by a removal of all import duties excepting those on liquor, arms, and salt. The annual loss to the Indian revenues rose to £1,219,000.

Equally damaging was the loss caused after 1873 by the depreciation of silver and the consequent augmentation in the amount of remittances to England. This depreciation followed the adoption of the gold standard by Germany, and subsequently by Denmark, Norway, Sweden, and Holland. This reduced the demand for silver for the purposes of currency. Before 1873, the operation of a bimetallic system had maintained a stable ratio of $15\frac{1}{2}$ to 1 between silver and gold, but the link between the two metals was broken and silver began to slump in 1874 when France, Belgium, Switzerland, and Italy also switched to a monometallic system by a suspension of the free coining of silver. Since India had to make remittances to England in terms of gold standard, the rate of exchange fell by 1885 from 2s. to a rupee to 1s. $6\frac{1}{4}d$. 'The loss by exchange was only Rs. 90 lakhs in 1873, but it rose to 3 crores in 1878, and to 4.3 crores in 1885.'[28] The decline in the rate of exchange did not stop here but fell to 1s. 1d. in 1894, with a corresponding increase in the amount of home charges, which rose to Rs. 15 crores.[29] A Royal Commission on Indian Expenditures made inquiries during 1895–1900 and attributed the dislocation of the Indian finances to military spending, loss by exchange, and tariffs. It was in these circumstances that Curzon realized the need to introduce certain countervailing duties on imports. The imposition of a sugar duty was a recognition of this need, but was an inadequate palliative. It was not until the establishment of a Tariff Board under the recommendations of the Fiscal Commission of 1921–2 that an era of protection really began.

In the period of unbridled *laissez-faire* the main burden of taxation had thus to be borne by the agricultural classes. The land revenue of the Government, which amounted, to Rs. 15 crores in

[28] Ibid. p. 211.   [29] Ibid. p. 242.

1858, rose to 33.4 crores in 1929, although considering the amount of public expenditure it accounted for 50 per cent. of the total revenues of India in the former year as compared to 19 per cent. in the latter. Customs revenues remained insignificant for most of the period before 1905, accounting for only 3.3 per cent. of the total in 1880. The Herschell Committee appointed in 1893 realized the need to reimpose import duties on cotton goods so as to counteract the loss by exchange. The new duties, however, brought in no more than Rs. 11 lakhs. The Secretary of State, against dissentient voices in his Council, used his authority to exclude British cotton yarn and cotton fabrics from the list of dutiable goods. Even in 1914 customs duties constituted only 7.7 per cent. of the total Indian revenues, rising to 31.2 per cent. in 1929 because of the protective tariffs introduced by the Tariff Board established in 1923.

THE HELPLESSNESS OF THE GOVERNMENT OF INDIA

Considerable evidence exists to show that the Government of India protested against the policy of the Secretary of State in favouring Britain's imperial interest at the cost of India. In 1867, for instance, he ordered Indian troops to be sent to Abyssinia, the cost to be charged to the Indian revenues. Lawrence objected to this in a letter of 2 January 1868. 'I am sure', he said, 'that the general feeling in India, especially among the natives, will be that it is unjust to charge India with the cost of the ordinary expenses of the troops.' He further stressed this point by saying that India must on no account be forced to pay for a war in Abyssinia 'in which it has really and truly no interest'.[30] But he could not prevent it.

The interests of private British companies in India was another subject of contention under Lawrence. They exercised pressure on the Secretary of State and weakened the authority of the Government of India. For example, the irrigation company in Orissa resented any attempt on the part of the Government to regulate its affairs so as to give relief to the agriculturists.[31] Lawrence's objection to private British companies also arose from the difficulty of controlling their expenditure and of ensuring the just treatment of

[30] Lawrence to Northcote, Lawrence Papers, ix, no. 2, f. 3.
[31] Lawrence to Cranborne, 22 Nov. 1866, vii, no. 5.

Indians travelling by railways. In a letter of 31 August 1866 Lawrence pointedly brought to the notice of the Secretary of State his inability to keep them under proper check:

One of the great objections which I see to the increase of Private Companies in India, representing large amounts of capital, and comprising many wealthy and influential persons in England is the disadvantage at which they place the Govt. in India. The agents and officials of these companies have a strong tendency to look to their Boards in England, rather than to the local Govt., and thus powerful corporations grow up which that Govt. have difficulty in controlling. So long as the Govt. go with the agents in India, all is plain sailing; but the case becomes very different when we exhibit a desire to control or check them. This is shown very clearly when we try to reduce expenditure; to secure a really effective audit of accounts, to insure proper treatment of natives travelling by Rail.[32]

In a previous letter of 17 May Lawrence had already referred to the maltreatment of Indians travelling by rail. 'The whole native community', he had said, 'are open-mouthed at the way native travellers are treated on many of the Railways; and the complaints are corroborated by many of our own officers and officials. Unless some remedy of real efficacy is applied, sooner or later, great mischief will ensue.'[33] Nothing, however, seemed to have been done by the Secretary of State, for the Viceroy later complained:

The Govt. of India has of late years become comparatively weak, and appears to me to be becoming yearly still weaker. The G.G. in particular, while responsible for everything, is shackled and trammeled so that his action, no matter how resolute he may be by nature, can do little . . . We are, indeed a Govt. without the powerful support of a Govt.[34]

The dominance of the Secretary of State and his policy of imperial preference was felt even more bitterly by Strachey, as Finance Member of the Viceroy's Council. His bitterness arose from the insistence of the Secretary of State on priority payment of loans raised in England on account of the Government of India for productive public works, such as railways and irrigation projects. Whenever the Government of India effected savings for these pur-

---

[32] Ibid. no. 31.   [33] Ibid. no. 20.
[34] Ibid. 2 Sept. 1867, ibid. viii, no. 51.

poses, the Secretary of State stepped in to earmark these for home payment. Hence Strachey's comparison of the relationship between London and Calcutta to the wolf and the lamb in the fable.[35] This comment is significant in that it shows how the Government of India had to submit, against its will, to the pressure of the Secretary of State.

Even a powerful and strong Viceroy like Lord Curzon could do nothing beyond protesting against what he regarded as unreasonable and excessive military expenditure incurred for extra-Indian defence projects. An occasion arose when the Defence Committee of the British Government asked the Government of India, without any previous consultation, to add eighteen battalions to the existing strength of the British army in India.

I may tell you [wrote Curzon to the Secretary of State], that I think we shall fight against this tooth and nail. Have you calculated the expense? Barracks alone at 16 to 20 lakhs per regiment could amount to 3 crores; while the recurring annual cost of the regiments would be 180 lakhs. We would sooner run our present risk than pay this heavy premium.[36]

To this must be added the demand which the home Government made for the supply of military officers at India's own cost.

The Government at home [replied Curzon], are breaking our backs. . . . Whether it is South Africa, or the West Coast, or Uganda, or Somaliland, or Egypt, or China, or Siam, we are being increasingly called upon to run the Empire. I have pushed complacency to the point of what many people would call folly . . . We cannot go on doing this any longer—least of all when our requests for corresponding help from home, in the directions where we think it most necessary, are continually refused.[37]

What Curzon wanted was that if India fought 'the battles of the Empire', Britain should meet 'a portion of the charge'.[38] But the Imperial Government paid no heed to this.

In our various bargains with the Imperial Government [he complained to the Secretary of State], we do not come off with such even honours

---

[35] See above, p. 220.
[36] Curzon to Hamilton, MSS. Eur. D. 510/10, f. 139. The emergency had arisen out of the Boer War in South Africa.
[37] Ibid. ff. 137-8. [38] Ibid. 510/12, f. 99.

as to justify us in consenting to this incessant squeeze. There must be give as well as take. Only last week I read a telegram from Lansdowne assuming, as a matter of course, that the Government of India would pay half of the cost of the Consulate Guards at Ispahan. Within the past few days we have consented to take 3,000 more Boer prisoners in India at the cost of great trouble and some risk to ourselves. *There is no time in history when India has been so indented upon and drained before*: and though you will never have a Viceroy more willing to subordinate Local to Imperial interests, I say advisedly that you may not again have a Viceroy who can afford to assume these risks. . . . I feel compelled to utter this note of emphatic warning, because it is my duty, and because I think that undue trespass is being made upon our goodwill.[39]

If the resolutions of the Indian National Congress, especially from 1891 onwards, are examined, it will be found that so far as its opposition to the increased cost of civil and military administration was concerned, there was practically no difference of opinion between the Congress and the Government of India. Both consistently protested against India being forced to fight the battles of the Empire at its own cost. The difference, however, was that while Congress expressed its opposition to British policy publicly, the Government appeared to remain either helpless or complacent. Moreover, the Congress demand for legislative control of the Indian finances was viewed with distrust by the Government. The expansion of the Legislative Councils was therefore regarded as fraught with risk. In a letter of 16 October 1886 Dufferin clearly pointed out this danger to Northbrook, stating that

If we take native opinion as it now exists, we should find it hostile to the annexation of Burmah, to the increase of the army, to the railways and fortifications on our North-West frontier, to our subsidies to the Ameer, and indeed to every class of expenditure which is likely to increase taxation without bringing in an obvious and immediate return.[40]

OBJECTIONS TO COSTS OF ADMINISTRATION

Though suggesting to the Government the expediency of reducing the costs of administration and meeting deficits by an imposition of countervailing duties on imports, the business and professional

---

[39] Ibid. 510/10, f. 139.
[40] Northbrook Coll., MSS. Eur. C. 144, v, no. 17.

classes were themselves unwilling to make any contribution to the public taxes. They opposed the levy of any excise duty or any system of direct taxation such as licences or income-tax. It was in the teeth of great opposition that the Central Legislative Council passed an Act in 1877 introducing a licence tax on trade and dealing. The business classes were among those who benefited most from roads, railways, and communications, and yet they grudged payment of any direct tax.

Their opposition was not in vain. The licence tax operated as income-tax payable in fees on the size of the income arising from trade and dealing, but since the taxable minimum was reduced to as low as Rs. 500 a year, the poorer class of business men were pressed most heavily. In his budget speech of 1886 the Finance Member of the Government, Sir Auckland Colvin, clearly acknowledged the inequitable nature of the tax, saying:

It is open to the vital objection that it presses most heavily on the poorer among the trading, mercantile and commercial classes, and leaves the wealthier besides other whole classes of the upper part of the population comparatively or absolutely unassessed.[41]

Colvin referred to the exemption which the holders of property and the professional classes enjoyed in India. His Income Tax Bill of 1886, which brought into the fold of direct taxation the classes so far exempted, involved controversies which throw considerable light on the selfish character of the Indian middle classes. Besides trade and dealing, this Bill was designed to tax all non-agricultural incomes arising from office, profession, or property, such as house rent and the like. Though amenable to the proposed measure as a temporary expedient to stave off the financial crisis arising from loss by exchange, the Indian members of the Council opposed it as a permanent measure.

While introducing the Bill Colvin referred, among other things, to what he called 'a grievous blot on our Indian administration', which consisted in exempting from taxation the classes that had in the past enjoyed 'the sunshine' of British rule, and risen into prosperity at the cost of the poor agricultural classes. His comments indicated the manner in which the upper middle classes had flourished as a consequence of their freedom from taxation:

[41] I.O. Legis. Proc. (India), 4 Jan. 1886, vol. 2771, no. 114, f. 31.

In spite of what has gone before and in spite of what remains to be said . . . one great fact remains established; one great blot on our administration not only still unremoved, but aggravated by the course of events in recent years. It is this, that, putting aside those who derive their income from land in the temporarily-settled districts, the classes in this country who derive the greatest security and benefit from the British Government are those who contribute the least towards it.

He said that while various opinions had been expressed as to the advantages or disadvantages of British rule, even the most en-venomed and hostile of its critics were agreed on one point, 'that it has given greater security to life, property, and trade, and to the amassing, therefore of wealth, than any Government that ever preceded it'. But it was precisely the mercantile and professional classes, to whom this had brought 'such an abundant harvest', who contributed least towards the support of the Government.[42]

Two of the lawyer members of the Council, V. N. Mandlik and Peari Mohan Mukerji, moved amendments to the Bill. One of these was to limit the period of its operation to a year or two; for in the words of Mandlik it was 'unsuited to the country' and 'past history was against it'.[43] However, the Viceroy, Lord Dufferin, supported Colvin's views and made certain comments which also throw light on the character of the middle classes in India. He said:

We look abroad, and we see that the peasant pays his salt tax, which though it has been reduced, still supplies us with a yearly net revenue of £6,000,000; that the landowner pays his land tax and his cesses; that the tradesman and the merchant pays his licence tax; but that the lawyer or doctor, the members of the other learned professions, the officers of Government, and other persons occupying an analogous status, and the gentleman at large pay little or nothing. I look around this very table, and what do I see? that there is not one of us into whose pocket Sir Auckland Colvin is able to get so much as his little finger. For instance, take my friend Mr. Mandlik, a most eminent and dis-tinguished member of the legal profession. He will admit, I am sure, that his qualifications to rank as a tax-payer are of the most microscopic proportions. The same may be said of my friend Mr. Peari Mohan Mukerji, except in so far as he may be a landowner; but whatever revenues he derives from land are exempted from the operation of this Bill. I might make the same appeal to most of our other colleagues, and, what is equally sad, I am forced to make an identical confession in

[42] Ibid. f. 31.   [43] Ibid. f. 56.

regard to myself and to the members of the Government. There is not one of us who pays any really serious sum from his income into the Imperial Exchequer.[44]

The Income Tax Act of 1886 provided annually for about £620,000, in addition to £500,000, being the yield of the licence tax. Together they taxed nearly 300,000 persons, the taxable minimum being Rs. 500 as before. Of these, only 80,000 new persons were brought under the operation of the Income Tax Act.[45] They were for the most part members of the public services and the learned professions. The remaining 220,000 were traders and dealers. If all are regarded as members of the middle classes, upper and lower, commercial and professional, in a population of 180 million for British India, this gives 1 middle-class person to 600 of the population. This was, however, exclusive of the landed interests which did not come under the purview of this Act.

The Act, it is true, brought the professional and service classes under direct taxation, but as under the licence tax the burden of taxation pressed much more heavily on the lower income groups. While incomes below Rs. 2,000 paid an average assessment of 2 per cent., or 4 pies in the rupee, the rate at and above Rs. 2,000 was only a little over $2\frac{1}{2}$ per cent., or 5 pies in the rupee.[46]

Even in matters of import duties there had been a shift in the burden of taxation from the rich to the poor. The Indian Taxation Enquiry Committee of 1924–5 analysed import duties so as roughly to distinguish articles consumed mainly by the richer classes from those consumed by the population as a whole. It reported:

In the case of articles of direct consumption there has been an increase in the case of those consumed by the population as a whole, from 430 lakhs to 1,746 lakhs, or by 307 per cent., and in the case of articles, mainly of luxury, consumed by the richer classes, from 400 lakhs to 1,416 lakhs or by 254 per cent. So far as these figures go, they tend to indicate a certain amount of shifting of the burden from the

[44] I.O. Legis. Proc. (India), 4 Jan. 1886, vol. 2771, no. 114, f. 35.
[45] Ibid. f. 32.
[46] This position continued in the present century. Dr. John Matthai, a leading Indian economist, stated before the Indian Taxation Enquiry Committee of 1924–5, 'The richer classes in India contribute relatively so small a proportion of the consumption taxes' (*Evidence*, vii. 2).

richer classes to the general population. The duty chiefly responsible for this appears to be that on sugar, which was imposed for the first time in 1894 at 5 per cent., raised to 10 per cent. in 1916, to 15 per cent. in 1921, and is now fixed at 25 per cent., at which figure it yields 14 per cent. of the total customs revenue.

This was part of the policy of protection, but it must not be forgotten, the *Report* added, that it had also 'the effect of raising the price of country sugar as well as that of imported sugar', which tended to 'increase the burden of taxation on the poorest class, who are large consumers of both kinds'.[47]

In the field of excise duties too the middle classes stood by the interests of Indian mill owners. In 1894, for example, when the Government of India levied an excise duty on cotton manufactures in India, Congress passed a resolution recording its 'emphatic protest' against what it considered 'the injustice on cottons manufactured in British India'. It declared the levy as designed to 'cripple seriously the mill industry of this country'. Though composed largely of the professional and literary classes, Congress had in fact emerged as a superior ally of the Indian bourgeoisie, superior not because of wealth so much as education, political influence, and traditional social prestige. The holding of an industrial conference simultaneously with the annual session of Congress in 1905 and the launching of the boycott of British goods in 1906 were by far the most significant expressions of the alliance between the intelligentsia and the bourgeoisie.

RELIGIOUS REVIVALISM AND MIDDLE-CLASS SPLIT

The rise of religious revivalism and the beginning of a split in the rank of the middle classes formed yet another of the characteristic features of the period to 1905. The necessity of resorting to religion as a political weapon arose partly from the failure of the British adequately to provide jobs for the educated, especially the lower middle classes whose number, as has been seen, had been steadily increasing since 1870 and who suffered as a consequence of the inequitable burden of taxation. There were, however, other important causes which went deeper. Religious nationalism was in

[47] Vol. i, p. 120, para. 145.

fact an expression of the cultural crisis produced as a cumulative consequence of British rule.

The middle-class split, the signs of which had begun to appear and accumulate in the 1890's, was due basically to the two different reactions to Western influences, which were either of the reformist or of the revivalist character. In their emphasis on the need to reform the traditional social order both agreed in principle. Both were influenced by English education, by the rule of law, by Christian missions, their methods of work and organization. But while the reformists responded favourably to Western influences, the revivalists regarded them as a serious affront to India's cultural heritage and intellectual pride.

Reformist Movements and their Approach

The Brahma Samaj in Bengal and the Prarthana Samaj in Bombay were two of the main reformist movements. They were supported by better-class English-educated Indians, especially those in the higher employment of the Government. They advocated legislative action as a means to social reform.

Ram Mohan Rai, the founder of the Brahma Samaj, was a typical example of a reformist leader. He co-operated with the British in the spread of Western education and in the abolition of social evils through legislative enactment. Ishwarchandra Sharma, Brahman principal of the Sanskrit College at Calcutta, was another of the early social reformers who sought the co-operation of the British to reform their traditional society. At his instance the Government enacted a law in 1856 sanctioning the remarriage of widows.

Bengal also took the initiative in securing the abolition of Hindu polygamy. Between 1855 and 1857 numerous petitions were presented for the introduction of legislation to prevent that abuse.[48] Babu Ramaprasad Ray and Sir John Grant, a senior member of the Council, prepared a Bill for this purpose, but the Mutiny which broke out soon afterwards delayed it. In 1863 Raja De Narain Singh of Benares submitted a draft Bill on the subject and asked permission to introduce it in the Central Legislative Council, but the proposal was dropped. In 1866 the Government of Bengal took the matter up and, on the basis of the memorials already presented, prepared a draft Bill.

[48] See I.O. Home Proc. (Legis.), 1866, r. 436, vol. 53, ff. 257–8.

A study of the documents connected with this measure shows that the upper castes of Bengal had become notorious for social degeneration. In a petition of 27 December 1855 the Maharaja Bahadur of Burdwan, for instance, referred to the degradation of the respectable class of Brahmans called Kulins, a distinction supposed to have been given to them by Raja Ballal Sen of Bengal shortly before the Muhammadan conquest. Certain Brahmans and Kayasths, who had probably migrated from Upper India, were distinguished as Kulins or superior to the rest of their tribes in the province. Though contrary to the doctrines of Hinduism, which insisted on monogamy except under special circumstances, the Kulins indulged in plural marriages.

The Maharaja Bahadur, himself a Brahman colonist, pointed out that the traditional Kulins were, under pain of degradation, prohibited from marrying their daughters to Brahmans of an inferior class. Such of the inferior Brahmans as had amassed wealth under the Company's rule, however, proceeded to buy social prestige by an attempt to marry their daughters to persons belonging to Kulin families by paying large sums of money to procure such alliances. This produced inflationary conditions in the matrimonial market of the province, conditions which adversely affected the interest especially of inferior Brahmans or Kayasths who were not rich.

Pointing out the evils of the system the Maharaja Bahadur remarked:

Those Koolins who cannot get persons of equal caste willing to effect matrimonial alliances with them, nor afford the large marriage gratuities which are demanded, are obliged to let their daughters arrive at old age without being married. Inferior Brahmins are unable to get wives from inability to pay those large gratuities, and many of them are forced to sell the whole of their property for the purpose. Koolin Brahmins never marry without receiving large donations, and multiply wives for the sake of obtaining those gratuities without knowing or caring what becomes of the women to whom they are united by the most solemn rites of their religion. They have been known to marry more than a hundred wives each; and it is customary with them, immediately after going through the nuptial ceremonies and receiving their gratuities, to leave the houses of the girls they have married, never to see their faces more.[49]

[49] See I.O. Home Proc. (Legis.), 1866, r. 436, vol. 53, f. 260.

The enlightened section of educated Bengalis thus wished to remove this stigma by means of legislation. A statement on the object of the Bill sent by the Maharaja to the Secretary of the Government of India commented:

The unlicenced liberty to marry a plurality of wives had led to many deplorable abuses. Men of wealth and intemperance, heedless of the grave responsibility of the act, often contract a fresh marriage from an impulse of the moment; and among the middle classes, too, instances are not of unfrequent occurrence of men multiplying their wives without the semblance of any reasonable cause, and even in cases where they are unable to afford suitable maintenance to their living consorts.

It specially deplored the Bengal Kulins who for paltry gains visited 'village after village, accepting the hands of scores of maidens, the great majority of whom are destined never to enjoy the blessings of a wedded life'.[50]

As the matter involved issues of a religious nature, the Lieutenant-Governor of Bengal requested the Government of India to enact the measure. The latter, however, viewed it as fraught with risk; for it might not have the approval of the people outside Bengal, especially of the Muhammadans.[51] The measure remained unenacted. The hesitancy of the Government to legislate on a subject involving religious views was understandable. The Brahma Samaj therefore became all the more insistent on the liberation of marriage from the shackles of Kulinism. Its attack on caste was similarly directed towards the removal of such barriers as obstructed social mobility.

Though its inspirational source was not so strongly Western in flavour, the Prarthana Samaj was a comparable movement in the Presidency of Bombay, where the upper ranks of the educated classes favoured the idea of co-operation with the Government as the best means of social reform. A Parsi reformist, Behramji Malbari, for example, moved the Government to enact a law to suppress child marriage. In 1890 the Central Legislative Council accordingly sponsored a Bill fixing the minimum marriageable age of girls at twelve. Cohabitation below that age became a penal offence, and a wife married in infancy was declared entitled to have her marriage dissolved.

[50] See I.O. Home Proc. (Legis.), 1866, r. 436, vol. 53, ff. 265-6.
[51] Ibid. ff. 267-78.

The Bill received the support of such eminent liberals as M. G. Ranade, who later became a judge of the Bombay High Court; R. G. Bhandarkar, a great Orientalist; K. P. Gadgil, a barrister; and G. K. Gokhale, a leader of the moderates. All were life members of the Deccan Education Society established in 1884 at Poona, with Lord Ripon, then Viceroy, and Sir James Fergusson, then Governor of Bombay, as patrons. But Bal Gangadhar Tilak, the leader of the revivalist group, opposed this measure. Originally a life member of the Deccan Education Society and professor of mathematics at Fergusson College, he had resigned and taken over the editorship of the *Kesari* and the *Mahratta* in 1890. Through these journals he organized opposition to any attempt on the part of the Government to interfere with the social and religious institutions of the Hindus. The Bill nevertheless became law in 1892, but Tilak made it into a basis of anti-Western agitation.

Factors of Revivalism

Unemployed Malcontents. It has been seen that revivalist nationalism was in general a lower middle-class movement whose rank and file had received some English and vernacular education rather than university education. It was a result of educated unemployment which increased with the growth of education among such priestly and literary classes as could not maintain themselves by an exclusive dependence on land. As early as 1880 some British officials pointed out the dangers of purely literary education and, as has been seen, suggested the opening of technical schools to give further opportunities for employment. But nothing significant came out of this recommendation. On the contrary, when education became a free enterprise in the 1880's it produced the class Dufferin called 'Babu politicians' who by the end of that decade had become 'professional agitators'.

Even those of the lower middle classes who engaged in trade or had a salaried employment were not happy with a system of taxation that pressed most heavily on them.

Dissatisfaction among Graduates. The employment policy of the British gave cause for dissatisfaction to the first rank of university graduates as well. The rules framed under the Charter Act of 1833 had declared all public careers open to competition regardless of caste, creed, or colour, but since competitive examinations were held in England, the system operated as a bar to Indians entering the covenanted civil service in appreciable numbers. There was no bar to the employment of any Indian who might be best fitted to fill any particular situation. Instances had occurred in which the authorities in India had deemed it better to appoint Indians to places specifically reserved for the members of the civil service. Act 24 & 25 Vict., c. 54 had been passed to confirm such appointments made in India. But recruitment to the regular cadre of the covenanted civil service was definitely viewed with disfavour.

In a letter of 17 August 1867 Lawrence clearly admitted to the Secretary of State that the exclusion of Indians from a share in the higher civil service 'was the intention of the framers of the law'. It was a political issue, for, he added:

> The chief objection to a change is that of policy. We conquered India mainly by force of arms, though policy and good government have largely aided us. In like manner we must hold it. The Englishmen must always be in the front rank, holding the post of honour and of power as the condition of our retaining our rule.[52]

Lawrence was especially opposed to the inclusion of 'the Bengalees' who had 'most benefited by education because they had the greatest opportunities'. He questioned their quality of 'courage' and 'self-reliance' and pointed out that 'Punjabees and other vigorous races are no more willing to be managed by Bengalees than are Englishmen.'[53]

To defeat the object of the competitive system and to exclude the Bengalis, the Secretary of State introduced a Bill in Parliament in 1869. It became Act 33 Vict., c. 3 in 1870. Under this Act the Viceroy in consultation with the Secretary of State was to frame rules to nominate Indians to any office specifically reserved for covenanted civil servants. Obviously, this was an extension of the principle recognized under Act 24 & 25 Vict., c. 54.[54] The Secretary of State made no secret of his intention to secure the exclusion of the educated classes, especially the Bengalis.

In a competitive examination [he said in one of his dispatches to India], the chances of a Bengalee would probably be superior to the

---

[52] I.O., Lawrence Papers, iv, let. no. 48.   [53] Ibid.
[54] See I.O., Sels. from Desp. to Ind. (Educ.), 8 Apr. 1869, paras. 6–8, pp. 369–70.

chances of a Pathan or Sikh. It would nevertheless be a dangerous experiment to place a successful student from the Colleges of Calcutta in command over any of the martial tribes of Upper India.

The Government of India was advised to select candidates from among the taluqdars of Upper India, 'disconnected as much as possible with the tests of mere literary examinations'.[55] This was to be what came to be known as the Statutory Civil Service.

It took more than eight years to lay down rules of nomination, and when these were finalized with the object of forming a 'close native civil service', the scope of nomination was limited to a few inferior appointments previously reserved for covenanted servants. Moreover, the statutory civil servants were to be remunerated at a rate lower than that of covenanted servants. The statute was in fact designed to preserve the political interest of the Empire 'by restricting the most important executive posts to Europeans' and to do something by way of fulfilling 'the pledges implied in the various Acts of Parliament and the declarations of policy' made ever since the Charter Act of 1833. Indeed the passing of the statute was a device to exclude educated Indians from higher positions in the civil service. The lowering in 1876 of the minimum age of recruitment from 21 to 19 had a similar purpose. The removal of Surendranath Banerjea from the Indian Civil Service in 1874 for what the Secretary of State called being 'guilty of falsehood' and 'a palpable abuse of his judicial powers', occurred more or less in a similar context.[56]

Following the recommendations of the Aitchison Indian Public Service Commission of 1886–7, the Statutory Civil Service was abolished. New cadres of provincial and subordinate civil service were introduced in 1892 to secure a more extensive employment of Indians in government service. But the holding of the examination in England continued to be a serious handicap to Indians until provision was made in 1923 to hold simultaneous examinations in England and in India.

Arrogance of European Civil Servants. The arrogance of the European members of the Indian Civil Service added insult to the injury caused by the prejudicial treatment of educated Indians. A case of 1882 may be quoted to illustrate this. One Dosabhai Framji, a Parsi of the uncovenanted service and Presidency magistrate, was

[55] Ibid. paras. 7–8.   [56] Ibid. para. 2.

appointed to act as Collector of Bombay and Superintendent of Stamps and Stationery. The European civil servants of Bombay resented this and presented memorials 'remonstrating against the appointment'. Their remonstrances were rejected by the Secretary of State, but their attitude naturally caused irritation to Indians.

Northbrook, who had earlier presided over the administration of India, bore testimony to this arrogance. In one of his private letters he warned Dufferin, before the latter took over as Viceroy in 1885:

> You will soon see that the Anglo-Indians[57] have little or nothing of what is really India, and that the Civil Servants, with all their magnificent qualities, have strongly ingrained in their minds, excepting some of the very best of them, like Mount Stewart [sic] Elphinstone and George Clerk [sic] of old, and Aitchison, Lt.-Governor of the Punjab now, that no one but an Englishman can do anything. So that . . . you will find a good deal of quiet opposition to any efforts you may make to employ largely educated Natives.

He nevertheless advised Dufferin to employ Indians extensively to counteract disaffection among them.

> This [he continued], is an absolute necessity; as the Natives acquire an education nearly equal to ours, go to our Universities, and are called to our Bar, there must be serious discontent if we do not manage to satisfy their legitimate ambition by giving them a fair share in the Government of their own Country. Ripon's main lines of policy in these respects have my cordial support.[58]

But in spite of this advice or even of the views of such liberal administrators as Munro, Malcolm, and Elphinstone, 'the higher Government officials formed a closer caste than had even the mansabdars of Akbar'.[59]

RELIGIOUS AND CULTURAL REACTION

The educated unemployment which arose in the main from the inadequacy of economic development and the rapid expansion of purely literary education, however, was limited in the area it

[57] Meaning at this date the English in India.
[58] I.O. MSS. Eur. C. 144, v, no. 2, 8 Sept. 1884, ff. 10–12.
[59] H. Dodwell, *A Sketch of the History of India* (1925), p. 209.

affected. What set the great mass of the people against the British was not so much economic discontent as religious suspicion. The educated classes may be said to have used religion to satisfy their economic interest. But that is not the whole truth; it was the behaviour of the educated classes themselves, especially in Bengal, that first provoked reaction against Western culture. The influence of the West in fact seemed to sap the foundation of India's traditional culture and way of life. For example, the educated Bengalis prided themselves on the use of wine and champagne, pipes and beefsteak. The orthodox Hindus viewed these tendencies with abhorrence. To English-educated Indians, who in Bengal were for the most part Brahma Samajists, everything Indian looked primitive and barbarous, dirty and odious. The founder of the Brahma Samaj himself was no friend of Sanskrit. He was chief among the opponents of the Sanskrit College established at Calcutta in 1823.

Dwarkanath Tagore's son, Debendranath Tagore, who took over the leadership of the Samaj in 1843, endeavoured to check these secular tendencies. He emphasized the principle of the *Vedanta* as the kernel on which the Brahma Samaj had been founded. But he was superseded by Keshab Chandra Sen, a rabid radical who came to dominate the Samaj in the 1860's.

Orthodox Hindus in fact regarded the Brahma Samaj as something alien to Hinduism. Its followers were deemed comparable to Christians. A number of educated Bengali Brahmans had embraced Christianity, whereas in Madras Christian missions failed to convert any but members of low castes. The Brahma Samajists seemed emotionally more attached to the West than to their own country, and revivalism was a reaction against what was considered a psychological surrender.

The political consequences of religious fear arising from proselytization have already been pointed out.[60] Nevertheless, the proselytizing activity of Christian missions did not cease. Some of the scholarly bishops in India expressed a sense of disapproval at conversion being used as a yardstick to measure the progress of Christianity. They suggested that instead of zealous missionaries Christian scholars should be sent to India to popularize Christianity on an intellectual plane, but nothing came of these suggestions. Zealous missionaries continued to operate. They reaped a good

[60] See above, pp. 195–210.

harvest especially in the years of recurrent famines, when they maintained homes for famine-stricken orphans and poor people whom they brought up as Christians.[61]

During the famine of 1896–7 the missionaries of the North-Western Provinces and Oudh desired that the Government should subsidize their efforts to give relief to the people. But the local government could not do this 'without giving rise to accusation of proselytism'.[62] The missionaries took advantage of their association with the administration of the famine fund created in 1877 to provide relief to sufferers. During 1896–7 it was proposed 'to create a Fund to be administered entirely by Missionaries'.[63] The Lieutenant-Governor of the North-Western Provinces and Oudh, Sir A. P. MacDonnell, however, raised serious objection to this. In view of past experience he did not approve the idea of any missionary being appointed even to serve on a relief committee.

If the cry of proselytism were raised [he said], I do not know what the effect would be. Doubtless many would sooner starve than be helped at the cost of their religion, and thus the movement would defeat its object. The Government *cannot* get mixed up with Missionaries. We employ them to distribute relief among their own flocks: and I have no great objection to their being on committees, (though I should prefer not to have them even there). But I do sincerely trust that we may be saved from the complications of any more intimate or effective connexion.[64]

Indeed the state of contemporary Hindu society was such that conversion to Christianity or to any other religion became relatively easy since restrictions on commensality and social mixing were so rigid that any violation involved loss of caste and therefore of religion. For example, a voyage to England was considered an act of pollution which involved excommunication. One of the reasons which impelled the British Indian Association in 1886 to petition Parliament to hold the I.C.S. examination simultaneously in England and in India was that a journey to foreign countries, besides being difficult and expensive, entailed 'the loss of social position to all but the small minority who break with the Indian society from

[61] See Elgin to Hamilton, 3 Feb. 1897, I.O. MSS. Eur. D. 509/4, f. 47.
[62] Ibid.   [63] Encl. in Elgin to Hamilton, 10 Feb. 1897, ibid. f. 61.
[64] Encl. in Elgin to Hamilton, 10 Feb. 1897, ibid. f. 63.

personal motives, and are unable to faithfully reflect its sentiments by reason of their isolation'.[65]

In Christianity or Islam low-caste Hindus found a refuge from the tyranny of Hinduism. Steeped in superstition and guided by a false notion of prestige, the upper-caste Hindus opposed their employment even for the purposes of disinfecting houses to counteract the spread of bubonic plague, which broke out in 1897 in Bombay. The *Bangvasi*, a Bengal journal, suggested on 25 March 1899 that 'low-caste men should never be employed in disinfecting Hindu houses. It is because disinfection was carried out by low-caste men in his house that a Brahman of Belgam committed suicide.'[66]

Hinduism was indeed faced with a crisis of culture. It arose from British policy to build, on the foundation of a traditionally caste-ridden agricultural society, an educational, legal, and political system which had in the West resulted basically from the Industrial Revolution and a flexible social system. It was difficult for Indians to make a choice. The acceptance of the Western concept of social mobility constituted a real challenge to Brahmanism and the exclusive concept of its caste order. Its rejection, on the other hand, involved the negation of British rule and a reversal of what that rule had achieved over a period of more than 100 years. The aim of revivalism was to restore Brahmanism in a modified form by an exclusion of British rule and the influences that operated under it. To revivalists political liberty was essential for cultural and religious freedom.

GROWTH OF RACIALISM

The growth of racial animosity in India supplied food for religious revivalism. The European planting community was especially responsible for it. Planters made a mockery of the rule of law. As an instance, in a letter of 3 December 1866 the Secretary of State admitted that the English agents of Assam flogged coolies 'unwatched' and they were 'apt to maltreat natives' without fear of punishment.[67] Whenever a European came up for trial for mis-

[65] I.O., Sels. from Desp. to Ind. (Public), 15 July 1886, para 8, p. 310.
[66] Encl. in Curzon to Hamilton, 13 Apr. 1899, I.O., MSS. Eur. D. 510/1, para. 15.
[67] Cranborne to Lawrence, I.O. Lawrence Papers, iii, no. 45.

demeanour or breach of the law, the magistracy departed from the principles of justice. A serious case arose in the beginning of Lord Lytton's Government. One Fuller, a European barrister at Agra, beat his coachman in the stomach, which resulted in his death. The English magistrate at Agra punished him by a fine of Rs. 30. The Viceroy intervened when the Calcutta press condemned the whole thing as a gross miscarriage of justice. The matter reached the Secretary of State, but nothing came of it.

It was quite common for planters to assault their Indian workmen. Even a strong Viceroy such as Curzon could do nothing beyond deploring what he called 'lamentable assault cases'.[68] Two English planters in Travancore,

in order to obtain a confession of theft from a native Syce or groom, tied him up to a tree and flogged him to such an extent that he died in the evening of the same day. They then carried off his body to a distance of two miles and buried it, in the hope of escaping discovery.

The matter, however, leaked out and finally came before the Madras High Court. The planters, as Curzon wrote to the Secretary of State, had subscribed 'a thousand pounds for the defence of the accused men'. The Viceroy expressed a sense of helplessness and added that 'there will probably remain nothing for me but to watch with impotent indignation the successive stages in the development of the case'.[69]

His comment on the Travancore murder case was not unjustified. In a subsequent letter of 21 August 1901 he informed the Secretary of State that he had never seen 'a more transparent case of murder' brought to a court. But he was shocked to find that the punishment of the Madras High Court did not extend beyond three years of simple imprisonment.[70] In another case, in Curzon's own words,

an English overseer in one of the mills at Cawnpore kicked a coolie on the backside and knocked him down. The man lay there on the ground for three hours unattended, was then picked up and taken away to his house, where he died in the course of the evening. The medical evidence showed conclusively that death resulted from the kick. Nevertheless,

[68] Curzon to Hamilton, 10 Jan. 1901, I.O. MSS. Eur. D. 510/7, f. 15.
[69] Curzon to Hamilton, 5 June 1901, ibid. 510/8, f. 95.
[70] Ibid. ff. 316 and 329.

the overseer was let off with a fine of Rs. 200, the Magistrate taking credit to himself for having inflicted an exceptionally heavy sentence, and remarking that he had also taken into account the remorse which the prisoner must naturally feel.[71]

The planters were specially powerful in Assam where they owned and managed tea gardens. The degree of influence they exercised on the Government may be judged from the fact that even Curzon was forced to recall Mr. Cotton, the Chief Commissioner of Assam, who showed a bias against the planters for their abominable acts. In a letter to the Secretary of State of 11 September 1901, Curzon admitted that

on many plantations harsh and cruel and abominable things go on, and that the coolies get nothing like the wage which is stipulated for by the law. It is also true . . . that when cases of collision come before the District Magistrates, or before the Sessions Judges, or even before the High Court there is one scale of justice for the planter and another for the coolie.

Nevertheless Cotton was recalled because he represented the planters 'as a lot of inhuman monsters'.[72]

Much of the unpopularity of the Government proceeded from the iniquitous conduct of the planters. They were the people who were involved in the Ilbert Bill Controversy of 1882. They had a profound contempt for Indians, and they brought all their organized influence to oppose the Bill which aimed at authorizing Indian magistrates to try all offences, including those of Europeans. The Government realized that their opposition was unjust, but it could not ignore them. The effect of the original Bill was watered down. Normally Indians would have swallowed white arrogance, but the growth of the educated middle classes, improved communications and a free press united them together on a common platform. The Ilbert Bill controversy was followed immediately by the organization of the National Conference in 1883 and its merger with the Indian National Congress in 1886. The moderate leaders of Congress, however, had no mass backing. The mass appeal of Indian nationalism proceeded from revivalist leaders.

[71] Curzon to Hamilton, 10 June 1901, ibid. f. 316.
[72] Ibid. 510/9, f. 3.

THE REVIVALIST LEADERS

Swami Dayanand Saraswati

The first of these leaders was Swami Dayanand Saraswati (1824–83), whose aim was to restore Indian culture to its pristine dignity by securing 'India for the Indians'. Dayanand, whose early name was Mula Shanker, belonged to the Indian state of Morvi in Kathiawar in the Presidency of Bombay. Brought up in the rigid atmosphere of an orthodox Brahman family, Mula Shanker became a tenacious Hindu. While a boy of 14 he had learnt by heart a large number of Vedic hymns and rules of Sanskrit grammar. His father, Amba Shanker, was a town jamadar, a small police officer, and money-lender. He was a follower of Shiva, whose idol he worshipped as a devoted Hindu. He desired that his son should become a religious man and follow the tradition of the family. To his great surprise, however, Mula Shanker became a rationalist, hostile to idolatry and family tradition.

In his autobiography Dayanand tells the story of how one night he was asked to fast and keep a long vigil with others in the temple of Shiva, a night of dedication and worship called *Shivaratri*. By midnight the temple servants and other devotees, including his father, had fallen asleep, but as he had been taught that by sleeping he might forfeit the effect of his fasting and devotion, Dayanand remained awake. In the silent hours of the night he saw a number of mice, in search of food, running about upon the idol of Shiva, whom the people invoked as the creator of the universe. He awoke his father and asked him how it was that an omnipotent living god like Shiva suffered his body to be polluted by the mice without the slightest protest on his part. The father tried to explain away the incident, but unsuccessfully. Dayanand devoted himself to serious studies. At the age of 22 his parents determined to get him married, but he fled from home in pursuit of knowledge, of an answer to his question.

In 1860 Dayanand came in contact with a blind scholar of the Vedas, Swami Virajanand, who lived at Mathura near Delhi, who influenced his ideas. Virajanand attached a social purpose to the education he imparted to him, and advised him to dedicate himself to the service of the country which he called *Bharatvarsha*.

The Vedas have long ceased to be taught in Bharatvarsha [he said], go and teach them; teach the true *shastras*, and dispel, by their light, the darkness which the false creeds have given birth to. Remember that, while works by common men are utterly misleading as to the nature and attributes of the one true God, and slander the great *rishis* and *munis*, those by the ancient teachers are free from such a blemish. This is the test which will enable you to differentiate the true ancient teaching from the writings of ordinary men.[73]

Dayanand took this advice. He made an assessment of the relative value of scriptural literature, stripping it of its later accretions and retaining what he considered to be original and genuine. In 1866 he came into contact with Christian missionaries with whom he held important disputations. He soon started preaching against idolatry, first in Sanskrit, but later on in Hindi, a language through which he could spread his message to the mass of the people. The first edition of his famous book called the *Satyartha Prakash* came out in Hindi in 1874. It was a scientific view of Hindu religion. It also contained chapters criticizing Christianity and Islam.

The Brahma Samaj influenced Dayanand in forming a plan of social reform. Towards the close of 1872 he went to Calcutta where he spent nearly four months in lecturing and discussion. He, however, differed from the leaders of the Brahma Samaj in that his inspiration was genuinely indigenous and his approach uncompromisingly revivalist. In 1874 he went to Bombay where he met the leaders of the Prarthana Samaj. It was here that he founded his Arya Samaj in 1875. In 1877 he visited Ludhiana and Lahore in the Punjab, which later became the rallying-point in the movement after the death of its founder in 1883. The Hindus, who dominated the mercantile interest in that province, found in his movement an opportunity to counteract, on a religious plane, the feudal influence of great landholders who were generally Muhammadans. The success of the Arya Samaj in the Punjab illustrates the manner in which religion contributed to the rise of capitalism.

But while capitalism in the West rid itself of its religious moorings, it failed to do so in India. It became an important basis of politics. A year before his death Dayanand had formed an association for the protection of cows. He had also published a book on this subject called *Gokarunanidhi*. The object was to mobilize

[73] Quoted in Farquhar, p. 107.

Hindu public opinion as much against Christians and Muhammadans as against the Government who had no scruple on the question of cow-killing. Thus in his attempt to revive the ancient glory of Hindu culture Dayanand disregarded two of the main strands in India's cultural development, Islam and Christianity. He dismissed them as extraneous.

In the words of Dr. Griswold of Lahore, 'the watchword of Pandit Dayanand was "Back to the Vedas".' With this watchword another was implicitly, if not explicitly, combined, 'India for the Indians'. Both together enunciate the principle, that 'the religion of India as well as the sovereignty of India ought to belong to the Indian people; in other words, Indian religion for the Indians, and Indian sovereignty for the Indians'.[74] From the character of its founder the Arya Samaj tended to exclude, both religiously and politically, extra-Indian influences such as Islam, Christianity, and British Government.

Bal Gangadhar Tilak

The revivalist leader who openly carried religion into politics was Bal Gangadhar Tilak (1856–1920), a Chitpavan Maratha Brahman born at Ratnagiri, a coastal town in the Presidency of Bombay. He was the son of Gangadhar Ramchandra Tilak, a schoolmaster who taught mathematics in a school of his home town at Rs. 25 a month. He supplemented his income by writing textbooks. On the death of his father in 1872 Tilak received a bequest of Rs. 5,000 in addition to the copyright on the textbooks. Tilak thus belonged to a lower middle-class family.

Tilak married at the age of 15 and passed his matriculation examination a year later. He entered the Deccan College at Poona as a resident scholar and got a first class in his B.A., without distinctions. He was, however, a voracious reader. In addition to Sanskrit, mathematics, and Marathi literature, he studied Hegel, Kant, Mill, Bentham, Voltaire, and Rousseau. After graduation Tilak took a law degree and did not proceed to M.A. His aim was to adopt a political career and serve the people instead of the Government. Among his intimate friends at the Deccan College was one Agarkar who determined to join him in his mission, which was to

[74] *Indian Evangelical R.*, Jan. 1892, quoted in Farquhar, pp. 111–12.

open private educational institutions with the object of inculcating a spirit of patriotism, service, and sacrifice.

The kind of school Tilak had in mind was established in 1879. It was the work of one Vishnushastri Chiplonkar, who had resigned from government service to found his new English school under Tilak's inspiration. Tilak began his public career as one of its teachers. The missionary zeal and the efficiency of its workers earned the school the reputation of one of the finest high schools in the country, and it became the nucleus of the Deccan Education Society established at Poona in 1884 and of the Fergusson College, where Tilak taught mathematics until he resigned and took to journalism in 1890. His resignation was the result of differences with G. K. Gokhale and other liberal leaders who did not approve of his rigid and puritanical view of public service and politics.

Tilak chose journalism as a more effective means to awaken the country to a new sense of responsibility. To him this responsibility meant a combination of cultural renaissance and political freedom. His associates had in 1881 already launched the *Kesari* (meaning deep red) in Marathi and the *Mahratta* in English, the former being designed to serve the lower, and the latter the more advanced section of the community. On his resignation Tilak took over the sole proprietorship of these newspapers and was their chief editor.

Through these journals he organized opposition to any interference on the part of the Government with Hindu social and religious institutions. He, like Dayanand, regarded political freedom as a necessary condition for religious revival. For him religion and politics were indistinguishably intermingled. The one could not flourish without the other. Unlike Dayanand, however, Tilak was not a pure Orientalist. He was a supporter of English education which he used in the liberation of India from British rule. In 1892 a section of the Arya Samaj also came to accept this point of view. This section took the initiative in establishing a network of Anglo-Vernacular schools and colleges named after Dayanand. The old ideological emphasis on the Vedic religion nevertheless continued unabated. Its object was to ensure that the young generation educated in Western science and literature remained basically attached to the Indian view and way of life.

A remarkable and distinct feature of Tilak's movement was that it exploited the idolatrous beliefs of the Hindus and abetted incitement to violence in the preservation of those beliefs. Even in his college days Tilak was, for example, one of the admirers of Wasudeo Balwant Phadke, who had established a secret society where young men learnt shooting. His hostile criticism of government anti-plague measures led to violence in 1897 when Mr. Rand, a special plague officer, was shot dead at Poona on 22 June, having become unpopular because of the steps he took to segregate plague-stricken areas and to disinfect houses. Tilak's outright condemnation of the action of the plague committee led the Government to suspect that he was perhaps the moving spirit behind the murder; and the Governor of Bombay ordered his arrest. He was charged with seditious writings against the Government. The papers connected with his trial showed how he and his writings had fired the imagination of the youths and stirred them to take active part in politics.[75] He was convicted and sentenced but released on condition that he would do nothing to stir up disaffection against the Government. The Secretary of State advised his local governments in India to see that students were restrained from associating with political activity.[76] Nevertheless, Rand's murder ushered in an era of religious fanaticism and political violence, which continued until Gandhi came forward to condemn both in the 1920's.

Lala Lajpat Rai

Lala Lajpat Rai may be said to be another of the revivalist leaders who viewed politics from a religious angle. The son of a petty official, Munshi Radhakrishnan, Lajpat Rai joined the legal profession at Lahore in the 1890's and worked as a lecturer in history at the Dayanand Anglo-Vedic College there. One of the founders of the College and a devout follower of Dayanand, he became one of the uncompromising advocates of the nationalist cause. Under his leadership the Arya Samaj grew into a powerful movement which denounced idolatry and caste and promoted education of the lower levels of society. In the beginning he counselled an evolutionary, not a revolutionary, approach to politics. It was only when he was convinced that no amount of prayers, resolutions, and protests could move the British that he proceeded to recommend a firm attitude and a boycott of British goods.

[75] See I.O., Sels. from Desp. to Ind., (Public), no. 148, 16 Dec. 1897.
[76] I.O., Sels. from Desp. to Ind. (Educ.), no. 19 of 1897.

Bepin Chandra Pal

Bepin Chandra Pal was a revivalist leader of Bengal. He belonged to a high-caste Hindu family. His father, Ramchandra Pal, was a petty landholder, and he himself an assistant librarian in the Imperial (now National) Library of Calcutta.

Unlike Bombay and the Punjab, revivalism grew in strength in Bengal only after its partition in 1905. It is true that the writings of Bankim Chandra Chatterjee were replete with the religious fervour of Dayanand, but the Bengalis assumed an attitude of open hostility to the British only after the partition. *The New Spirit*, Pal's important work which represented his view on cultural and political thought in India, came out in 1907.

Pal's basic concept of *swaraj* or self-government was not comparable to that of a dominion within the British Commonwealth. It was not to be realized by an expansion of the Councils or the Indianization of the public services. It signified full freedom, a complete exclusion of the British from both cultural and political points of view. This freedom was not to be a gift, but the result of a struggle until the British were compelled to submit to the will of the Indian people. The Swadeshi movement and the boycott of government offices were the means he suggested to achieve independence. The boycott movement was to be a substitute for war, a political expedient rather than an instrument of economic development.

In his cultural and political thought Pal was more comparable to Tilak. He viewed religion 'not as one of the many departments of human life and duty', but

as the Ideal Goal of all the activities of man—the Regulative Idea that shapes them all. . . . It is when every movement in the physical world, as every event in history is viewed as a revelation of the Thought and Love of God, that historical characters and epochs become objects of religious idealisation and the commemoration of these assumes the sanctity and significance of a religious sacrament.

His religious concept was, however, not exclusive. He included both Hindus and Muhammadans, though he invariably used *Om*, a Vedic symbol of divinity, in his writings. He realized the complexity of Indian national life and recognized all religions that went to its making. He said:

In India, this national life is of a very complex composition. It is partly Hindu, and partly Mahomedan, partly Zoroastrian, and partly Christian. The sacraments of our civic life, therefore, cannot be identified with any particular sect or religion. . . . They must have reference to the past history and achievements of all these communities.[77]

THE MUSLIM RELIGIOUS REVIVAL

Revivalist Hinduism was a counterpart of revivalist Islam in modern times. The latter began earlier than the former, but in their effect they were more or less alike. Both Hindu and Muhammadan revivalists used religion in their attempts to widen the basis of their political appeal, but since the two religions were mutually exclusive, any resort to religion as a basis of politics tended to cause communal violence.

The revivalist movement in Islam started at Delhi after the death in 1707 of the Mughal emperor Auranzeb. The leader of this movement was Shah Waliullah (1703–62). He was educated in the Delhi Madrasa established by his father, Shah Abdur Rahim, and named after him as Madrasa-i-Rahimia. At the age of 16 Waliullah became a teacher in this Madrasa. Later he went to Mecca to perform *hajj* or pilgrimage and there studied under Shah Abu Tahir, a famous Islamic scholar. Waliullah's public life began on his return from Mecca in 1730. He appealed to his coreligionists to look back and concentrate on the basic teachings of the Quran, and to sink the sectarian differences which divided the Indian Muslims as Shiahs and Sunnis, or as Sufis and orthodox Ulema. His was a pan-Islamic movement. He wanted to unite the Muslims in a single organization.

Waliullah's son, Shah Abdul Aziz, carried on the mission of his father. The leaders who used the pan-Islamic movement for political purposes were Aziz's nephew, Ismail, and Syed Ahmed of Bareilly in Oudh. They declared *jihad* or revolt against the Sikhs in the Punjab to supplant them politically, but they approached politics from a religious angle. Syed Ahmed declared himself as an enemy of *kafirs* or non-believers. The Wahabis of Patna in Bihar

---

[77] B. C. Pal, *The New Spirit* (1907), pp. 196–7.

were also revivalists. Their leaders, Walayat Ali and Inayat Ali, were inspired by the teachings of Shah Waliullah, but their activities were directed against the British who had replaced the political influence of Indian Muslims. They were involved in the Mutiny of 1857 in Bihar, where they were tried for sedition and their leader, Ahmedullah, was sentenced to transportation. Maulavi Karamat Ali, another revivalist leader, belonged to Bengal.

The traditional orthodoxy of Islam and the time-lag in the English education of the Muhammadan community made the Islamic revival a relatively stronger force, but the economic and political decline of that community under the early years of British rule was perhaps as important a factor. Apart from the political dominance of their coreligionists, Muhammadans had in the pre-British days enjoyed the benefit of land grants in addition to preferential employment in the judicial, executive, and military branches of the Mughal service. Under the British their position deteriorated until after 1870 the spread of English education among them began to effect some improvement. The reason was that the Muhammadans had generally no control of the commercial and financial interests of the country even under Mughal rule, which were for the most part in the hands of Hindus, who also managed the revenues of Government. They were the people who gained most with the expansion of trade and industry under the British. The Muhammadans lost not only politically, but in many other ways as well. For example, the reduction of the military establishments of the Nawab of Bengal threw out of employment a large number of Muhammadans who served in the Nawab's army. The Mughal faujdars were supplanted by European magistrates in 1781. The judges of criminal courts, who before 1790 had been exclusively Muhammadan, were as a class removed by Cornwallis in the Diwani provinces. The operation of the same rule was extended to the North-Western Provinces in the beginning of the nineteenth century. Muhammadan qazis and muftis were of course continued, but the introduction of trial by jury in 1832 and the substitution of Persian by English in 1837 greatly reduced their importance. The posts of law officers were themselves abolished on the establishment of High Courts in 1862.

It was in the North-Western Provinces, especially in Oudh, that the Muhammadans were able to retain most of their traditional superiority in the higher ranks of the public service. This was due chiefly to the fact that the Bengal system was not extended in its entirety to these provinces, and that the indigenous pattern of Muslim administration had continued in Oudh right up to 1856. In spite of the fact that the percentage of Muhammadans in the total population was 13.4 in 1886, for example, they held 45.1 per cent. of the total number of posts in the judicial and executive service of the North-Western Provinces and Oudh. The Hindus held only 50.2 per cent. of these posts although they constituted 86.2 per cent. of the total population.[78] This predominance of Muhammadans in the public service continued in subsequent years.[79] The establishment of the Anglo-Muhammadan College at Aligarh which later grew into a university, and the encouragement of Muhammadan education by the British in the years following 1870, went a long way to preserve their traditional place in the public service of these provinces.

Elsewhere the representation of Muhammadans in the public service remained poor and inadequate, decidedly not consistent with the degree of political influence that this community had exercised in pre-British times. In Madras, for instance, the percentage of Muhammadans in the total population in 1886 was 6.2, but they held only 0.4 per cent. of the total number of judicial and executive posts. In Bombay they formed 18.8 per cent. of the total population, but held only 5.4 of these posts. In Bengal, which also included Bihar and Orissa, Muhammadans formed 31.3 per cent. of the total population, but held only 8.5 per cent. of the posts in the judicial and executive services. Their position was even worse in Assam where they held only 0.9 per cent. of these posts although they constituted 26.9 per cent. of the total population.[80]

The revival of Islam gave Muhammadans a pan-Islamic consciousness and sustained their morale despite their economic and political decline. The growth of English education among them in the meantime created a class of Muhammadans not only conscious of a distinct and separate nationality but also able to forward their interests either with the help of the Government or the backing of their own community. Such a class emerged largely in the United Provinces of Agra and Oudh where, as has been said, Muham-

[78] Ind. Public Service Com., 1886–7, *Rep.*, p. 31.
[79] See *Census of India, 1901*, vol. i, para. 366.   [80] Ibid.

madans had retained much of their old power and influence. Sir Syed Ahmed, a great champion of English education and founder of the Anglo-Muhammadan College at Aligarh, represented the aspirations of educated Muhammadans. He dissociated himself from the Congress demand for responsible government, for he realized that representative government in India would be essentially Hindu in composition and that his community would become subject to Hindu rule. He created conditions for the establishment in 1906 of the All-India Muslim League, a communal organization designed basically to restore the political importance of Indian Muslims.

It is of interest to note that earlier among the Muhammadans the educated were generally those who belonged to a higher order of society, the descendants of purely foreign Muslims who had migrated under Mughal rule. They had superior interests in land or government service, especially in Oudh. The bulk of the Indian Muhammadan converts belonged originally to the lower orders of Hindu society, who were economically poor and socially depressed. And since the middle-class elements in land, government service, and the professions were of indigenous origin, there remained a wide gap between the educated class of Muhammadans and the bulk of their community, which remained landed and bureaucratic in character, especially because there were so few members of the business classes. It was the religious revivalists who narrowed this gap. Educated Muhammadans used them for political purposes. As religious leaders they could rally the masses successfully.

XIII

The Period After 1905

THE character of the middle classes in the period after 1905 became more and more complex, for besides the religious approach, an economic approach to social divisions and political struggle emerged from the growth of modern capitalism. For example, the industrial population of Calcutta, Bombay, Cawnpore, and Jamshedpur seemed obviously divided into capitalists and labourers rather than Hindus and Muhammadans. There were the professional classes as well, but instead of being grouped as members of distinct and exclusive castes, their general tendency was to regard themselves as members of specific professions, divided into income hierarchies instead of castes, again an economic concept. The religious and economic concepts of social division began to operate side by side. But since religion had the backing of tradition and general acceptance, it dominated the economic concept which was after all new and still embryonic.

It is true that the increasing infiltration of education and the consequent rise of consciousness at the lower levels of society tended to strengthen the theory that disparity in the distribution of wealth was a basic cause of social inequality. But since the great bulk of the population remained still illiterate and the economy still undeveloped in rural areas, the religious approach to social problems continued more or less unchanged except in big cities and industrial towns. In censuses, for instance, the educated among low castes returned themselves as belonging to one or other higher caste, a tendency which has only in recent years received a check because of the special educational facilities and reserved posts in the services for the depressed classes called *harijans* who alone are entitled to such favours perhaps from political considerations, but who would forfeit them if they claimed higher caste.

The complexity of religious and economic interaction in the social and political life of India in the present century is a subject of considerable interest. It deserves thorough research and separate treatment. This book makes no pretension whatsoever to do this; the aim here is simply to review a few of the main trends of development in the period after 1905, particularly with reference to their bearing on the character and role of the middle classes.

DEMOCRACY AS THE LIBERATOR OF THE SOCIALLY DEPRESSED

The first of these trends was the downward filtration of education and with it the extension of the franchise and growth of parliamentary democracy, which were of great social significance. The educated among the backward classes, especially untouchables, used the franchise in the context of their caste loyalty as a political weapon to wrest social equality and places in the legislature and government service. Democracy tended to exercise a liberating influence in so far as the downtrodden were concerned. Their leaders could make use of it to withdraw the political support of their castes from those who were loath to recognize the legitimate aspirations of the backward to rise in social estimation. The educated middle classes, who consisted for the most part of higher caste groups, were not slow to realize the importance of this new trend. The Congress movement to secure temple entry for untouchables and the Poona Pact of 1932 to provide special seats for them in local and central legislatures within the framework of the general Hindu electorate were two of the main examples illustrating this.

POLITICAL VIOLENCE AND COMMUNAL RIOTS

The growth of representative institutions was, however, preceded by political violence and revivalist nationalism which led to communal riots. These constituted another significant feature of the period after 1905.

Political violence started with Bombay, where Bal Gangadhar Tilak had introduced two religious festivals as a means of mobilizing the masses against the British. The first of these was in honour

of the Hindu god Ganpati, an elephant-shaped popular idol universally worshipped by orthodox Hindus. The other was in honour
of Shivaji, the Maratha leader who had raised the standard of
revolt against the Muhammadan rulers of the country. On these
occasions young men were organized, given military training, and
armed with sticks. During the festivals they paraded the streets of
Poona with bands and sang songs calculated to intensify hostility
towards Government and Muhammadans. Though originally
domestic, these festivals assumed a public character in 1894. The
celebration of that year lasted for ten days, particularly because a
Hindu-Muslim riot had broken out in the previous year in Bombay,
and the leaders of the movement realized the possibility of widening
their organizational basis.

The actual beginning of political violence may be traced to
Rand's murder in 1897.[1] It later spread to Bengal after its partition
in 1905 and mounted towards a climax in the form of what is known
as *gadar* or the rebellion of 1915. It is not relevant to the purpose of
this book to trace a history of what developed into a revolutionary
movement in the first decade of the present century; it is relevant
to review its social character.

The leaders and supporters of this movement in Bombay were
for the most part Brahmans. They viewed British rule as a serious
challenge to the social and political influence which they had in the
past exercised. They defended orthodoxy by violent means. For
example, presiding over the Shivaji festival ten days before Rand's
murder, Tilak quoted the *Bhagavad Gita* in support of his argument
that no blame attached to any person who killed even his teachers
and kinsmen provided he were not actuated by a desire for personal
gain.[2] As has been seen, his writings and speeches prepared the
way for the rise of extremism and political violence, especially
among the ranks of college students and teachers. But the persons
who made them flare into revolutionary and secret activities were
the Savarkar brothers, Ganesh and Vinayak, two of the earliest and
most famous Brahman revolutionaries of Nasik in Bombay. Vinayak, a graduate of Fergusson College, had left India in 1906 to
organize an anti-British movement from Paris. Ganesh was involved in the Nasik conspiracy of 1909 when one Jackson, a British
officer, was murdered at a farewell party given in his honour.

[1] See above, p. 384.   [2] Ind. Sedition Committee, 1918, *Rep.*, p. 2.

In the different conditions in Bengal, the educated class of Bengalis called *bhadralok* (respectable people) had been a peaceful people, for they had benefited most from the early expansion of education and unlimited opportunity for employment. The *bhadralok* consisted of Brahmans, Kayasths, and Vaidyas, three of the higher castes of Bengal. From the peculiar land system known as patni tenure they were more interwoven with the landed classes than the English-educated Indians in other provinces. The increasing fragmentation of land, however, tended to reduce the *bhadralok* to the status of lower middle classes, especially when the opportunity of their employment shrank gradually with the spread of English education in other parts of the country. The Sedition Committee of 1918 took note of this steady decline in the economic condition of the educated classes of Bengal, stating:

Originally they predominated in all offices and higher grade schools throughout Upper India. They were also, with the Parsees, the first Indians to send their sons to England for education, to qualify for the Bar or to compete for the higher grades of the Civil and Medical services. When, however, similar classes in other provinces also acquired a working knowledge of English, the field for Bengali enterprise gradually shrank. In their own province *bhadralok* still almost monopolise the clerical and subordinate administrative services of Government. They are prominent in medicine, in teaching and at the Bar. But, in spite of these advantages, they have felt the shrinkage of foreign employment. . . . Their hold on land too has weakened owing to increasing pressure of population and excessive sub-infeudation. Altogether their economic prospects have narrowed, and the increasing numbers who draw fixed incomes have felt the pinch of rising prices. On the other hand, the memories and associations of their earlier prosperity, combined with growing contact with Western ideas and standards of comfort, have raised their expectations of the pecuniary remuneration which reward a laborious and, to their minds, a costly education. Thus as *bhadralok* learned in English have become more and more numerous, a growing number have become less and less inclined to accept the conditions of life in which they found themselves on reaching manhood.[3]

Nevertheless, religion was not mixed up with politics in Bengal before 1905. There had been an orthodox religious movement led by a Bengali ascetic, Ram Krishna, who died in 1886. He was a

[3] *Report*, pp. 11–12.

strong defender of Hinduism, even of idolatry, particularly of the goddess *Kali* whom he regarded as an emblem of divine strength (*Śakti*). But he decried bigotry and taught that all religions were universally true. His doctrines were preached by his disciples, chief among whom was a graduate of Calcutta University, Narendranath Datt, who became known as Swami Vivekanand. He attended the Parliament of Religions in Chicago and founded in the United States a Vedant society to disseminate the teachings of the Vedas. He returned to India in 1897, and with the help of a band of his followers organized centres of philanthropic and social service under the supervision of a society called the Ram Krishna mission. Though a Hindu organization, the mission became known for its liberal and universal appeal.

An attempt was made before 1905 to excite violence against the British. It was initiated by Barindra Kumar Ghosh, who had returned from England in 1902 with the object of spreading revolutionary ideas among the youths of Bengal. He came to Baroda where his brother, Aurobindo Ghosh, who had also been educated in England, was Vice-President of the Gaekwar's College. With a first-class Classical Tripos from Cambridge, Barindra Kumar Ghosh had passed for the Indian Civil Service, but was rejected at the final examination for his inability to ride. He went to Calcutta and tried to arouse anti-British feelings among the educated classes, but was disappointed with the poor response he received from the *bhadralok*. He returned to Baroda, convinced that purely political propaganda would not serve his purpose, and that politics had to be raised to the rank of religion.[4] That required a suitable opportunity, which Curzon provided in 1905 by dividing Bengal into two separate charges, one including East Bengal and Assam, and the other comprising West Bengal, Bihar, and Orissa. In this Curzon appears to have been guided by administrative considerations. Disturbed as he was by the conduct of European planters and by the existence of what he called two different scales of justice, in 1902 he appointed a Police Commission to recommend measures of reform. The Commission recommended that the police force should be augmented, that the authority of the District Officers should be increased, and that the police administration as a whole should be brought finally under the control of a

[4] *Report*, p. 11.

civil servant acting as Inspector-General of Police. The idea was to strengthen the bureaucratic apparatus of the state to secure a due maintenance of law and order.

Considering the utter neglect to which the eastern districts of Bengal had been subject for several decades, and the inadequacy of the police force necessary for the preservation of law and order over an extensive and thickly-populated rural area of poor Muhammadan agriculturists, Curzon did two things. He increased the strength of the administrative staff and partitioned the province to intensify control. The partition, however, seriously affected the interests of the educated classes, who were for the most part Hindus. They found a further shrinkage of the area within which they could exercise their interests, particularly at a period when the expansion of the Legislative Councils in India was talked of. They feared that they would remain in a minority in both the Bengal Legislative Councils, being outnumbered in East Bengal by the Assamese and Muhammadans, and in West Bengal by Biharis and Oriyas. Feelings therefore ran high. Ghosh, the Sedition Committee report says, came to Calcutta in 1904 when the talks for partition were going on, and his brother, Aurobindo, in 1905, the year of the partition. The movement for the boycott of British goods started in 1906. This was followed by attempts to establish national schools and colleges as a mark of protest against English education. Politics had become coloured by considerations of religion and race. Once raised to the height of religion, politics became a mass movement, a prelude to the outbreak of violence in Bengal.

The revolutionary movement of Bengal and Bihar, which subsequently spread to the United Provinces and the Punjab, was essentially a middle-class movement. Of 186 persons convicted of revolutionary crimes until 1917, as many as 165 were of the Brahman, Kayasth, and Vaidya castes, with 152 belonging to the first two. Professionally speaking, 68 out of the 186 convicted were students, 16 teachers, 42 small landowners and traders, 20 clerks and persons in government service, 25 persons of no fixed occupation, 7 doctors and dispensers, 5 newspapermen, and 2 others.[5] Evidently they were for the most part members of the lower middle classes.

[5] *Report* (Annexure).

The non-violent non-cooperation movement which Ghandi introduced early in the 1920's reduced the importance of the revolutionary movement as a political weapon. It nevertheless remained significant in many other ways. The Indian revolutionaries were the first to have built up an organizational hierarchy which functioned at central, provincial, district, and local levels. Their members were of different categories, and they had precise rules for the conduct of each. They also introduced an element of regimentation in the private life of individual members. An important feature of their organization was that they built up a common stock with the help of the money and other things they obtained from different sources.[6] The religious character of the oath they administered before the goddess Kali was later given up by the other revolutionary parties. But their organizational discipline and party secrecy continued to inspire those who did not believe in democratic methods.

Based as it was on resurgent Hindu nationalism, the revolutionary movement, especially in the first two decades of the present century, was exclusive in its appeal. The Muhammadans viewed it with suspicion and gave no support to it. In fact it widened the gulf between the two major communities of India.

THE RISE OF WORKING-CLASS AND PEASANT MOVEMENTS

When, by 1921, Indian capitalism had emerged as an independent force, the growth of indigenous as well as foreign capitalist interests in the country led to a considerable increase in the industrial population. The non-agricultural population in 1891, for example, amounted to nearly 18 per cent. of the total population. It subsisted on industry, commerce, and the various professions, including government service.[7] It rose to 30 per cent. in 1951 for India alone, exclusive of Pakistan, of whom 10 per cent. depended upon industry, 6 upon commerce, 2 upon transport, and 12 upon the services and the miscellaneous professions.[8] The percentage employed in industrial and other non-agricultural occupations continued to rise in spite of the considerable increase in India's popula-

---

[6] *Report*, ch. 5.   [7] *Census of India, 1891*, pp. 112–13.
[8] India, Min. of Inf., *India, 1953*, p. 7.

tion, which went up from 279 million in 1891 to 389 million in 1941, and 360 million in 1951 for India alone. The report of the Census of India, 1951, showed that although the percentage of rural population declined from 88.7 in 1921 to only 82.7 in 1951, the urban population increased from 11.3 to 17.3 per cent. during the same period.[9]

In addition to increasing the number of industrial workers, the growth of industries and urbanization brought into being a considerable number of salaried employees below the managerial and supervisory levels. They added to the problem of the lower middle classes whose strength increased with the increasing number of schools and colleges. A new leadership sprang from among these classes. There came into existence a hierarchy of labour leaders whose interest it was to forward the claims of their own class by an alliance with industrial and other workers. This alliance necessitated the organization of trade unions and factory legislation. Industrial strikes became an additional weapon designed not only to wrest economic concessions but also to threaten the continuance of foreign rule.

Peasant movements were also the work of the lower middle classes. They resulted from a number of factors which have already been noticed. By far the most important of these was the transfer of land into the hands of money-lenders, which tended to create an army of landless labourers. Forcible eviction and arbitrary enhancement of rent were other causes of growing agrarian discontent. Then there was the evil arising from subinfeudation in the permanently settled provinces, especially in Bengal and parts of Madras, where as a result of sub-letting there came into existence a numerous class of agents, contractors, and managers in whose interest it was to oppress the cultivators. The system of subinfeudation, which stimulated the growth of absentee landlords, finally squeezed the tillers of the soil. Above all was the increase of pressure on land and the consequent growth of uneconomic holdings.

These factors contributed to the complexity of land problems. They gave birth to a number of peasant movements which approached these problems, and still do so, from the angle of their respective political philosophies. Their demands ranged from the

[9] Ibid. p. 6.

abolition of zamindari and redistribution of land to co-operative and collective farming.[10]

Thus in the urban as well as rural areas economic factors had in the 1920's begun to assume an importance which called for an approach different from religious or racial chauvinism. It was to be an economic approach based on the conflicting interests of the social classes. It may be of interest to note that there had already developed a sound basis for this in the past. Law and legislative authority had already developed on contractual principles. The definition of the rights of agricultural classes and the establishment of a hierarchy of courts to enforce those rights had already produced conditions for the growth of class-consciousness. The enactment of tenancy legislation and income-tax controversies had already paved the way for the development of an economic concept of society. Western education itself helped its growth.

THE COUNTER-FORCE OF REVIVALIST NATIONALISM

The growth of revivalist nationalism was by far the most effective counter-force. It did not diminish in face of the rise of proletarian and peasant movements; it was stimulated by the rising influence of the Muslim League and the rigidity of British policy towards the Hindu middle classes. While economic thinking was blurred as a consequence of communal riots, constitutional methods were discredited as a result of delay in the recognition of the demand for responsible government.

The Montagu-Chelmsford reforms of 1919 partially recognized the middle-class demand for responsible government. Elected representatives of the people were entrusted with the administration of certain subjects of a developmental nature. But this came too late, and when it came, it was half-hearted. It took no notice, for example, of the interests of the lower middle classes, of industrial workers and peasants who suffered most from rising prices and unemployment. The non-recognition of these new forces perhaps made compromise with the British impossible. But what ruined the chance of a compromise was the British policy of repres-

---

[10] The zamindari system has since been abolished. Vinoba Bhave, the originator of the *bhudan* or land-grant movement, has, since independence, been trying through persuasion to provide land for the landless.

sion which forced the issue to a choice between non-cooperation
and civil disobedience on the one hand and an abject surrender on
the other. The National Congress chose the former, and in an
attempt to build a united national front allowed politics to dominate the question of economic development. A class approach to
India's economic and social problems was given up. In the years
that followed the civil disobedience movement of 1921–2, socialist
leaders like Acharya Narendra Deo and Jai Prakash Narain worked
with the Congress.

Politics, however, had to be raised to the height of religion in
order to form a mass movement. Without it there was no chance of
success, as past experience had shown. Any movement on a mass
scale had to appeal to the people in a language intelligible to them,
the language of religion. Gandhi used a religious approach both
because it was his personal faith and as a political weapon. He tried
to rid it of violence, racial hatred, and communal jealousy. When
he took over the leadership of the Congress after Tilak's death in
1920, he endeavoured to convert it into an instrument intended not
only to fight for political freedom but also to reconcile, through a
religious approach, the conflicting interests of labour and capital,
landlord and tenant, Hindu and Muslim, Brahman and *Harijan*.
But since the mass of the people could not distinguish between
religion, race, or communalism, a resort to religion as the basis of
political appeal produced both political violence and communal
riots.

IDEOLOGICAL OBSESSION AND THE DIVISION OF INDIA

The success of the Russian Revolution in 1917 and the growth
of revolutionary nationalism in India were two of the chief factors
which created ideological obsession in the minds of Indian leaders.
The rigidity of British policy hardened it all the more. Nationalism
became the core of the Indian struggle against the British, but
while the radicals combined with it an overdose of socialist doctrine, the conservatives imbued it with a revivalist fervour. Both
were carried away by emotions and swayed by doctrinal considerations. Maulana Abul Kalam Azad, who served as President of the
Indian National Congress during 1939–46 and conducted most of
the political negotiations with the British in that period, describes

how rigid adherence to political dogmas intensified communal rift and led to the division of India in 1947. India won freedom but was divided.[11] Both freedom and division were the work of the middle classes.

[11] See Abul Kalam Azad, *India Wins Freedom* (1959), pp. 160–1.

Appendix

Returns to the House of Commons Relative to Education in India[1]

RETURN of the Number and Caste of the SCHOLARS in the EDUCATION ESTABLISHMENTS, maintained at the Public Expense, in the several Presidencies of *British India*.

NORTH-WESTERN PROVINCES, on 30th April 1845.

NAME OF INSTITUTION	CASTE OF STUDENTS				TOTAL
	Christians	Hindoos	Mahomedans	Other than these Three	
Ghazeepore School	10	40	157	—	207
Benares College	16	293	9	—	318
Allahabad School	1	94	23	—	118
Saugor ditto	3	317	44	—	364
Jubbulpore ditto	3	136	20	—	159
Bareilly ditto	3	144	48	—	195
Agra College	31	274	60	—	365
Delhi ditto	15	299	146	—	460
	82	1,597	507	—	2,186

[1] P.P. 48(20) of 1847–8.

LOWER PROVINCES, on 30th April, 1845.

NAME OF INSTITUTION	CASTE OF STUDENTS				TOTAL
	Christians	Hindoos	Mahomedans	Other than these Three	
Calcutta Sanscrit College	—	189	—	—	189
Calcutta Hindoo ditto	—	516	—	—	516
Calcutta Patshullah ditto	—	188	—	—	188
Calcutta School Society's School	—	469	—	—	469
Calcutta Madrissa	—	—	152	—	152
Calcutta Medical College	20	56	3	2	81
Calcutta Secondary School	1	14	66	—	81
Hooghly College of Mohamed Mohsin	10	598	208	—	816
Hooghly Branch School	3	252	48	—	303
Hooghly Infant ditto	—	40	1	—	41
Hooghly Seetapore ditto	—	95	41	—	136
Ramree School	2	2	51	26	81
Moulmein ditto	22	6	9	42	79
Midnapore ditto	1	136	4	—	141
Cuttack School	19	90	12	—	121
Dacca College	17	301	24	—	342
Comillah School	4	119	18	1	142
Chittagong	16	72	14	—	102
Sylhet	5	45	3	—	53
Jessore	—	96	3	—	99

					Total
Chotangpore [*sic*]	2	41	26	41	110
Chyebassa	—	48	1	11	60
Nizamut College, Moorshedabad:					
Sahibzadah's Department	—	—	23	—	23
General ditto	—	—	17	—	17
Bauleah School	3	138	3	—	144
Bhaugulpore United School	2	87	31	73	193
Patna College	25	62	15	—	102
Mozufferpore School	1	20	—	—	21
Russapuglah Zemindary	—	—	36	—	36
Assam:					
Gowahatty School	1	104	76	11	192
Seebsaugor ditto	—	—	—	117	117
Vernacular Schools:					
Kamroop Division	—	—	—	996	996
Durrung ditto	—	321	5	31	357
Nowgong ditto	—	—	—	—	—
Seebsaugor ditto	—	—	—	267	267
Luckimpore ditto	—	81	17	171	269
	154	4,186	907	1,789	7,036

FORT ST. GEORGE

(see p. 410.)

BOMBAY, to 30th April 1844.

NAME OF INSTITUTION	Number of Schools		Christians	Hindoos	Mahomedans	Other than these Three	TOTAL
			CASTE OF STUDENTS				
Elphinstone Native Education Society:							
English Department							
Vernacular Schools	—	—	—	533	18	—	551
	1	Central Muratkee	—	261	1	—	262
	2	Kapoorwady ditto	—	104	—	—	104
	3	Tailor's-lane ditto	—	70	—	—	70
	1	Central Goozerattee	—	174	4	—	178
	2	Fort ditto	—	82	—	—	82
	3	Paidhonic ditto	—	61	—	—	61
	1	Hindoostanee	—	—	22	—	22
	1	Persian	—	10	25	—	35
		NAMES OF TOWNS					
Government English Schools at:							
	—	Poona	—	139	—	—	139
	—	Surat	—	81	—	—	81
	—	Tanna	—	50	—	—	50
Government District Vernacular Schools:							
Poona Collectorate	1	Poona, No. 1	—	103	2	—	105

Poona Collectorate—(continued)

No.						
2	Poona, No. 2	—	95	—	—	95
3	Poona, No. 3	—	91	—	—	91
4	Poona, No. 4	—	119	—	—	119
5	Poona, No. 5	—	41	1	—	42
6	Jooneer	—	154	3	—	157
7	Indapoor	—	88	1	—	89
8	Sassoor	—	65	—	—	65
9	Cotoor	—	70	—	—	70
10	Tullehgaom	—	54	2	—	56
11	Kher	—	71	—	—	71
12	Narrayengaom	—	41	—	—	41
13	Soopa	—	47	6	—	53
14	Pullasdeo	—	46	1	—	47
15	Ghoreh	—	83	4	—	87
16	Chakun	—	35	6	—	41
17	Pabul	—	32	1	—	33
18	Kullus	—	34	2	—	36
19	Pour	—	48	3	—	51
20	Chass	—	61	—	—	61
21	Kher Shivapoor	—	51	1	—	52
	Jejooree	—	81	3	—	84
(Supplementary)						
1	Ahmednuggur, No. 1	—	114	3	—	117
2	Ahmednuggur, No. 2	—	112	—	—	112
3	Ahmednuggur, No. 3	—	69	12	—	81
4	Nassick	—	141	—	—	141
5	Yesleh	—	97	9	—	106

Ahmednuggur Collectorate

BOMBAY—*continued*

NAME OF INSTITUTION	Number of Schools	NAMES OF TOWNS	Christians	Hindoos	Mahomedans	Other than these Three	TOTAL
Ahmednuggur Collectorate—(*continued*)	6	Sungurnair	—	118	1	—	119
	7	Jamkair	—	44	3	—	47
	8	Akoleh	—	123	2	—	125
	9	Sheogaom	—	56	4	—	60
	10	Trimbuck	—	88	—	—	88
	11	Rahooree	—	69	—	—	69
	12	Niphan	—	57	—	—	57
	13	Nimon	—	61	4	—	65
	14	Kotool	—	71	—	—	71
	15	Seroor	—	56	1	—	57
	16	Parnair	—	66	1	—	67
	17	Seroor Bhalgaom	—	35	3	—	38
	18	Newaseh	—	62	1	—	63
	19	Rajoor	—	51	—	—	51
	20	Rahateh	—	58	—	—	58
	21	Hindoostanee school at Nassick	—	45	—	—	45
Sholapoor Collectorate	1	Sholapoor	—	116	6	—	122
	2	Barsee	—	109	3	—	112
	3	Mahra	—	74	3	—	77

Sholapoor Collectorate—(continued)							
4	Mohol	33	—	—	—	33	—
5	Mungolee	33	—	—	—	33	—
6	Indee	44	—	—	—	44	—
7	Bagehwarree	17	—	1	—	17	—
8	Moodebehal	24	—	—	—	23	—
9	Hipurgee	51	—	—	—	51	—
Candeish Collectorate							
1	Dhooliah	108	—	—	—	108	—
2	Errundole	106	—	—	—	106	—
Rutnagherry Collectorate							
1	Rutnagherry, No. 1	208	—	5	—	203	—
2	Rutnagherry, No. 2	91	—	1	—	90	—
3	Guhagur	49	—	—	—	49	—
4	Chiploon	56	—	—	—	56	—
5	Murud	50	—	—	—	50	—
6	Rajapoor	34	—	—	—	34	—
7	Malwan	81	—	—	—	81	—
8	Kulmuth	34	—	—	—	34	—
9	Dabhol	30	—	—	—	30	—
10	Hurnai	105	—	—	—	105	—
11	Someshwur	74	—	3	—	71	—
12	Khed	56	—	—	—	56	—
13	Palgad	102	—	—	—	102	—
14	Kilshie	98	—	—	—	98	—
Belgaum Collectorate							
1	Belgaum (Murattee)	92	—	2	—	90	—
2	Belgaum (Canarese)	81	—	—	—	81	—

BOMBAY—*continued*

NAME OF INSTITUTION	Number of Schools	NAMES OF TOWNS	CASTE OF STUDENTS				TOTAL
			Christians	Hindoos	Mahomedans	Other than these Three	
Belgaum Collectorate —(*continued*)	3	Chikodi	—	64	—	—	64
	4	Sadalya	—	63	—	—	63
	5	Yaumkanmardi	—	49	3	—	52
	6	Gokak	—	144	1	—	145
	7	Kula-ghi	—	33	3	—	36
	8	Savadatti	—	61	3	—	64
	9	Sampgaom	—	54	—	—	54
	10	Naisurgi	—	28	—	—	28
	11	Bidi	—	61	—	—	61
	12	Nandigad	—	49	—	—	49
	13	Khanspoor	—	100	—	—	100
Dharwar Collectorate	1	Dharwar (Murattee)	—	168	15	—	183
	2	Ditto (Canarese)	—	116	13	—	129
	3	Hoobly (Murattee)	—	138	1	—	139
	4	Ditto (Canarese)	—	91	5	—	96
	5	Havery	—	45	—	—	45
	6	Rani Benone	—	40	4	—	44
			—	7,916	222	—	8,138

GRAND TOTAL

NORTH-WESTERN PROVINCES	82	1,597	507	—	2,186
LOWER PROVINCES	154	4,186	907	1,789	7,036
FORT ST. GEORGE (*see below*)	—	—	—	—	—
BOMBAY	—	7,916	222	—	8,138
	236	13,699	1,636	1,789	17,360

MEMORANDUM on the Course of Instruction at the Education Establishments, maintained at the Public Expense in the several Presidencies of *British India*

IN the Lower Provinces, the Madrissa of Calcutta affords instruction in the literature and law of the Mahomedans and the books read are those usually studied by the young men of that religion, mostly in the Arabic language. The Hooghly College has also a department in which Arabic and Persian are studied.

The Sanscrit Calcutta College is intended to teach Sanscrit literature and Hindoo law. English classes are attached to both the Sanscrit College and Madrissa.

The Patshala was founded for the cultivation of the Bengali language.

In the North-Western Provinces the Colleges of Delhi and Agra have Oriental departments, chiefly for Arabic and Persian, but in which the vernacular languages are also cultivated. The Benares College was founded for the instruction of Hindoos in Sanscrit literature and Hindoo law, and has a class for Persian also.

The object of the remaining seminaries is instruction in the English language and literature, and in the sciences of Europe.

(True Extracts)

East India House, ⎫
5 October 1846 ⎭

T. L. Peacock,
Examiner of Indian Correspondence

EXTRACT, FORT ST. GEORGE PUBLIC DIARY TO CONSULTATION OF 18TH MAY 1847

Received the following Letter, from *R. G. Clarke*, Esq., Officiating Secretary, Council of Education, to the Chief Secretary to Government, Fort St. George, dated 22d April 1847.

Sir,

I AM directed by the Council of Education to acknowledge the receipt of extract from Minutes of Consultation, dated 8th January last, No. 34, forwarding copy of a despatch from the Court of Directors and of its enclosure, requiring, for the purpose of being laid before the House of Commons, a Return showing the number of scholars, and the system of instruction pursued in the several schools, and other establishments for education maintained at the public expense, in this presidency; and to state that it has been ascertained upon inquiry that there are no* such educational establishments in existence in this presidency.

I have, &c.

(signed)   *R. G. Clarke,*
Officiating Secretary

Fort St. George, 22 April 1847

(No. 447)

Ordered, That a copy of the foregoing letter be forwarded to the Honourable Court, with reference to their despatch No. 27, in this department, dated 21st October 1846.

(True Extract)

(signed)   *R. G. Clarke,*
Deputy Secretary to Government

Fort St. George, 12 May 1847

* With the exception of the Madras High School, where the number of pupils is as follows:

Hindoos	133
Mussulmans	2
Christians	21
	156

MADRAS HIGH SCHOOL

Syllabus of Study

Grammar	The whole.
Geography (Modern)	The whole generally.
Abridged History of Rome	To the fall of Carthage.
Ditto of Greece	To the fall of the Macedonian Empire.
Ditto of England	From commencement to end of Geo. 3.
Robinson's Charles V	Books 1, 2, 3, 4, and part of Book 5.
Norton's Rudimentals	Lectures 1, 2, 3 and 4.
Smith's Moral Sentiments	
Locke on the Understanding	
Marcet's Political Economy	
Calcutta Poetical Reader	No. 4.
Selections from the English Poets	

Arithmetic	The whole generally.
Algebra	Books 1 to 6, and 11 to Proposition 21.
Euclid	Plane and spherical; the whole generally.
Trigonometry	
Conic Sections	
Newton's Principia	Sections 1 to 3.
Differential Calculus	The whole generally.
Herschell's Astronomy	The whole, excepting cap. 2.
Elements of Optics	Generally.
Principles of Stereostatics and Hydrostatics	

MADRAS HIGH SCHOOL—*continued*

Marcet's Chemistry
Elements of Electricity

Vernacular:
    Teloogoo Studies:
Gooroomoorty's Grammar
Punchatranta
Campbell's Grammar
Synonymes from Campbell's Dictionary, with English explanations
Arabian Nights
Morris's Selections
Vickramarka Tales
English and Teloogoo Exercises

    Mahratta Studies:
Balmuttera
Grammar
Necticutthee
Bodecutthee
Bodewachanum
Grant Duff's History of the Mahrattas, about 200 pages

(True Extracts)

T. L. Peacock,
Examiner of Indian Correspondence

East India House,
25 November 1847

Glossary of Most Commonly Used
Indian Terms[1]

Amil: Officer in charge of a division of a province; in Mughal times, land-revenue officer.

Amin: Trustee or commissioner, specially used for native commissioners appointed in 1777 to investigate resources of the country and more generally for men appointed to manage estates on removal or recusancy of zamindar.

Crore: 10 million or 100 lakhs (of rupees).

Devasthan: Land granted for support of a temple.

Dustuk: Permit to pass by road or river duty free.

Faujdar: District executive officer, commander of a military force, who had to put down smaller rebellions, disperse or arrest robber gangs, &c.

Ghatwali tenure: A grant to a *ghatwal*, a chief or other person who applied the land revenue to support a force for protecting the passes and preventing raids from hill tribes.

Gomastah: Paid agent of the E.I. Company or mercantile or banking houses.

Inam (hence inamdar): a holding free of land revenue given to a noble, usually a Brahman.

Izafat: Term used in the N. Konkan when the grantee is allowed to take the revenue as a personal benefit; he may be a revenue farmer appointed to realize 'increased' revenue.

Jagir: Assignment of land revenue of a territory to a chief or noble for specific service (to support troops, police, &c.) or to maintain the state and dignity of the grantee, originally for life, but often became permanent and hereditary.

Lakh: 100,000 (rupees).

[1] In the main, excluding those which appear in the Shorter Oxford English Dictionary.

Kanungo   A district accountant-registrar in charge of the land
  (*qanungo*):   records.
Lambardar: Headman of a village or section of a village.
Mahal: An estate of group of lands regarded as a unit for the
                   assessment of land revenue (hence mahalwari settle-
                   ment).
Mamlatdar: Native land-revenue officer in charge of a taluq or
                   division of a district.
Mansabdar: An officer of state who had a mansab, or official appoint-
                   ment of rank and profit, and was bound to supply a
                   number of troops for the service of the state. The
                   mansabdars formed the official nobility of the Mughal
                   state.
Mirasdar: Holder of a permanent and hereditary tenure.
Mukarrari
  (*muqarrari*):   Fixed-rent tenure.
Munshi: A vernacular officer clerk.
Munsif   Indian judicial functionary of the lowest order who
                   previously tried petty cases on commission; later
                   absorbed as judicial officer of inferior courts.
Pargana: A subdivision of a district containing a varying number
                   of villages.
Patni: A permanent farm of the management and rent col-
                   lection of a part of a zamindari (hence patnidar.)
Patwari: Village officer who keeps the accounts and records, &c.
Poddar
  (*potdar*):   A treasurer or treasury clerk.
Saranjam: An assignment of revenue to meet expenses of troops,
                   police, &c. (Maratha equivalent of jagir).
Serishtadar: Officer superintendent who holds the files of cases
                   pending.
Soyurghal: Life grant of land revenue, not of land.
Tahsildar: Revenue officer of local subdivision of district.
Taluq: A landholding or tenure which is subordinate to a
                   landlord or superior, so taluqdar.
Vakil (*waqil*):   A native attorney or barrister; a pleader in the Hindu
                   law courts.

Select Bibliography

A. MANUSCRIPT SOURCES

BRITISH MUSEUM

Additional MSS.: Papers relating to Warren Hastings, Elijah Impey, and the Marquess of Wellesley.

INDIA OFFICE LIBRARY

Hamilton Collection, MSS. Eur. D. 508–10.
Lawrence Papers (being listed).
Lytton Papers:
  MSS. Eur. E. 218/23 (Native Civil Service, 1876–7).
  MSS. Eur. E. 218/519 (Correspondence in India, 1876–80, 13 vols).
Northbrook Collection, MSS. Eur. C. 144, containing correspondence between Lord Northbrook and Lord Dufferin between 1884 and 1886.
Minor Collections, MSS. Eur. E. 173, dealing with the administration of the North-Western Provinces immediately after acquisition from the Nawab of Oudh in 1801.

INDIA OFFICE (NOW COMMONWEALTH RELATIONS OFFICE) RECORDS DEPT.

Board's Collections, no. 273 of 1809–10 (Register no. 6095) and no. 319 of 1811–12 (Reg. no. 7257) relating to police reforms during 1793–1813.
Home Miscellaneous Series, vols:
  351 History of revenue collection in Bengal.
  352 and 353 Courts of Judicature in Bengal.
  369 Public offices and establishments in Bengal.
  421–2 Extracts from Bengal Revenue Proceedings dealing with judicial and legal matters.
  521/4 James Cumming's Papers.
Collections to Educational Despatches to India, 1859–79.

Collections to Revenue Despatches to India, 1859–79.

Proceedings (India) Public, Nov. 1898, rel. to complaint of British Indian Association against the rising influence of the Indian middle classes.

S.P.G. ARCHIVES, LONDON

Letters received from Calcutta and Madras; Despatches to Calcutta and Madras and Proceedings.

B. PRINTED SOURCES[1]

1642–54. Foster, William. The English Factories in India. Vols. for 1642–5; 1646–50; 1630–3; 1651–4.

1772. Bengal Govt. Records. Committee of Circuit, Proceedings, 1772. 3 vols. in one. Cal., 1926.

1792–3. E.I.Co. Court of Directors. Sel. Com. on Export Trade from G.B. to E. Indies. Reports 1–3, with Fourth Report upon subject of Cotton Manufactures of G.B. (I.O., P.B. Coll. 28.)

1819–21. N.W.P. Govt. Records. Selections from the Revenue Records of the North-West Provinces:

Vol. i, 1819–20. Cal., 1866.

Vol. ii, 1822–33. Allahabad, 1872.

Vol. iii, 1807, 1808, 1821. Allahabad, 1873.

1850. Bengal. Memorial of the Hindoo Inhabitants of Bengal and Bihar to the E.I.Co. to repeal Act 21 of 1850. Cal., 1850.

1866. Papers connected with the Trial of Moulvie Ahmedoolah of Patna, and others, for conspiracy and treason. Cal., 1866.

1869. Elliott, C. A. Report on Influence of Caste on Rates of Rent. . . . Beng. Govt., Sel. V, vol. 2, no. 15.

1875. Deccan Riots Commission. Report of Commissioners of Inquiry on Deccan Riots in 1875 and their Connection with the Revision of the Assessment. C. 2071 (1878).

1880–1. Indian Famine Commission (Chairman: Gen. Sir R. Strachey). Report. 3 pts. Cs. 2591, 2735, 3086.

1881–91. Condition of the Lower Classes in India; various reports. (I.O., P.B. Coll. 220.)

1883–4. Indian Education Commission. Report.

1884. Extracts from Papers connected with the Bengal Rent Bill. Cal., 1884.

[1] For Parliamentary Committees, Select Committees, and Sessional Papers see below, pp. 418 and 419.

1885. Corresp. rel. to Vernacular Education in the Lower Provinces of Bengal. Cal., 1885.

1886. Corresp. on Education of Mahomedan Community and their Employment in the Public Service Generally. Sel. 1, no. 205.

1887–90. Indian Public Service Commission. Report and Correspondence. Cs. 5327, 5926.

1888. Condition of the Agricultural Population in India, Confidential Reports. (I.O., P.B. Coll. 221.)

1890–1. Report of the Committee on the Reform of the Bengal Police.

1893–4. Indian Currency Committee (Pres.: Lord Herschell). Report. C. 7060.

1898. Currency Committee, 1898–91 (Pres.: Sir H. Fowler). Mins. of Evidence, &c. Cs. 9037, 9222, 9736, 9390, 9421.

— Famine Commission (Pres.: Sir J. Lyall). Report. C. 9178.

— Papers rel. to Reorganisation of the Educational Service in India, 1891–7. Cal., 1898.

1901. Famine Commission (Pres.: Sir A. P. MacDonnell). Report. Cd. 876.

1902–3. Indian Police Commission (Pres.: A. H. L. Fraser). Report. Cd. 2478, 1905.

1905–12. Papers relating to Bengal Administration. Cds. 2658, 2746, 5979.

1907–9. Rl. Commission on Decentralisation in India (Chairman: C.E.H. Hobhouse). Report. 10 vols. Cds. 4360–9.

1916–18. Indian Industrial Commission (Pres.: Sir T. H. Holland). Report. 5 vols. Cds. 51, 234–8 (1919).

1917–19. Calcutta University Commission (Pres.: Sir M. Sadler). Report, Evidence & Documents. 13 vols.

1918. Sedition Committee (Pres.: S. A. T. Rowlatt). Report. Cd. 9190.

1921–2. Indian Fiscal Commission (Pres.: Hon. Sir I. Rahimtoola). Report. Simla, 1922.

1924. Rl. Commission on Superior Civil Service in India (Chairman: Viscount Lee of Fareham). Report. Cmd. 2128.

1924–5. Indian Taxation Enquiry Committee (Pres.: Sir C. Todhunter). Report. 7 vols. Cal., 1925–6.

1926–7 Unemployment Committee (Pres.: G. F. Paddison). Report on the Question of Unemployment among the Educated Middle Classes. Madras, 1927.

1928. Rl. Commission on Agriculture in India (Chairman: Lord Linlithgow). Abridged Report.

1931. Rl. Commission on Labour in India (Chairman: J. H. Whiteley). Report. Cmd. 3883.

1935. Unemployment Committee, U.P. (Chairman: Sir T. B. Sapru). Report. Allahabad, 1936.

1937. Abbott, A. and S. H. Wood. Report on Vocational Education in India. Delhi, 1937.

1948–9. University Education Commission (Chairman: Sir S. Radhakrishnan). Report. 2 vols. Delhi, 1949–51.

1955. India, Min. of Finance. Progress of Joint Stock Companies in India. New Delhi, 1955.

Parliamentary Committees and Select Committees

The following four items are reprinted in Reports from Committees of the House of Commons, 1803, 15 vols., folio:

1772–3. Committee of the HC appointed to enquire into the Nature, State, and Condition of the E.I. Co. and of British Affairs in the East Indies. Reports 1–5, 27 May 1772 to 18 June 1773. (Vol. iii.)

1772–3. Com. of Secrecy, HC, appointed to enquire into the State of the E.I. Co. Reports 1–9, 7 Dec. 1772 to 30 June 1773. (Vol. iv.)

1781. Com. HC on Petitions of Mr. Touchet and Irving . . . and of Warren Hastings, Philip Francis, &c. re the Administration of Justice &c. in India. Report, 8 May 1781. (Vol. v.)

1782–3. Sel. Com. HC appointed to take into consideration the State of the Administration of Justice in the provinces of Bengal, Bahar, and Orissa. Reports 1–11, 5 Feb. 1782 to 18 Nov. 1783. (Vol. v.)

1808–12. Sel. Com. HC on Affairs of the E.I. Co. Reports 1–4, with appendices, and 5th Report . . . on the Administration of Revenue and Justice, 1812.

1831–2. Sel. Com. HC on Affairs of the E.I. Co. Report, with Gen. App. and Index, and 6 vols of Mins. of Evidence, with app. and index, dealing with I. Public; II. Finance and Accounts—Trade (2 pts.); III. Revenue; IV. Judicial; V. Military; VI. Political and Foreign. (8 (734); 9–14 (735 I–VI.) (Another set, large 4to, printed for E.I. Co. Court of Directors.)

1848. Sel. Com. HC on Sugar and Coffee Planting in India. Reports 1–8.

1852. Sel. Com. HC on Indian Territories. Reports, with proceedings mins. of evidence, app., and index (10 (533)).

1852. Sel. Com. HL on Indian Territories, to whom were referred the petition of G. J. Gordon re education and of C. H. Cameron re establishment of universities. (19 (88)).

1852–3. Sel. Com. HC on Indian Territories. Reports 1–6 with mins. of evidence and app. (27–29 (426, 479, 556, 692, 768, 897)).

1857–8. Sel. Com. HC on Colonisation and Settlement of India. Reports 1–4, with procs., mins. of evidence and app. (7 (261, 326, 415, 461)).

1876. Sel. Com. HC on Depreciation of Silver. Report with procs., mins. of evidence, app. &c. (8 (338)).

Other Parliamentary Sessional Papers

1810. HC 5 (288–9). Private Trade between India and Europe, the Importation of Cotton from India (1797) &c.

1812–13. HC 8 (152). Bullion and Merchandise Exported by the Co. to India and China: Statistics, 1708–11.

— HC 8 (194). Mutiny of Native Troops at Vellore, &c.

— HL 64 (23). Letter fr. Marquess of Wellesley, together with several reports on private trade and commerce of Calcutta from 1797–8 to 1799–1800.

— HL 65 (163). Residence of Europeans not in the Service of the Co.: Corresp.

1824. HC 23 (443). Burning of Hindoo Widows: Corresp.

— HC 23 (426). Infanticide: Corresp.

1830. HC 28 (550). Suttee: Proposed Regulations for the Suppression of the Practice.

1833. HC 23 (390). Gold and Silver Coin and Bullion Imported into and Exported from India and China.

1841. HC 17 (328). Religious Ceremonies of Natives of India (Separation of Govt. from all share in management of Native Temples): Desp. 31 Mar. 1841.

1845. HC 34 (664). Native Religious Institutions and Ceremonies and Payments to the support of the Juggernauth Temple.

— HC 34 (216). Education Order of G.O.I. for the Establishment of the Council of Education.

— HC 34 (327). Railway Communications: Desp. from Court of Directors, 7 May 1845.

1847–8. HC 48 (20). Education: Return of no. of Scholars maintained at the Public Expense in the Presidencies of British India, specifying Hindoos, Mussulmans, and Christians.

— HC 51 (473). Judicial and Legal Officers: No. and Names of Persons appointed to any Judicial or other Legal Office in the E. Indies and British Colonies, since 1st Jan. 1832.

1852–3. HC 36 (361). Education: Return of no. of Scholars, specifying College and Schools &c.

— HL 11 (105E). Civil Servants: Nos. in 1834 and 1851 on the Retired and Active and Furlough Lists respectively.

— HL 11 (110C). Natives employed in the Civil Administration of British India, 1828 and at the Present Time.

1854. HC 47 (393). Education: Desp. dated 19th July 1854 to the G.O.I.

1857–8. HC 11 (111). Police and Judicial: Social Condition of the Rural Population of Bengal; Desp. from the Court of Directors.

— HC 42 (71). Missionaries and the Support or Countenance of Public Officers: Corresp., 1847–8.

— HC 42 (190). Education in Behar: Letter from Court of Directors, dated 13th Apr. 1858.

— HC 42 (201VI). Natives Employed in Civil Administration: Return of No. and Salaries, 1851 and 1857.

— HL 11 (283). Education: Letter, dated 28th Apr. 1858. from Lord Ellenborough, and Memo. by Sir G. Clerk, dated 29th Mar. 1858.

1859. HC 18 (143). Lands Held in Enam (Madras), Corresp.

— HL 6 (115). Education: Desp. dated Apr. 1859 and Report on Public Instruction in Lower Provinces of Bengal, 1857–8.

— HC 25 (158). Disturbances in Travancore: Caste Restrictions and Petitions regarding Arrears of Salaries of Public Servants, Acts against Converts to Christianity, &c.

1860. HC 52 (27). Education in India, Minute by Lt. Gov. of Bengal on Letter from Earl of Ellenborough.

— HC 52 (89). Disturbances in Tinnevelley against Christian Converts from Low Castes.

— HC 52 (157). Police of the Patna Division, Report of the Commissioner for 1857.

— HC 49 (605). Income Tax Bill: Copy.

1861. HC 42 (199). Admission of Natives to the Medical Dept. of the Army.

— 45 (291). Disputes between the Indigo Planters and Ryots of Lower Bengal: Further Orders and Corresp.

1862. HC 40 (372). High Court at Calcutta: Charter and Desp. rel. to its Establishment.

1867–8. HC 51 (200). Uncovenanted Service in India: No. of Appointments with Salary of £500 p.a. and Upwards, held by Europeans and Natives of India respectively.

1870. HC 52 (397). Education. Report and Corresp. showing the progress of Education in India since 1866.

1872. HC 44 (161). Wahabees at Patna: Copy of Minutes by Lord Dalhousie in 1852 rel. to the Precautionary Measures to be Adopted.

1874. HC 47 (184). Native Appointments: Return showing Appointments of Natives of not less than 150 rupees a month ... 1867–71.

1877. HC 63 (173). Trial of Mr. Fuller, for an assault on a Native: Corresp. &c.

1883 HC 51 (C. 3512). Native Jurisdiction over European British Subjects: Corresp. over Proposed Alteration of the Provisions of the Code of Criminal Procedure.

1887. HC 62 (340). Agricultural Banks in India, Corresp.

1892. HC 58 (188). Behar Cadastral Survey, Corresp. 1893–4 HC 63 (448), Ditto.

1899. HC 65 (C. 9190). Educational Progress from 1892–3 to 1896–7. 3rd Quinquennial Rev. by J. S. Cotton.

1900. HC 58 (13). Wars on or beyond the Borders of British India since 1849: Return.

1902. HC 71 (C. 1089). Land Revenue System: Resol. of G.O.I. dated 16th Jan. 1902 and Memorial to the Sec. of State for India.

C. TRAVELS

Barbosa, Duarte. The Book of Duarte Barbosa, ed. M. L. Dames. 2 vols. London, 1918–21. (Hak. Soc. Ser. 2, A9.)

Bernier, François. Travels in the Mogul Empire, 1656–68, ed. A. Constable. London, Constable, 1891.

Linschoten, J. H. van. Voyage of John Huyghen van Linschoten to the East Indies, ed. A. D. Burnell. London, 1885. (Hak. Soc. 70–71.)

Manrique, S. The Travels of Fray Sebastien Manrique, 1629–43, tr. by C. E. Luard and H. Hosten. Oxford, 1927. 2 vols. (Hak. Soc. ser. 2, 59 & 61.)

Manucci, Niccolao. Manucci's Storia do Mogor or Mogul India, tr. and ed. by W. Irvine. London, Murray, 1907–8. 4 vols.

Mundy, Peter. Travels of Peter Mundy in Europe and Asia, 1608–67, ed. R. C. Temple. Vol. ii: Travels in Asia, 1628–34. London, 1914. (Hak. Soc. ser. 2, 35.)

Pyrard of Laval, François. Voyage . . . to the East Indies, Maldives, Moluccas and Brazil, tr. and ed. A. Gray and H. C. P. Bell. London, 1887–8. 2 vols. (Hak. Soc. 76, 77, 80.)

Tavernier, Jean Baptiste. Travels in India, tr. and ed. by V. Ball. London, 1889. 2 vols.

Terry, Edward. A Voyage to East India. London, 1655; reprint 1777.

Roe, Sir Thomas. The Embassy of Sir Thomas Roe to the Court of the Great Mogul, 1615–19, ed. W. Foster. London, 1899. 2 vols. (Hak. Soc. 1 and 2.)

Valle, Pietro della. Travels . . . in India, from the Old Eng. trans. of 1664, by G. Havers, ed. E. Grey. London, 1892. (Hak. Soc. 84–85.)

D. SECONDARY SOURCES

Abu Fazl. The Ain i Akbari, tr. by H. Blochmann. Cal., 1873–94. 3 vols.

Adam, William. Adam's Reports on Vernacular Education in Bengal and Behar, submitted to Government in 1835, 1836, and 1838. With a brief view of its past and present condition by the Rev. J. Long. Cal., 1868.

— 1st–3rd Reports. Cal., 1835–8.

Ambedkar, B. R. Annihilation of Caste: Speech. Bombay, 1936.

Azad, Abul Kalam. India Wins Freedom. Bombay, 1959.

Blochmann, H. 'A Chapter from Muhammadan History', Calcutta Review, Apr. 1871.

Chesney, Sir G. T. Indian Polity: a View of the System of Administration in India. London, 1868.

Child, Sir Josiah. A Treatise wherein is Demonstrated that the East India Trade is the Most National of all Foreign Trades. London, 1681.

Chirol, Sir Valentine. Indian Unrest. London, 1910.

Choksey, R. D. The Aftermath . . . 1818–26. Bombay, 1950.

Crawford, D. G. A History of the Indian Medical Service, 1600–1913. London, 1914. 2 vols.

Deshmukh, Sir C. D. Economic Development in India, 1946–56. Bombay, 1957.

Curzon of Kedleston, Marquess of. Lord Curzon in India; being a Selection from his Speeches as Viceroy and G.-G. of India, 1888–1905, ed. by Sir T. Raleigh. London, 1906.

Dixon, Lt.-Col. C. G. Sketch of Mairwara. London, 1850.

Dodwell, H. H. A Sketch of the History of India, 1858–1918. London, 1925.

Elphinstone, M. The History of India. 3rd ed. London, 1849.

Farquhar, J. N. Modern Religious Movements in India. New York, 1918.

Fawcett, Sir C. The First Century of British Justice in India. Oxford, 1934.

Field, C. D. A Digest of the Law of Landlord and Tenants. Cal., 1879.

Forrest, Sir G. W., ed. Selections from State Papers of the Governors-General of India: Lord Cornwallis. Oxford, 1926.

Furber, H. John Company at Work. Cambridge, 1948.
— 'Early American Trade with India', New England Quarterly, ii. (1938).
Gadgil, D. R. The Industrial Evolution of India in Recent Times. Bombay, 1942.
Ghate, B. G. Changes in the Occupational Distribution of the Population. Delhi, 1940.
Ghose, L. N. The Modern History of the Indian Chiefs, Rajas, Zamindars, &c. Cal., 1879–81. 2 vols.
— Memoirs of Maharaja Mubkissen Bahadur. Cal., 1901.
Hamilton, Walter. Description of Hindostan and its Adjacent Countries. London, 1815. 2 vols.
Heber, Reginald. Narrative of a Journey through the Upper Provinces of India . . . 1824–5. 3rd ed. London, 1828. 2 vols.
Howell, A. Education in British India prior to 1854. Cal., 1872.
Hume, A. O. Agricultural Reform in India. London, 1899.
Hunter, W. W. Annals of Rural Bengal. 7th ed. London, 1897.
— Bengal MSS. Records, 1782–1807. London, 1894. 4 vols.
— The Indian Musulmans. London, 1871.
— Imperial Gazetteer of India. 2nd ed. London, 1885–7.
Irwin, H. C. The Garden of India, or Chapters in Oudh History and Affairs. London, 1880.
Iyengar, S. S. Land Tenures in the Madras Presidency. Madras., 1921.
Jain, L. C. Indigenous Banking in India. London, 1929.
Johnston, J. Abstract and Analysis of the Report of the Indian Education Commission. London, 1884.
Keith, A. B. Speeches and Documents on Indian Policy, 1750–1921. London, 1922. 2 vols.
Lambton, A. K. S. Landlord and Peasant in Persia. London, 1953.
Long, Rev. J., ed. Selections from Unpublished Records of Government for the years 1748–67. Cal., 1869.
[MacDonnell, A. P.] Agricultural and Administrative Reform in Bengal, by a Bengal Civilian. London, 1883.
McCully, B. T. English Education and the Origins of Indian Nationalism. New York, Columbia U.P., 1940.
Mehta, M. M. Structure of Indian Industries. Bombay, 1955.
Milburn, W. Oriental Commerce, or the East India Trader's Complete Guide. London, 1813. 2 vols.
Mises, Ludwig von. Bureaucracy. New Haven, Yale U.P., 1944.
Misra, B. B. The Central Administration of the East India Company, 1773–1834. Manchester U.P., 1959.

Misra, B. B. The Judicial Administration of the East India Company in Bengal, 1765–82. Patna, 1952.
— 'The Administration of Bihar, 1757–1947', in Bihar Govt., Bihar through the Ages.
Misra, B. R. Indian Provincial Finance, 1919–39. London, 1942.
— Land Revenue Policy in the United Provinces under British Rule. Benares, 1942.
Mitra, K. C. Memoirs of Dwarka Nath Tagore. Cal., 1870.
Moreland, W. H. India at the Death of Akbar. London, 1920
— The Revenue Administration of the United Provinces. Allahabad, 1911.
— From Akbar to Auranzeb. London, 1923.
— The Agrarian System of Moslem India. Cambridge, 1929.
Morrison, M. B. My Experience of Agricultural Behar and Benarees, and Some Thoughts on the Bengal Tenancy Bill. Cal., 1884.
Mozoomdar, P. C. The Life and Teachings of Keshub Chunder Sen. Cal., 1887.
Mullens, Joseph. A Brief Review of Ten Years' Missionary Labour in India between 1852 and 1861. London, 1863.
Murray, Hugh. Historical and Descriptive Account of British India. 4th ed. Edinburgh, 1843. 3 vols.
Naoroji, D. Poverty and Un-British Rule in India. London, 1901.
Nicholls, G. Sketch of the Rise and Progress of the Benares Pathshalla or Sanskrit College. Allahabad, 1907.
Niyogi, J. P. The Evolution of the Indian Income Tax. London, 1929.
Pal, Bepin Chandra. The New Spirit. Cal., 1907.
— The Soul of India. 3rd ed. Cal., 1940.
Pal, Radhabinod. The History of the Law of Primogeniture. Cal., 1929.
Pelsaert, F. Jahangir's India, tr. W. H. Moreland and P. Geyl. Cambridge, 1925.
Philips, C. H. The East India Company, 1874–1834. Manchester U.P., 1940.
Royle, J. F. An Essay on the Antiquity of Hindoo Medicine. London, 1837.
— On the Culture and Commerce of Cotton in India. London, 1850.
Saran, P. The Provincial Government of the Mughals, 1526–1658. Allahabad, 1941.
Sinha, H. C. Early European Banking in India. London, 1927.
Sketch of the Commercial Resources and Monetary and Mercantile System of British India. London, 1837.
Smith, W. C. Modern Islam in India; a Social Analysis. London, 1946.
Syed Mahmood. A History of English Education in India. Aligarh, 1895.

Thacker's Bengal Directory, 1869–84. (Earlier Calcutta; Thacker's Post Office Directory, 1863-4; Thacker's Directory, 1865–8.)

Thacker's Indian Directory, 1885.

Thomas, P. J. The Central Problem of Indian Economy. Madras, 1938.

— The Growth of Federal Finance in India. London, 1939.

Thornton, E. Statistical Papers relating to India, printed for the Court of Directors of the E.I. Co. London, 1853.

Thornton, R. Memoir on the Statistics of Indigenous Education, North Western Provinces of the Bengal Presidency. Cal., 1850.

Trevelyan, C. E. On the Education of the People of India. London, 1838.

Walter, C. K. M. Gazetteer of Marwar. Cal., 1877.

Ward, William. A View of the History, Literature, and Religion of the Hindus. London, 1817–20. 4 vols.

Weber, Max. The Religion of India, tr. and ed. by H. H. Gerth and Don Martindale. Glencoe, Ill., 1958.

West, Sir A. Sir Charles Wood's Administration of Indian Affairs from 1859 to 1866. London, 1867.

Whitehead, H. Indian Problems in Religion, Education, Politics. London, 1924.

Wilson, C. R. The Early Annals of the English in Bengal. Vol. i. London, 1895.

Wise, Dr. T. A. A Commentary on the Hindu System of Medicine. Cal., 1845.

— Review of the History of Medicine. London, 1867. 2 vols.

Woodrow, H. Macaulay's Minutes on Education in India, written in the Years 1835, 1836, and 1837. Cal., 1862.

Index

Abbott, A., 297–9
Abdul Aziz, *Shah*, 386
Abdul Qadir, 63
Abdur Rahim, *Shah*, 386
Abu Fazl, *Ain-i-Akbar*, 43, 45–46, 58, 62
Abwabs (Cesses), 122
Adam, William, 58; reports on education, 147 f., 154, 185
Agarkar, G. G., 382
Agarwal & Co., 250
Agency houses, 13–14, 87–90, 96, 115, 227; Parsis in, 98; changes, 99; decline, 223, 229
Agra, 39, 136; trade, 23; early travellers, 27, 35, 40, 54, 76; calico, 36; judicial officers, 191; Mutiny, 201; banking, 246, racialism, 378
Agra & United Service Bank, 225
Ahmedabad, 12, 23; cotton, 249, 251
Ahmed, *Sir* Syed, 386, 389
Ahmedullah, 387
Aitchison, *Sir* C. U., 373–4
Ajodhia Bank, Fyzabad, 246 n.
Akbar, 32, 36, 41, 43, 45; mansabs, 57, 374; scholarship, 62–63
Alexander & Co., 88–90, 114
Aligarh university, 293, 388–9
All-India Muslim League, 389
Allahabad, 74 f., 136; land admin., 137 f., 264; judicial officers, 191, 279; banking, 246; currency circulation, 247; colleges, 286; university, 287, 294, 348; graduates, 301, 326; High Court, 329
Allahabad Trading & Banking Corp., 246 n.
Altekar, A. S., 55
Amini Commission (1776), 127, 187
Amins, 177, 187, 413
Amir Ali, Syed, 347
Amirs, 41, 45–46; in hierarchy, 57–58, 308
Anderson, David, 187
Anglo-Indians (Eurasians), 192–4; employment, 215, 252–5; in P.W.D., 291–2; uncovenanted servants, 316; in law, 327–9

Apprenticing Soc., Calcutta, 193
Armenians, 85, 98
Army, Indians in, 186–7
Artisans, 35–41
Arya Samaj, 16, 381–4
Asiatic Society of Bengal, 203
Assam: agency offices, 224; banks, 245; colonization, 259; racialism, 377, 379; Muhammadans, 388; Bengal partition, 394–5
Assam Co., 224
Astrologers, 54–55, 59, 61, 64
Auckland, *Lord*, 178
Aungier, Gerald, 72
Aurangzeb, 8, 47, 72, 386; Hindus, 63
Azad, *Maulana* Abul Kalam, 399

Baden-Powell, B. H., 55
Banajee, Cavasjee, 117
Banerjea, Surendranath, 349, 354, 373
Bangvasi (Bengal journal), 377
Bank of Bengal, 99 n.
Bank of Hindostan, 90
Banking: rise of joint-stock banks, 215, 223–8, 231–4, 241; segregation of banks, 245–6; saving, 247; money-lenders, 277; *see also* Shroffs
Banyans, 26 n., 29–33, 65, 76, 78, 82, 103–4; under British, 124–5, 130, 132, 209; rise of, 227; money-lending, 278
Baptist College, Serampur, 158
Baptists, *see* Missionaries
Barbosa, Duarte, 28–29
Barlow, *Sir* George H., 83
Baroda, *Gaekwar of*, 354–5
Barwell, Richard, 111
Bauker Ally Khan, 138
Bayley, *Sir* Steuart, 347
Bayley, C. S., 352, 354
Begg Sutherland & Co., 251
Benares, 29, 31, 35, 230; Hindu & Sanskrit studies, 62, 147, 150, 209, 293, 330; trade, 83, 111; Br. resident, 84; Chait Singh, 127; Rajputs, 136, 138; law studies, 167, 169, 173, 174; medical studies, 181; admin. 177, 179; judicial admin., 189–91;